Flower of Life 3

Fumi Yoshinaga

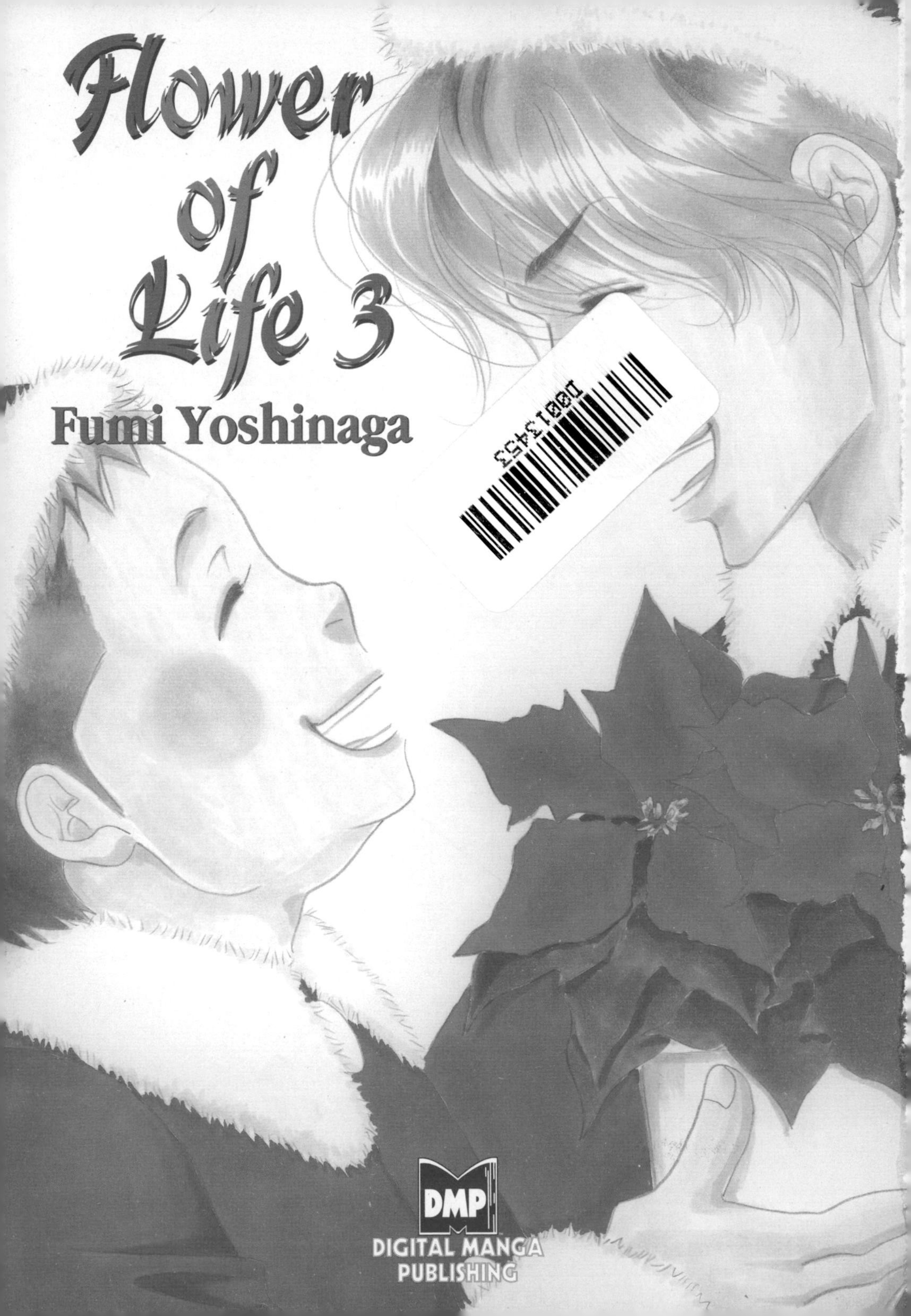

DMP
DIGITAL MANGA PUBLISHING

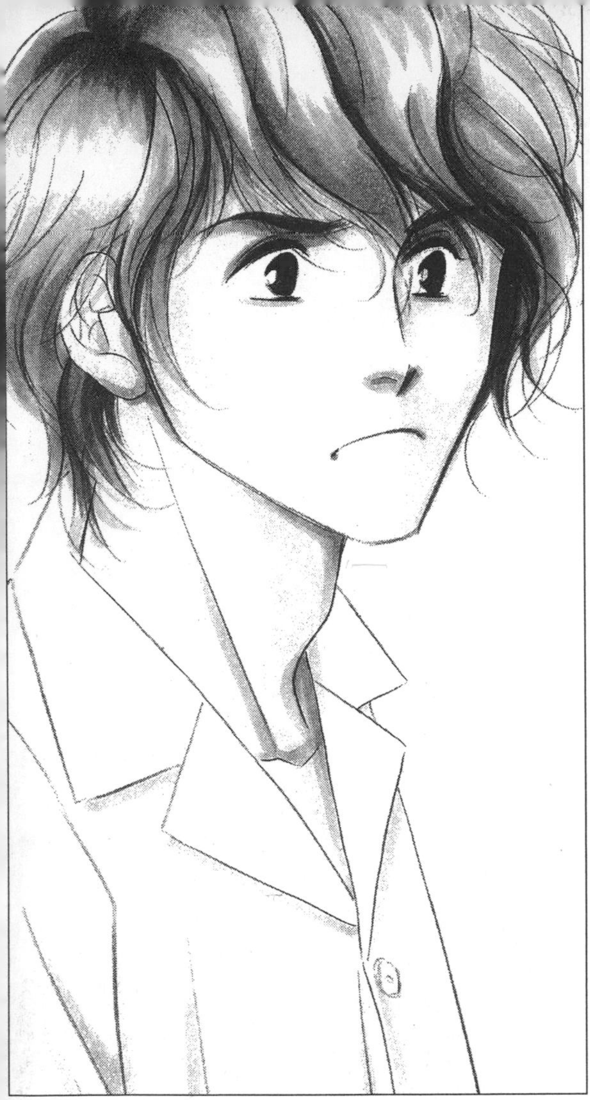

HARUTARO HANAZONO

BECAUSE OF HIS BATTLE WITH LEUKEMIA, ENROLLS IN HIGH SCHOOL A YEAR AND ONE MONTH LATE. CURRENTLY, HOWEVER, THERE IS NO LONGER ANY SIGN OF HIS ILLNESS, AND THIS BOY WITH THE SUPER-OUTGOING, HIGH-ENERGY, STRAIGHT-DOWN-THE-MIDDLE PERSONALITY IS ENJOYING SCHOOL LIFE TO THE FULLEST.
GOOD QUALITY: HONESTY.
BAD QUALITY: SIMPLICITY.
HIS OTHER FAMILY MEMBERS INCLUDE A FATHER, MOTHER (CURRENTLY WORKING OVERSEAS), AND AN OLDER SISTER.

STORY

DUE TO AN ILLNESS, HARUTARO HANAZONO ENTERS HIGH SCHOOL A YEAR AND ONE MONTH LATE. IN CHARGE OF HARUTARO'S HOMEROOM IS SHIGERU SAITO, THE FEMALE TEACHER WHO SEEMS AND ACTS MORE LIKE A GAY MAN. THE FIRST FRIEND HARUTARO MAKES IS THE ADORABLY CHUBBY LITTLE MANGA AFICIONADO, SHOTA MIKUNI. THE NEXT PERSON HARUTARO BEFRIENDS -- WELL, NOT REALLY, SINCE HE HATES THE GUY -- IS THE OLD-LOOKING, BESPECTACLED OTAKU OF STEEL, KAI MAJIMA. HARUTARO, MIKUNI AND MAJIMA ARE THE ONLY THREE MEMBERS IN THE MANGA CLUB. BUT COMPARED TO HARUTARO AND MIKUNI, WHO SPEND THEIR SUMMER VACATION IN FUN TOGETHER, MAJIMA BUSIES HIMSELF WITH PART-TIME JOBS AND A CERTAIN MAJOR EVENT. NOW THAT AUTUMN IS OVER, WHAT'S NEXT IN STORE FOR THEM...?

SHOTA MIKUNI

HARUTARO'S FIRST FRIEND. WITH A PERSONALITY TO MATCH HIS CUDDLY-CUTE APPEARANCE, MIKUNI IS GENTLE, EASY-GOING AND A LITTLE BIT SHY.
GOOD QUALITY: GENTLENESS.
BAD QUALITY: TIMIDITY.
LIVES WITH HIS FATHER AND MOTHER.

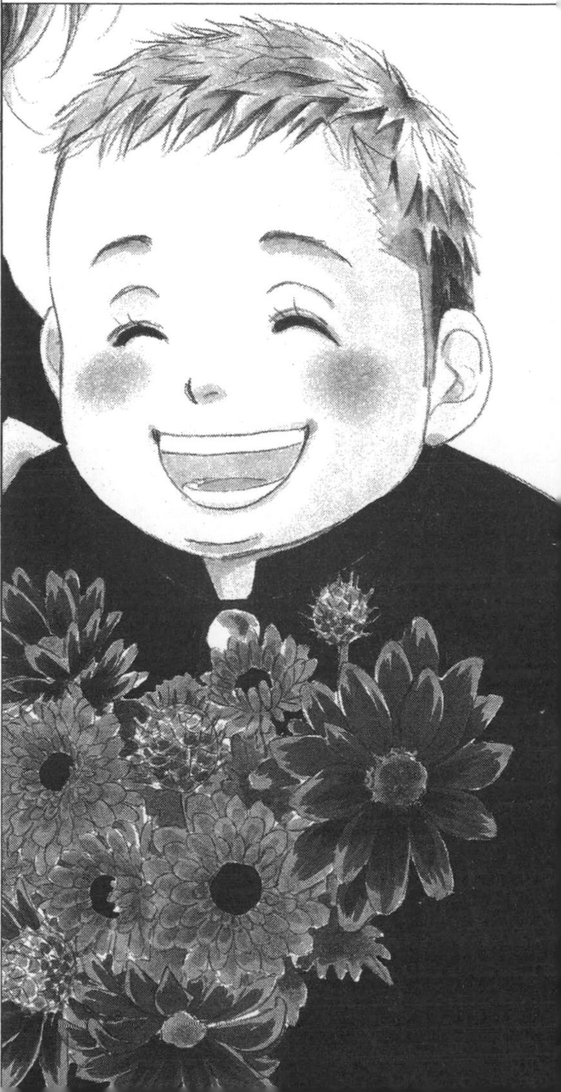

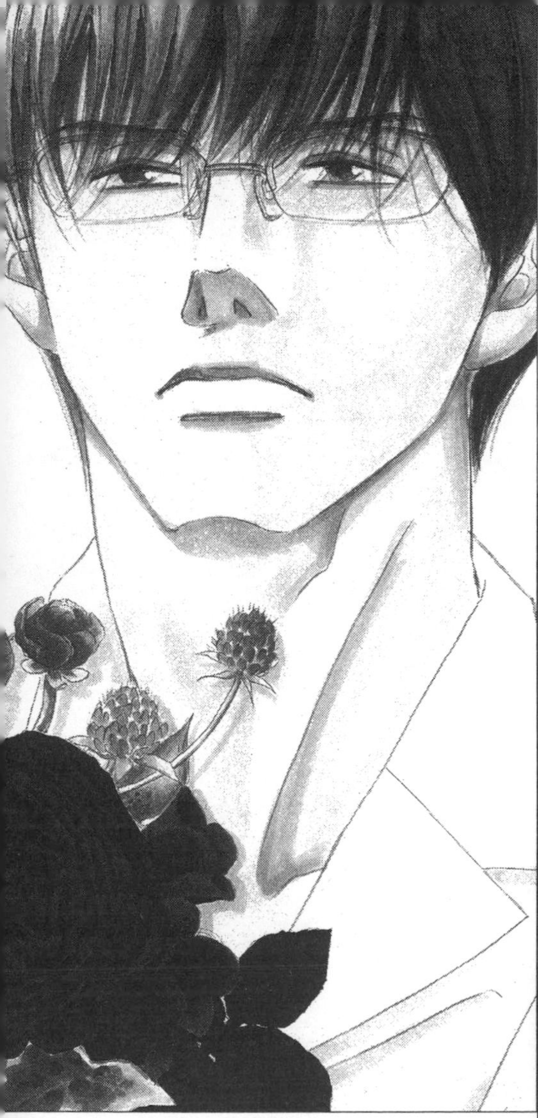

KAI MAJIMA

CLASSMATE OF HARUTARO AND MIKUNI. A HIGH SCHOOL STUDENT WHO HAS ALREADY REACHED THE FINAL STAGE AS THE ULTIMATE OTAKU. BOASTS A (USELESSLY) SCULPTED BODY AND IS (USELESSLY) TALENTED AT SPORTS. INTELLECTUALLY, HE IS A COMPLETE MORON.
GOOD QUALITY: ......DIFFICULT TO SAY...
BAD QUALITY: ARROGANCE.
HIS FAMILY LIFE IS SHROUDED IN MYSTERY.

Flower of Life 3

Translation	**Sachiko Sato**
Lettering	**Replibooks**
Graphic Design/Layout	**Daryl Kuxhouse/Fred Lui**
Editing	**Daryl Kuxhouse**
Editor in Chief	**Fred Lui**
Publisher	**Hikaru Sasahara**

English Edition Published by
DIGITAL MANGA PUBLISHING
A division of DIGITAL MANGA, Inc.
1487 W 178th Street, Suite 300
Gardena, CA 90248

www.dmpbooks.com

First Edition: July 2007
ISBN-10: 1-56970-829-0
ISBN-13: 978-1-56970-829-3

1 3 5 7 9 10 8 6 4 2

Printed in China

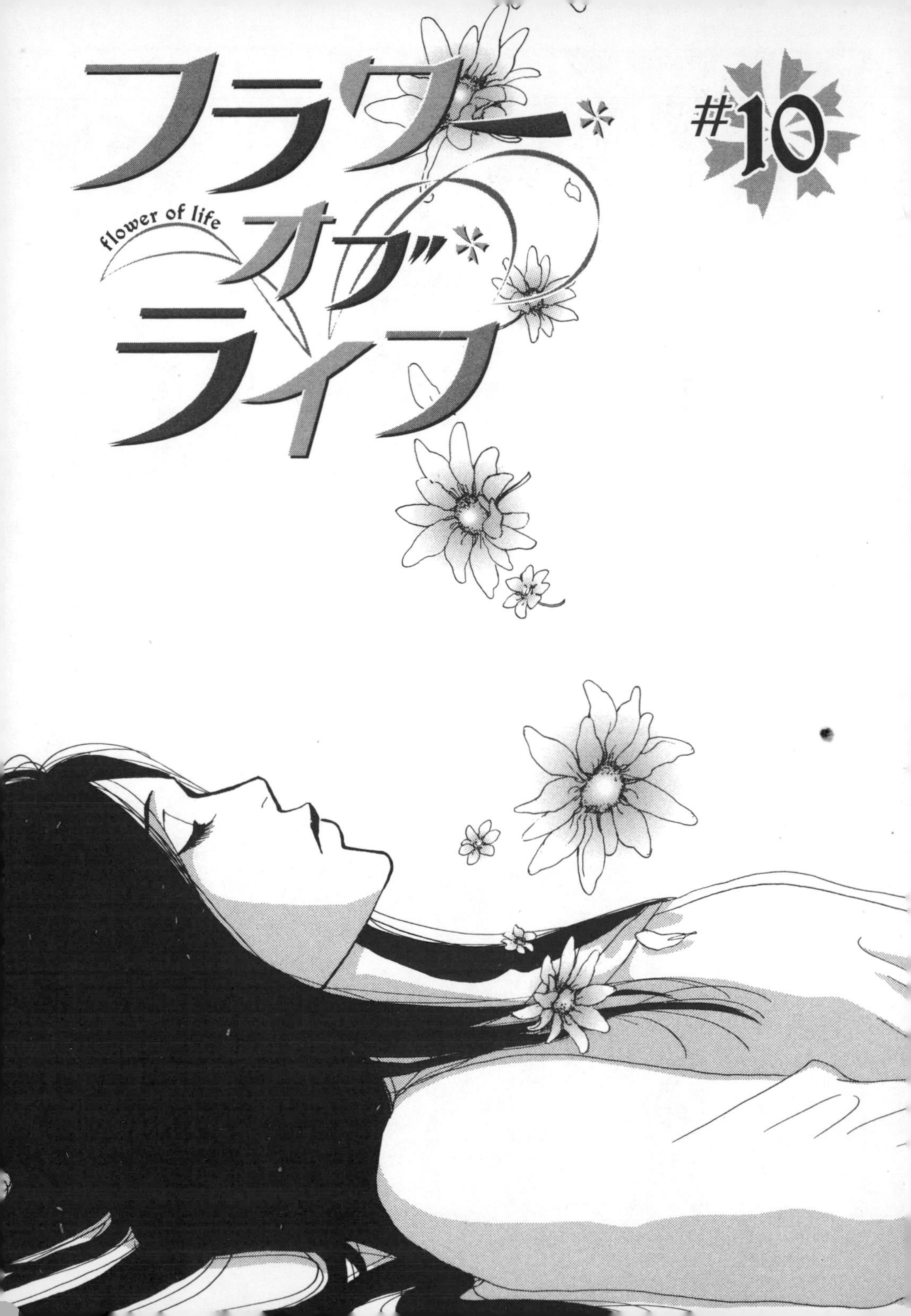
フラワー
オブ
ライフ
flower of life
#10

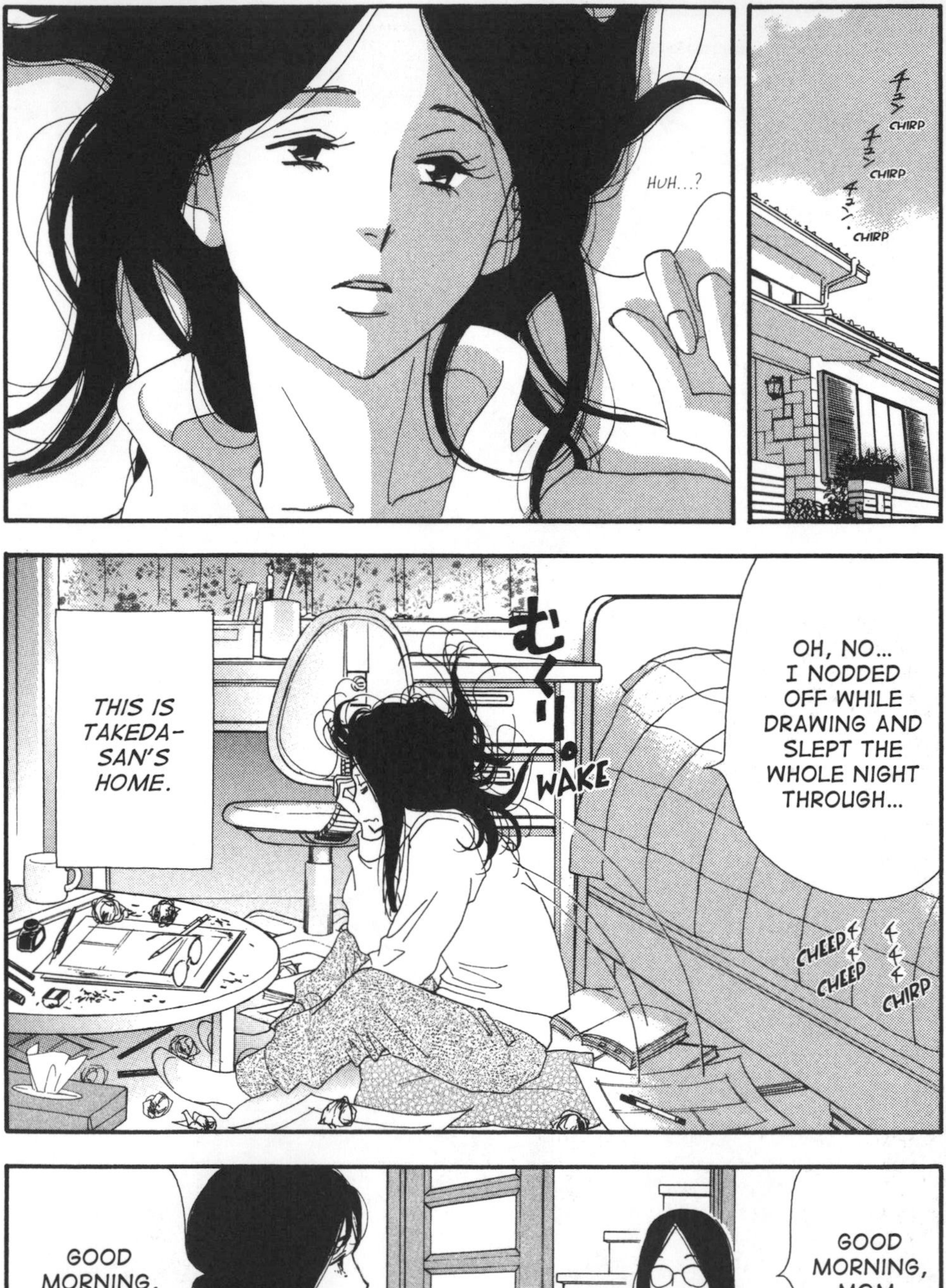

チュン CHIRP
チュン CHIRP
チュン・ CHIRP
HUH...?
OH, NO... I NODDED OFF WHILE DRAWING AND SLEPT THE WHOLE NIGHT THROUGH...
CHEEP CHEEP
CHIRP
むくり。 WAKE
THIS IS TAKEDA-SAN'S HOME.
GOOD MORNING, MOM.
GOOD MORNING, SUMI-CHAN.

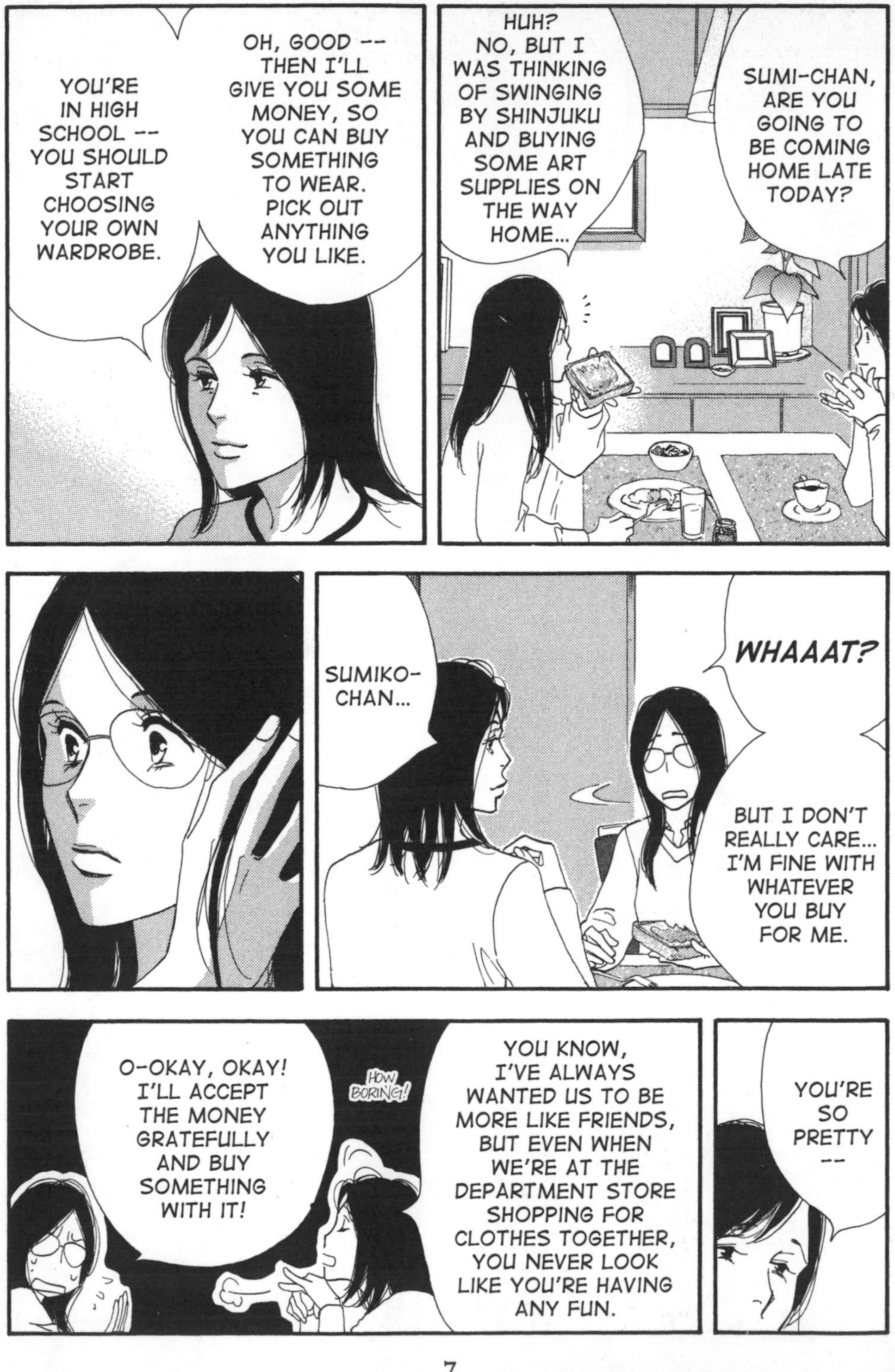
SUMI-CHAN, ARE YOU GOING TO BE COMING HOME LATE TODAY?
HUH? NO, BUT I WAS THINKING OF SWINGING BY SHINJUKU AND BUYING SOME ART SUPPLIES ON THE WAY HOME...
OH, GOOD -- THEN I'LL GIVE YOU SOME MONEY, SO YOU CAN BUY SOMETHING TO WEAR. PICK OUT ANYTHING YOU LIKE.
YOU'RE IN HIGH SCHOOL -- YOU SHOULD START CHOOSING YOUR OWN WARDROBE.
WHAAAT?
SUMIKO-CHAN...
BUT I DON'T REALLY CARE... I'M FINE WITH WHATEVER YOU BUY FOR ME.
YOU'RE SO PRETTY --
YOU KNOW, I'VE ALWAYS WANTED US TO BE MORE LIKE FRIENDS, BUT EVEN WHEN WE'RE AT THE DEPARTMENT STORE SHOPPING FOR CLOTHES TOGETHER, YOU NEVER LOOK LIKE YOU'RE HAVING ANY FUN.
HOW BORING!
O-OKAY, OKAY! I'LL ACCEPT THE MONEY GRATEFULLY AND BUY SOMETHING WITH IT!

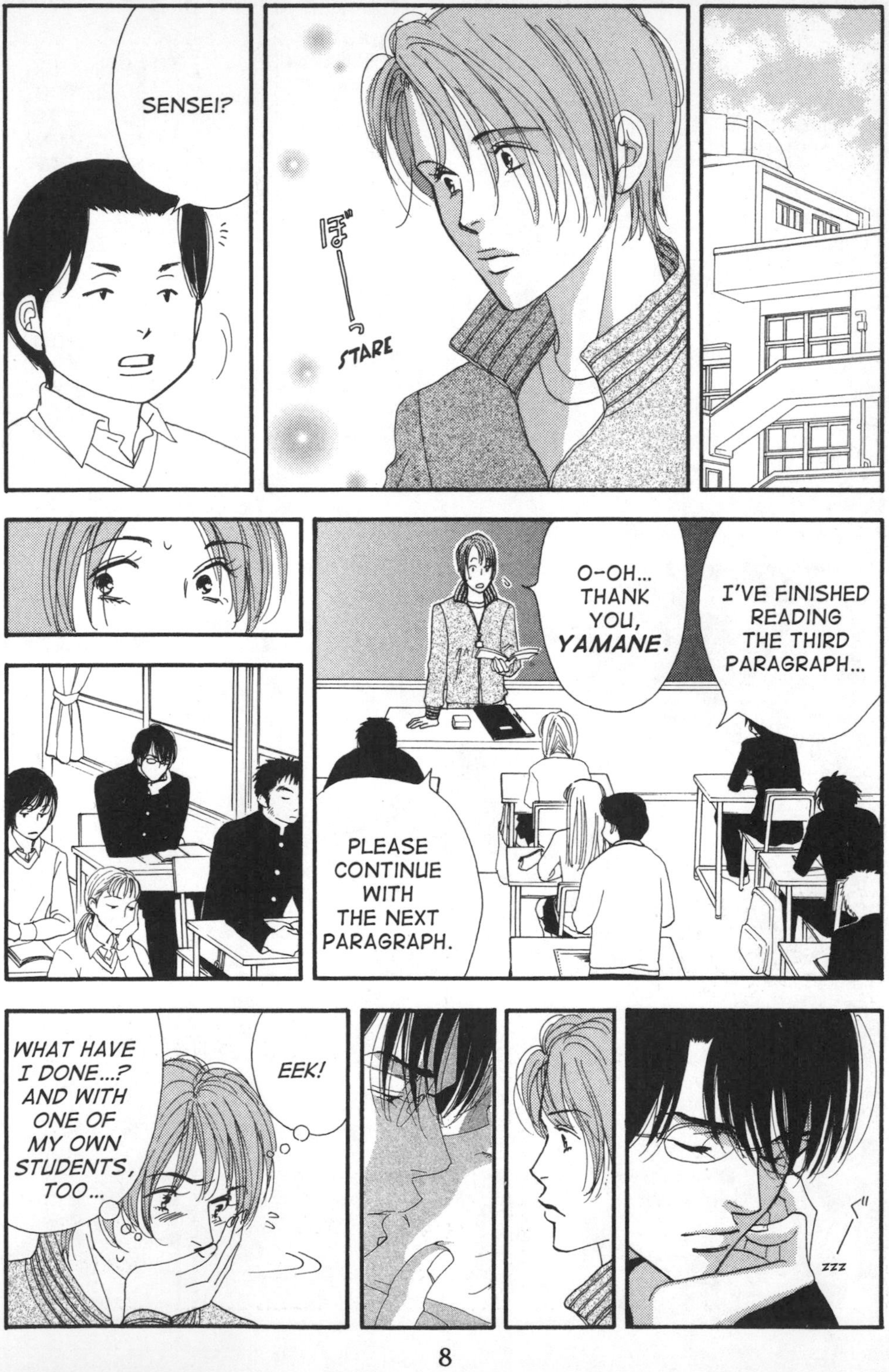
ぼーっ
STARE
SENSEI?
I'VE FINISHED READING THE THIRD PARAGRAPH...
O-OH... THANK YOU, YAMANE.
PLEASE CONTINUE WITH THE NEXT PARAGRAPH.
ZZZ
EEK!
WHAT HAVE I DONE...? AND WITH ONE OF MY OWN STUDENTS, TOO...

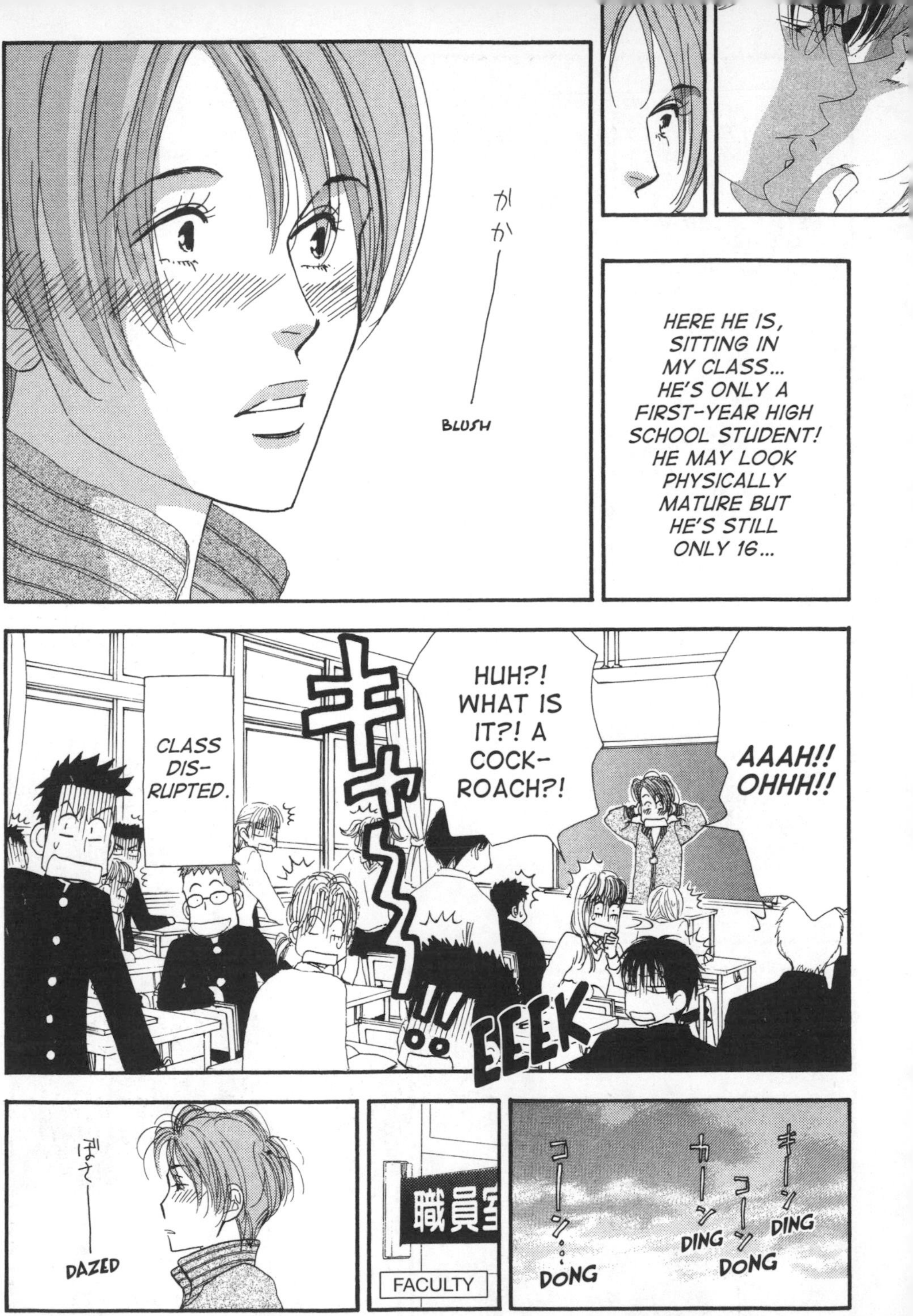
HERE HE IS, SITTING IN MY CLASS... HE'S ONLY A FIRST-YEAR HIGH SCHOOL STUDENT! HE MAY LOOK PHYSICALLY MATURE BUT HE'S STILL ONLY 16...
かか—
BLUSH
AAAH!! OHHH!!
HUH?! WHAT IS IT?! A COCKROACH?!
キャ～!!
EEEK
CLASS DIS-RUPTED.
キーン
DING
コーン
DONG
カーン
DING
コーン…
DONG
職員室
FACULTY
ぼて—
DAZED

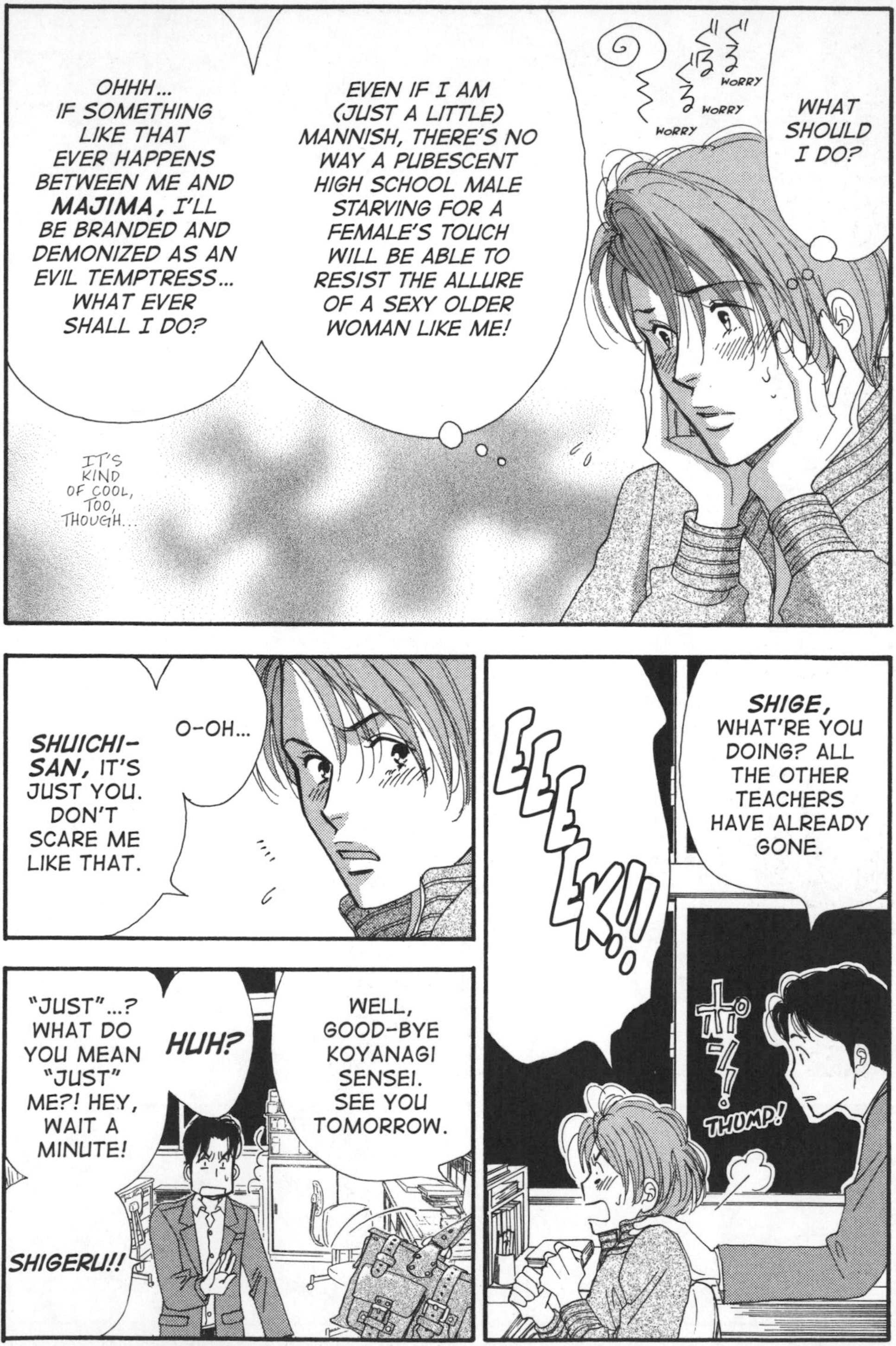
WORRY WORRY WORRY
WHAT SHOULD I DO?
EVEN IF I AM (JUST A LITTLE) MANNISH, THERE'S NO WAY A PUBESCENT HIGH SCHOOL MALE STARVING FOR A FEMALE'S TOUCH WILL BE ABLE TO RESIST THE ALLURE OF A SEXY OLDER WOMAN LIKE ME!
OHHH... IF SOMETHING LIKE THAT EVER HAPPENS BETWEEN ME AND MAJIMA, I'LL BE BRANDED AND DEMONIZED AS AN EVIL TEMPTRESS... WHAT EVER SHALL I DO?
IT'S KIND OF COOL, TOO, THOUGH...
SHIGE, WHAT'RE YOU DOING? ALL THE OTHER TEACHERS HAVE ALREADY GONE.
EEEEK!!!
THUMP!
O-OH...
SHUICHI-SAN, IT'S JUST YOU. DON'T SCARE ME LIKE THAT.
WELL, GOOD-BYE KOYANAGI SENSEI. SEE YOU TOMORROW.
HUH?
"JUST"...? WHAT DO YOU MEAN "JUST" ME?! HEY, WAIT A MINUTE!
SHIGERU!!

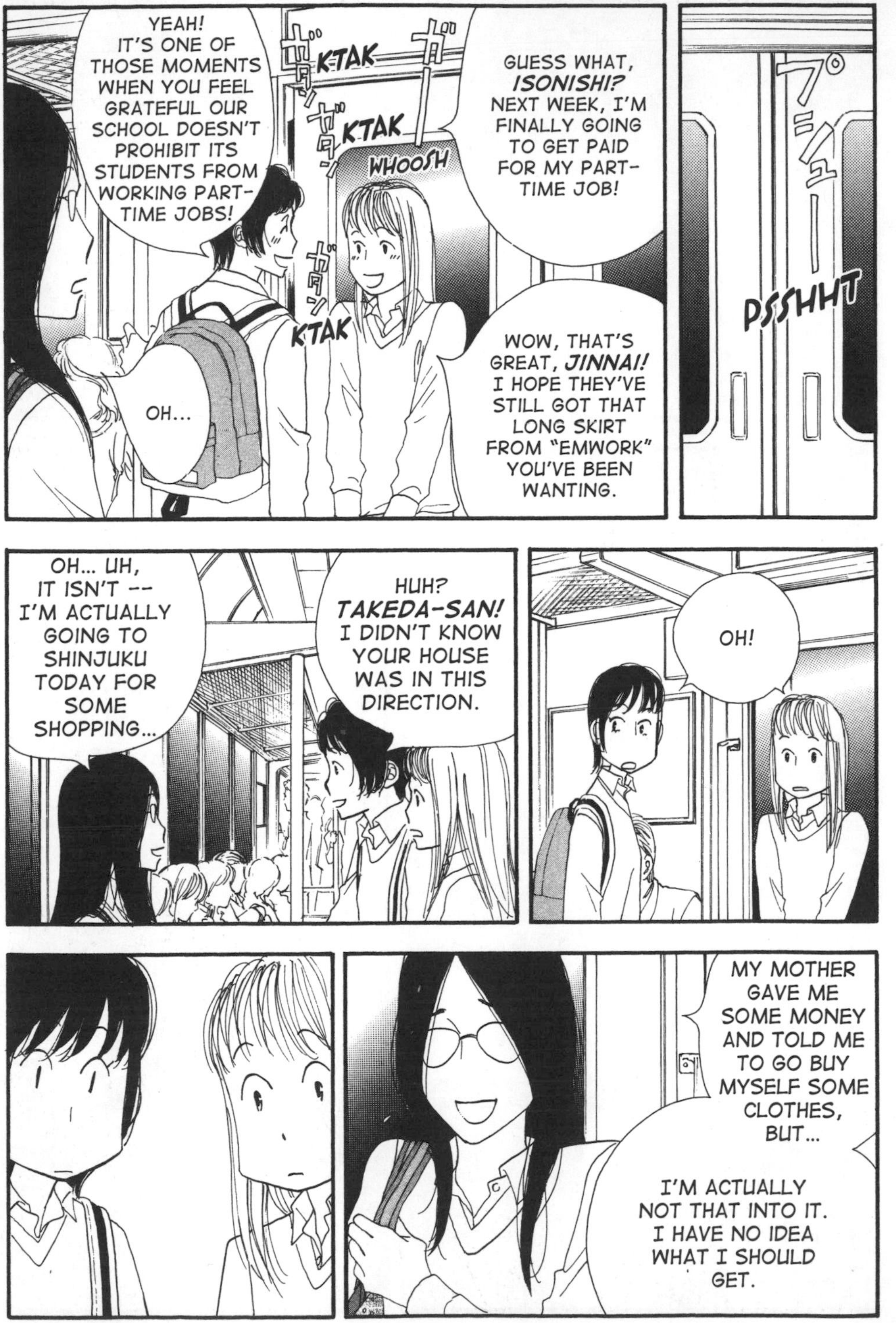
プシュー
PSSHHT
GUESS WHAT, *ISONISHI?* NEXT WEEK, I'M FINALLY GOING TO GET PAID FOR MY PART-TIME JOB!
YEAH! IT'S ONE OF THOSE MOMENTS WHEN YOU FEEL GRATEFUL OUR SCHOOL DOESN'T PROHIBIT ITS STUDENTS FROM WORKING PART-TIME JOBS!
KTAK
KTAK
WHOOSH
KTAK
WOW, THAT'S GREAT, *JINNAI!* I HOPE THEY'VE STILL GOT THAT LONG SKIRT FROM "EMWORK" YOU'VE BEEN WANTING.
OH...
OH!
HUH? *TAKEDA-SAN!* I DIDN'T KNOW YOUR HOUSE WAS IN THIS DIRECTION.
OH... UH, IT ISN'T -- I'M ACTUALLY GOING TO SHINJUKU TODAY FOR SOME SHOPPING...
MY MOTHER GAVE ME SOME MONEY AND TOLD ME TO GO BUY MYSELF SOME CLOTHES, BUT...
I'M ACTUALLY NOT THAT INTO IT. I HAVE NO IDEA WHAT I SHOULD GET.

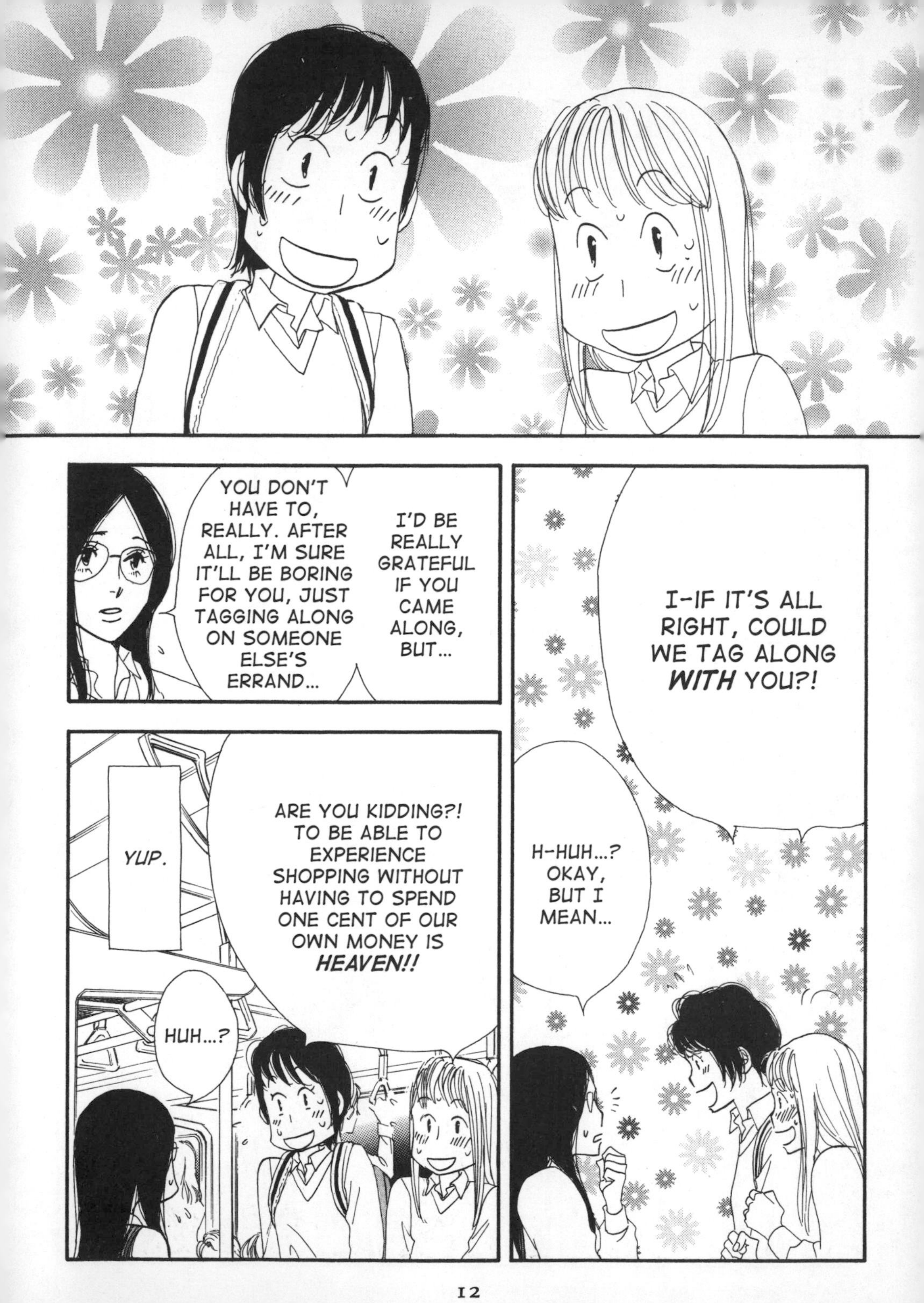
YOU DON'T HAVE TO, REALLY. AFTER ALL, I'M SURE IT'LL BE BORING FOR YOU, JUST TAGGING ALONG ON SOMEONE ELSE'S ERRAND...
I'D BE REALLY GRATEFUL IF YOU CAME ALONG, BUT...
ARE YOU KIDDING?! TO BE ABLE TO EXPERIENCE SHOPPING WITHOUT HAVING TO SPEND ONE CENT OF OUR OWN MONEY IS ***HEAVEN!!***
HUH...?
YUP.
I-IF IT'S ALL RIGHT, COULD WE TAG ALONG ***WITH*** YOU?!
H-HUH...? OKAY, BUT I MEAN...

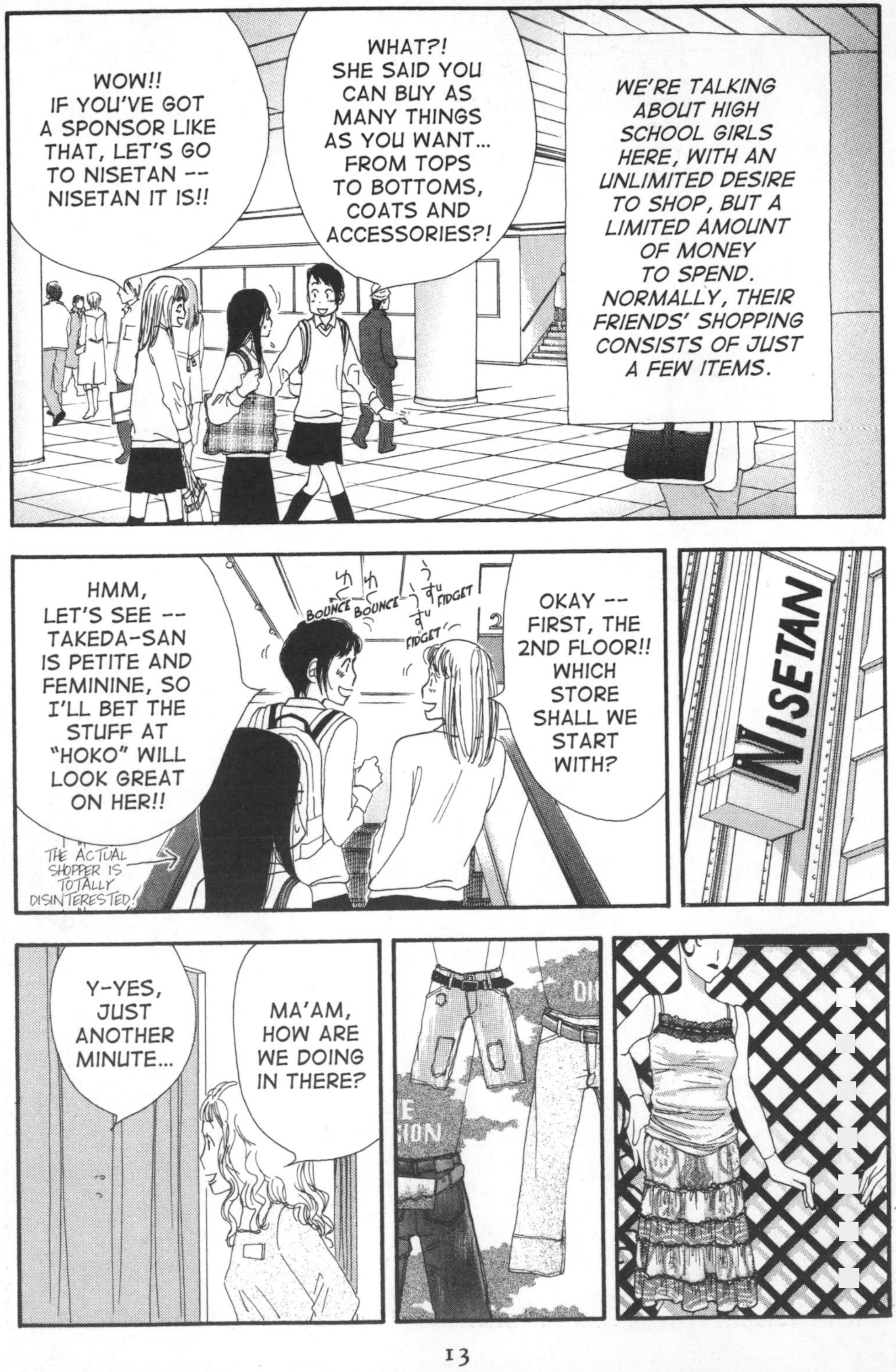
WE'RE TALKING ABOUT HIGH SCHOOL GIRLS HERE, WITH AN UNLIMITED DESIRE TO SHOP, BUT A LIMITED AMOUNT OF MONEY TO SPEND. NORMALLY, THEIR FRIENDS' SHOPPING CONSISTS OF JUST A FEW ITEMS.
WHAT?! SHE SAID YOU CAN BUY AS MANY THINGS AS YOU WANT... FROM TOPS TO BOTTOMS, COATS AND ACCESSORIES?!
WOW!! IF YOU'VE GOT A SPONSOR LIKE THAT, LET'S GO TO NISETAN -- NISETAN IT IS!!
NISETAN
OKAY -- FIRST, THE 2ND FLOOR!! WHICH STORE SHALL WE START WITH?
FIDGET FIDGET
BOUNCE BOUNCE
HMM, LET'S SEE -- TAKEDA-SAN IS PETITE AND FEMININE, SO I'LL BET THE STUFF AT "HOKO" WILL LOOK GREAT ON HER!!
THE ACTUAL SHOPPER IS TOTALLY DISINTERESTED!
MA'AM, HOW ARE WE DOING IN THERE?
Y-YES, JUST ANOTHER MINUTE...

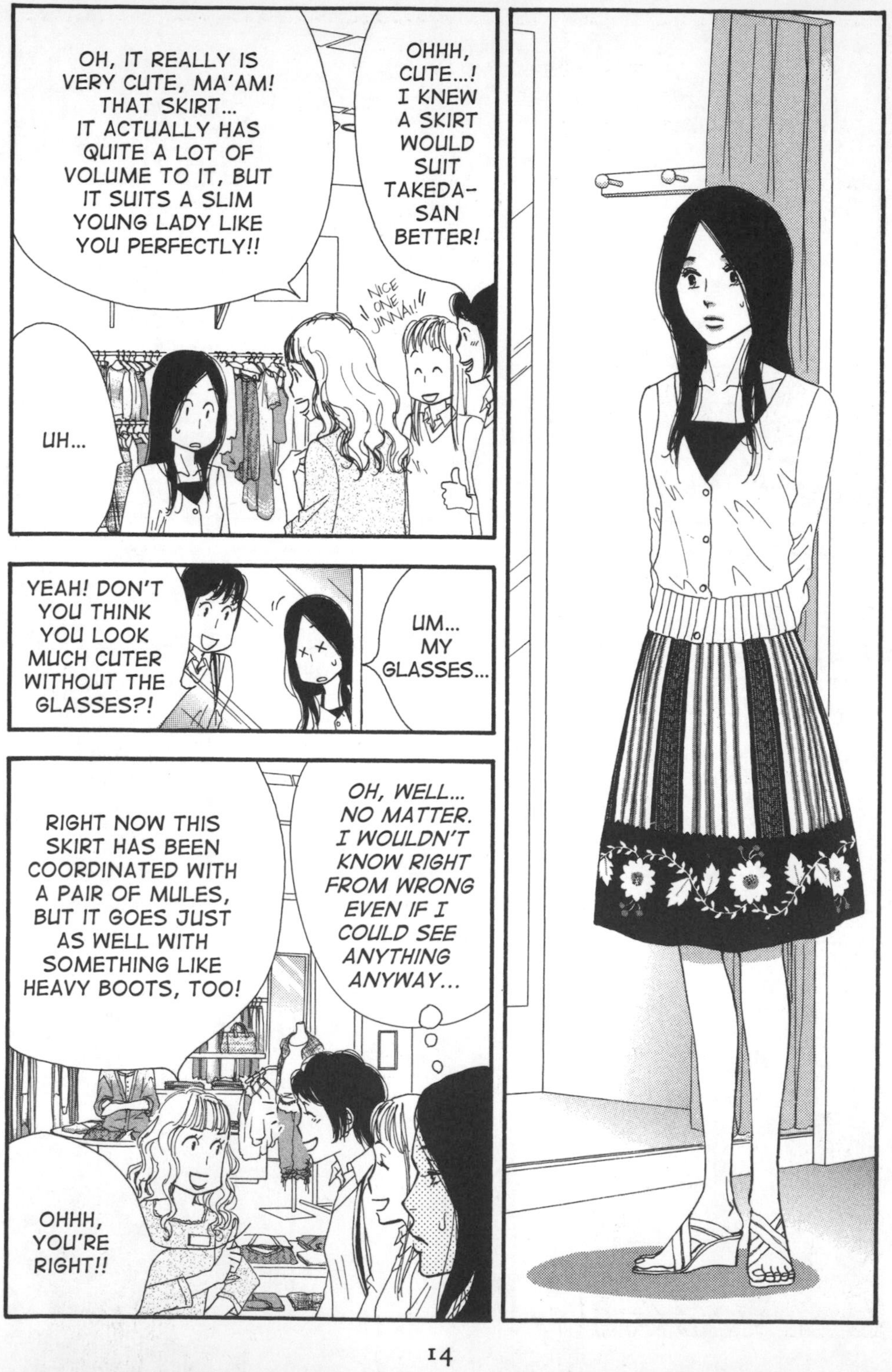
OHHH, CUTE...! I KNEW A SKIRT WOULD SUIT TAKEDA-SAN BETTER!
OH, IT REALLY IS VERY CUTE, MA'AM! THAT SKIRT... IT ACTUALLY HAS QUITE A LOT OF VOLUME TO IT, BUT IT SUITS A SLIM YOUNG LADY LIKE YOU PERFECTLY!!
NICE ONE JINNAI!!
UH...
UM... MY GLASSES...
YEAH! DON'T YOU THINK YOU LOOK MUCH CUTER WITHOUT THE GLASSES?!
OH, WELL... NO MATTER. I WOULDN'T KNOW RIGHT FROM WRONG EVEN IF I COULD SEE ANYTHING ANYWAY...
RIGHT NOW THIS SKIRT HAS BEEN COORDINATED WITH A PAIR OF MULES, BUT IT GOES JUST AS WELL WITH SOMETHING LIKE HEAVY BOOTS, TOO!
OHHH, YOU'RE RIGHT!!

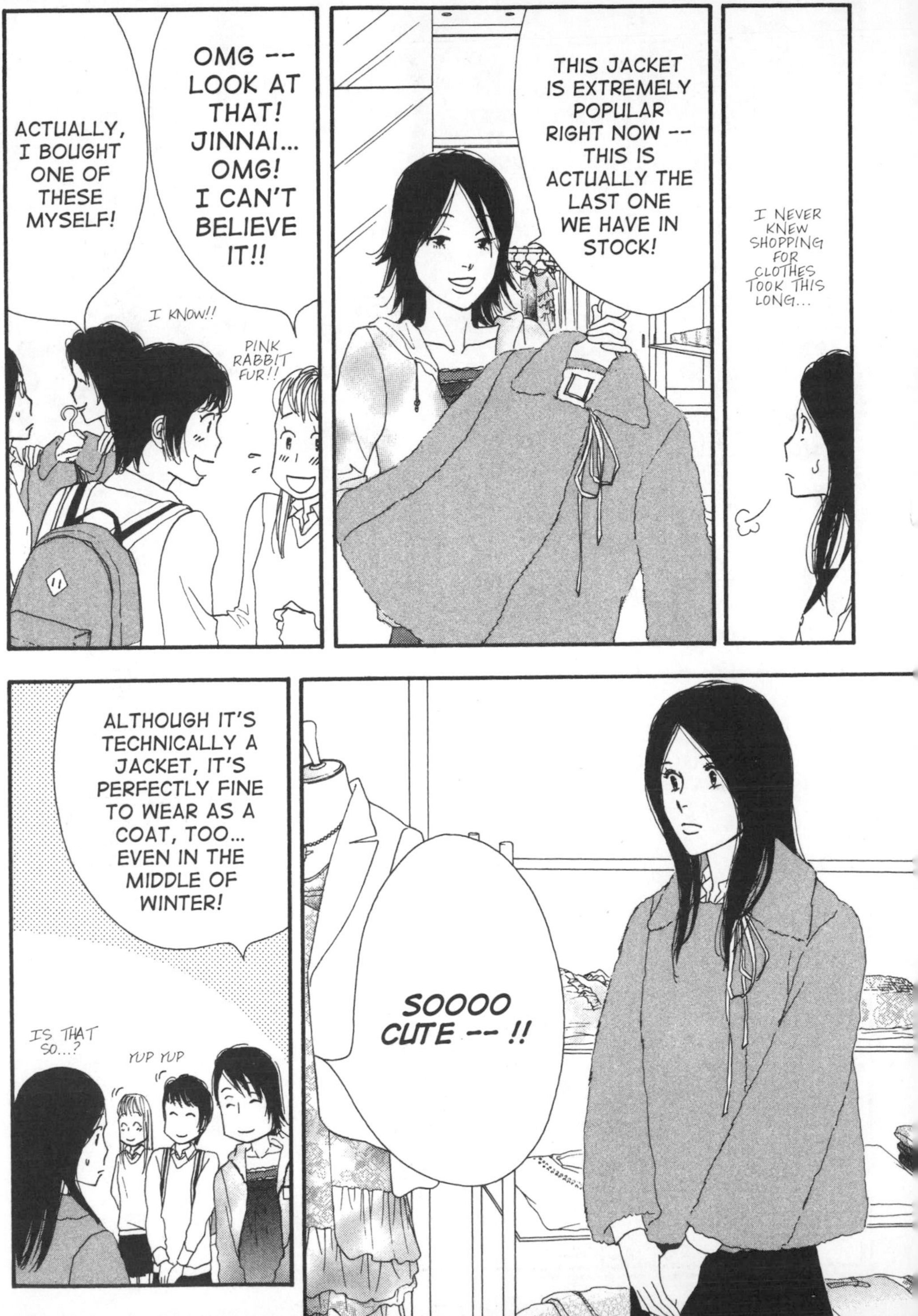

I NEVER KNEW SHOPPING FOR CLOTHES TOOK THIS LONG...
THIS JACKET IS EXTREMELY POPULAR RIGHT NOW -- THIS IS ACTUALLY THE LAST ONE WE HAVE IN STOCK!
OMG -- LOOK AT THAT! JINNAI... OMG! I CAN'T BELIEVE IT!!
ACTUALLY, I BOUGHT ONE OF THESE MYSELF!
PINK RABBIT FUR!!
I KNOW!!
SOOOO CUTE -- !!
ALTHOUGH IT'S TECHNICALLY A JACKET, IT'S PERFECTLY FINE TO WEAR AS A COAT, TOO... EVEN IN THE MIDDLE OF WINTER!
IS THAT SO...?
YUP YUP

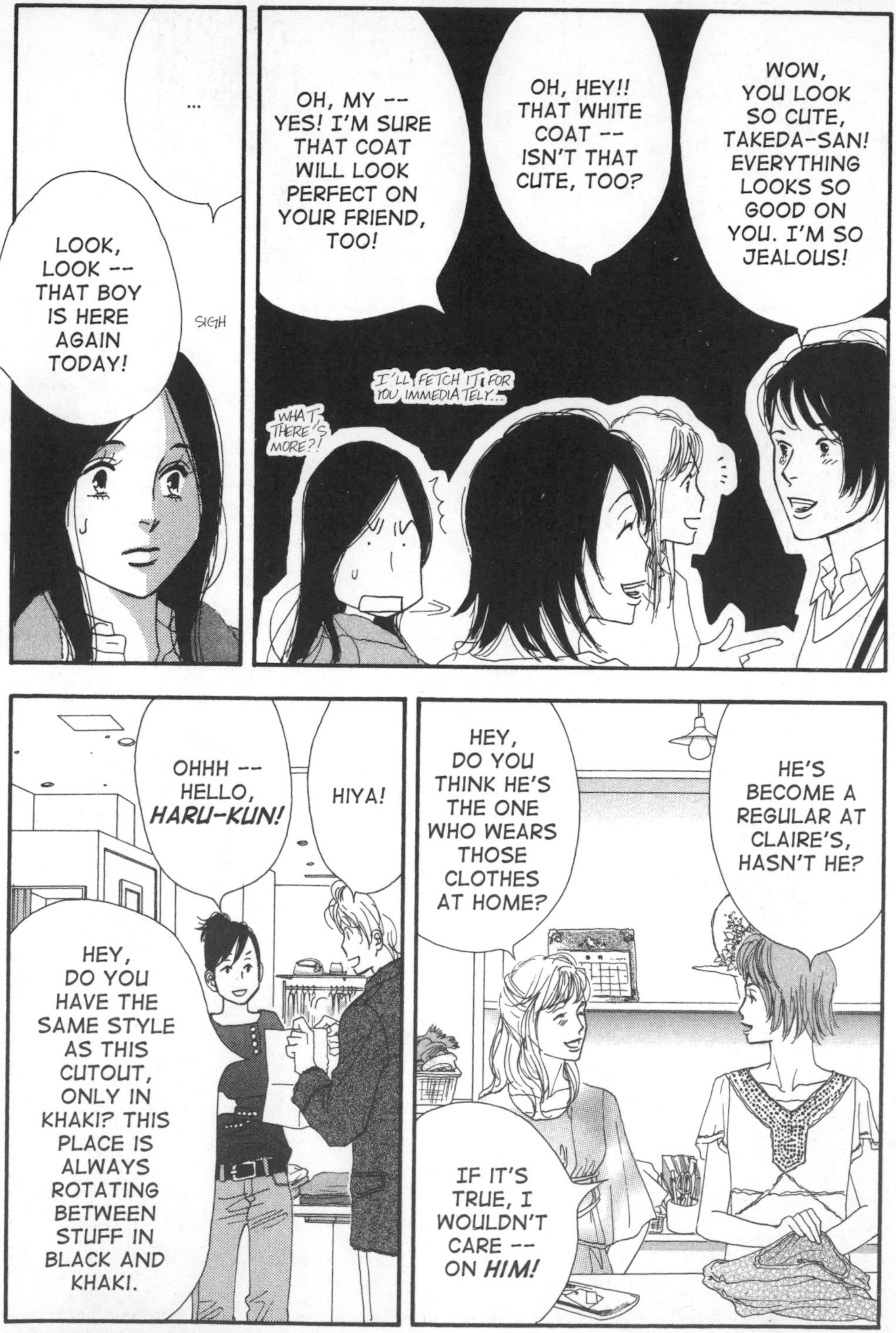
WOW, YOU LOOK SO CUTE, TAKEDA-SAN! EVERYTHING LOOKS SO GOOD ON YOU. I'M SO JEALOUS!
OH, HEY!! THAT WHITE COAT -- ISN'T THAT CUTE, TOO?
OH, MY -- YES! I'M SURE THAT COAT WILL LOOK PERFECT ON YOUR FRIEND, TOO!
I'LL FETCH IT FOR YOU IMMEDIATELY...
WHAT, THERE'S MORE?!
...
LOOK, LOOK -- THAT BOY IS HERE AGAIN TODAY!
SIGH
HE'S BECOME A REGULAR AT CLAIRE'S, HASN'T HE?
HEY, DO YOU THINK HE'S THE ONE WHO WEARS THOSE CLOTHES AT HOME?
IF IT'S TRUE, I WOULDN'T CARE -- ON *HIM!*
HIYA!
OHHH -- HELLO, *HARU-KUN!*
HEY, DO YOU HAVE THE SAME STYLE AS THIS CUTOUT, ONLY IN KHAKI? THIS PLACE IS ALWAYS ROTATING BETWEEN STUFF IN BLACK AND KHAKI.

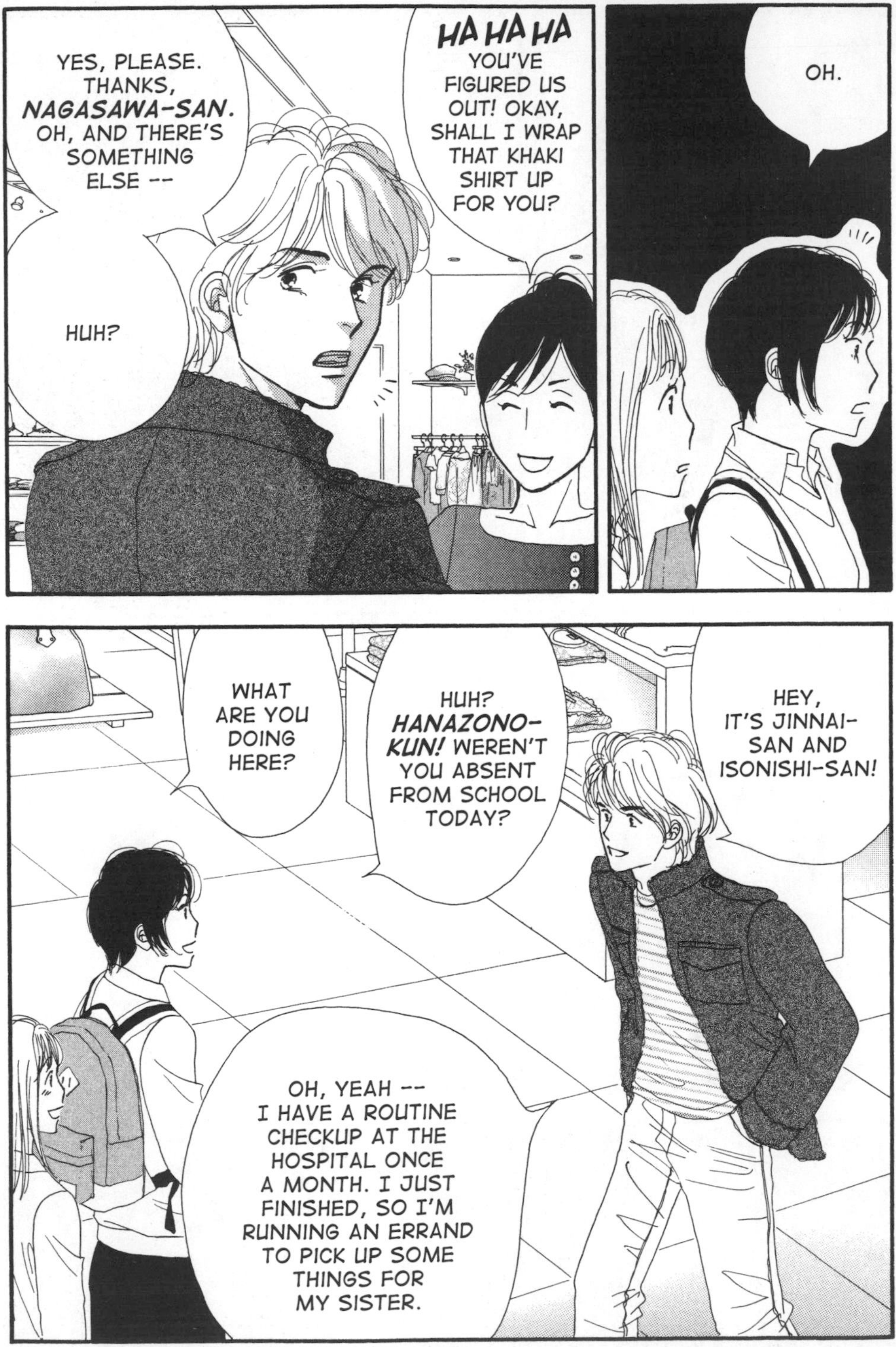
OH.
HA HA HA YOU'VE FIGURED US OUT! OKAY, SHALL I WRAP THAT KHAKI SHIRT UP FOR YOU?
YES, PLEASE. THANKS, NAGASAWA-SAN. OH, AND THERE'S SOMETHING ELSE --
HUH?
HEY, IT'S JINNAI-SAN AND ISONISHI-SAN!
HUH? HANAZONO-KUN! WEREN'T YOU ABSENT FROM SCHOOL TODAY?
WHAT ARE YOU DOING HERE?
OH, YEAH -- I HAVE A ROUTINE CHECKUP AT THE HOSPITAL ONCE A MONTH. I JUST FINISHED, SO I'M RUNNING AN ERRAND TO PICK UP SOME THINGS FOR MY SISTER.

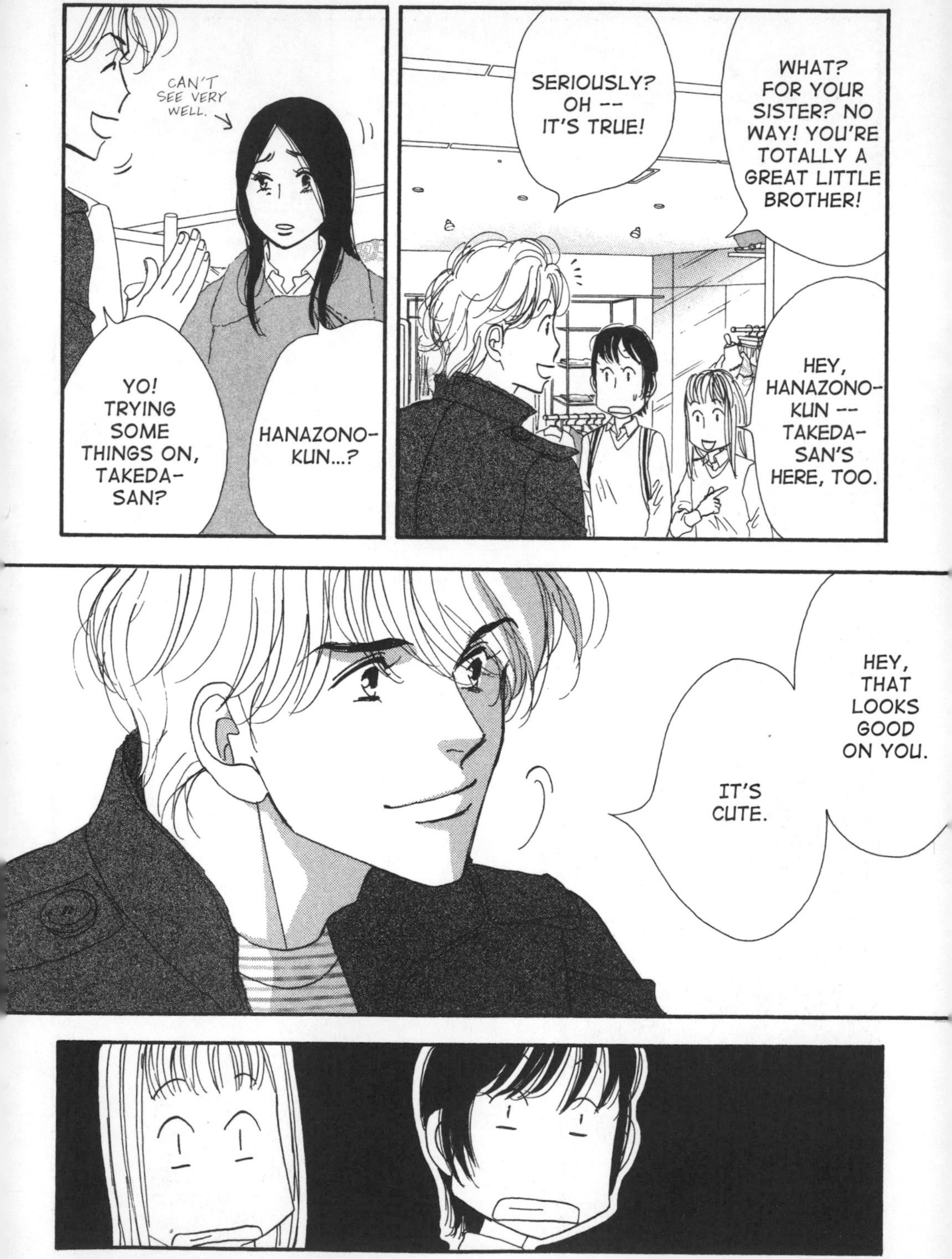
WHAT? FOR YOUR SISTER? NO WAY! YOU'RE TOTALLY A GREAT LITTLE BROTHER!
SERIOUSLY? OH -- IT'S TRUE!
HEY, HANAZONO-KUN -- TAKEDA-SAN'S HERE, TOO.
CAN'T SEE VERY WELL.
HANAZONO-KUN...?
YO! TRYING SOME THINGS ON, TAKEDA-SAN?
HEY, THAT LOOKS GOOD ON YOU.
IT'S CUTE.

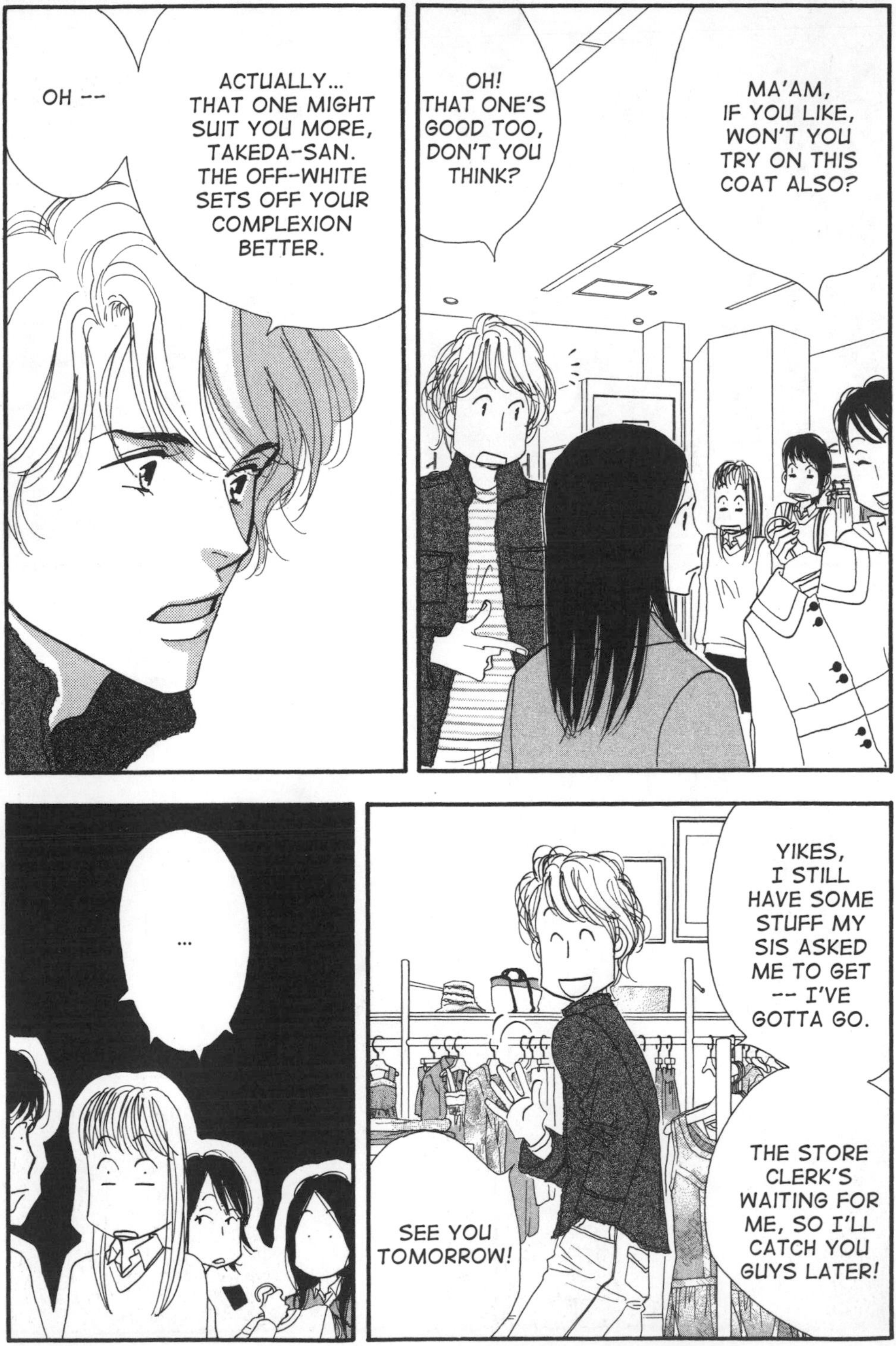
MA'AM, IF YOU LIKE, WON'T YOU TRY ON THIS COAT ALSO?
OH! THAT ONE'S GOOD TOO, DON'T YOU THINK?
OH --
ACTUALLY... THAT ONE MIGHT SUIT YOU MORE, TAKEDA-SAN. THE OFF-WHITE SETS OFF YOUR COMPLEXION BETTER.
YIKES, I STILL HAVE SOME STUFF MY SIS ASKED ME TO GET -- I'VE GOTTA GO.
THE STORE CLERK'S WAITING FOR ME, SO I'LL CATCH YOU GUYS LATER!
SEE YOU TOMORROW!
...

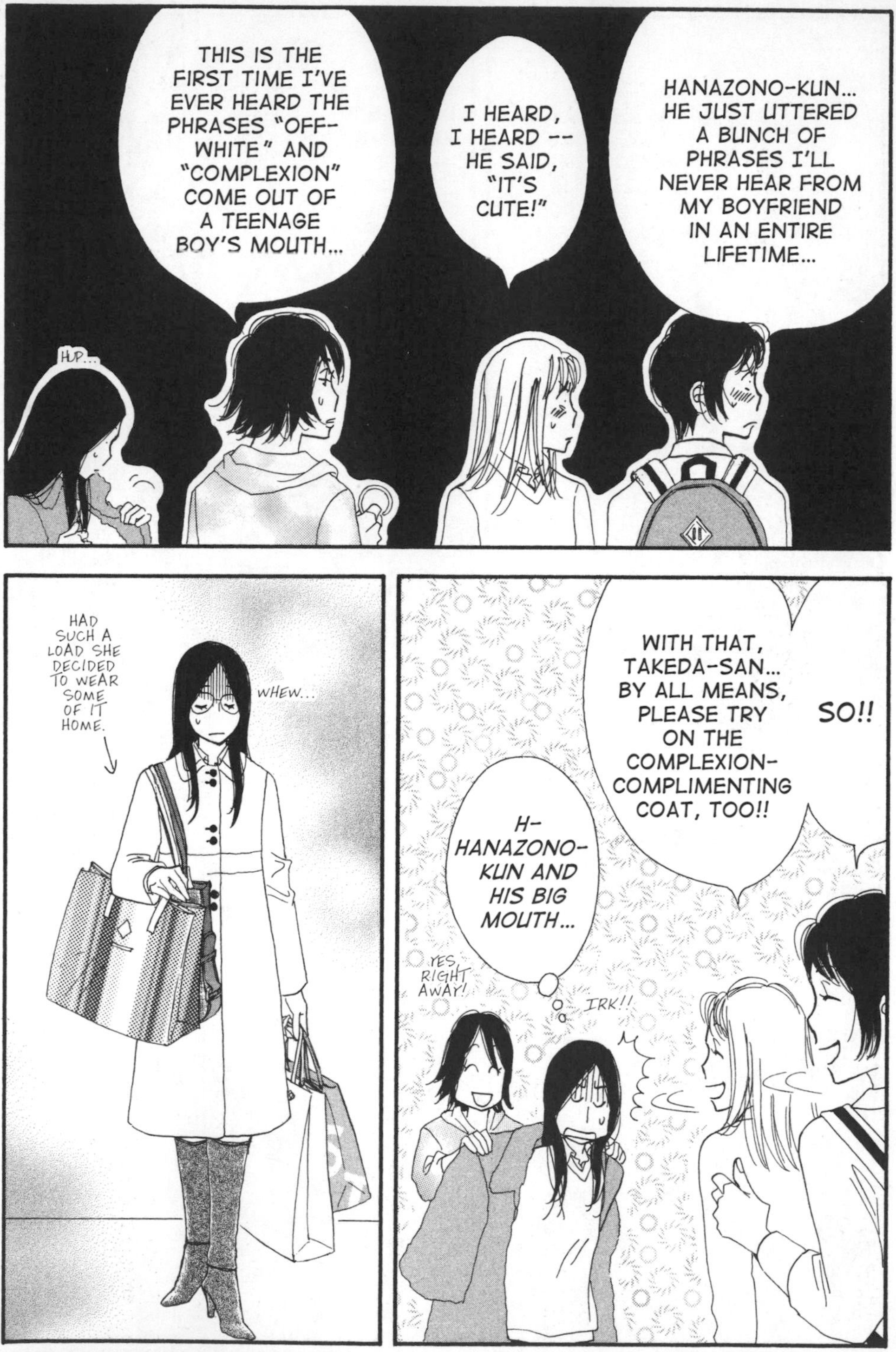
HANAZONO-KUN... HE JUST UTTERED A BUNCH OF PHRASES I'LL NEVER HEAR FROM MY BOYFRIEND IN AN ENTIRE LIFETIME...
I HEARD, I HEARD -- HE SAID, "IT'S CUTE!"
THIS IS THE FIRST TIME I'VE EVER HEARD THE PHRASES "OFF-WHITE" AND "COMPLEXION" COME OUT OF A TEENAGE BOY'S MOUTH...
HUP...
SO!!
WITH THAT, TAKEDA-SAN... BY ALL MEANS, PLEASE TRY ON THE COMPLEXION-COMPLIMENTING COAT, TOO!!
H-HANAZONO-KUN AND HIS BIG MOUTH...
IRK!!
YES, RIGHT AWAY!
WHEW...
HAD SUCH A LOAD SHE DECIDED TO WEAR SOME OF IT HOME.

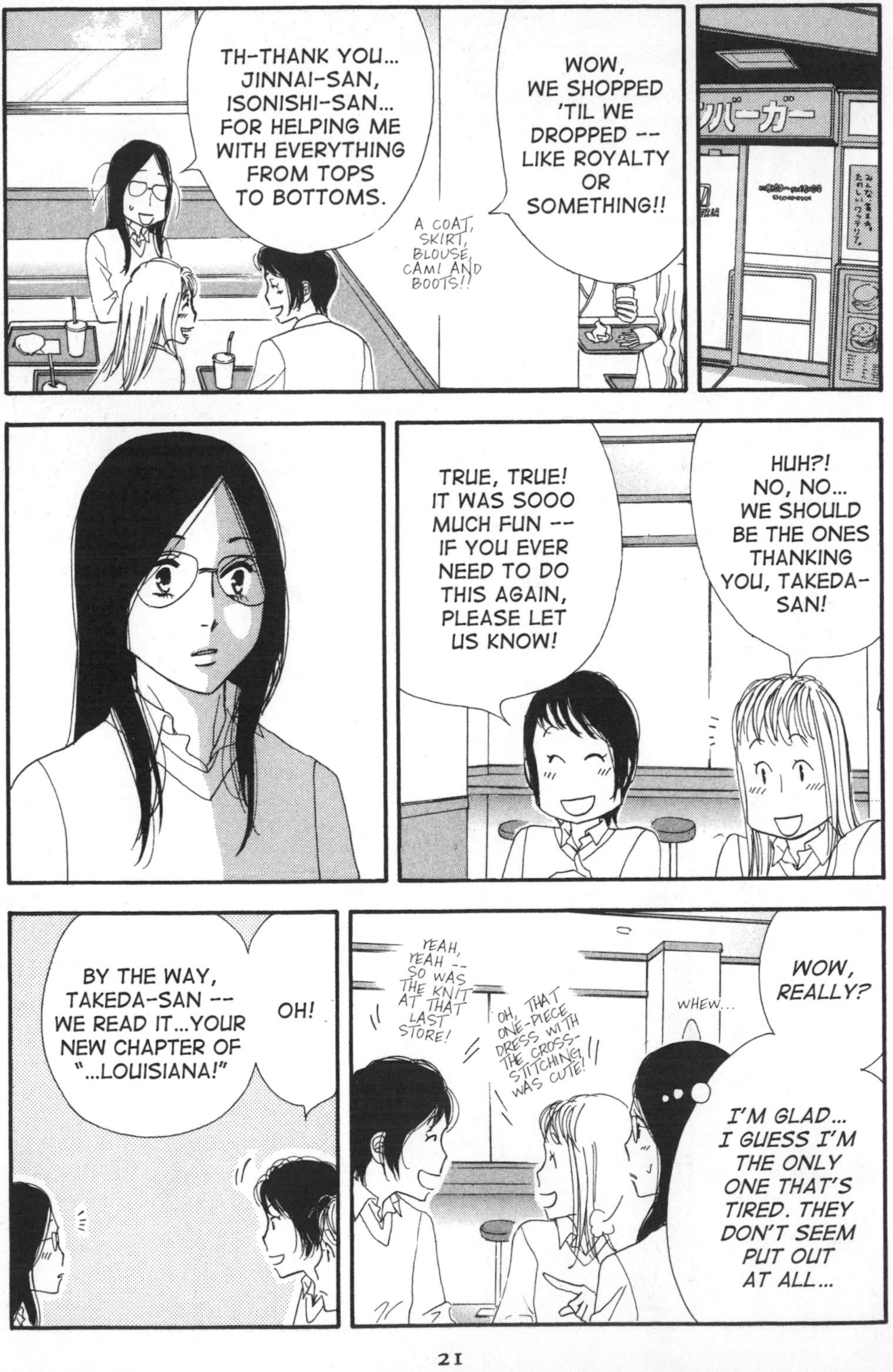
バーガー
WOW, WE SHOPPED 'TIL WE DROPPED -- LIKE ROYALTY OR SOMETHING!!
TH-THANK YOU... JINNAI-SAN, ISONISHI-SAN... FOR HELPING ME WITH EVERYTHING FROM TOPS TO BOTTOMS.
A COAT, SKIRT, BLOUSE, CAMI AND BOOTS!!
HUH?! NO, NO... WE SHOULD BE THE ONES THANKING YOU, TAKEDA-SAN!
TRUE, TRUE! IT WAS SOOO MUCH FUN -- IF YOU EVER NEED TO DO THIS AGAIN, PLEASE LET US KNOW!
WOW, REALLY?
I'M GLAD... I GUESS I'M THE ONLY ONE THAT'S TIRED. THEY DON'T SEEM PUT OUT AT ALL...
WHEW...
OH, THAT ONE-PIECE DRESS WITH THE CROSS-STITCHING WAS CUTE!
YEAH, YEAH -- SO WAS THE KNIT AT THAT LAST STORE!
OH!
BY THE WAY, TAKEDA-SAN -- WE READ IT...YOUR NEW CHAPTER OF "...LOUISIANA!"

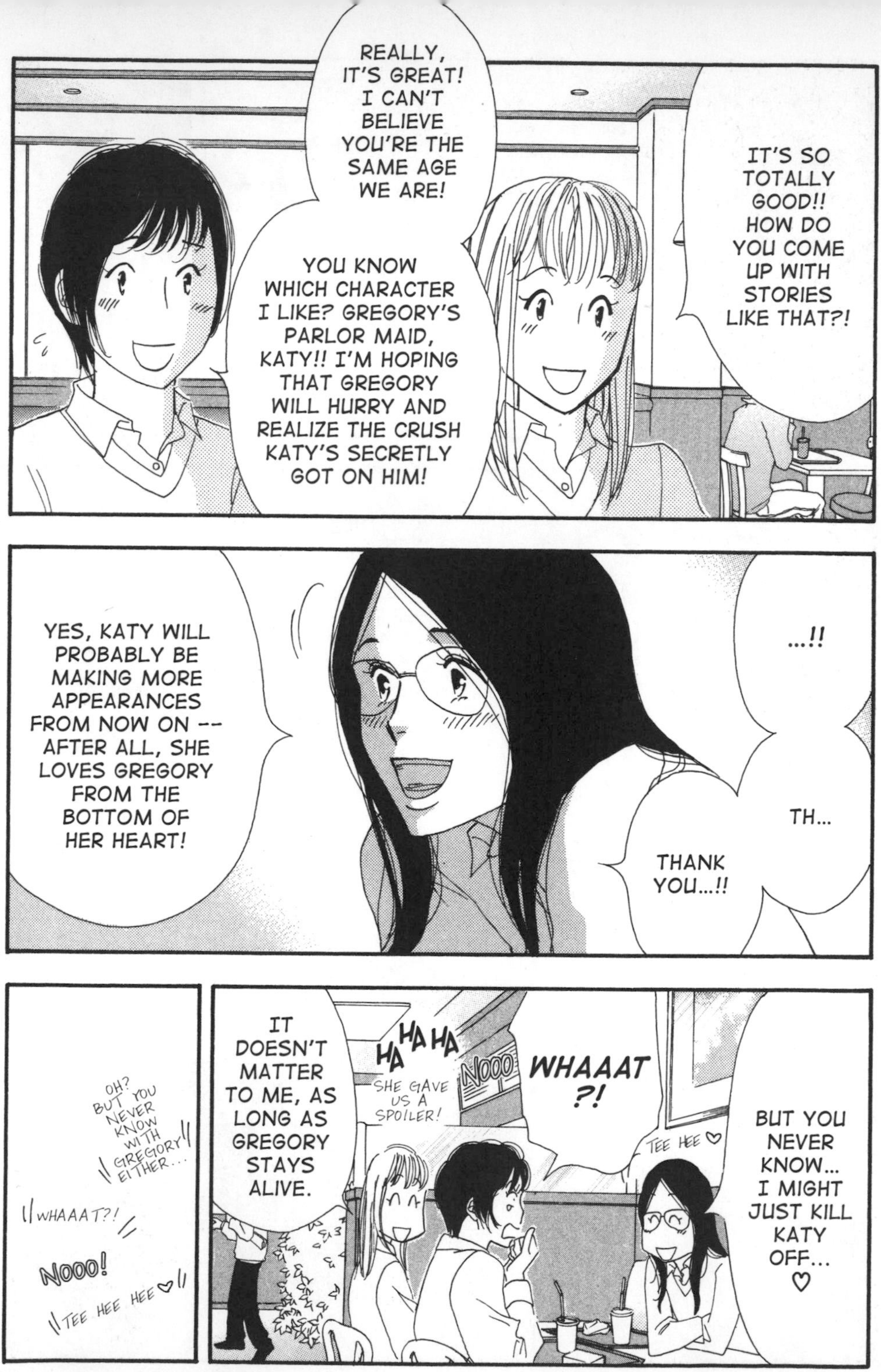
IT'S SO TOTALLY GOOD!! HOW DO YOU COME UP WITH STORIES LIKE THAT?!
REALLY, IT'S GREAT! I CAN'T BELIEVE YOU'RE THE SAME AGE WE ARE!
YOU KNOW WHICH CHARACTER I LIKE? GREGORY'S PARLOR MAID, KATY!! I'M HOPING THAT GREGORY WILL HURRY AND REALIZE THE CRUSH KATY'S SECRETLY GOT ON HIM!
...!!
TH...
THANK YOU...!!
YES, KATY WILL PROBABLY BE MAKING MORE APPEARANCES FROM NOW ON -- AFTER ALL, SHE LOVES GREGORY FROM THE BOTTOM OF HER HEART!
BUT YOU NEVER KNOW... I MIGHT JUST KILL KATY OFF... ♡
TEE HEE ♡
WHAAAT?!
NOOO
HA HA HA HA
SHE GAVE US A SPOILER!
IT DOESN'T MATTER TO ME, AS LONG AS GREGORY STAYS ALIVE.
OH? BUT YOU NEVER KNOW WITH GREGORY EITHER...
WHAAAT?!
NOOO!
TEE HEE HEE ♡

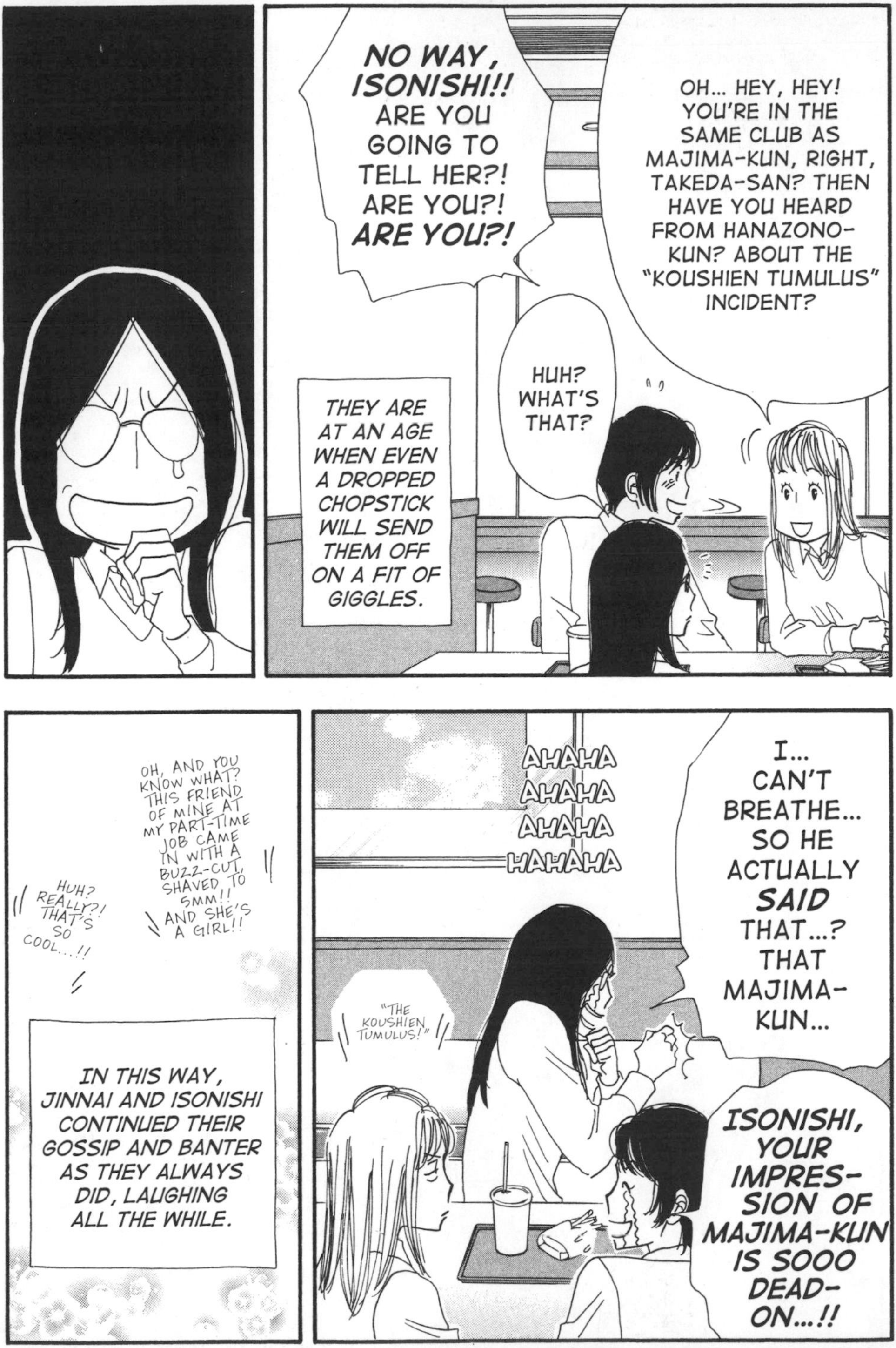
OH... HEY, HEY! YOU'RE IN THE SAME CLUB AS MAJIMA-KUN, RIGHT, TAKEDA-SAN? THEN HAVE YOU HEARD FROM HANAZONO-KUN? ABOUT THE "KOUSHIEN TUMULUS" INCIDENT?
NO WAY, ISONISHI!! ARE YOU GOING TO TELL HER?! ARE YOU?! ARE YOU?!
HUH? WHAT'S THAT?
THEY ARE AT AN AGE WHEN EVEN A DROPPED CHOPSTICK WILL SEND THEM OFF ON A FIT OF GIGGLES.
AHAHA AHAHA AHAHA HAHAHA
I... CAN'T BREATHE... SO HE ACTUALLY SAID THAT...? THAT MAJIMA-KUN...
"THE KOUSHIEN TUMULUS!"
ISONISHI, YOUR IMPRESSION OF MAJIMA-KUN IS SOOO DEAD-ON...!!
OH, AND YOU KNOW WHAT? THIS FRIEND OF MINE AT MY PART-TIME JOB CAME IN WITH A BUZZ-CUT, SHAVED TO 5MM!! AND SHE'S A GIRL!!
HUH? REALLY?! THAT'S SO COOL...!!
IN THIS WAY, JINNAI AND ISONISHI CONTINUED THEIR GOSSIP AND BANTER AS THEY ALWAYS DID, LAUGHING ALL THE WHILE.

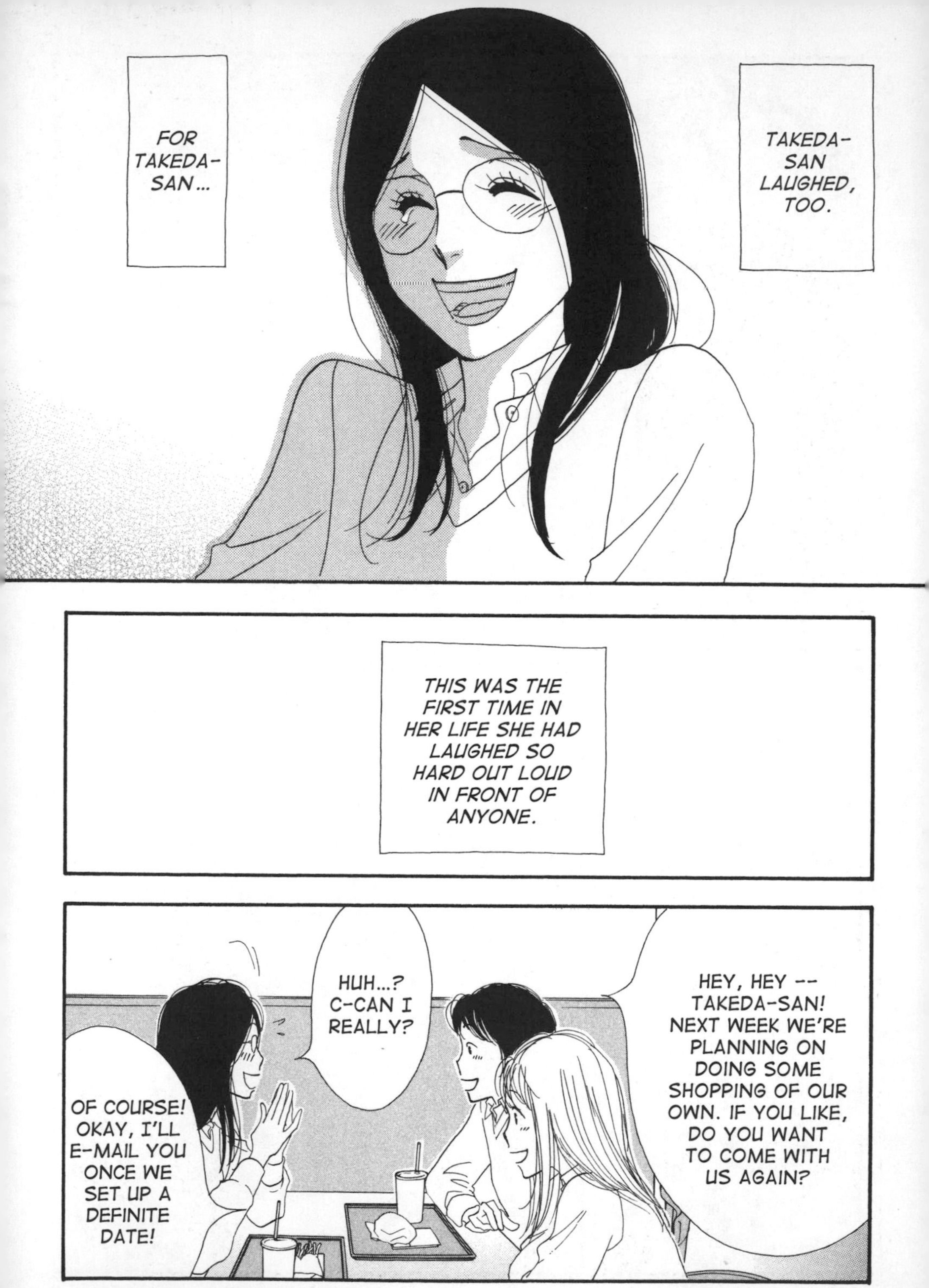
TAKEDA-SAN LAUGHED, TOO.
FOR TAKEDA-SAN...
THIS WAS THE FIRST TIME IN HER LIFE SHE HAD LAUGHED SO HARD OUT LOUD IN FRONT OF ANYONE.
HEY, HEY -- TAKEDA-SAN! NEXT WEEK WE'RE PLANNING ON DOING SOME SHOPPING OF OUR OWN. IF YOU LIKE, DO YOU WANT TO COME WITH US AGAIN?
HUH...? C-CAN I REALLY?
OF COURSE! OKAY, I'LL E-MAIL YOU ONCE WE SET UP A DEFINITE DATE!

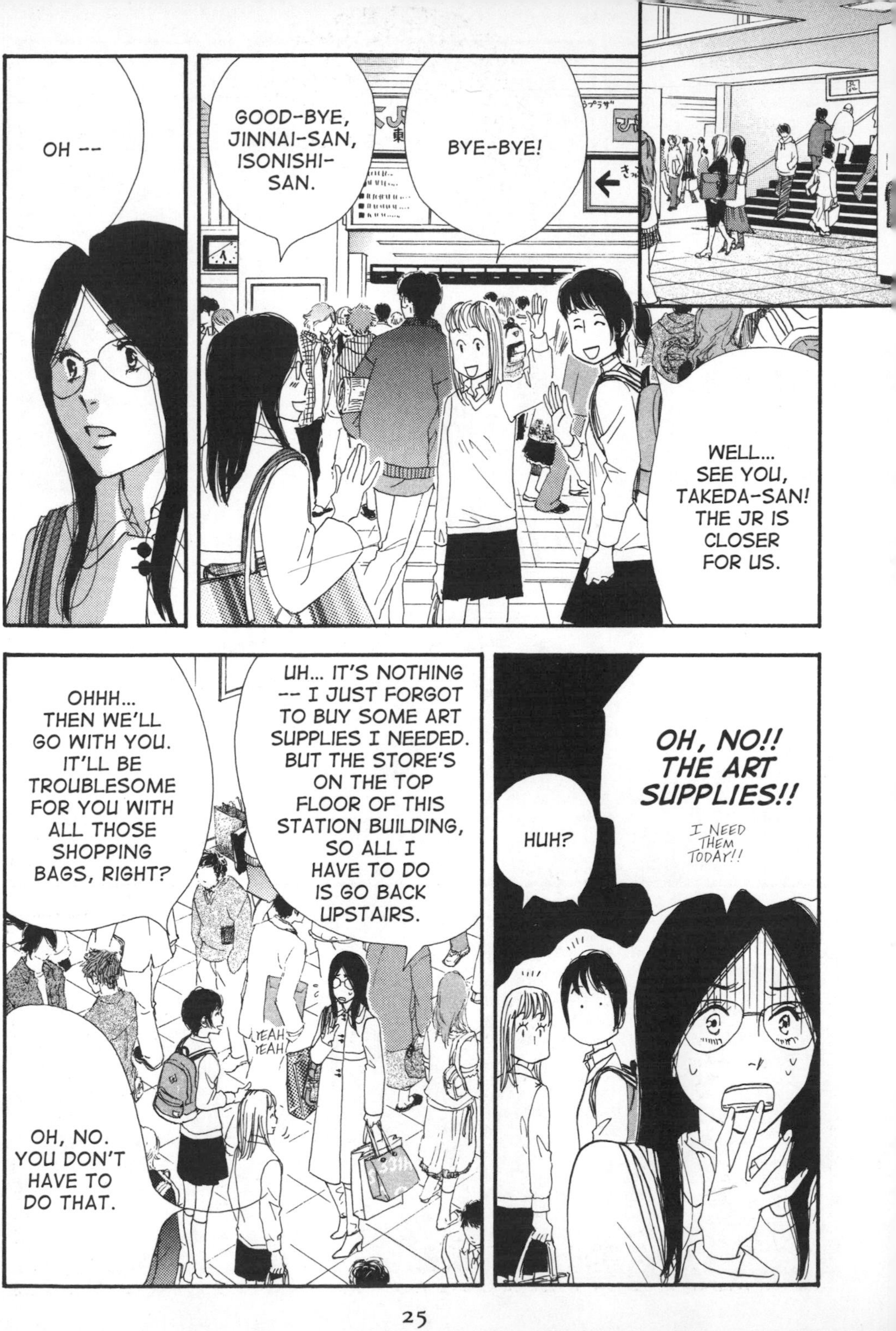
WELL... SEE YOU, TAKEDA-SAN! THE JR IS CLOSER FOR US.
BYE-BYE!
GOOD-BYE, JINNAI-SAN, ISONISHI-SAN.
OH --
OH, NO!! THE ART SUPPLIES!!
I NEED THEM TODAY!!
HUH?
UH... IT'S NOTHING -- I JUST FORGOT TO BUY SOME ART SUPPLIES I NEEDED. BUT THE STORE'S ON THE TOP FLOOR OF THIS STATION BUILDING, SO ALL I HAVE TO DO IS GO BACK UPSTAIRS.
OHHH... THEN WE'LL GO WITH YOU. IT'LL BE TROUBLESOME FOR YOU WITH ALL THOSE SHOPPING BAGS, RIGHT?
YEAH YEAH
OH, NO. YOU DON'T HAVE TO DO THAT.

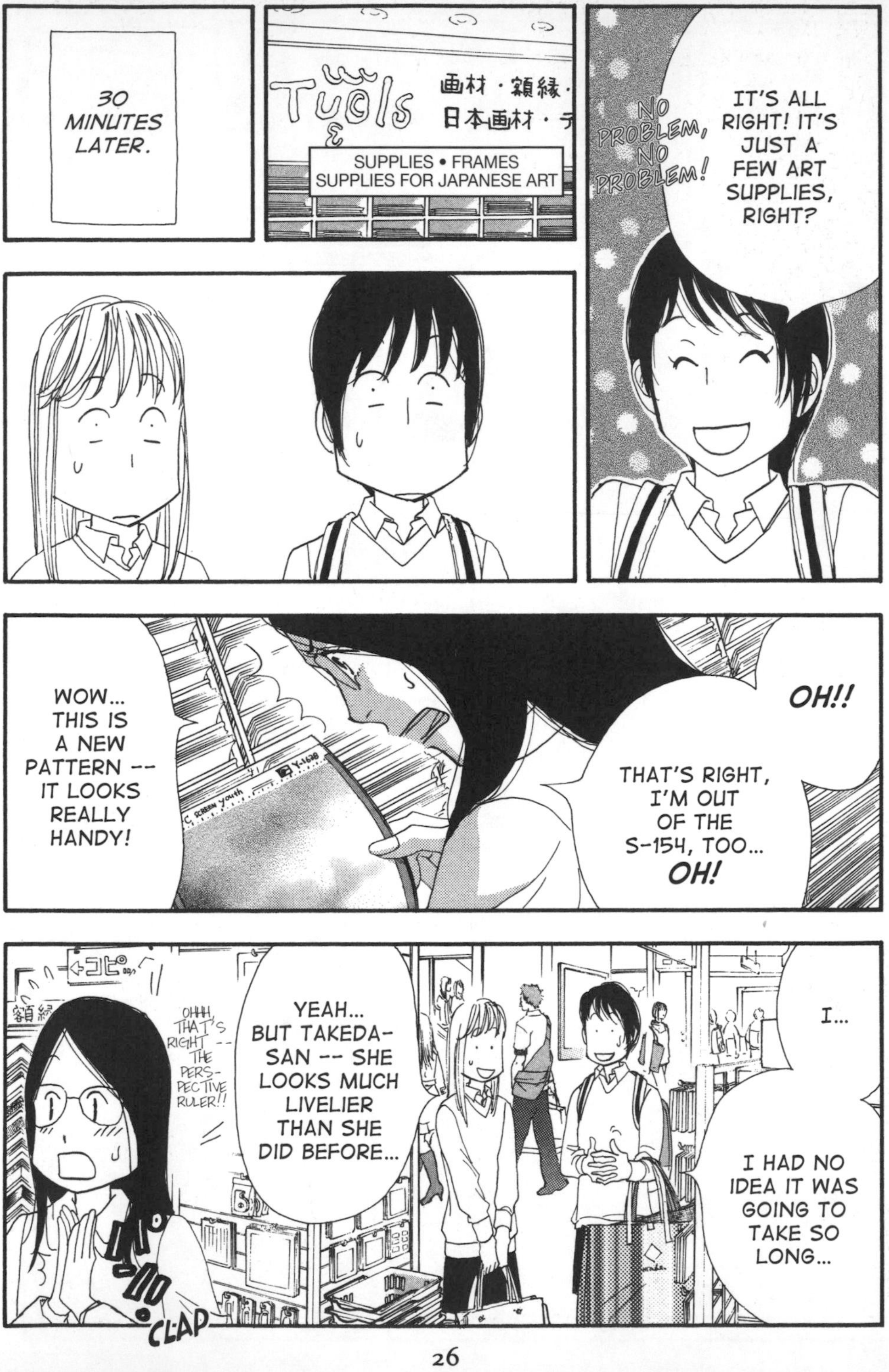
IT'S ALL RIGHT! IT'S JUST A FEW ART SUPPLIES, RIGHT?
NO PROBLEM, NO PROBLEM!
Tools
画材・額縁・
日本画材・テ
SUPPLIES • FRAMES
SUPPLIES FOR JAPANESE ART
30 MINUTES LATER.
OH!!
THAT'S RIGHT, I'M OUT OF THE S-154, TOO... OH!
WOW... THIS IS A NEW PATTERN -- IT LOOKS REALLY HANDY!
I...
I HAD NO IDEA IT WAS GOING TO TAKE SO LONG...
YEAH... BUT TAKEDA-SAN -- SHE LOOKS MUCH LIVELIER THAN SHE DID BEFORE...
OHHH, THAT'S RIGHT THE PERSPECTIVE RULER!!
CLAP

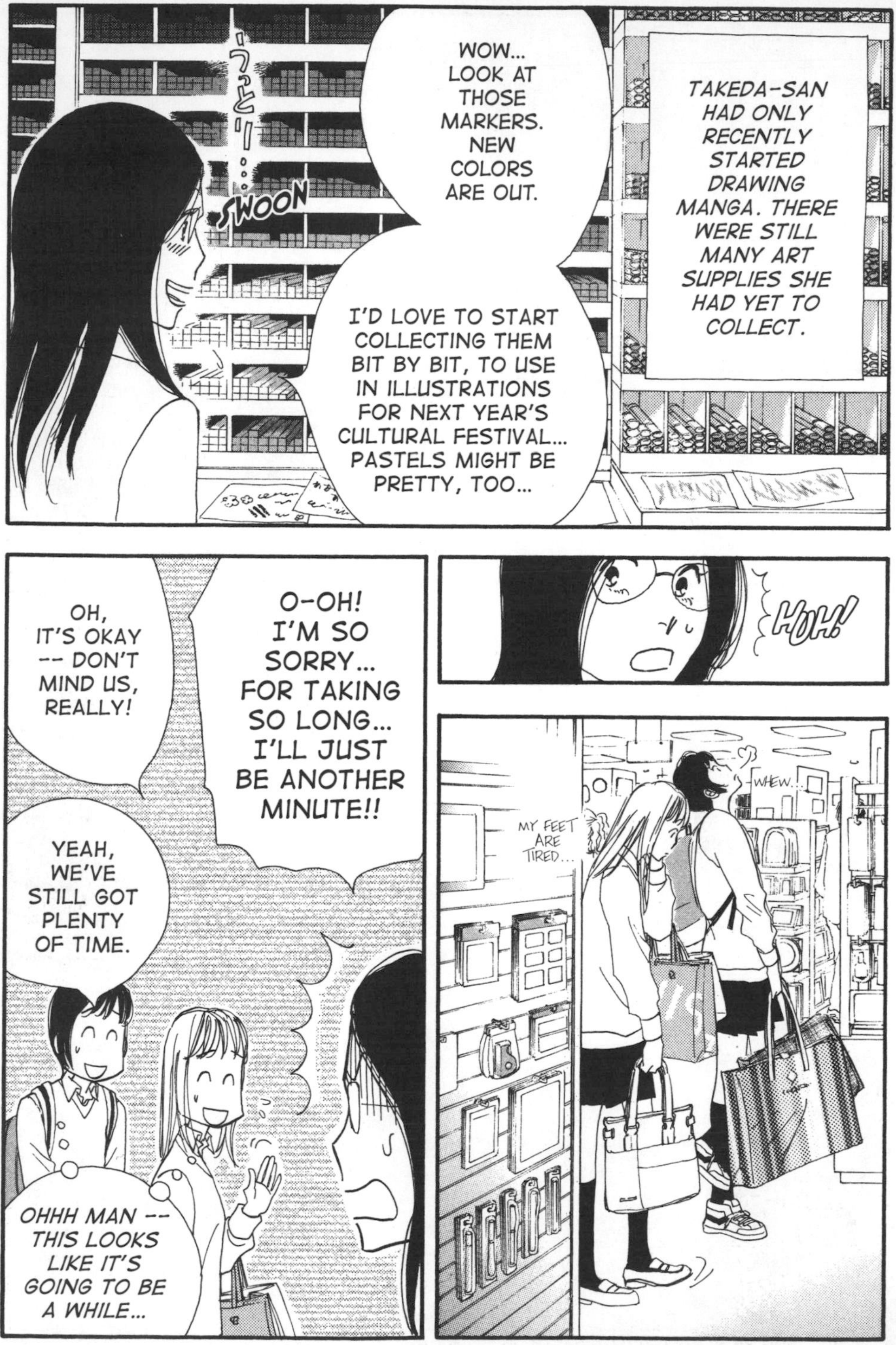
TAKEDA-SAN HAD ONLY RECENTLY STARTED DRAWING MANGA. THERE WERE STILL MANY ART SUPPLIES SHE HAD YET TO COLLECT.
WOW... LOOK AT THOSE MARKERS. NEW COLORS ARE OUT.
I'D LOVE TO START COLLECTING THEM BIT BY BIT, TO USE IN ILLUSTRATIONS FOR NEXT YEAR'S CULTURAL FESTIVAL... PASTELS MIGHT BE PRETTY, TOO...
SWOON
HUH!
WHEW...
MY FEET ARE TIRED...
O-OH! I'M SO SORRY... FOR TAKING SO LONG... I'LL JUST BE ANOTHER MINUTE!!
OH, IT'S OKAY -- DON'T MIND US, REALLY!
YEAH, WE'VE STILL GOT PLENTY OF TIME.
OHHH MAN -- THIS LOOKS LIKE IT'S GOING TO BE A WHILE...

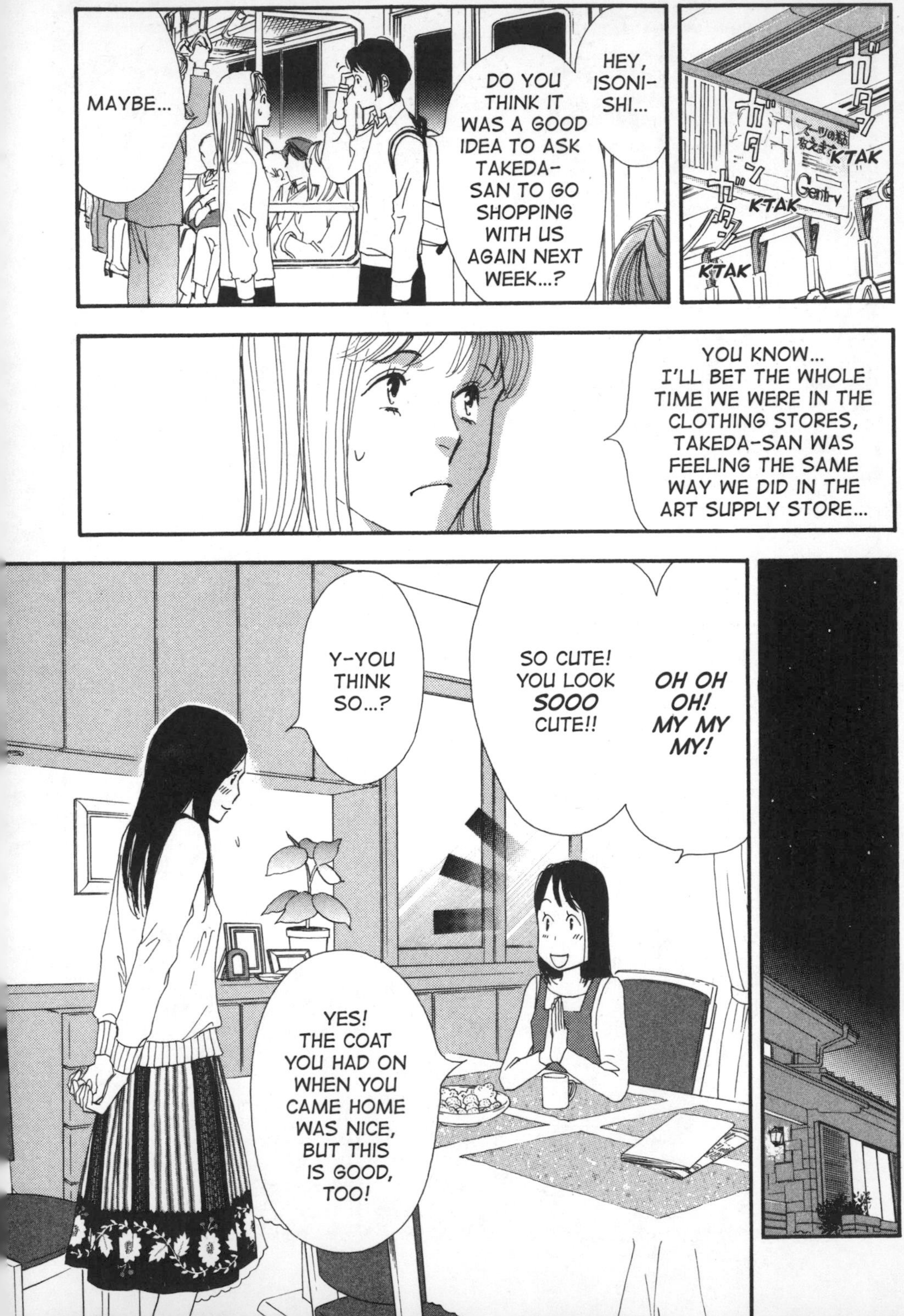
K'TAK
K'TAK
K'TAK
Gentry
HEY, ISONI-SHI...
DO YOU THINK IT WAS A GOOD IDEA TO ASK TAKEDA-SAN TO GO SHOPPING WITH US AGAIN NEXT WEEK...?
MAYBE...
YOU KNOW... I'LL BET THE WHOLE TIME WE WERE IN THE CLOTHING STORES, TAKEDA-SAN WAS FEELING THE SAME WAY WE DID IN THE ART SUPPLY STORE...
OH OH OH! MY MY MY!
SO CUTE! YOU LOOK SOOO CUTE!!
Y-YOU THINK SO...?
YES! THE COAT YOU HAD ON WHEN YOU CAME HOME WAS NICE, BUT THIS IS GOOD, TOO!

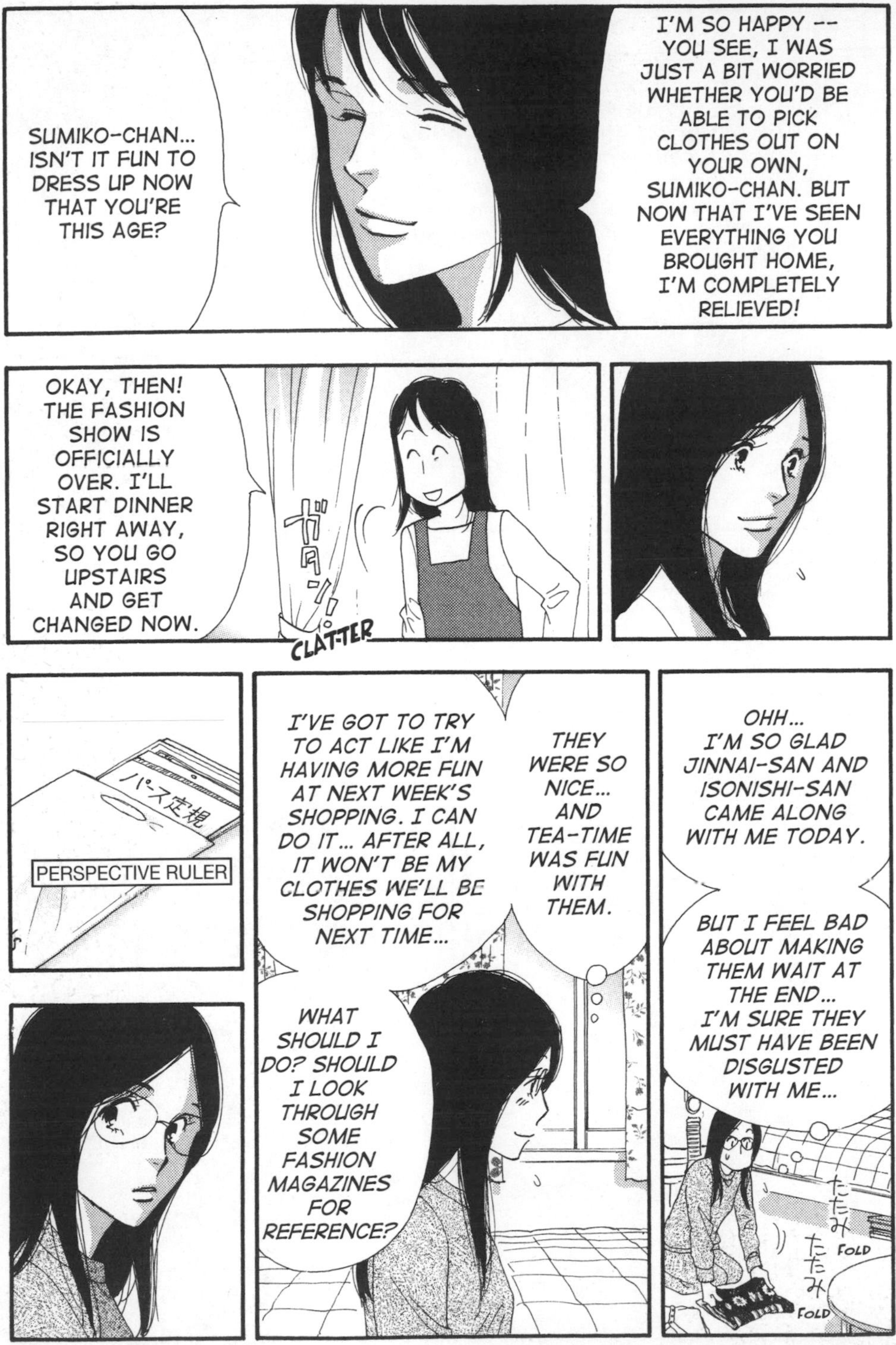
I'M SO HAPPY -- YOU SEE, I WAS JUST A BIT WORRIED WHETHER YOU'D BE ABLE TO PICK CLOTHES OUT ON YOUR OWN, SUMIKO-CHAN. BUT NOW THAT I'VE SEEN EVERYTHING YOU BROUGHT HOME, I'M COMPLETELY RELIEVED!
SUMIKO-CHAN... ISN'T IT FUN TO DRESS UP NOW THAT YOU'RE THIS AGE?
OKAY, THEN! THE FASHION SHOW IS OFFICIALLY OVER. I'LL START DINNER RIGHT AWAY, SO YOU GO UPSTAIRS AND GET CHANGED NOW.
ガタッ!
CLAT-TER
OHH... I'M SO GLAD JINNAI-SAN AND ISONISHI-SAN CAME ALONG WITH ME TODAY.
BUT I FEEL BAD ABOUT MAKING THEM WAIT AT THE END... I'M SURE THEY MUST HAVE BEEN DISGUSTED WITH ME...
たたみ
FOLD
たたみ
FOLD
THEY WERE SO NICE... AND TEA-TIME WAS FUN WITH THEM.
I'VE GOT TO TRY TO ACT LIKE I'M HAVING MORE FUN AT NEXT WEEK'S SHOPPING. I CAN DO IT... AFTER ALL, IT WON'T BE MY CLOTHES WE'LL BE SHOPPING FOR NEXT TIME...
WHAT SHOULD I DO? SHOULD I LOOK THROUGH SOME FASHION MAGAZINES FOR REFERENCE?
パース定規
PERSPECTIVE RULER

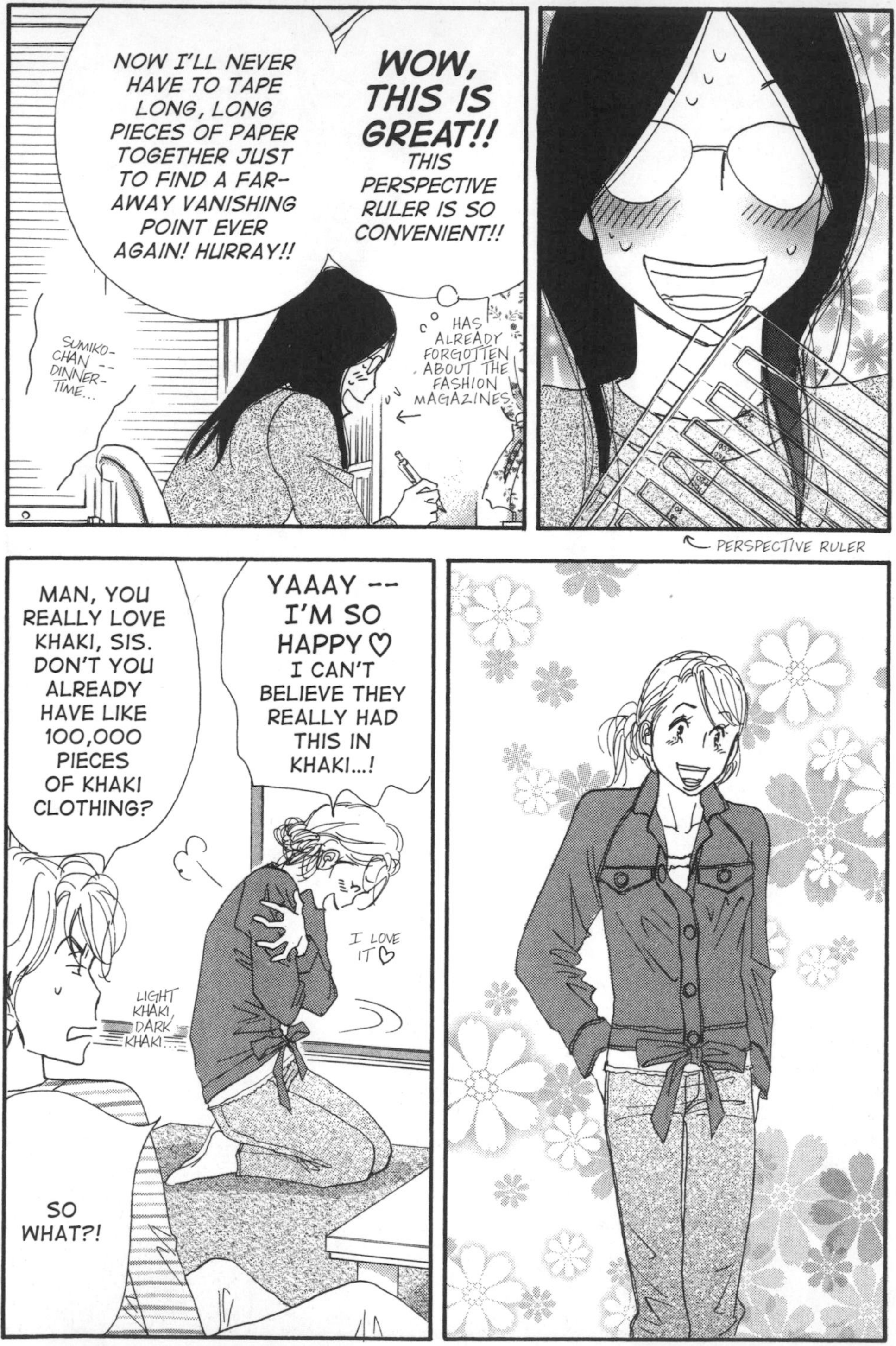
PERSPECTIVE RULER
WOW, THIS IS GREAT!!
THIS PERSPECTIVE RULER IS SO CONVENIENT!!
NOW I'LL NEVER HAVE TO TAPE LONG, LONG PIECES OF PAPER TOGETHER JUST TO FIND A FAR-AWAY VANISHING POINT EVER AGAIN! HURRAY!!
HAS ALREADY FORGOTTEN ABOUT THE FASHION MAGAZINES.
SUMIKO-CHAN -- DINNER-TIME...
YAAAY -- I'M SO HAPPY ♡ I CAN'T BELIEVE THEY REALLY HAD THIS IN KHAKI...!
MAN, YOU REALLY LOVE KHAKI, SIS. DON'T YOU ALREADY HAVE LIKE 100,000 PIECES OF KHAKI CLOTHING?
I LOVE IT ♡
LIGHT KHAKI, DARK KHAKI...
SO WHAT?!

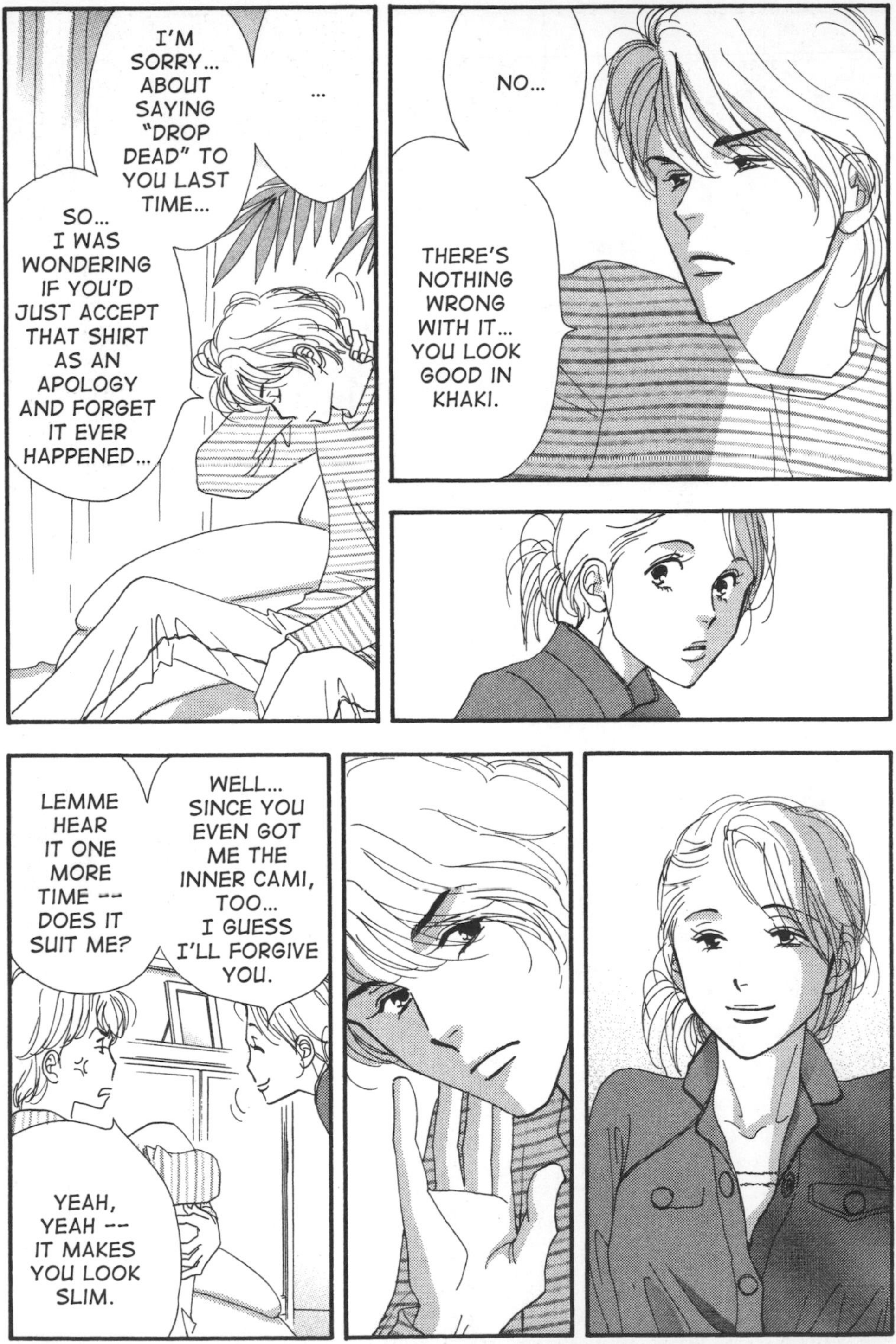
NO...
THERE'S NOTHING WRONG WITH IT... YOU LOOK GOOD IN KHAKI.
...
I'M SORRY... ABOUT SAYING "DROP DEAD" TO YOU LAST TIME...
SO... I WAS WONDERING IF YOU'D JUST ACCEPT THAT SHIRT AS AN APOLOGY AND FORGET IT EVER HAPPENED...
WELL... SINCE YOU EVEN GOT ME THE INNER CAMI, TOO... I GUESS I'LL FORGIVE YOU.
LEMME HEAR IT ONE MORE TIME -- DOES IT SUIT ME?
YEAH, YEAH -- IT MAKES YOU LOOK SLIM.

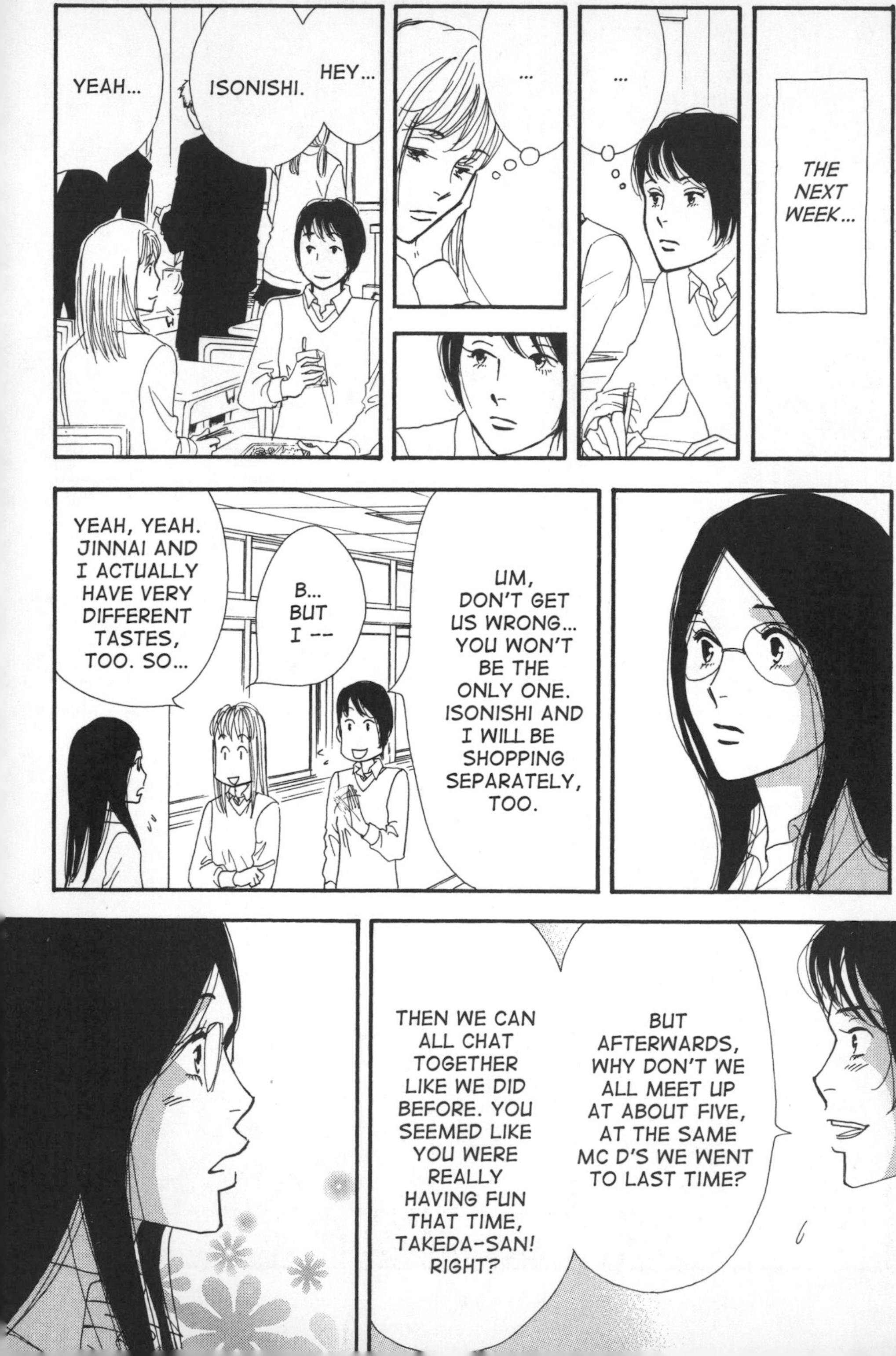
THE NEXT WEEK...
...
...
HEY...
ISONISHI.
YEAH...
UM, DON'T GET US WRONG... YOU WON'T BE THE ONLY ONE. ISONISHI AND I WILL BE SHOPPING SEPARATELY, TOO.
B... BUT I --
YEAH, YEAH. JINNAI AND I ACTUALLY HAVE VERY DIFFERENT TASTES, TOO. SO...
BUT AFTERWARDS, WHY DON'T WE ALL MEET UP AT ABOUT FIVE, AT THE SAME MC D'S WE WENT TO LAST TIME?
THEN WE CAN ALL CHAT TOGETHER LIKE WE DID BEFORE. YOU SEEMED LIKE YOU WERE REALLY HAVING FUN THAT TIME, TAKEDA-SAN! RIGHT?

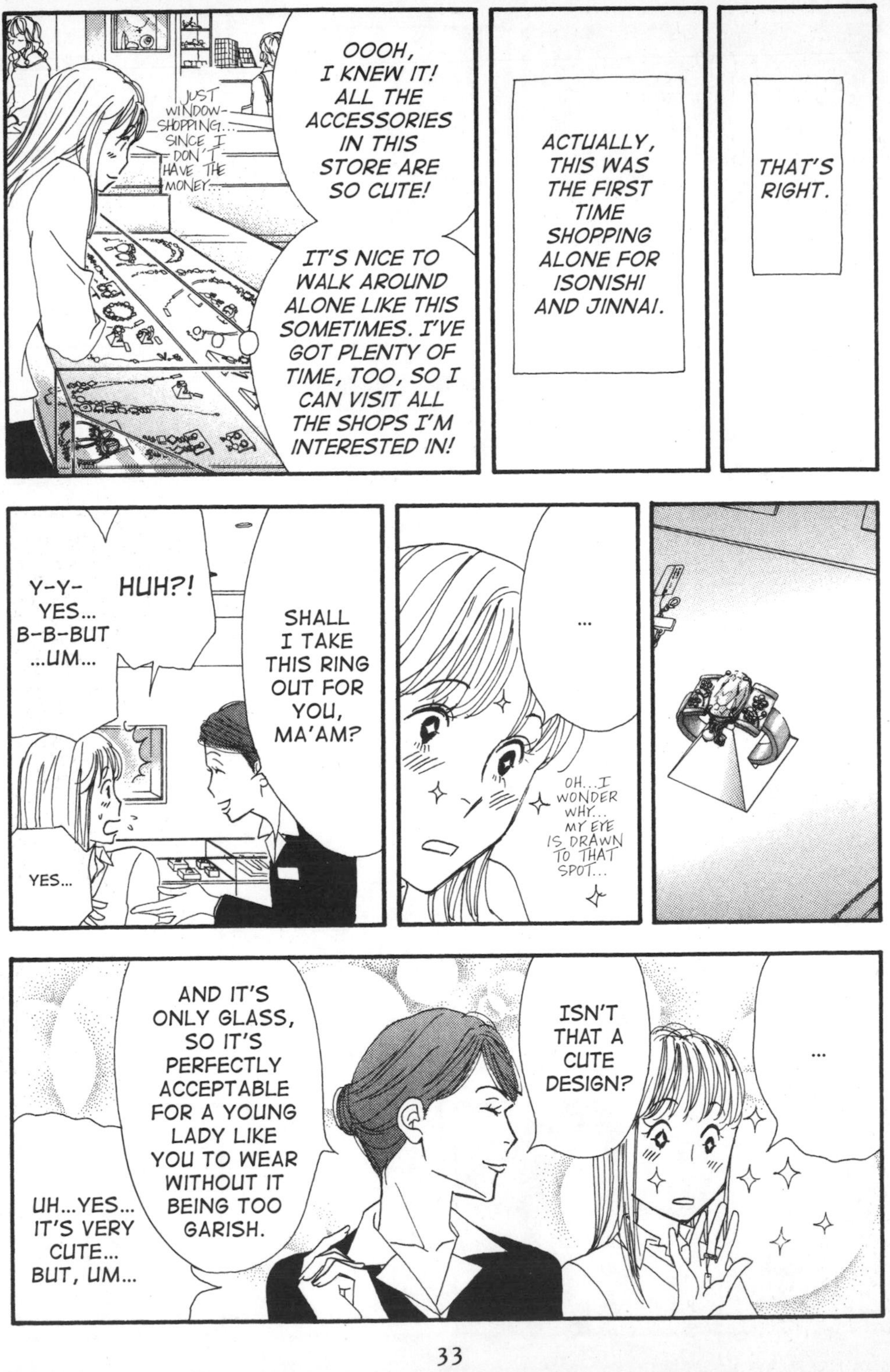
THAT'S RIGHT.
ACTUALLY, THIS WAS THE FIRST TIME SHOPPING ALONE FOR ISONISHI AND JINNAI.
OOOH, I KNEW IT! ALL THE ACCESSORIES IN THIS STORE ARE SO CUTE!
JUST WINDOW-SHOPPING... SINCE I DON'T HAVE THE MONEY...
IT'S NICE TO WALK AROUND ALONE LIKE THIS SOMETIMES. I'VE GOT PLENTY OF TIME, TOO, SO I CAN VISIT ALL THE SHOPS I'M INTERESTED IN!
...
OH... I WONDER WHY... MY EYE IS DRAWN TO THAT SPOT...
SHALL I TAKE THIS RING OUT FOR YOU, MA'AM?
HUH?!
Y-Y-YES... B-B-BUT ...UM...
YES...
...
ISN'T THAT A CUTE DESIGN?
AND IT'S ONLY GLASS, SO IT'S PERFECTLY ACCEPTABLE FOR A YOUNG LADY LIKE YOU TO WEAR WITHOUT IT BEING TOO GARISH.
UH...YES... IT'S VERY CUTE... BUT, UM...

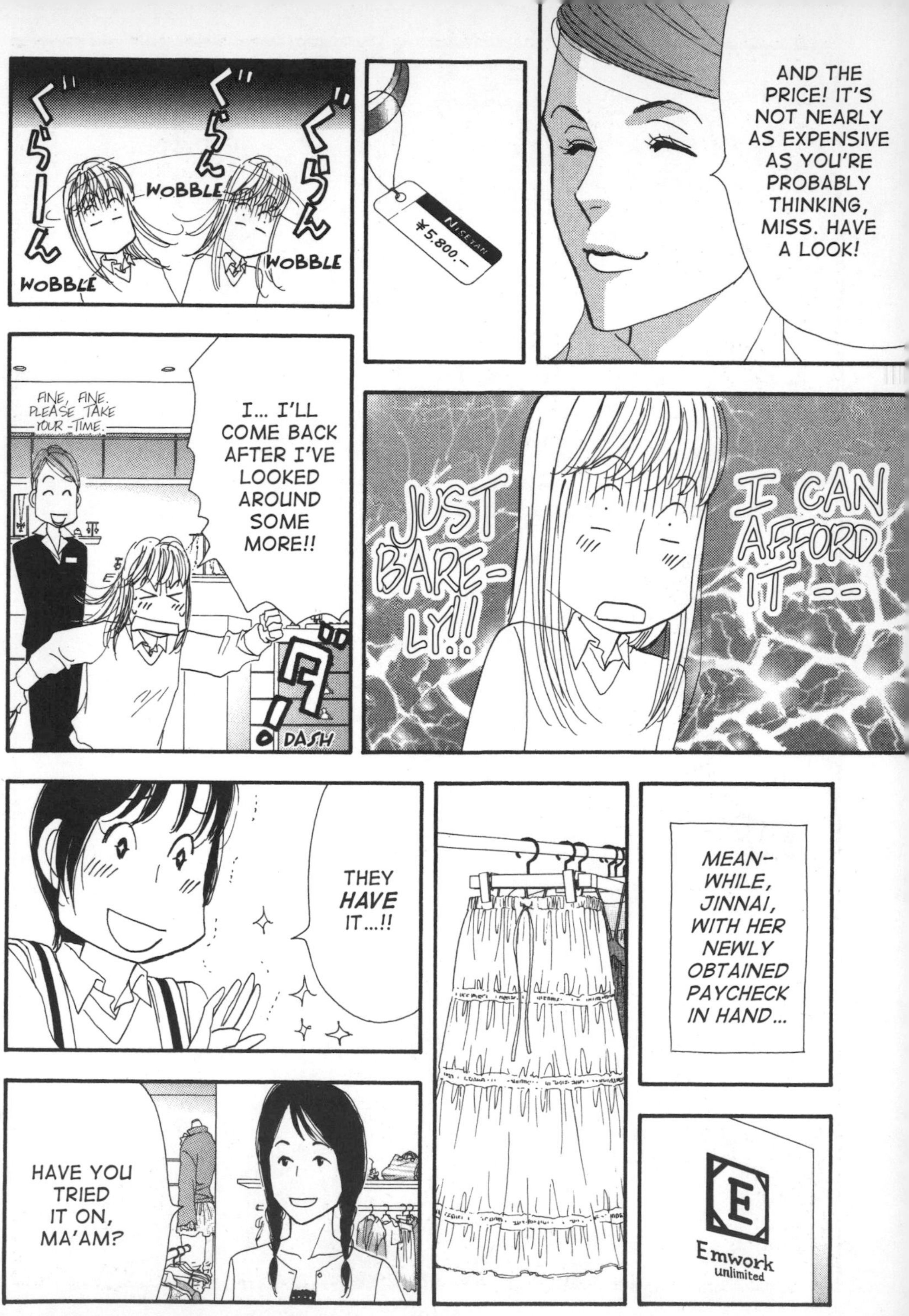

AND THE PRICE! IT'S NOT NEARLY AS EXPENSIVE AS YOU'RE PROBABLY THINKING, MISS. HAVE A LOOK!
NISETAN
¥5,800.–
ぐらん
ぐらん
ぐらーん
WOBBLE
WOBBLE
WOBBLE
I CAN AFFORD IT --
JUST BARE-LY!!
I... I'LL COME BACK AFTER I'VE LOOKED AROUND SOME MORE!!
FINE, FINE. PLEASE TAKE YOUR TIME.
ダッ
DASH
MEAN-WHILE, JINNAI, WITH HER NEWLY OBTAINED PAYCHECK IN HAND...
Emwork unlimited
THEY HAVE IT...!!
HAVE YOU TRIED IT ON, MA'AM?

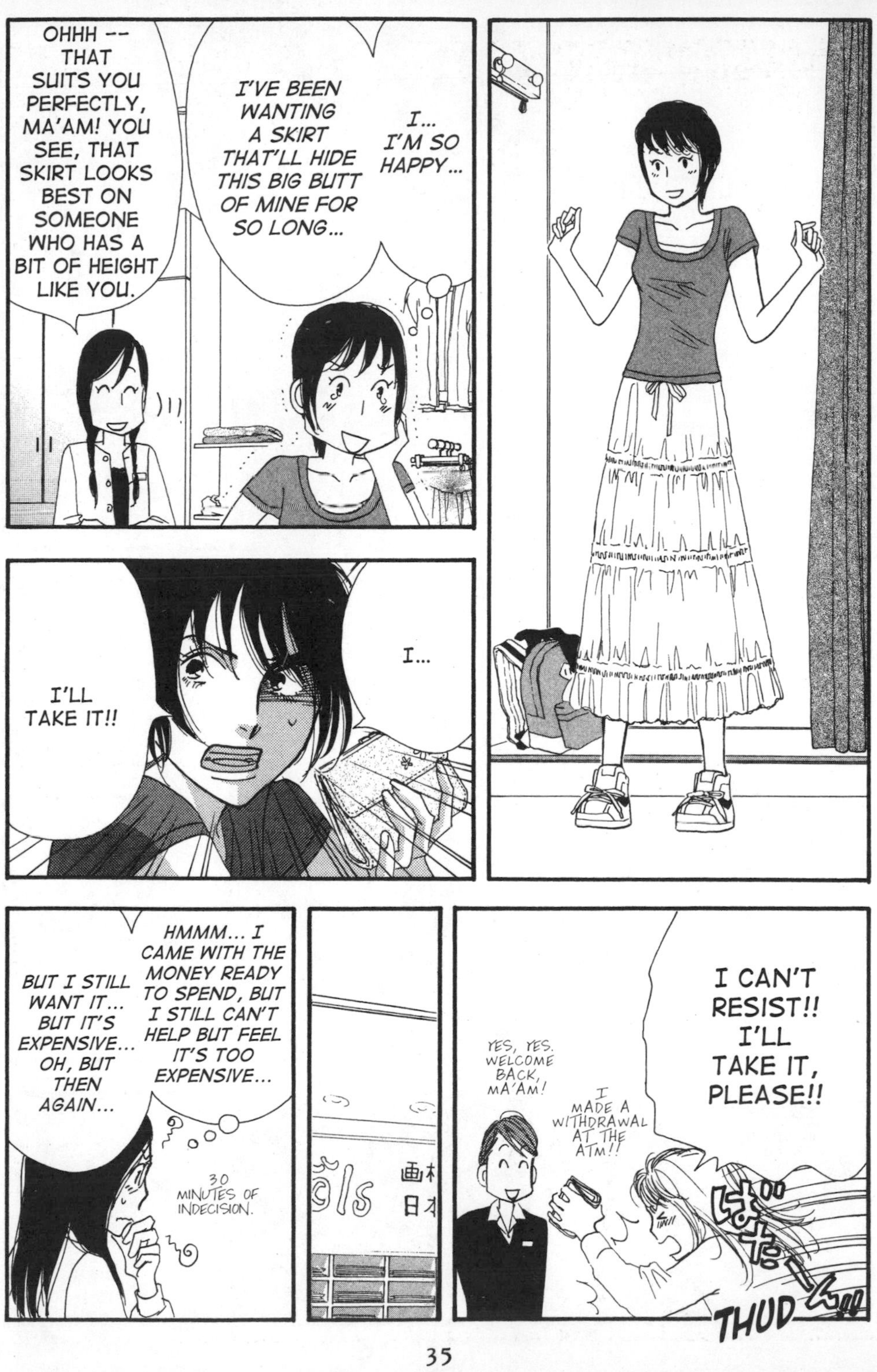
I... I'M SO HAPPY...
I'VE BEEN WANTING A SKIRT THAT'LL HIDE THIS BIG BUTT OF MINE FOR SO LONG...
OHHH -- THAT SUITS YOU PERFECTLY, MA'AM! YOU SEE, THAT SKIRT LOOKS BEST ON SOMEONE WHO HAS A BIT OF HEIGHT LIKE YOU.
I...
I'LL TAKE IT!!
I CAN'T RESIST!! I'LL TAKE IT, PLEASE!!
I MADE A WITHDRAWAL AT THE ATM!!
YES, YES. WELCOME BACK, MA'AM!
THUD
HMMM... I CAME WITH THE MONEY READY TO SPEND, BUT I STILL CAN'T HELP BUT FEEL IT'S TOO EXPENSIVE...
BUT I STILL WANT IT... BUT IT'S EXPENSIVE... OH, BUT THEN AGAIN...
30 MINUTES OF INDECISION.

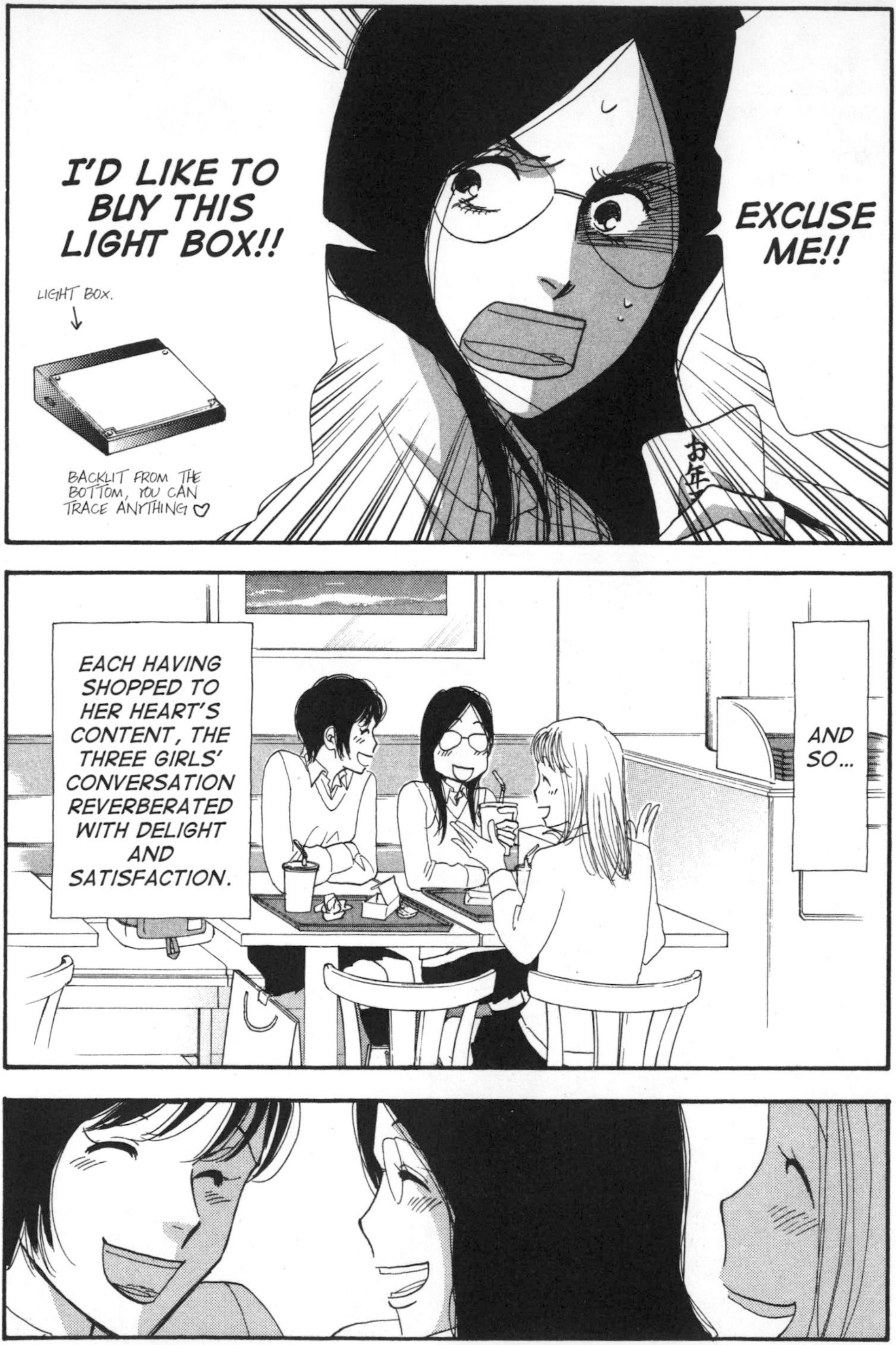
EXCUSE ME!!
I'D LIKE TO BUY THIS LIGHT BOX!!
LIGHT BOX.
BACKLIT FROM THE BOTTOM, YOU CAN TRACE ANYTHING ♡
AND SO...
EACH HAVING SHOPPED TO HER HEART'S CONTENT, THE THREE GIRLS' CONVERSATION REVERBERATED WITH DELIGHT AND SATISFACTION.

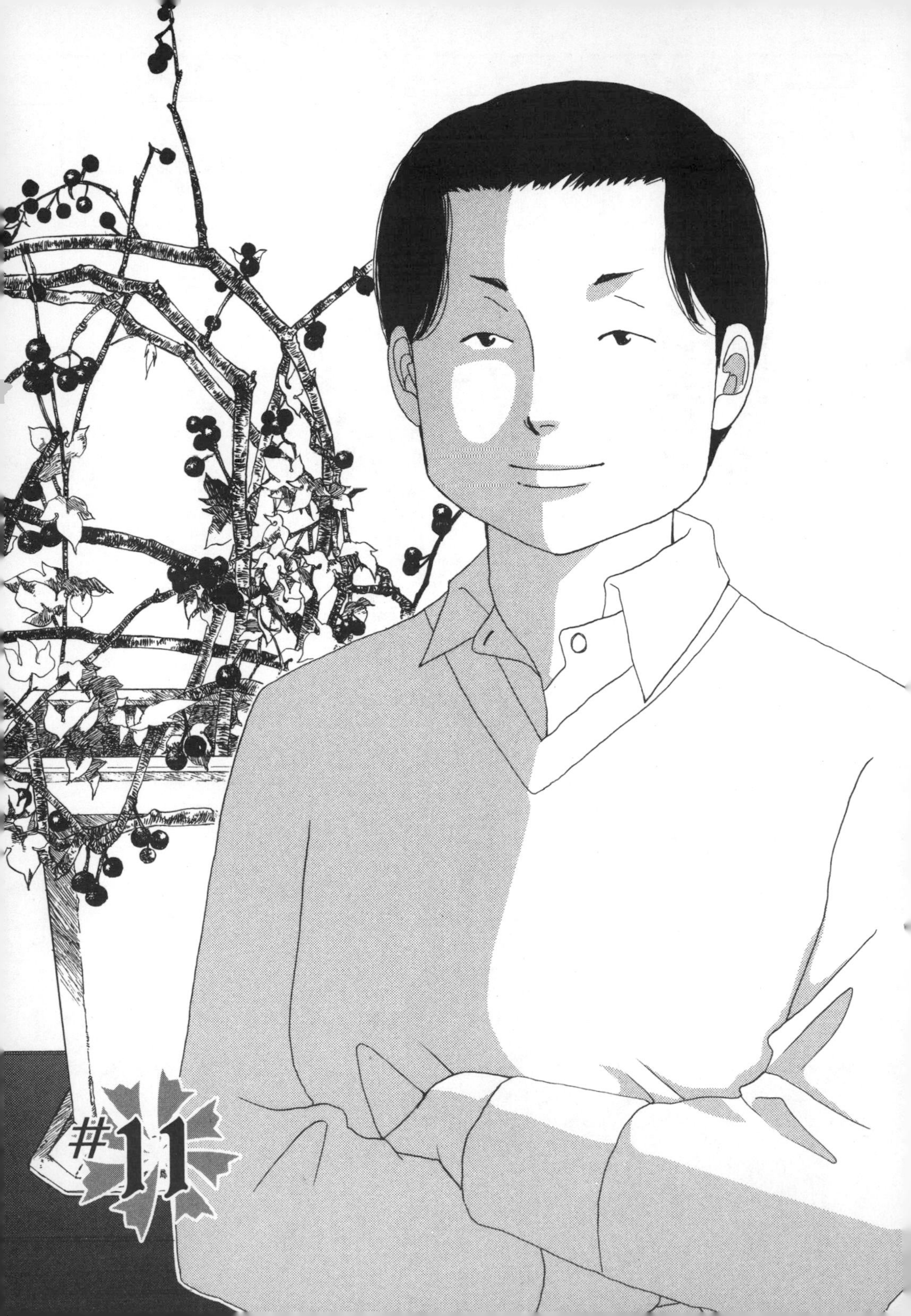
#11

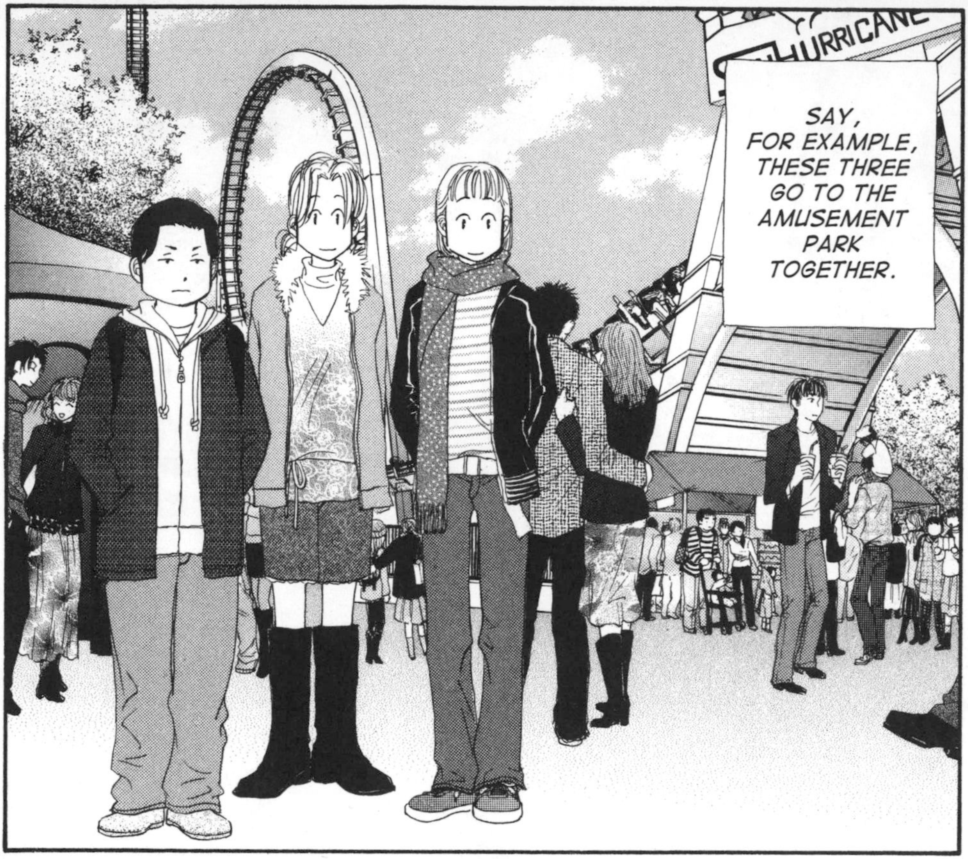
HURRICANE
SAY, FOR EXAMPLE, THESE THREE GO TO THE AMUSEMENT PARK TOGETHER.

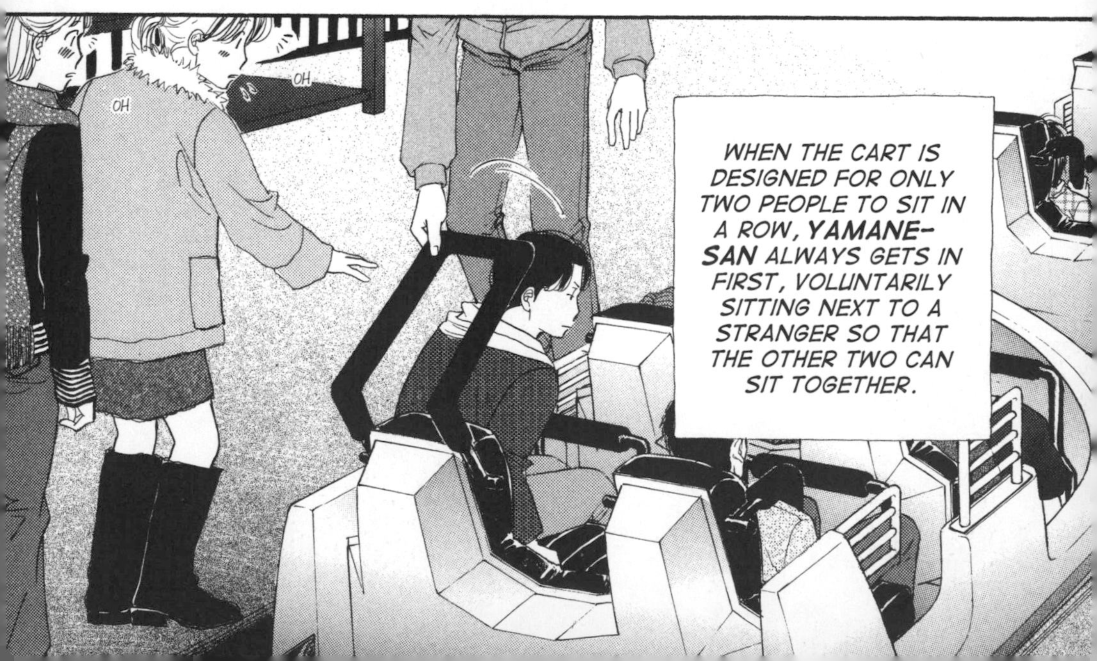
WHEN THE CART IS DESIGNED FOR ONLY TWO PEOPLE TO SIT IN A ROW, **YAMANE-SAN** ALWAYS GETS IN FIRST, VOLUNTARILY SITTING NEXT TO A STRANGER SO THAT THE OTHER TWO CAN SIT TOGETHER.
OH
OH

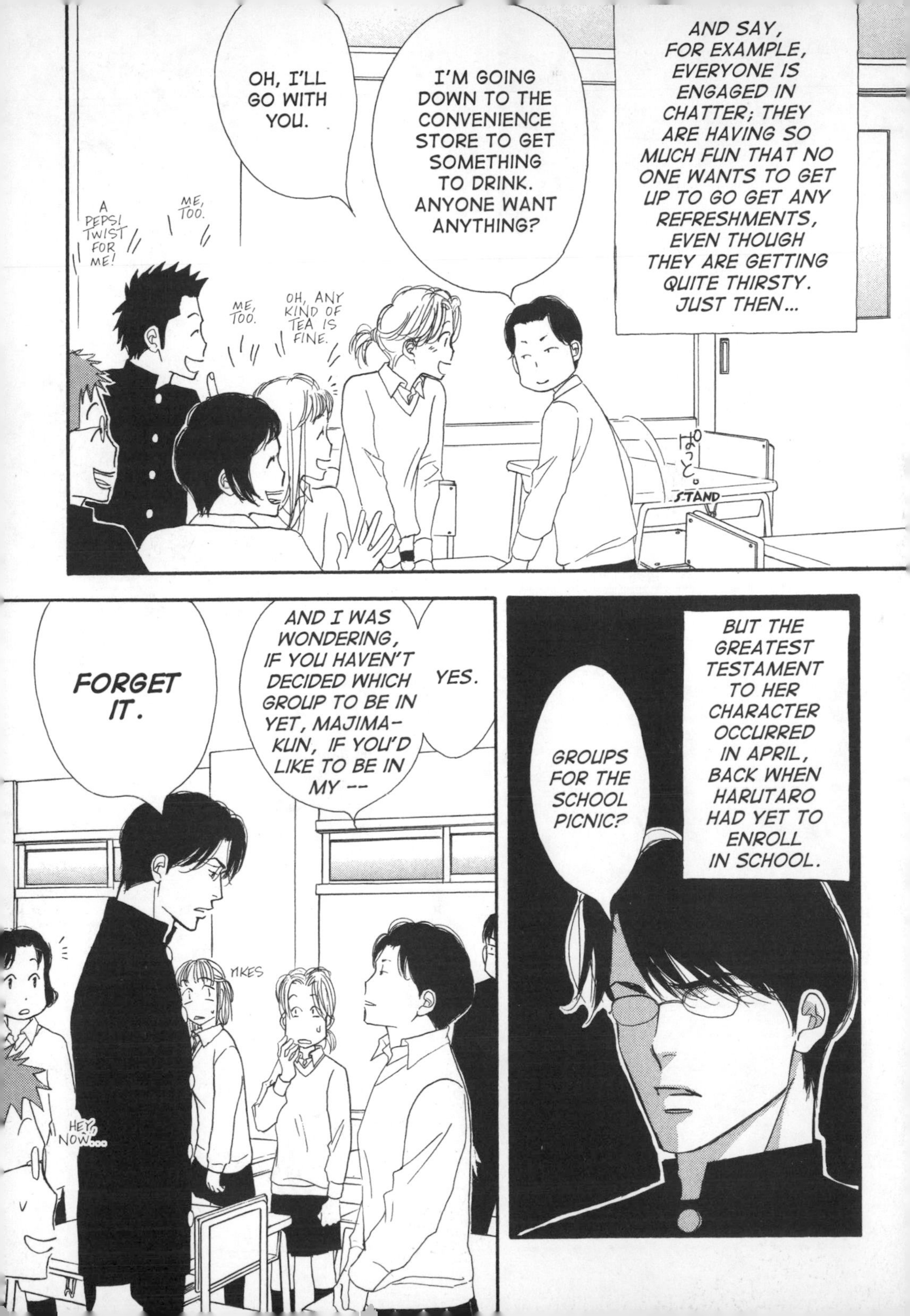
AND SAY, FOR EXAMPLE, EVERYONE IS ENGAGED IN CHATTER; THEY ARE HAVING SO MUCH FUN THAT NO ONE WANTS TO GET UP TO GO GET ANY REFRESHMENTS, EVEN THOUGH THEY ARE GETTING QUITE THIRSTY. JUST THEN...
I'M GOING DOWN TO THE CONVENIENCE STORE TO GET SOMETHING TO DRINK. ANYONE WANT ANYTHING?
OH, I'LL GO WITH YOU.
STAND
OH, ANY KIND OF TEA IS FINE.
ME, TOO.
ME, TOO.
A PEPSI TWIST FOR ME!
BUT THE GREATEST TESTAMENT TO HER CHARACTER OCCURRED IN APRIL, BACK WHEN HARUTARO HAD YET TO ENROLL IN SCHOOL.
GROUPS FOR THE SCHOOL PICNIC?
YES.
AND I WAS WONDERING, IF YOU HAVEN'T DECIDED WHICH GROUP TO BE IN YET, MAJIMA-KUN, IF YOU'D LIKE TO BE IN MY --
FORGET IT.
YIKES
HEY, NOW...

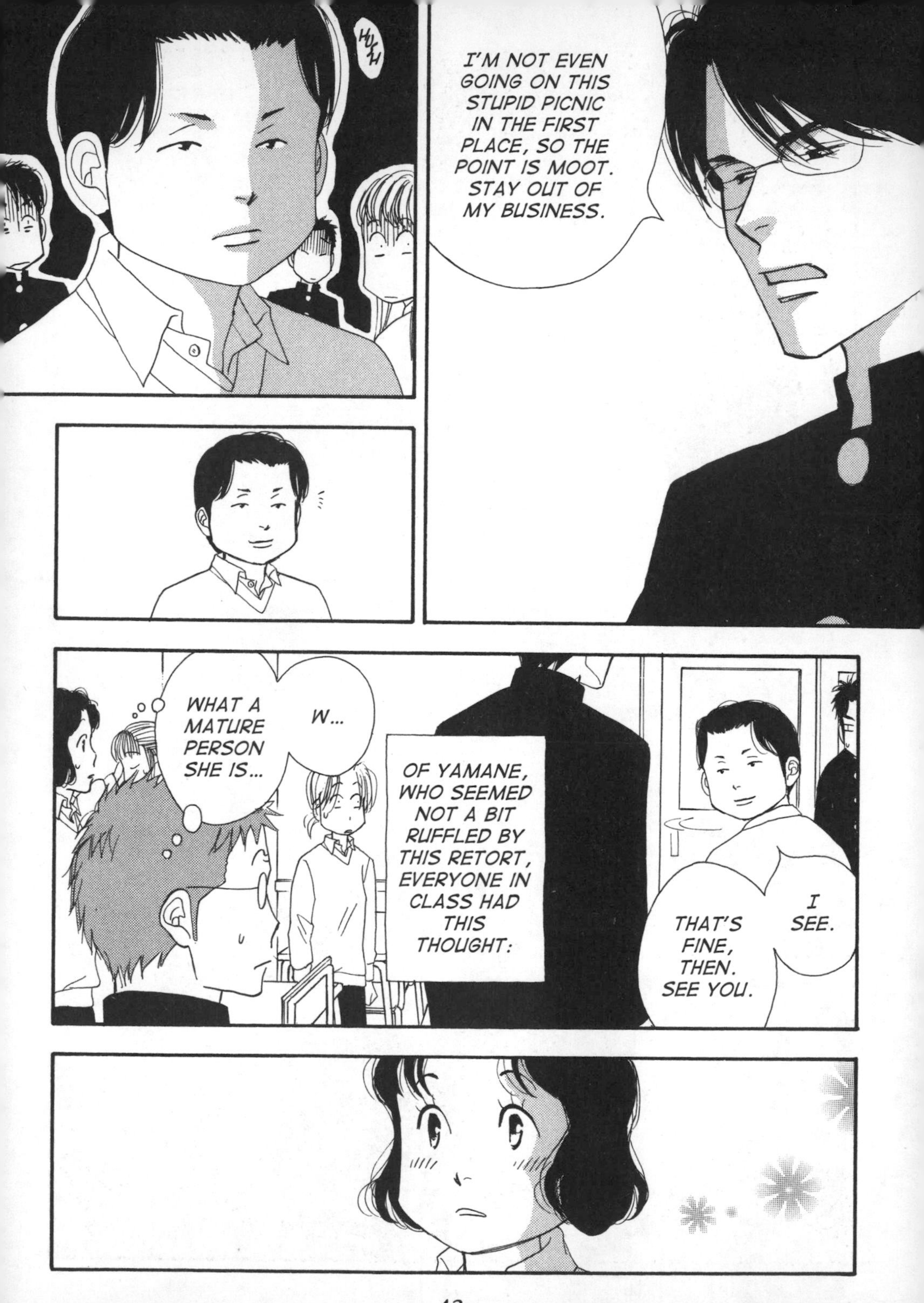
I'M NOT EVEN GOING ON THIS STUPID PICNIC IN THE FIRST PLACE, SO THE POINT IS MOOT. STAY OUT OF MY BUSINESS.
HUH
I SEE.
THAT'S FINE, THEN. SEE YOU.
OF YAMANE, WHO SEEMED NOT A BIT RUFFLED BY THIS RETORT, EVERYONE IN CLASS HAD THIS THOUGHT:
W...
WHAT A MATURE PERSON SHE IS...

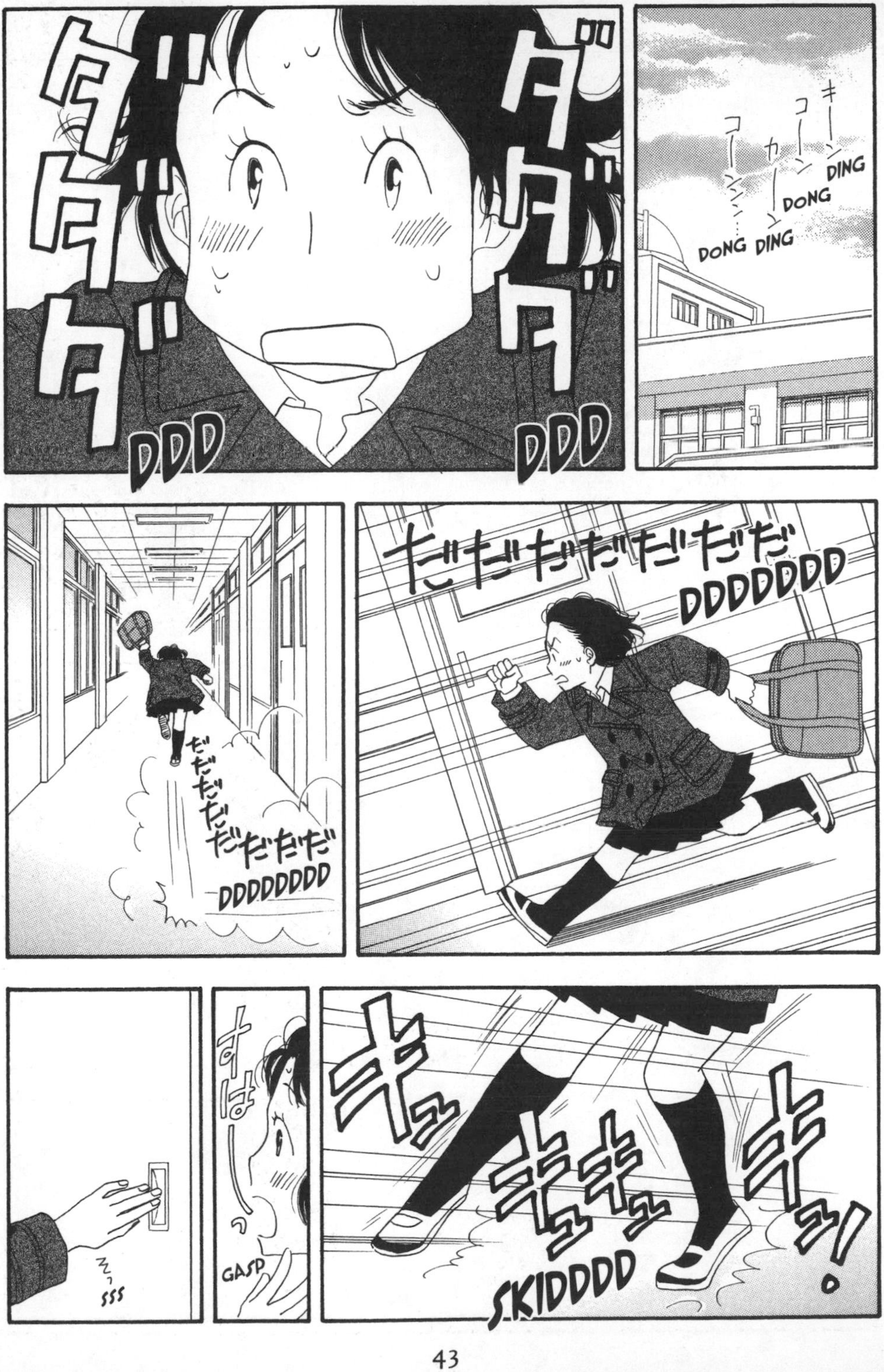
キーン
コーン
カーン
コーン…
DING
DONG
DING
DONG
ダダダダ
DDD
ダダダダ
DDD
だだだだだだだ
DDDDDDD
だだだだだだだ
DDDDDDDD
キュ
キュキュ
キュ!
SKIDDDD
すはーっ
GASP
そっ
SSS

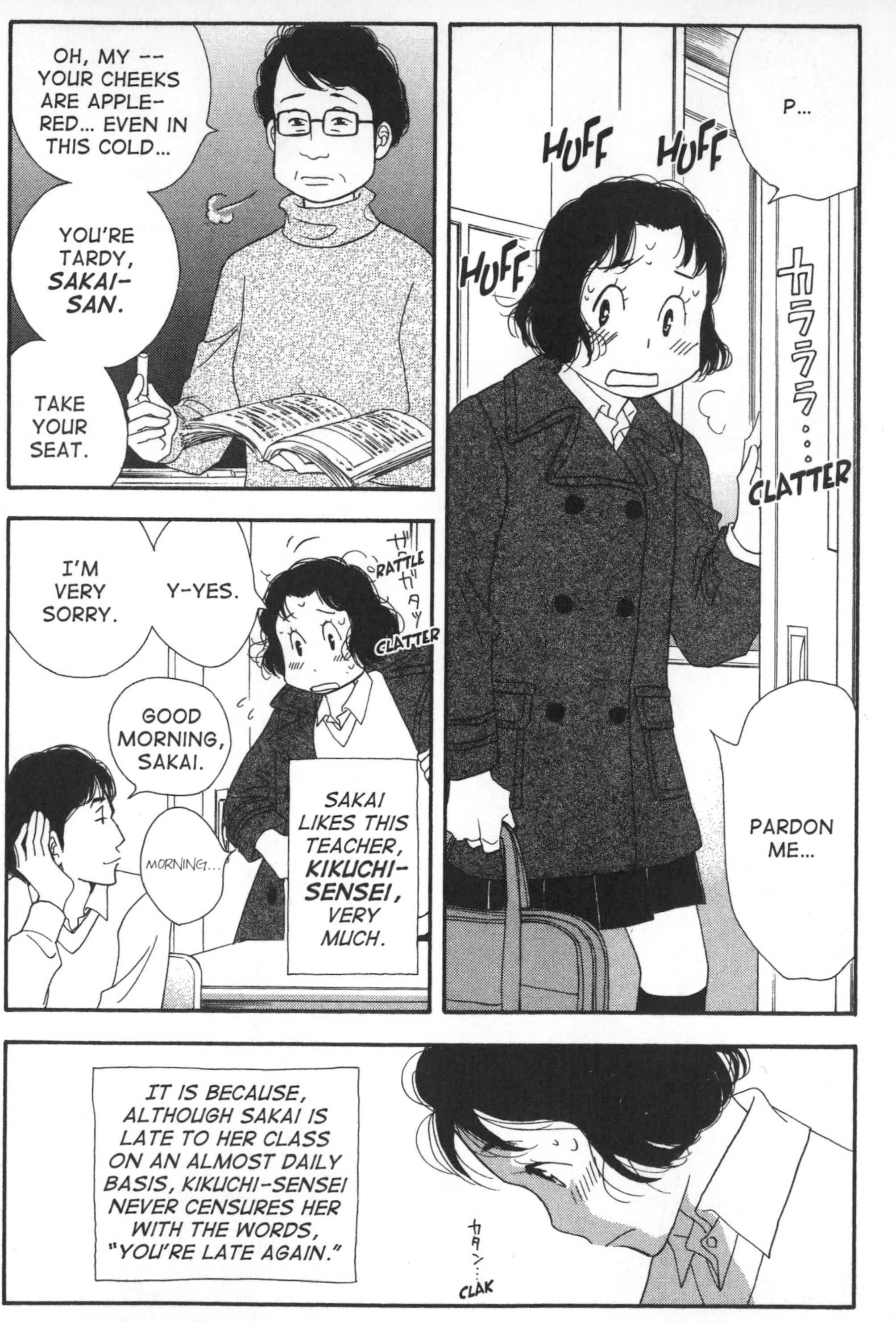
P...
HUFF
HUFF
HUFF
カララ…
CLATTER
PARDON ME...
OH, MY -- YOUR CHEEKS ARE APPLE-RED... EVEN IN THIS COLD...
YOU'RE TARDY, SAKAI-SAN.
TAKE YOUR SEAT.
Y-YES.
I'M VERY SORRY.
ガタッ
RATTLE
CLATTER
GOOD MORNING, SAKAI.
MORNING...
SAKAI LIKES THIS TEACHER, KIKUCHI-SENSEI, VERY MUCH.
IT IS BECAUSE, ALTHOUGH SAKAI IS LATE TO HER CLASS ON AN ALMOST DAILY BASIS, KIKUCHI-SENSEI NEVER CENSURES HER WITH THE WORDS, "YOU'RE LATE AGAIN."
カタン…
CLAK

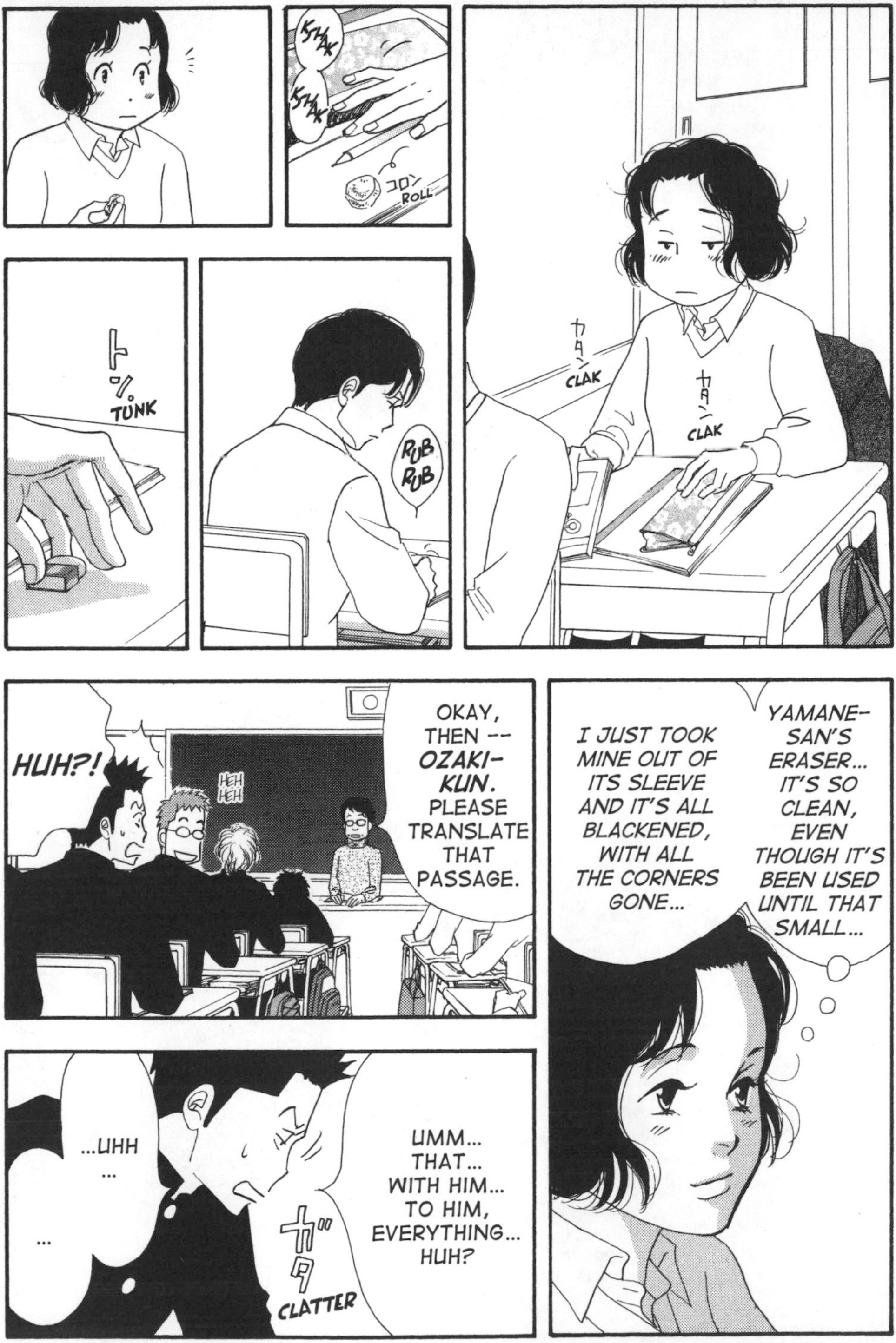
カタン
CLAK
カタン
CLAK
KSHAK
KSHAK
コロン
ROLL
RUB RUB
トン
TUNK
YAMANE-SAN'S ERASER... IT'S SO CLEAN, EVEN THOUGH IT'S BEEN USED UNTIL THAT SMALL...
I JUST TOOK MINE OUT OF ITS SLEEVE AND IT'S ALL BLACKENED, WITH ALL THE CORNERS GONE...
OKAY, THEN -- OZAKI-KUN. PLEASE TRANSLATE THAT PASSAGE.
HEH HEH
HUH?!
UMM... THAT... WITH HIM... TO HIM, EVERYTHING... HUH?
ガタ
CLATTER
...UHH ...
...

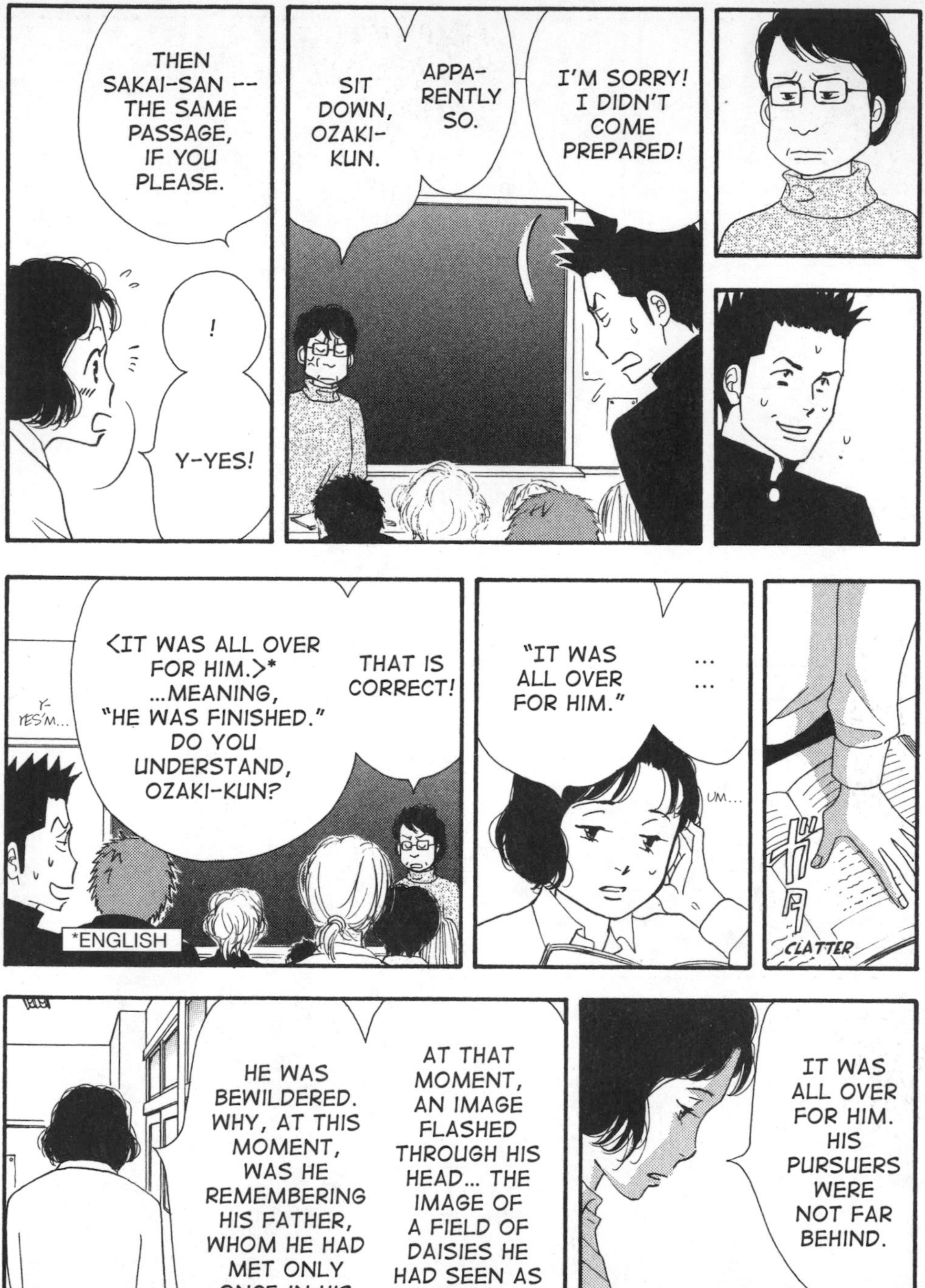

I'M SORRY! I DIDN'T COME PREPARED!
APPA-RENTLY SO.
SIT DOWN, OZAKI-KUN.
THEN SAKAI-SAN -- THE SAME PASSAGE, IF YOU PLEASE.
!
Y-YES!
ガタ
CLATTER
... ...
"IT WAS ALL OVER FOR HIM."
UM...
THAT IS CORRECT!
<IT WAS ALL OVER FOR HIM.>* ...MEANING, "HE WAS FINISHED." DO YOU UNDERSTAND, OZAKI-KUN?
Y- YES'M...
*ENGLISH
IT WAS ALL OVER FOR HIM. HIS PURSUERS WERE NOT FAR BEHIND.
AT THAT MOMENT, AN IMAGE FLASHED THROUGH HIS HEAD... THE IMAGE OF A FIELD OF DAISIES HE HAD SEEN AS A CHILD WITH HIS FATHER.
HE WAS BEWILDERED. WHY, AT THIS MOMENT, WAS HE REMEMBERING HIS FATHER, WHOM HE HAD MET ONLY ONCE IN HIS YOUTH?

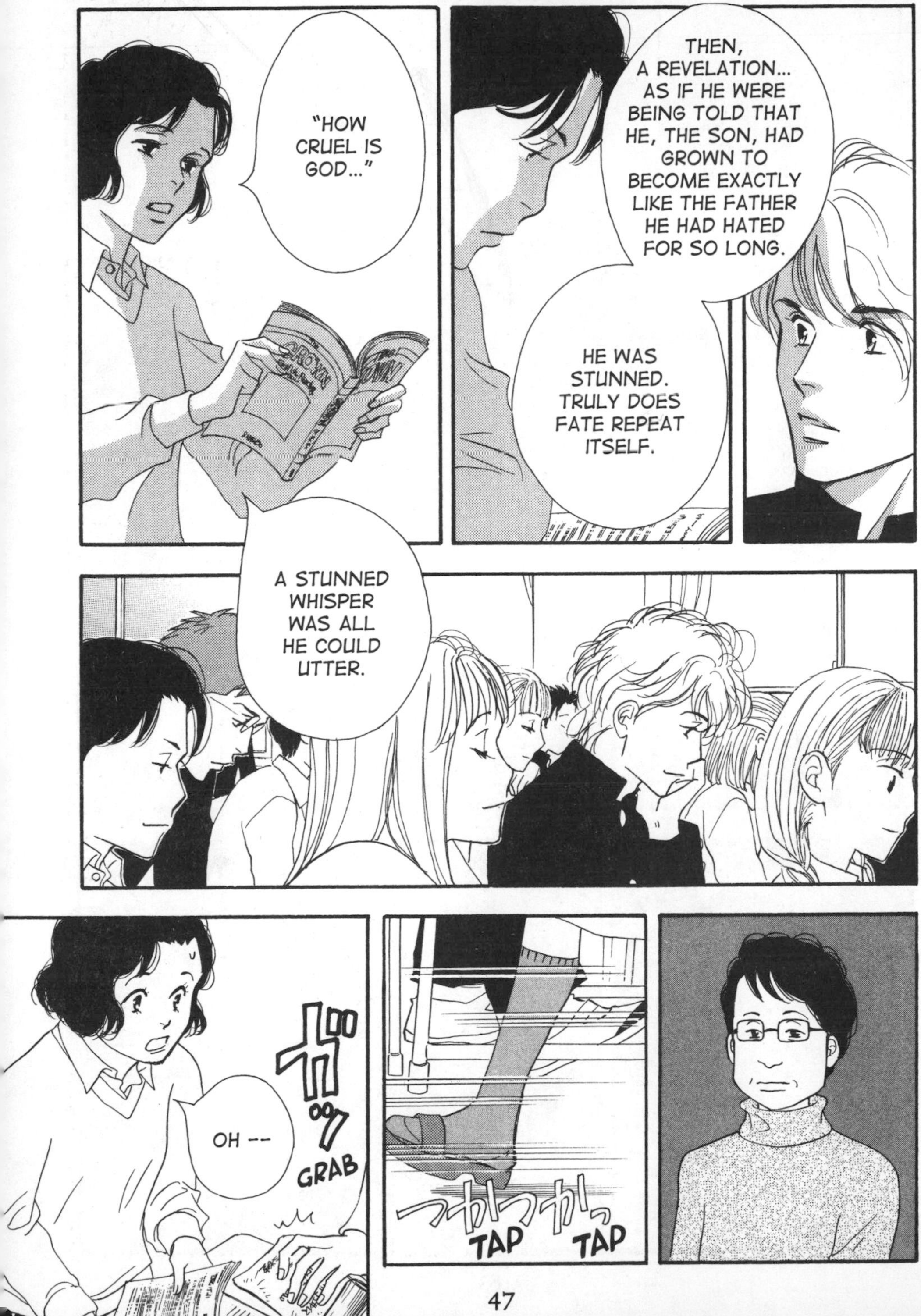
THEN, A REVELATION... AS IF HE WERE BEING TOLD THAT HE, THE SON, HAD GROWN TO BECOME EXACTLY LIKE THE FATHER HE HAD HATED FOR SO LONG.
HE WAS STUNNED. TRULY DOES FATE REPEAT ITSELF.
"HOW CRUEL IS GOD..."
A STUNNED WHISPER WAS ALL HE COULD UTTER.
TAP TAP
GRAB
OH --

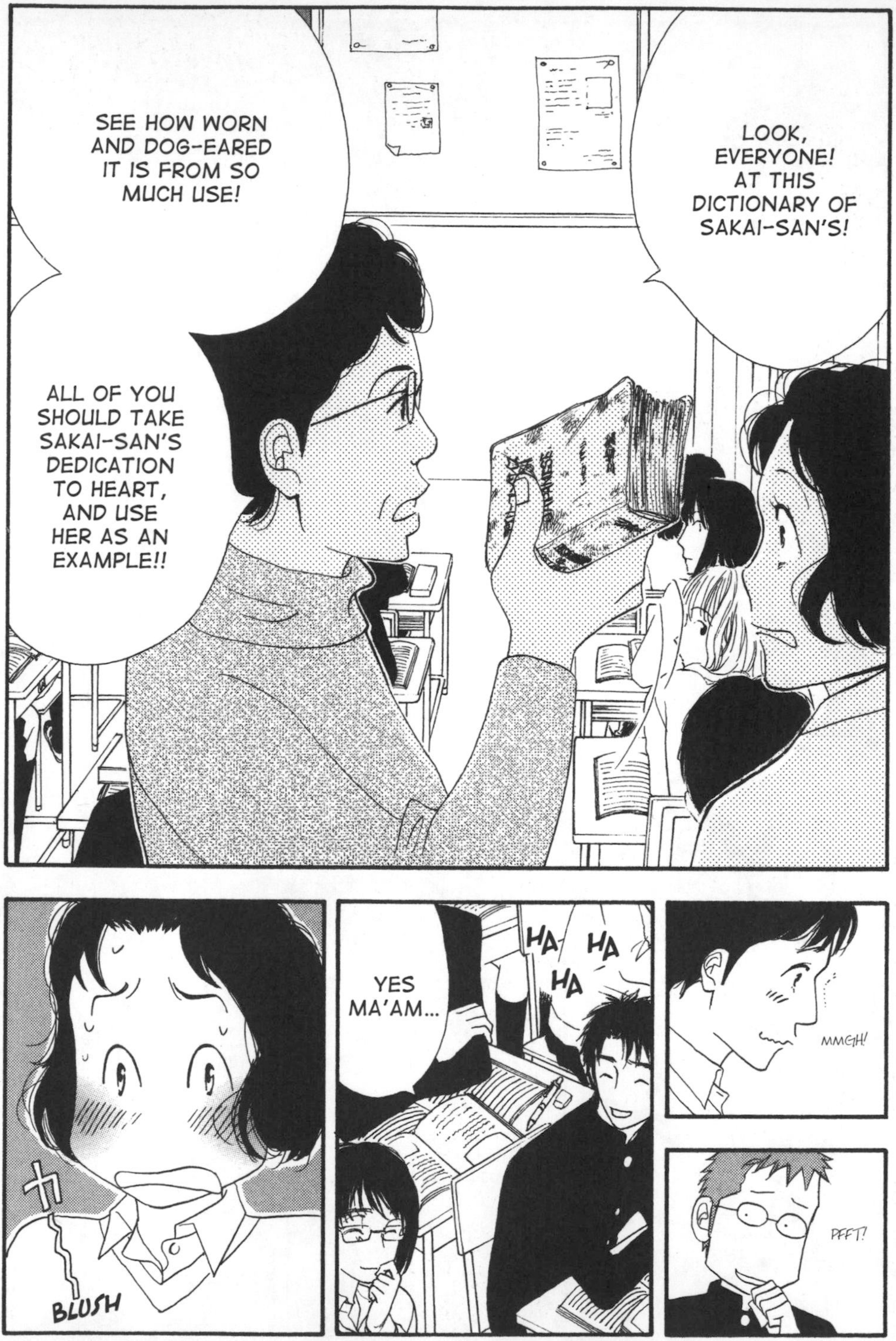
LOOK, EVERYONE! AT THIS DICTIONARY OF SAKAI-SAN'S!
SEE HOW WORN AND DOG-EARED IT IS FROM SO MUCH USE!
ALL OF YOU SHOULD TAKE SAKAI-SAN'S DEDICATION TO HEART, AND USE HER AS AN EXAMPLE!!
MMGH!
PFFT!
HA HA HA
YES MA'AM...
BLUSH

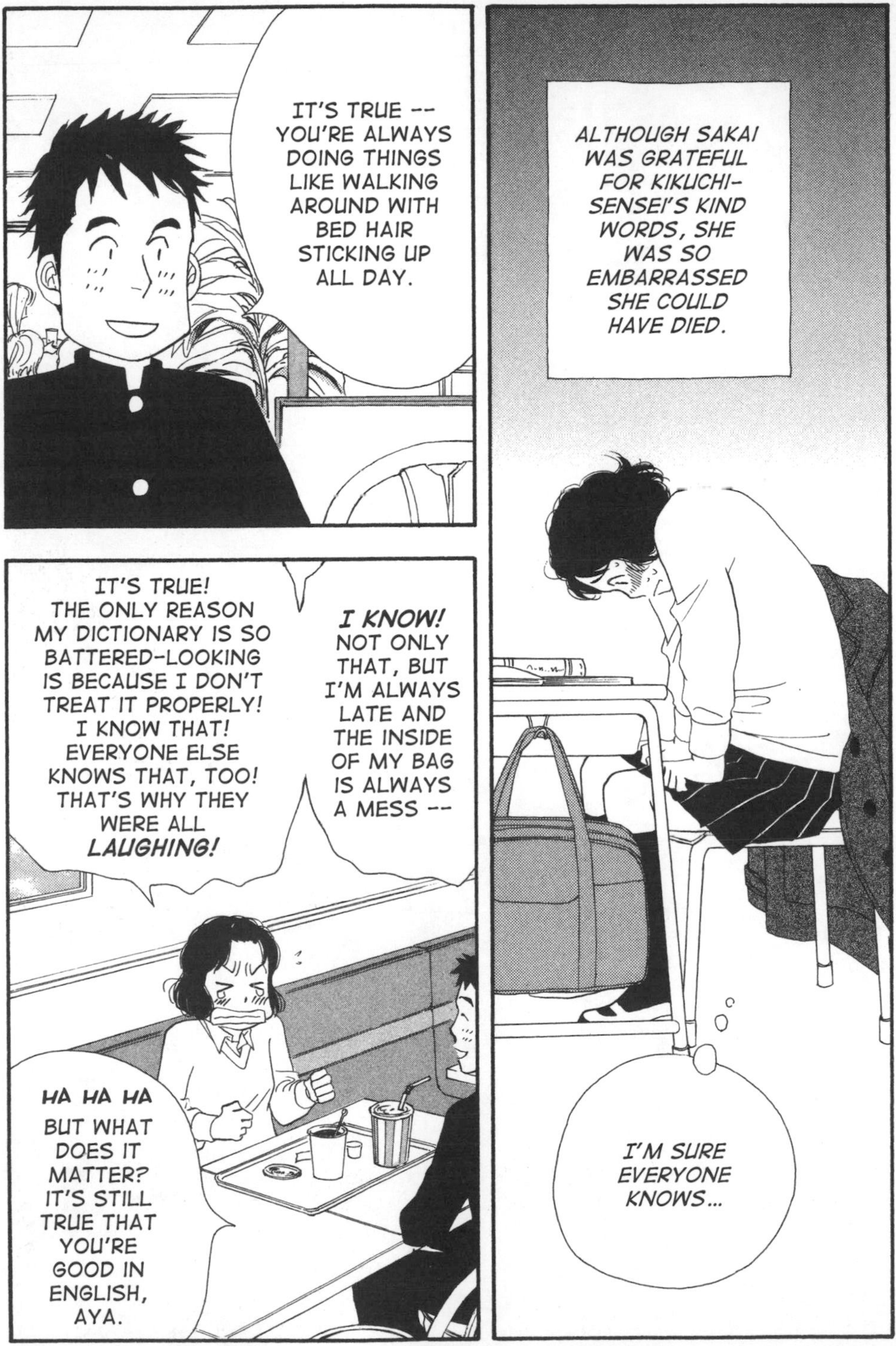
ALTHOUGH SAKAI WAS GRATEFUL FOR KIKUCHI-SENSEI'S KIND WORDS, SHE WAS SO EMBARRASSED SHE COULD HAVE DIED.
I'M SURE EVERYONE KNOWS...
IT'S TRUE -- YOU'RE ALWAYS DOING THINGS LIKE WALKING AROUND WITH BED HAIR STICKING UP ALL DAY.
I KNOW! NOT ONLY THAT, BUT I'M ALWAYS LATE AND THE INSIDE OF MY BAG IS ALWAYS A MESS --
IT'S TRUE! THE ONLY REASON MY DICTIONARY IS SO BATTERED-LOOKING IS BECAUSE I DON'T TREAT IT PROPERLY! I KNOW THAT! EVERYONE ELSE KNOWS THAT, TOO! THAT'S WHY THEY WERE ALL LAUGHING!
HA HA HA BUT WHAT DOES IT MATTER? IT'S STILL TRUE THAT YOU'RE GOOD IN ENGLISH, AYA.

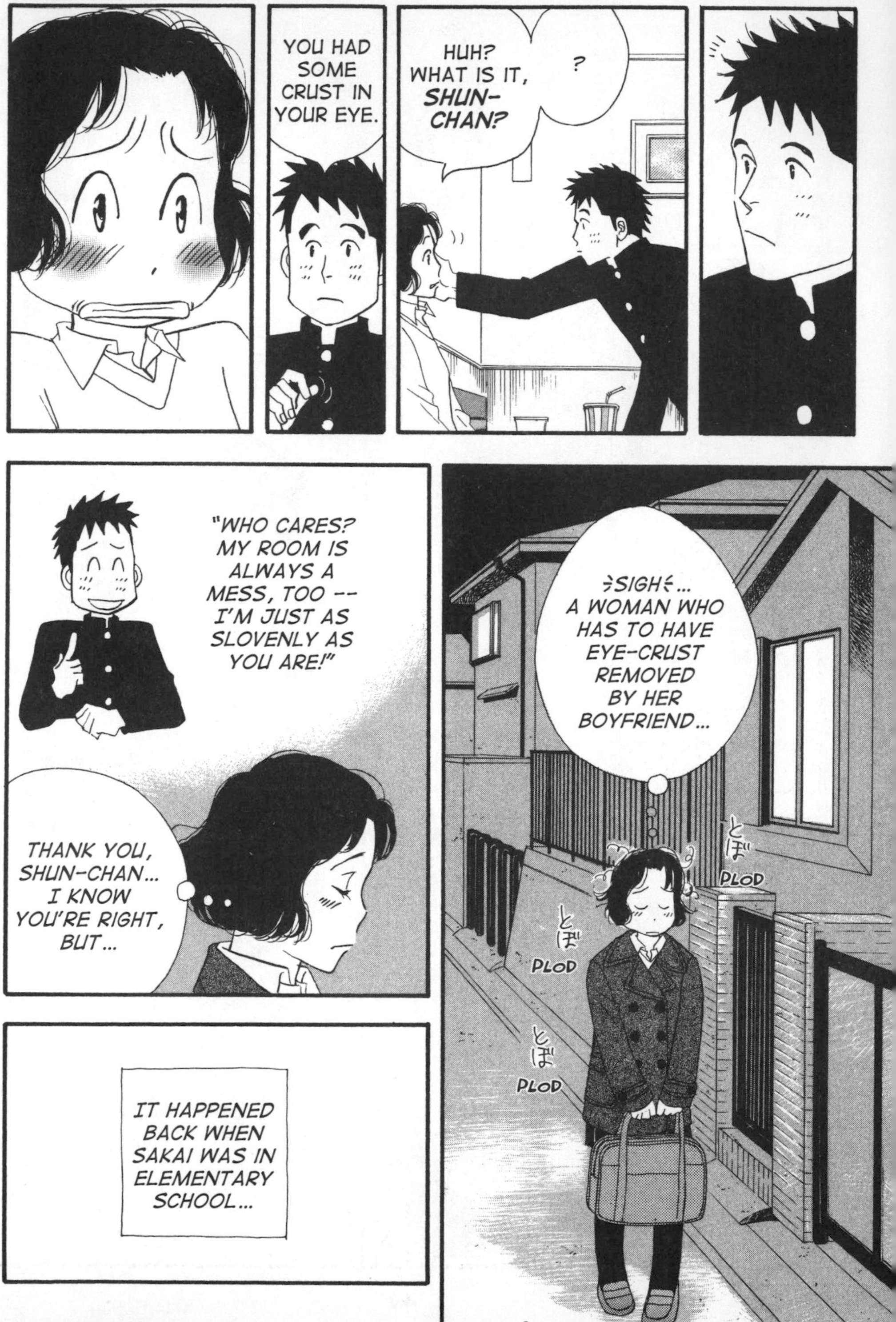
?
HUH? WHAT IS IT, SHUN-CHAN?
YOU HAD SOME CRUST IN YOUR EYE.
⋞SIGH⋟... A WOMAN WHO HAS TO HAVE EYE-CRUST REMOVED BY HER BOYFRIEND...
とぼ PLOD
とぼ PLOD
とぼ PLOD
"WHO CARES? MY ROOM IS ALWAYS A MESS, TOO -- I'M JUST AS SLOVENLY AS YOU ARE!"
THANK YOU, SHUN-CHAN... I KNOW YOU'RE RIGHT, BUT...
IT HAPPENED BACK WHEN SAKAI WAS IN ELEMENTARY SCHOOL...

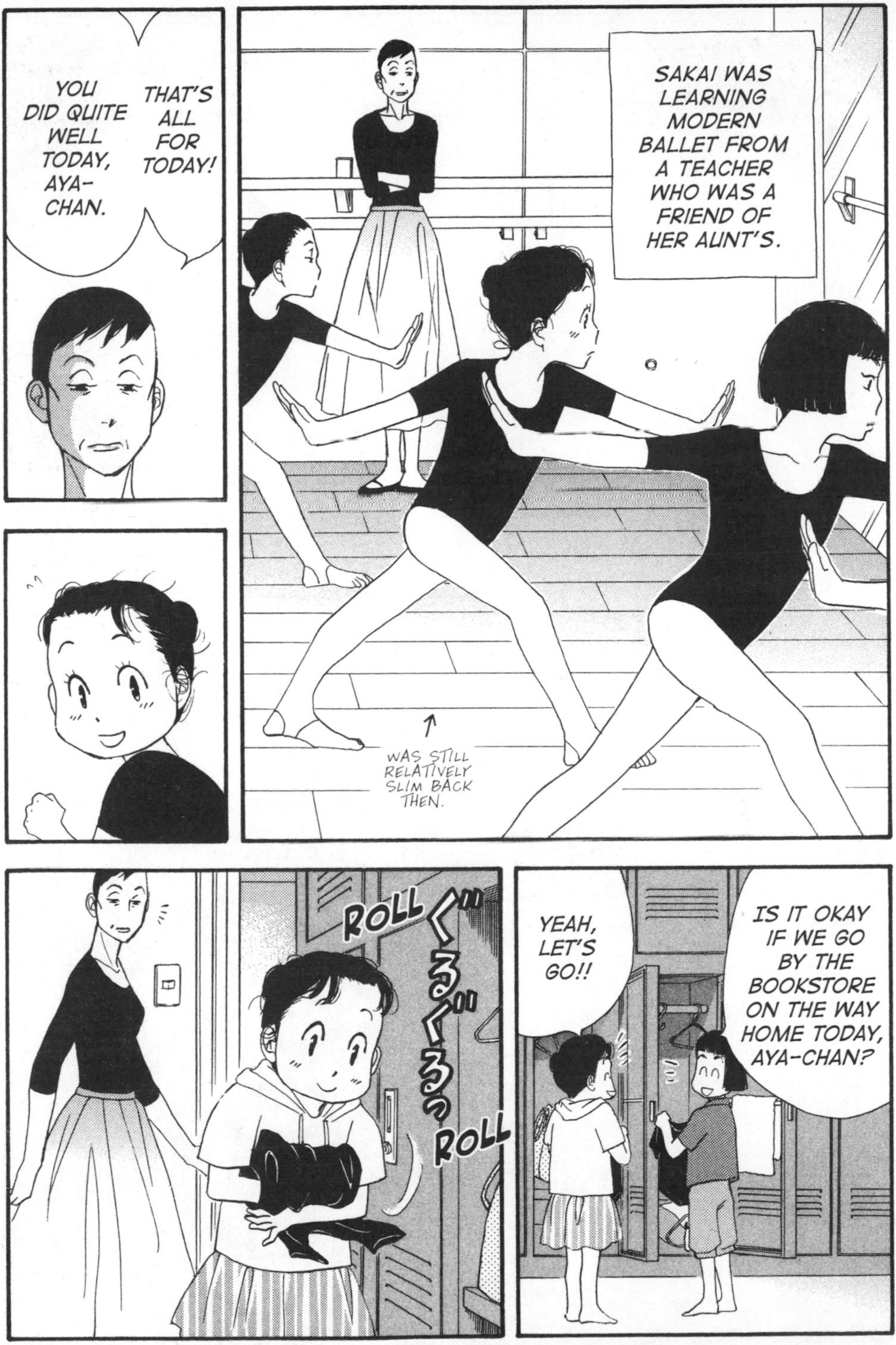
SAKAI WAS LEARNING MODERN BALLET FROM A TEACHER WHO WAS A FRIEND OF HER AUNT'S.
WAS STILL RELATIVELY SLIM BACK THEN.
THAT'S ALL FOR TODAY!
YOU DID QUITE WELL TODAY, AYA-CHAN.
IS IT OKAY IF WE GO BY THE BOOKSTORE ON THE WAY HOME TODAY, AYA-CHAN?
YEAH, LET'S GO!!
ROLL
ぐるぐるっ
ROLL

OH, DEAR! AYA-CHAN...

ROLLING YOUR LEOTARD INTO A WRINKLED MESS LIKE THAT -- WHAT A SLOVENLY CHILD YOU ARE!

どまーーん
JOLT

WHAT?

...

IT'S DIFFERENT FOR A GIRL... BEING TOLD YOU'RE SLOVENLY IS MUCH MORE OF A SHOCK THAN IT IS FOR A BOY...

DO YOU WANNA DRAW A MANGA TOGETHER AND PUT IT OUT AS A BOOK NEXT TIME? IN... UM... ONE OF THOSE DOUJINSHI THINGS!

LIKE I SAID...

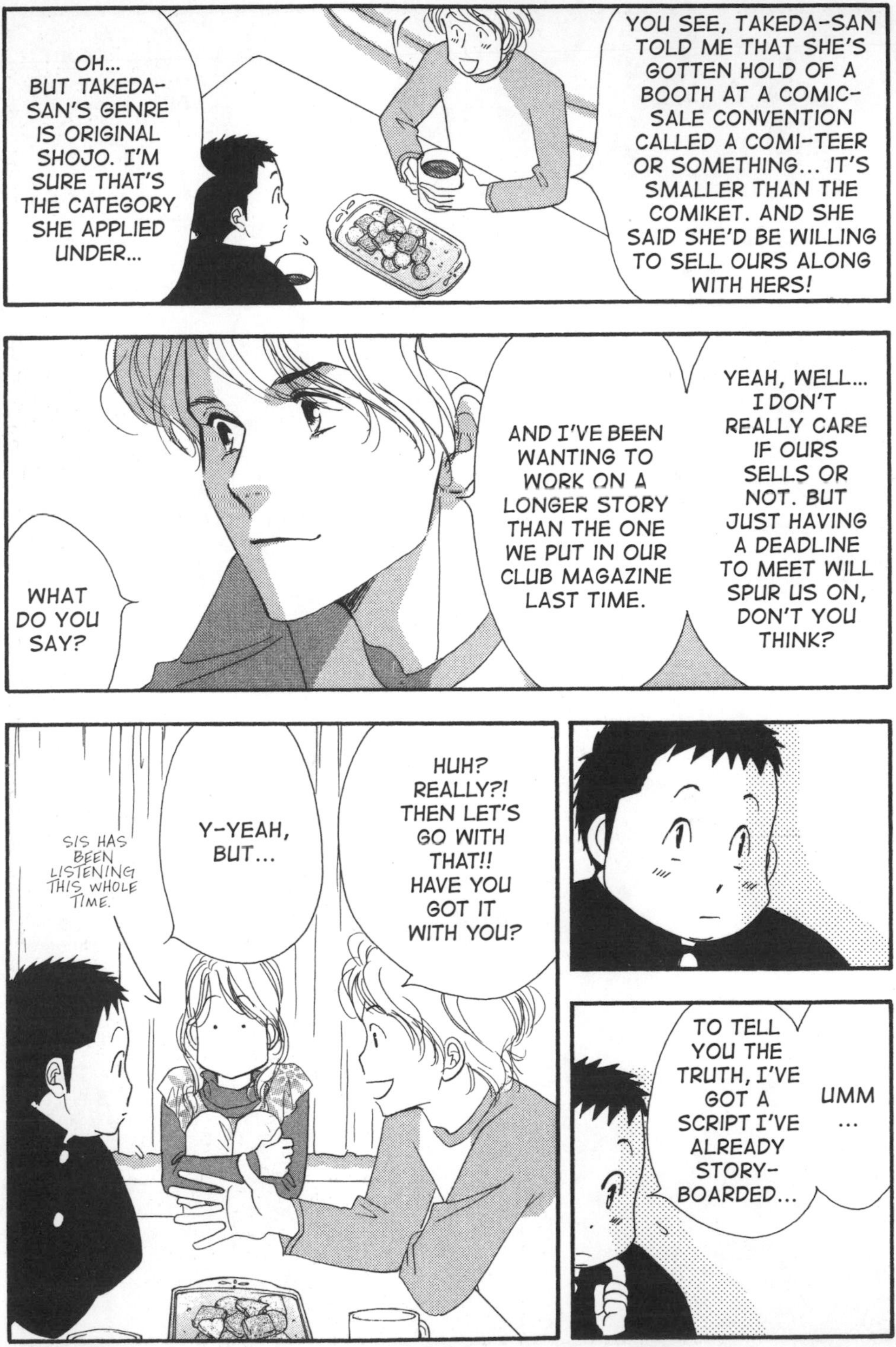
YOU SEE, TAKEDA-SAN TOLD ME THAT SHE'S GOTTEN HOLD OF A BOOTH AT A COMIC-SALE CONVENTION CALLED A COMI-TEER OR SOMETHING... IT'S SMALLER THAN THE COMIKET. AND SHE SAID SHE'D BE WILLING TO SELL OURS ALONG WITH HERS!
OH... BUT TAKEDA-SAN'S GENRE IS ORIGINAL SHOJO. I'M SURE THAT'S THE CATEGORY SHE APPLIED UNDER...
YEAH, WELL... I DON'T REALLY CARE IF OURS SELLS OR NOT. BUT JUST HAVING A DEADLINE TO MEET WILL SPUR US ON, DON'T YOU THINK?
AND I'VE BEEN WANTING TO WORK ON A LONGER STORY THAN THE ONE WE PUT IN OUR CLUB MAGAZINE LAST TIME.
WHAT DO YOU SAY?
UMM ...
TO TELL YOU THE TRUTH, I'VE GOT A SCRIPT I'VE ALREADY STORY-BOARDED...
HUH? REALLY?! THEN LET'S GO WITH THAT!! HAVE YOU GOT IT WITH YOU?
Y-YEAH, BUT...
SIS HAS BEEN LISTENING THIS WHOLE TIME.

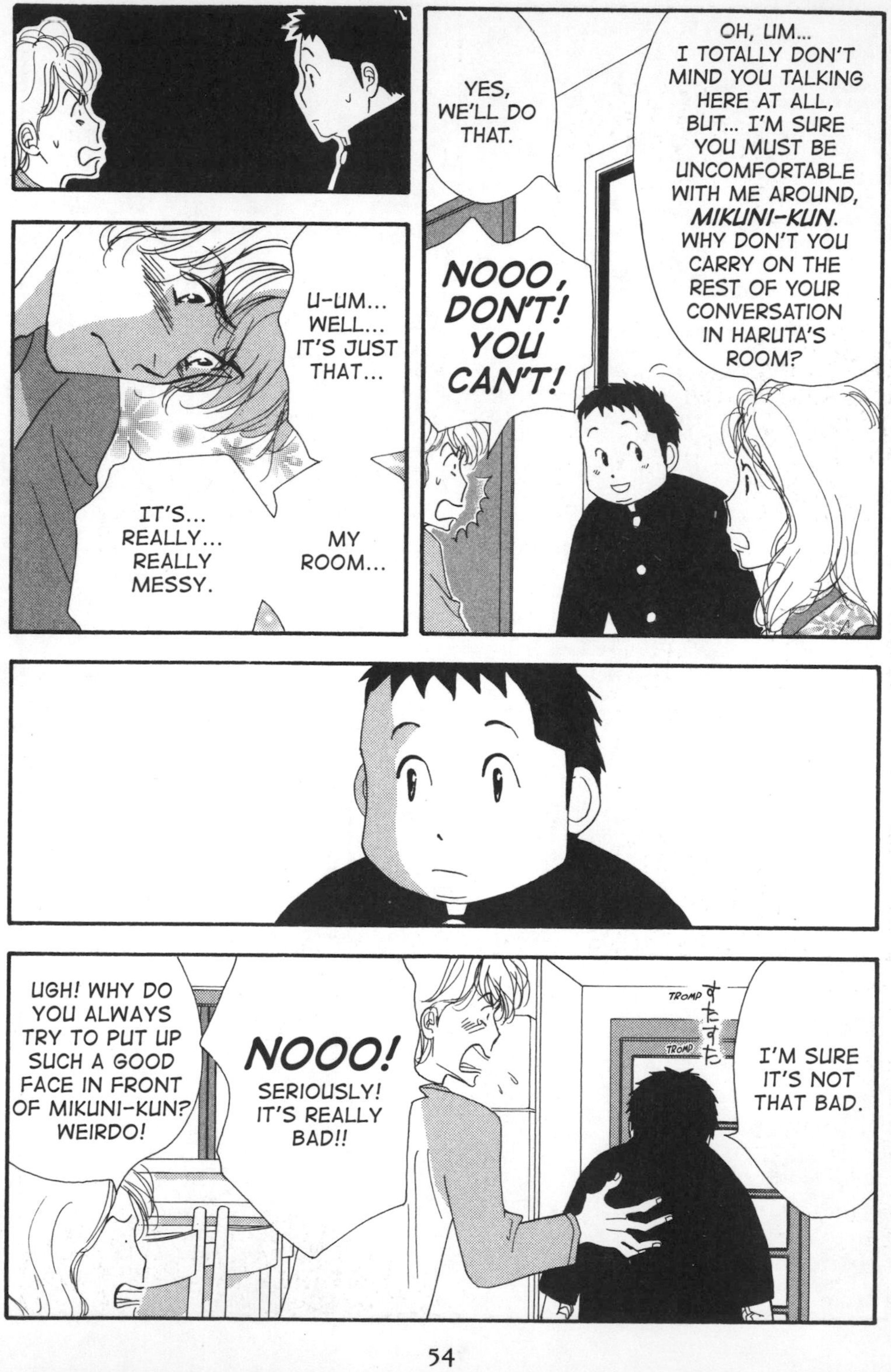
OH, UM... I TOTALLY DON'T MIND YOU TALKING HERE AT ALL, BUT... I'M SURE YOU MUST BE UNCOMFORTABLE WITH ME AROUND, MIKUNI-KUN. WHY DON'T YOU CARRY ON THE REST OF YOUR CONVERSATION IN HARUTA'S ROOM?
YES, WE'LL DO THAT.
NOOO, DON'T! YOU CAN'T!
U-UM... WELL... IT'S JUST THAT...
MY ROOM...
IT'S... REALLY... REALLY MESSY.
I'M SURE IT'S NOT THAT BAD.
すたすた
TROMP
TROMP
NOOO! SERIOUSLY! IT'S REALLY BAD!!
UGH! WHY DO YOU ALWAYS TRY TO PUT UP SUCH A GOOD FACE IN FRONT OF MIKUNI-KUN? WEIRDO!

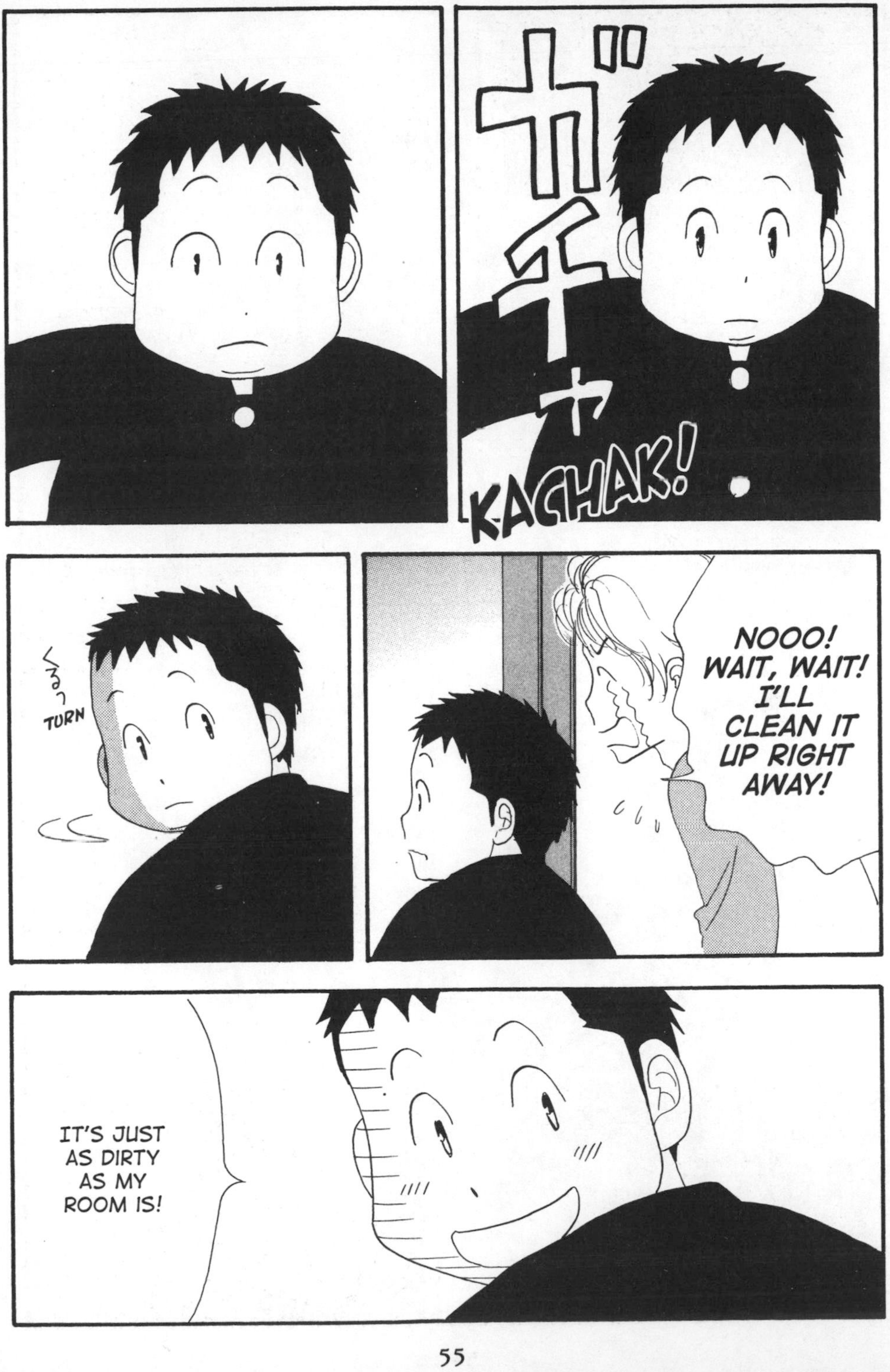
ガチャ
KACHAK!
NOOO! WAIT, WAIT! I'LL CLEAN IT UP RIGHT AWAY!
くるっ
TURN
IT'S JUST AS DIRTY AS MY ROOM IS!

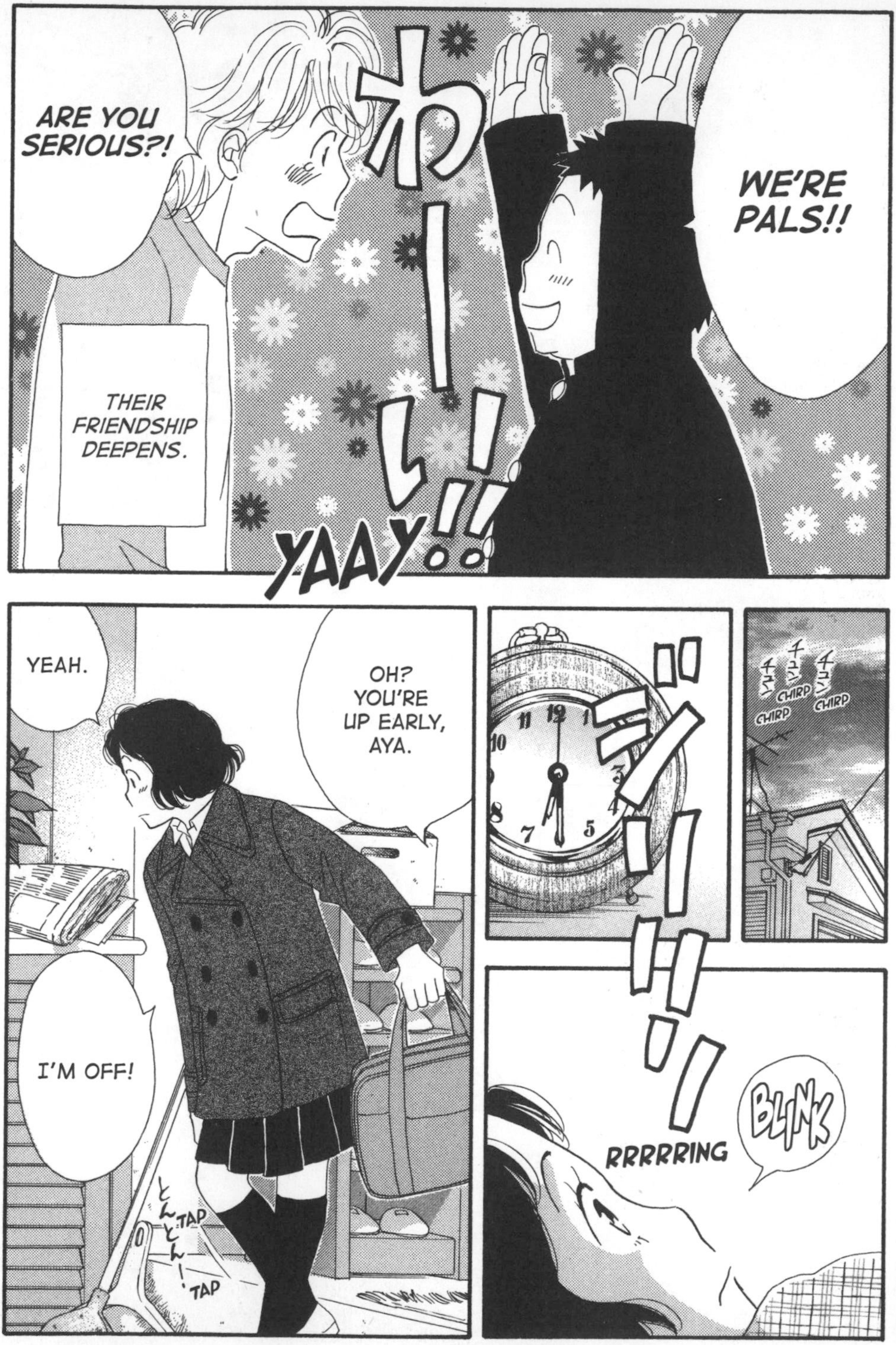
WE'RE PALS!!
わーい!!
YAAY!!
ARE YOU SERIOUS?!
THEIR FRIENDSHIP DEEPENS.
CHIRP
CHIRP
CHIRP
RRRRRING
BLINK
OH? YOU'RE UP EARLY, AYA.
YEAH.
I'M OFF!
とんとん
TAP
TAP

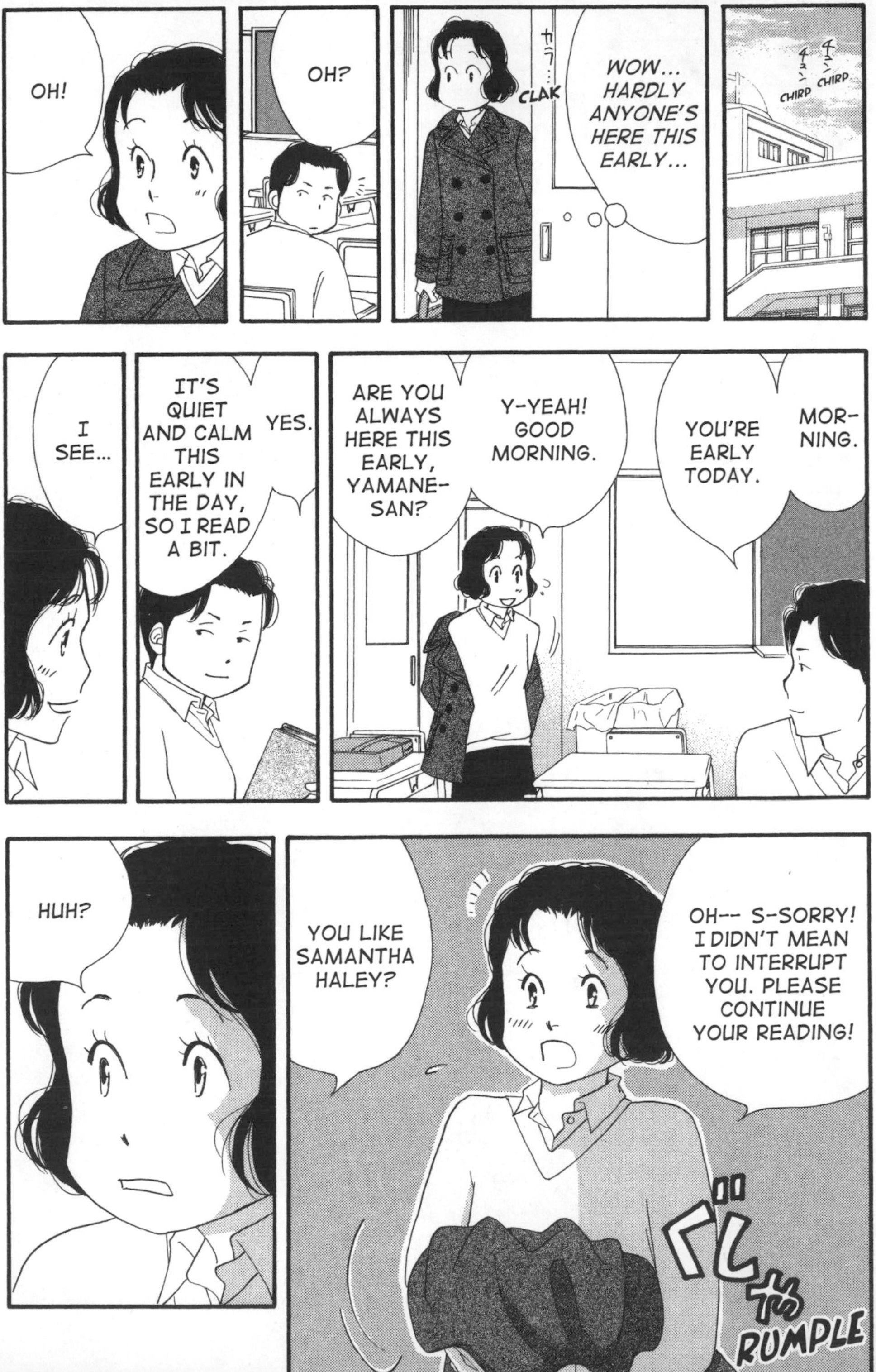
チュン チュン
CHIRP CHIRP
WOW... HARDLY ANYONE'S HERE THIS EARLY...
カラ…
CLAK
OH?
OH!
MORNING.
YOU'RE EARLY TODAY.
Y-YEAH! GOOD MORNING.
ARE YOU ALWAYS HERE THIS EARLY, YAMANE-SAN?
YES.
IT'S QUIET AND CALM THIS EARLY IN THE DAY, SO I READ A BIT.
I SEE...
OH-- S-SORRY! I DIDN'T MEAN TO INTERRUPT YOU. PLEASE CONTINUE YOUR READING!
ぐしゃ
RUMPLE
YOU LIKE SAMANTHA HALEY?
HUH?

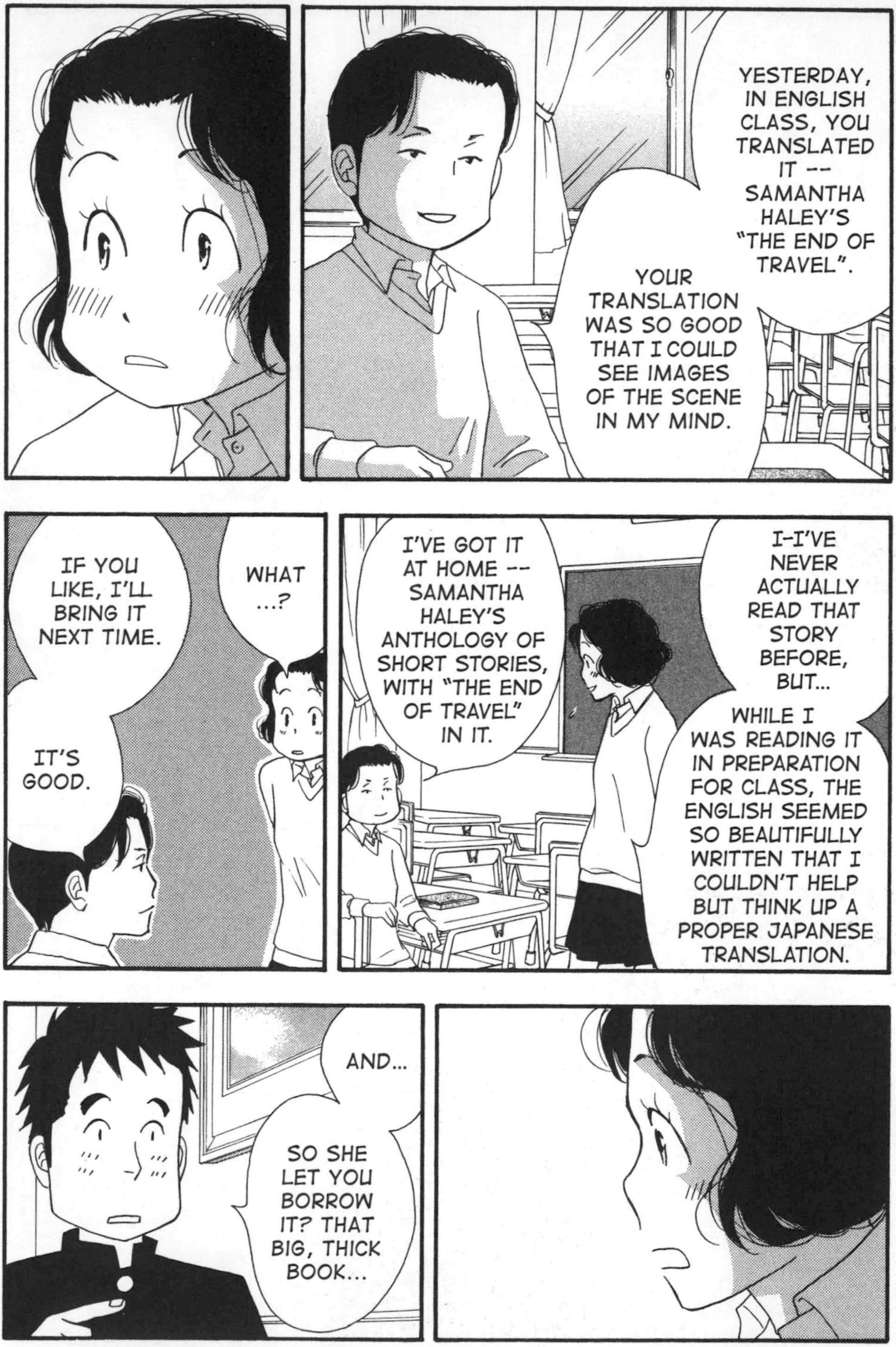
YESTERDAY, IN ENGLISH CLASS, YOU TRANSLATED IT -- SAMANTHA HALEY'S "THE END OF TRAVEL".
YOUR TRANSLATION WAS SO GOOD THAT I COULD SEE IMAGES OF THE SCENE IN MY MIND.
I-I'VE NEVER ACTUALLY READ THAT STORY BEFORE, BUT...
WHILE I WAS READING IT IN PREPARATION FOR CLASS, THE ENGLISH SEEMED SO BEAUTIFULLY WRITTEN THAT I COULDN'T HELP BUT THINK UP A PROPER JAPANESE TRANSLATION.
I'VE GOT IT AT HOME -- SAMANTHA HALEY'S ANTHOLOGY OF SHORT STORIES, WITH "THE END OF TRAVEL" IN IT.
WHAT ...?
IF YOU LIKE, I'LL BRING IT NEXT TIME.
IT'S GOOD.
AND...
SO SHE LET YOU BORROW IT? THAT BIG, THICK BOOK...

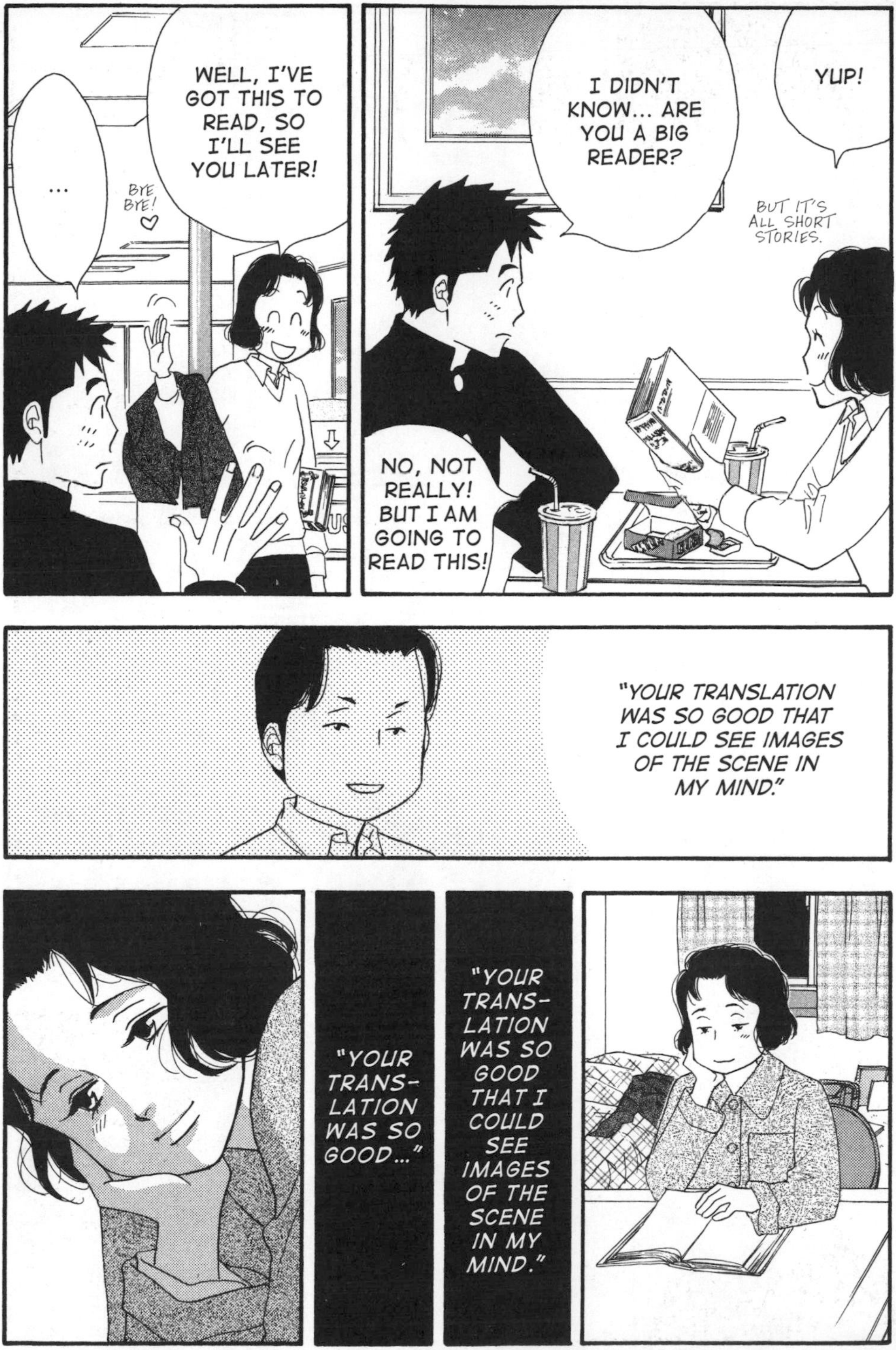
YUP!
I DIDN'T KNOW... ARE YOU A BIG READER?
BUT IT'S ALL SHORT STORIES.
NO, NOT REALLY! BUT I AM GOING TO READ THIS!
WELL, I'VE GOT THIS TO READ, SO I'LL SEE YOU LATER!
BYE BYE! ♡
...
"YOUR TRANSLATION WAS SO GOOD THAT I COULD SEE IMAGES OF THE SCENE IN MY MIND."
"YOUR TRANS-LATION WAS SO GOOD THAT I COULD SEE IMAGES OF THE SCENE IN MY MIND."
"YOUR TRANS-LATION WAS SO GOOD..."

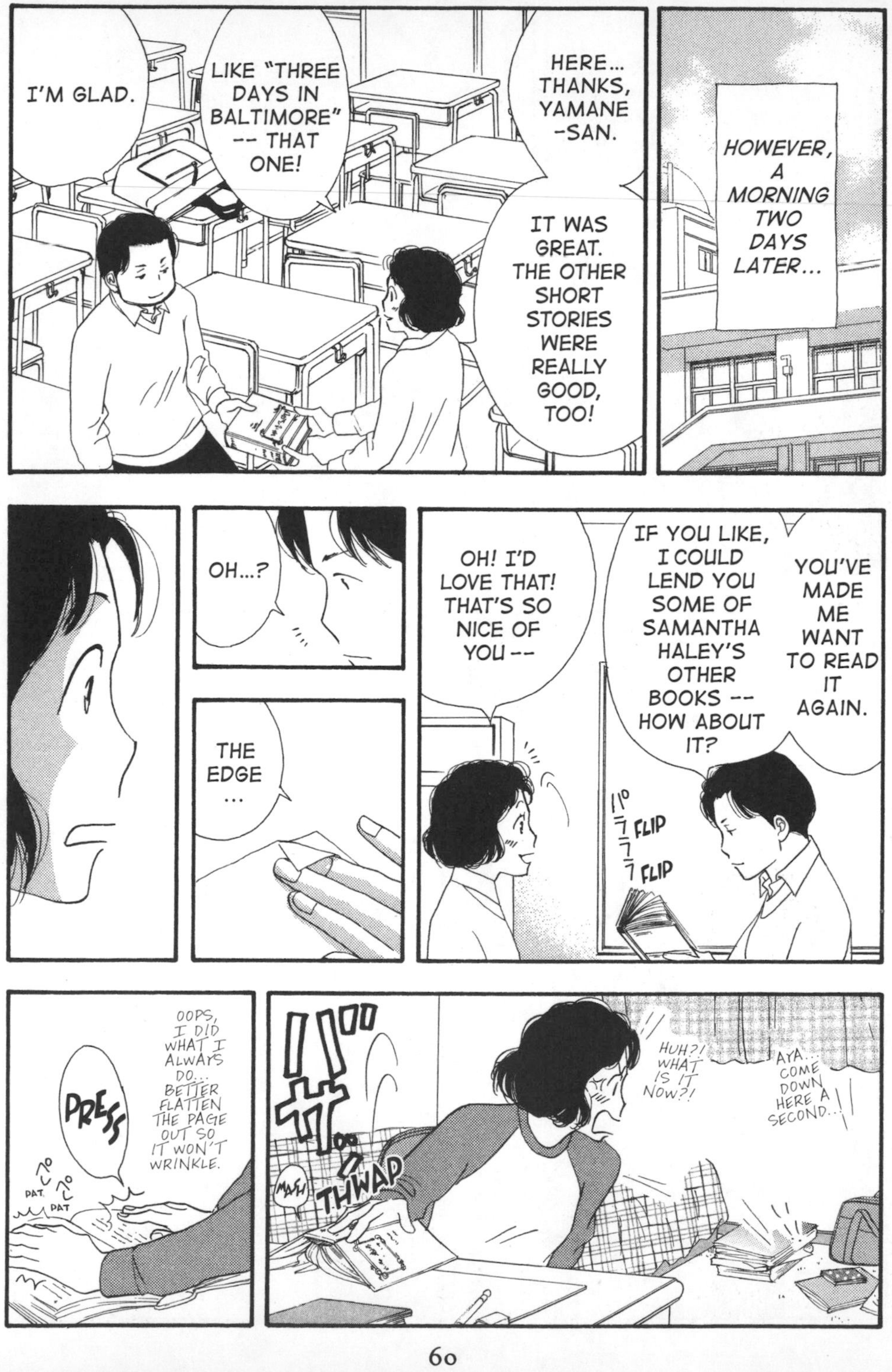
HOWEVER, A MORNING TWO DAYS LATER...
HERE... THANKS, YAMANE-SAN.
IT WAS GREAT. THE OTHER SHORT STORIES WERE REALLY GOOD, TOO!
LIKE "THREE DAYS IN BALTIMORE" -- THAT ONE!
I'M GLAD.
YOU'VE MADE ME WANT TO READ IT AGAIN.
IF YOU LIKE, I COULD LEND YOU SOME OF SAMANTHA HALEY'S OTHER BOOKS -- HOW ABOUT IT?
OH! I'D LOVE THAT! THAT'S SO NICE OF YOU --
FLIP
FLIP
OH...?
THE EDGE ...
AYA... COME DOWN HERE A SECOND...!
HUH?! WHAT IS IT NOW?!
THWAP
MASH
OOPS, I DID WHAT I ALWAYS DO... BETTER FLATTEN THE PAGE OUT SO IT WON'T WRINKLE.
PRESS
PAT
PAT

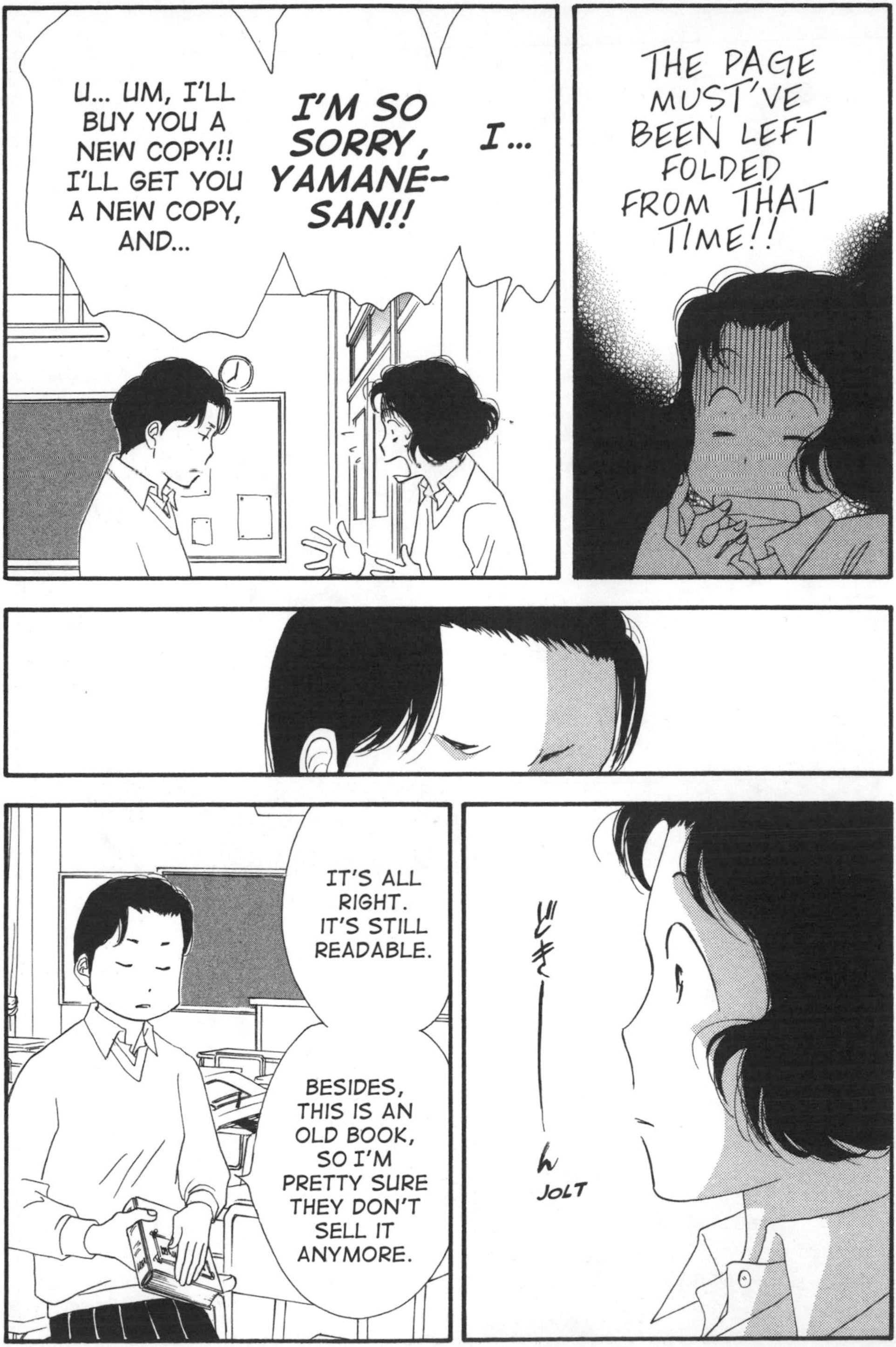
THE PAGE MUST'VE BEEN LEFT FOLDED FROM THAT TIME!!
I...
I'M SO SORRY, YAMANE-SAN!!
U... UM, I'LL BUY YOU A NEW COPY!! I'LL GET YOU A NEW COPY, AND...
どき——ん
JOLT
IT'S ALL RIGHT. IT'S STILL READABLE.
BESIDES, THIS IS AN OLD BOOK, SO I'M PRETTY SURE THEY DON'T SELL IT ANYMORE.

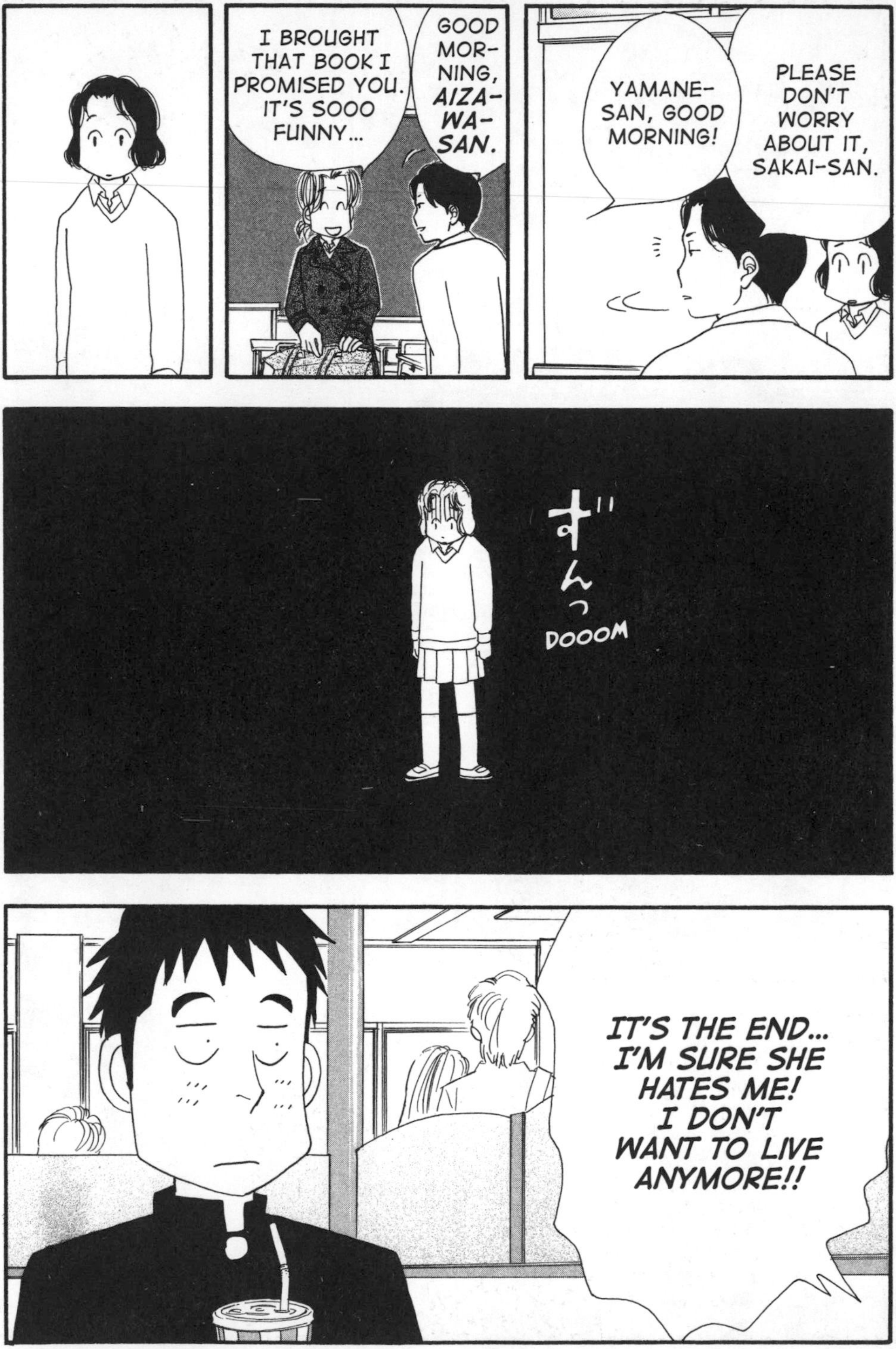
PLEASE DON'T WORRY ABOUT IT, SAKAI-SAN.
YAMANE-SAN, GOOD MORNING!
GOOD MORNING, AIZAWA-SAN.
I BROUGHT THAT BOOK I PROMISED YOU. IT'S SOOO FUNNY...
ずんっ
DOOOM
IT'S THE END... I'M SURE SHE HATES ME! I DON'T WANT TO LIVE ANYMORE!!

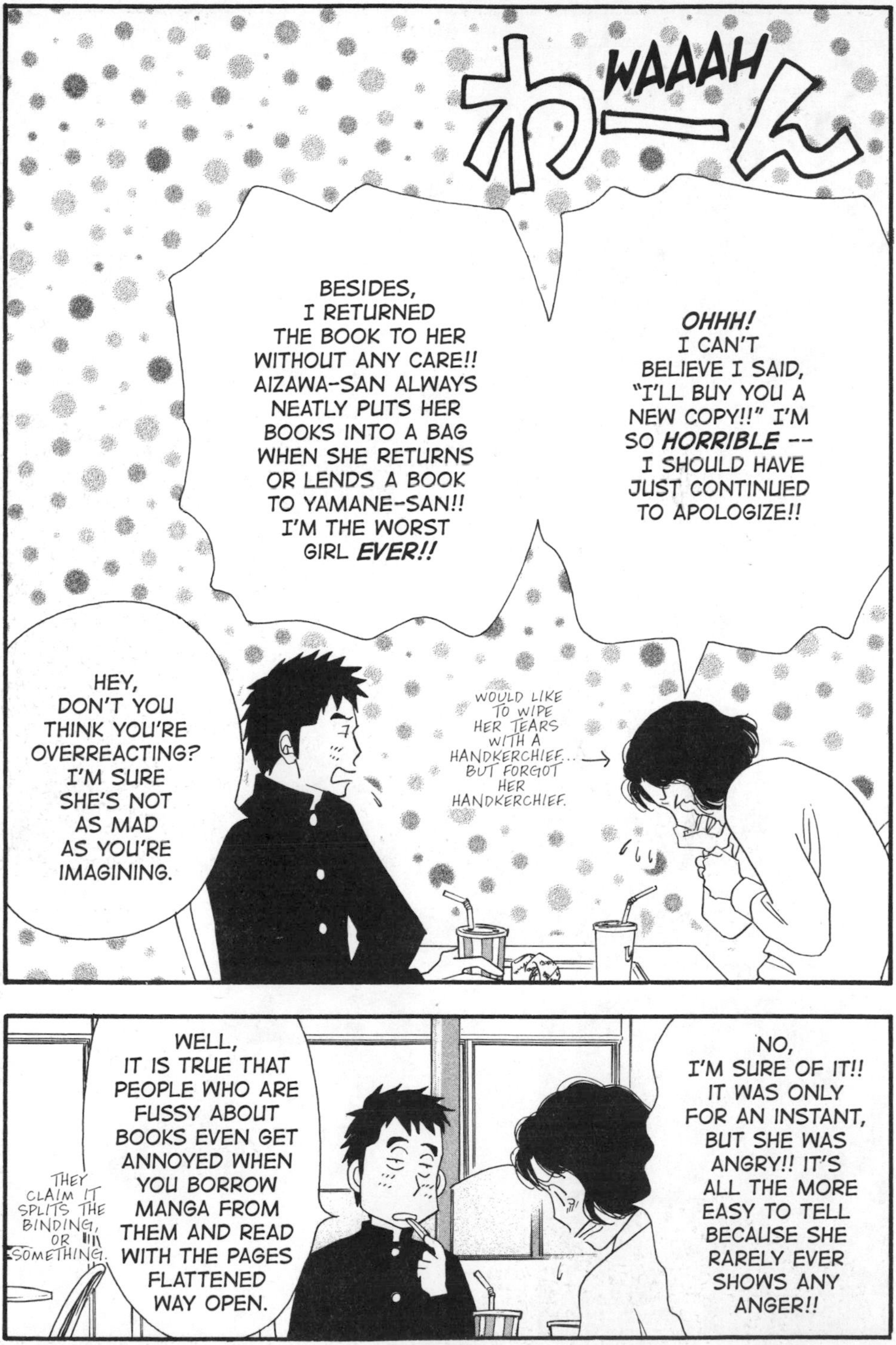

WAAAH
OHHH! I CAN'T BELIEVE I SAID, "I'LL BUY YOU A NEW COPY!!" I'M SO HORRIBLE -- I SHOULD HAVE JUST CONTINUED TO APOLOGIZE!!
BESIDES, I RETURNED THE BOOK TO HER WITHOUT ANY CARE!! AIZAWA-SAN ALWAYS NEATLY PUTS HER BOOKS INTO A BAG WHEN SHE RETURNS OR LENDS A BOOK TO YAMANE-SAN!! I'M THE WORST GIRL EVER!!
WOULD LIKE TO WIPE HER TEARS WITH A HANDKERCHIEF... BUT FORGOT HER HANDKERCHIEF.
HEY, DON'T YOU THINK YOU'RE OVERREACTING? I'M SURE SHE'S NOT AS MAD AS YOU'RE IMAGINING.
NO, I'M SURE OF IT!! IT WAS ONLY FOR AN INSTANT, BUT SHE WAS ANGRY!! IT'S ALL THE MORE EASY TO TELL BECAUSE SHE RARELY EVER SHOWS ANY ANGER!!
WELL, IT IS TRUE THAT PEOPLE WHO ARE FUSSY ABOUT BOOKS EVEN GET ANNOYED WHEN YOU BORROW MANGA FROM THEM AND READ WITH THE PAGES FLATTENED WAY OPEN.
THEY CLAIM IT SPLITS THE BINDING, OR SOMETHING.

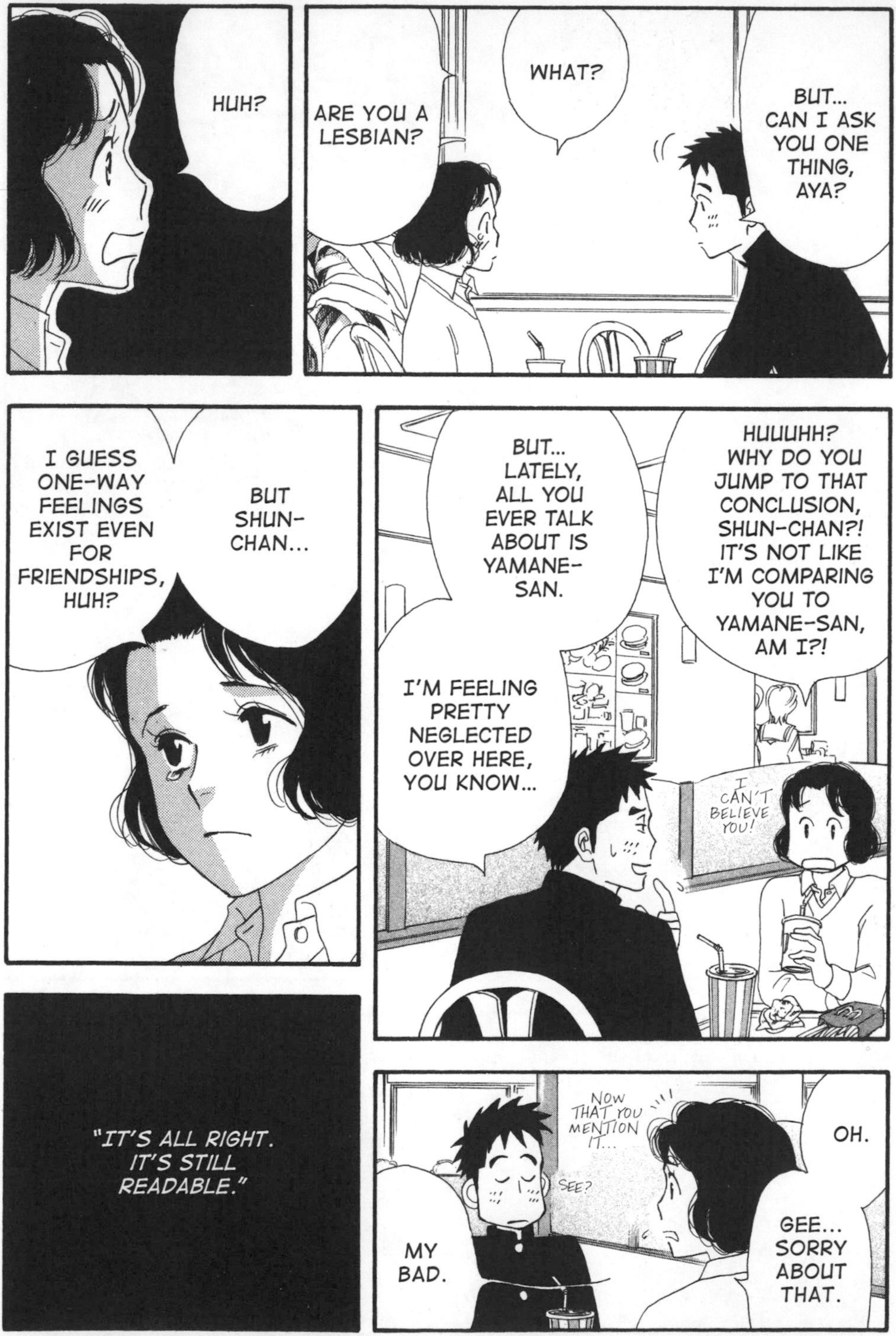
BUT... CAN I ASK YOU ONE THING, AYA?
WHAT?
ARE YOU A LESBIAN?
HUH?
HUUUHH? WHY DO YOU JUMP TO THAT CONCLUSION, SHUN-CHAN?! IT'S NOT LIKE I'M COMPARING YOU TO YAMANE-SAN, AM I?!
BUT... LATELY, ALL YOU EVER TALK ABOUT IS YAMANE-SAN.
I CAN'T BELIEVE YOU!
I'M FEELING PRETTY NEGLECTED OVER HERE, YOU KNOW...
BUT SHUN-CHAN...
I GUESS ONE-WAY FEELINGS EXIST EVEN FOR FRIENDSHIPS, HUH?
OH.
GEE... SORRY ABOUT THAT.
NOW THAT YOU MENTION IT...
SEE?
MY BAD.
"IT'S ALL RIGHT. IT'S STILL READABLE."

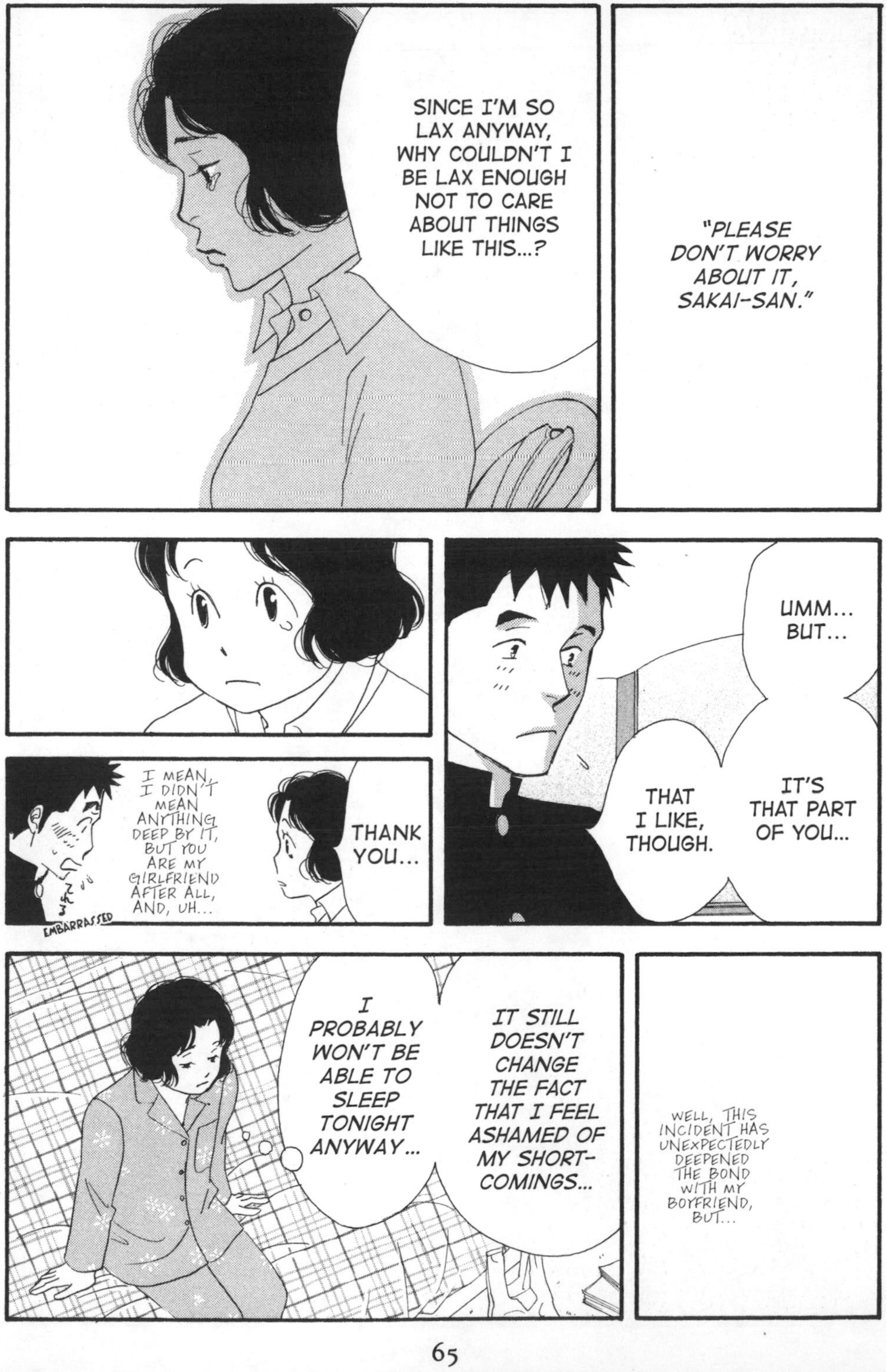
"PLEASE DON'T WORRY ABOUT IT, SAKAI-SAN."
SINCE I'M SO LAX ANYWAY, WHY COULDN'T I BE LAX ENOUGH NOT TO CARE ABOUT THINGS LIKE THIS...?
UMM... BUT...
IT'S THAT PART OF YOU...
THAT I LIKE, THOUGH.
THANK YOU...
I MEAN, I DIDN'T MEAN ANYTHING DEEP BY IT, BUT YOU ARE MY GIRLFRIEND AFTER ALL, AND, UH...
EMBARRASSED
WELL, THIS INCIDENT HAS UNEXPECTEDLY DEEPENED THE BOND WITH MY BOYFRIEND, BUT...
IT STILL DOESN'T CHANGE THE FACT THAT I FEEL ASHAMED OF MY SHORT-COMINGS...
I PROBABLY WON'T BE ABLE TO SLEEP TONIGHT ANYWAY...

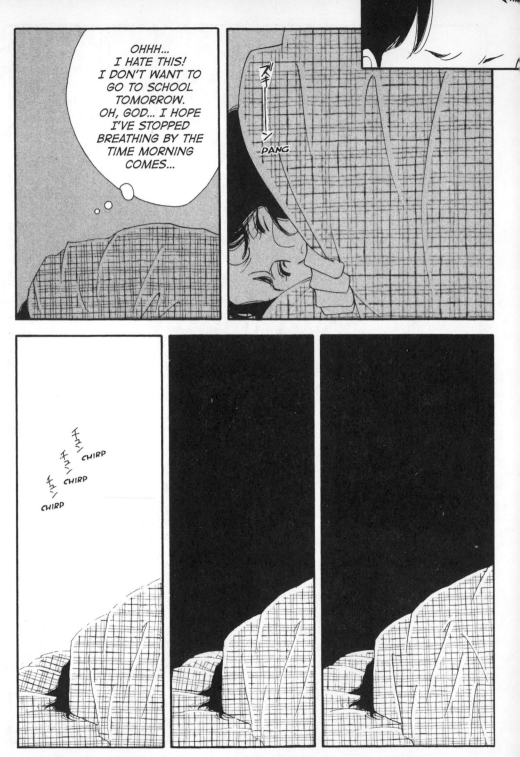

OHHH...
I HATE THIS!
I DON'T WANT TO
GO TO SCHOOL
TOMORROW.
OH, GOD... I HOPE
I'VE STOPPED
BREATHING BY THE
TIME MORNING
COMES...

PANG

CHIRP
CHIRP
CHIRP

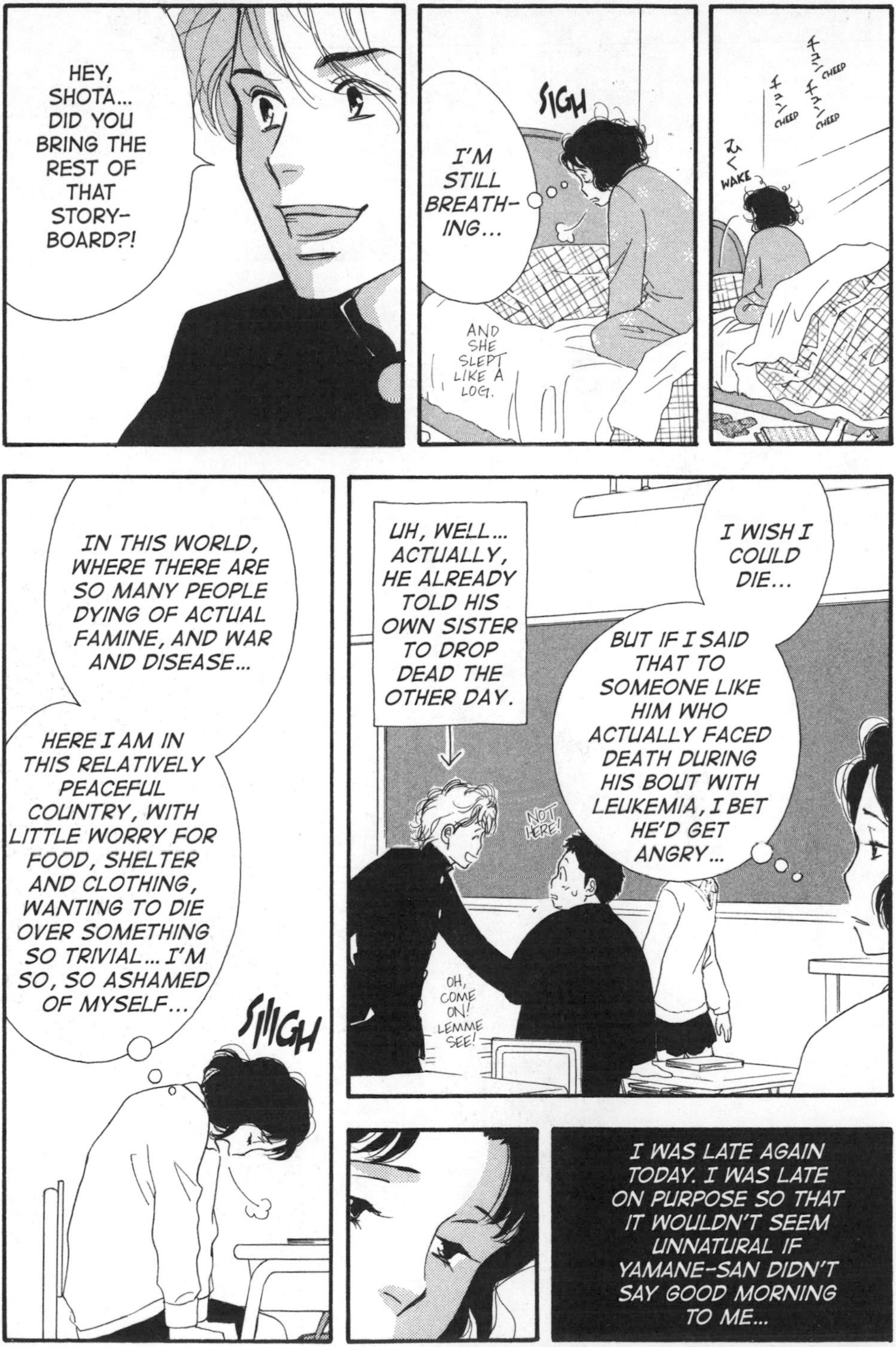
チュン CHEEP
チュン CHEEP
チュン CHEEP
むく WAKE
SIGH
I'M STILL BREATHING...
AND SHE SLEPT LIKE A LOG.
HEY, SHOTA... DID YOU BRING THE REST OF THAT STORY-BOARD?!
I WISH I COULD DIE...
BUT IF I SAID THAT TO SOMEONE LIKE HIM WHO ACTUALLY FACED DEATH DURING HIS BOUT WITH LEUKEMIA, I BET HE'D GET ANGRY...
UH, WELL... ACTUALLY, HE ALREADY TOLD HIS OWN SISTER TO DROP DEAD THE OTHER DAY.
NOT HERE!
OH, COME ON! LEMME SEE!
I WAS LATE AGAIN TODAY. I WAS LATE ON PURPOSE SO THAT IT WOULDN'T SEEM UNNATURAL IF YAMANE-SAN DIDN'T SAY GOOD MORNING TO ME...
IN THIS WORLD, WHERE THERE ARE SO MANY PEOPLE DYING OF ACTUAL FAMINE, AND WAR AND DISEASE...
HERE I AM IN THIS RELATIVELY PEACEFUL COUNTRY, WITH LITTLE WORRY FOR FOOD, SHELTER AND CLOTHING, WANTING TO DIE OVER SOMETHING SO TRIVIAL... I'M SO, SO ASHAMED OF MYSELF...
SIIIGH

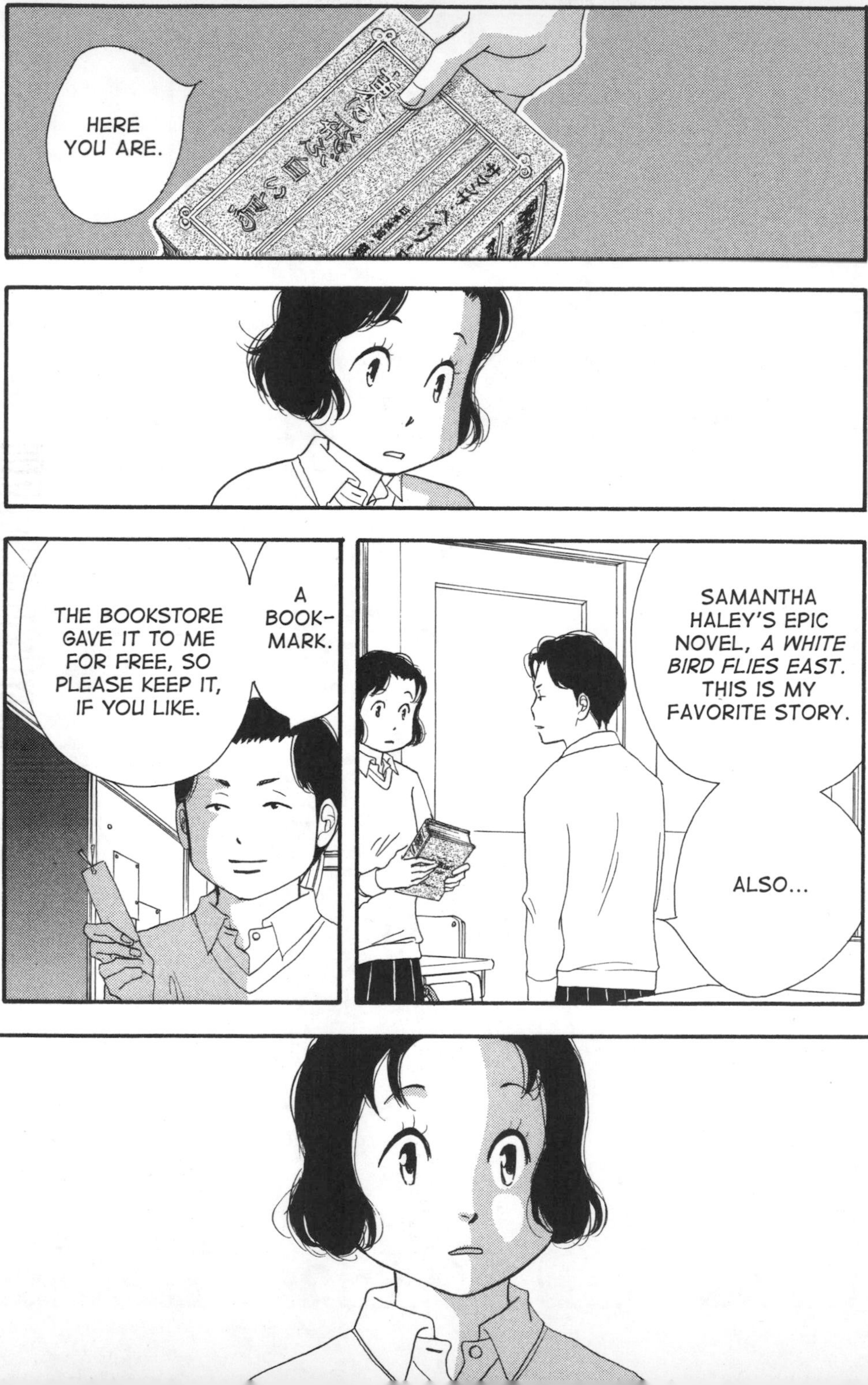
HERE YOU ARE.
SAMANTHA HALEY'S EPIC NOVEL, *A WHITE BIRD FLIES EAST*. THIS IS MY FAVORITE STORY.
ALSO...
A BOOK-MARK.
THE BOOKSTORE GAVE IT TO ME FOR FREE, SO PLEASE KEEP IT, IF YOU LIKE.

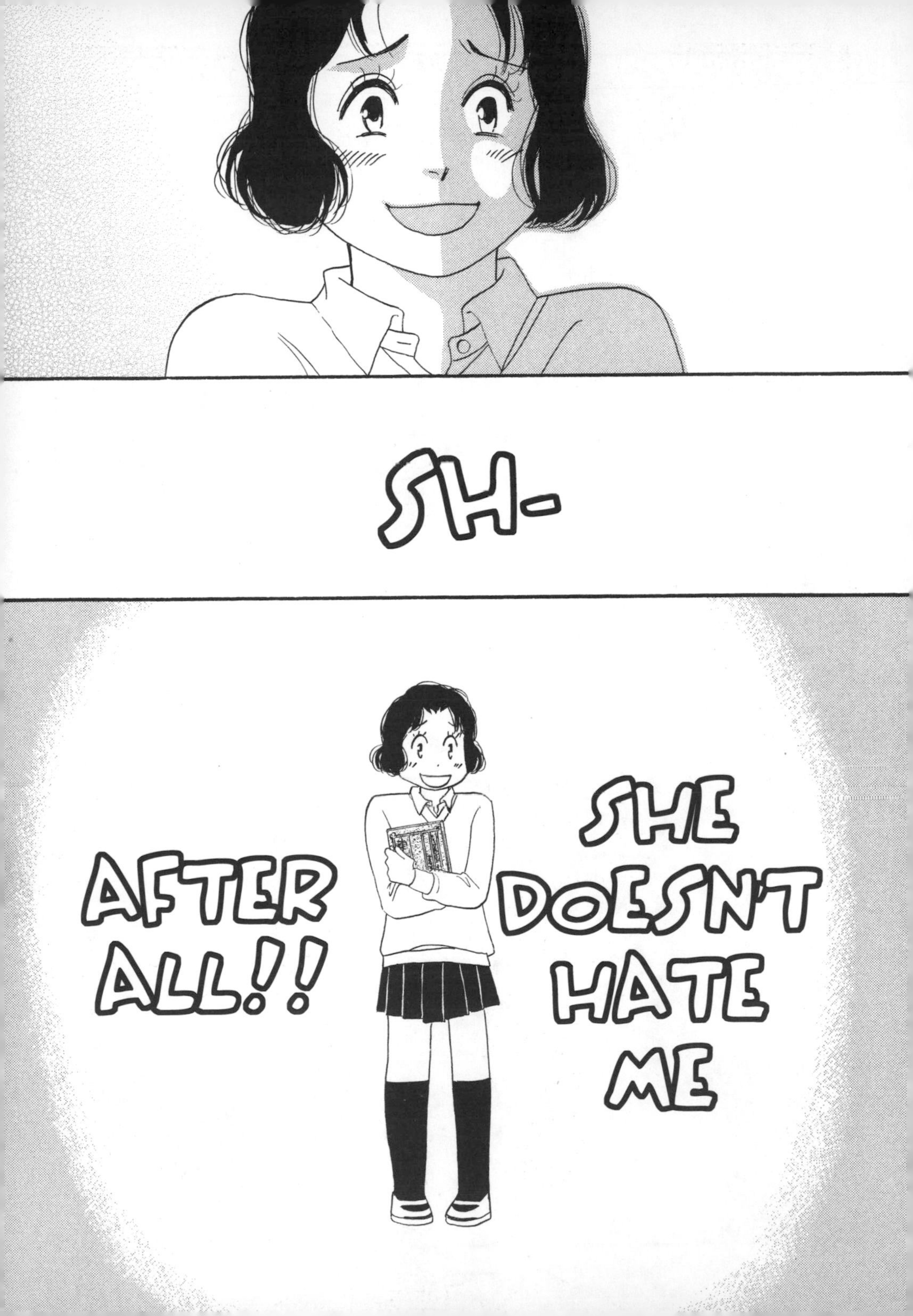
SH-
SHE DOESN'T HATE ME
AFTER ALL!!

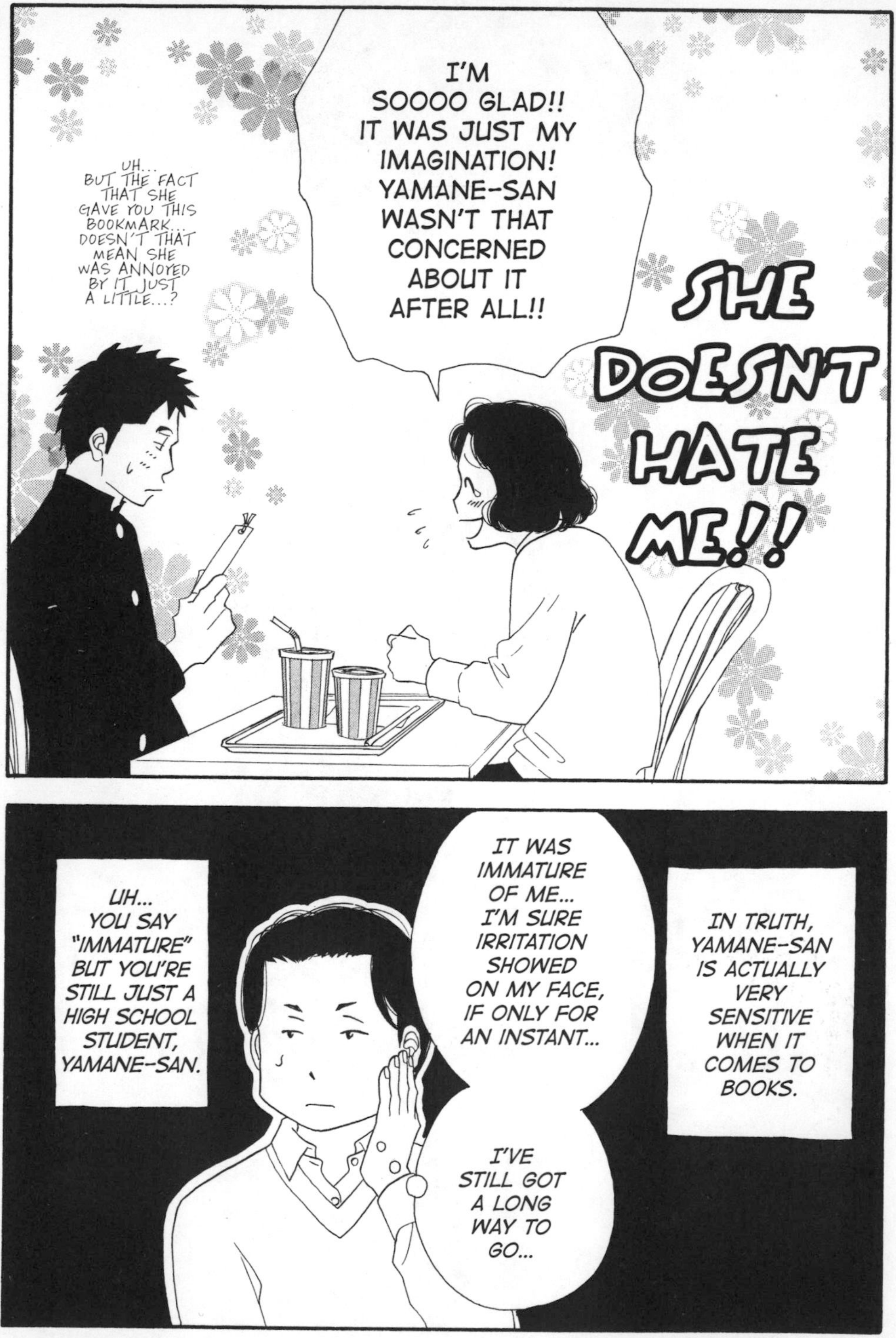

SHE DOESN'T HATE ME!!
I'M SOOOO GLAD!! IT WAS JUST MY IMAGINATION! YAMANE-SAN WASN'T THAT CONCERNED ABOUT IT AFTER ALL!!
UH... BUT THE FACT THAT SHE GAVE YOU THIS BOOKMARK... DOESN'T THAT MEAN SHE WAS ANNOYED BY IT JUST A LITTLE...?
IN TRUTH, YAMANE-SAN IS ACTUALLY VERY SENSITIVE WHEN IT COMES TO BOOKS.
IT WAS IMMATURE OF ME... I'M SURE IRRITATION SHOWED ON MY FACE, IF ONLY FOR AN INSTANT...
I'VE STILL GOT A LONG WAY TO GO...
UH... YOU SAY "IMMATURE" BUT YOU'RE STILL JUST A HIGH SCHOOL STUDENT, YAMANE-SAN.

どきーーん
JOLT

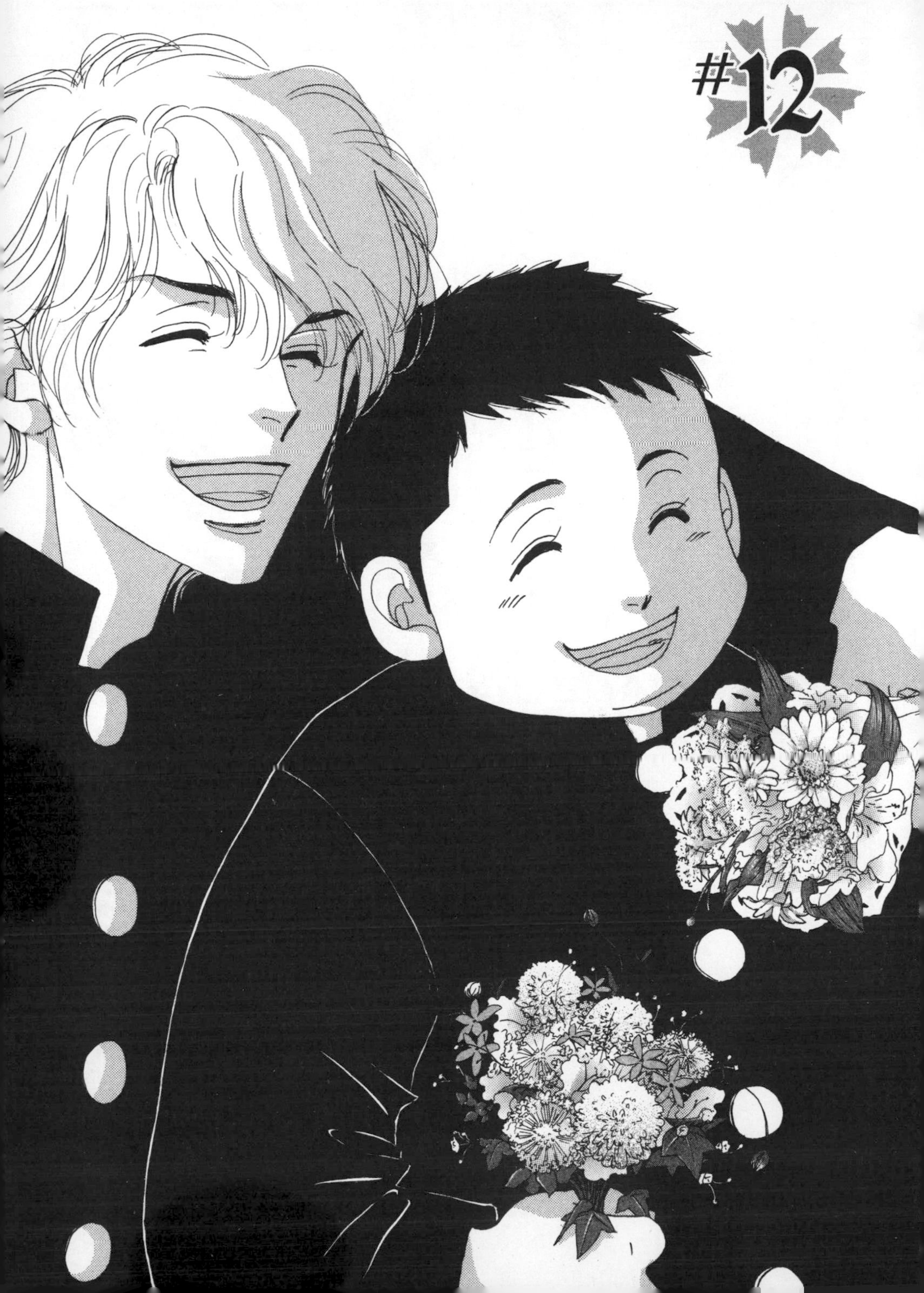
#12

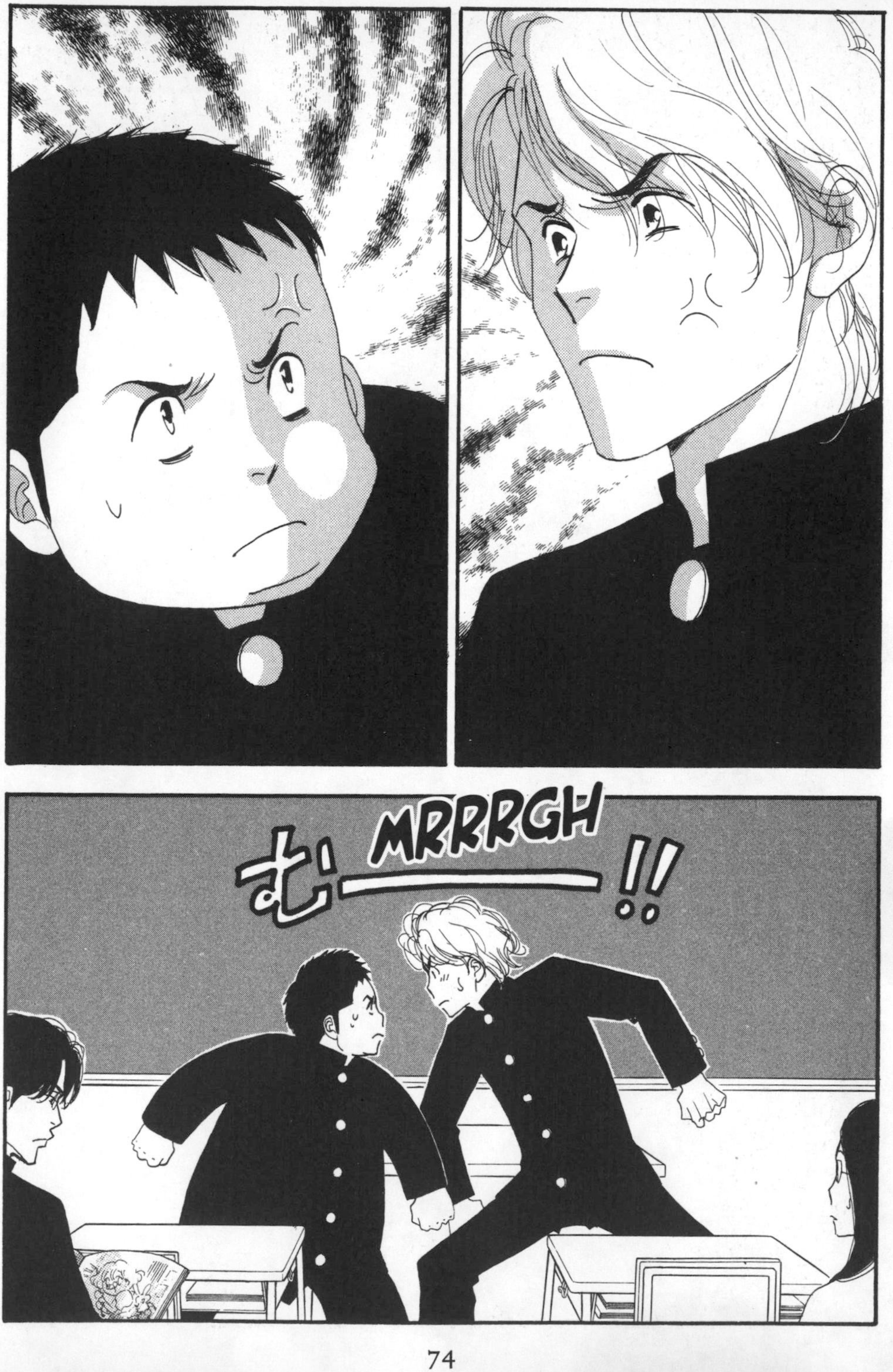
MRRRGH
む———!!

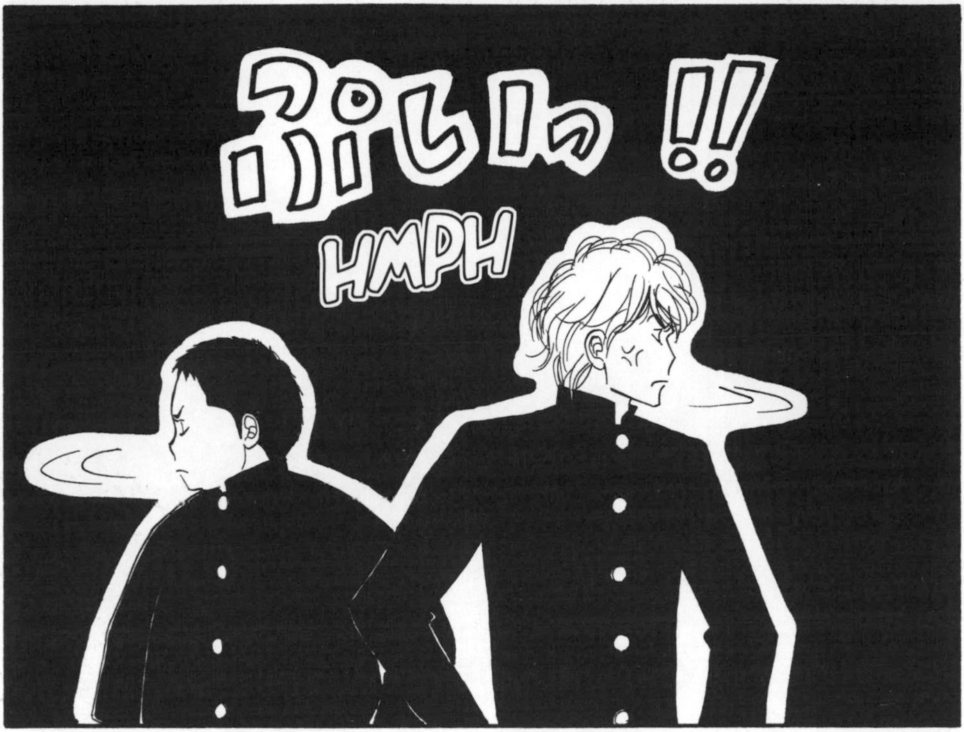
ぷいっ!!
HMPH

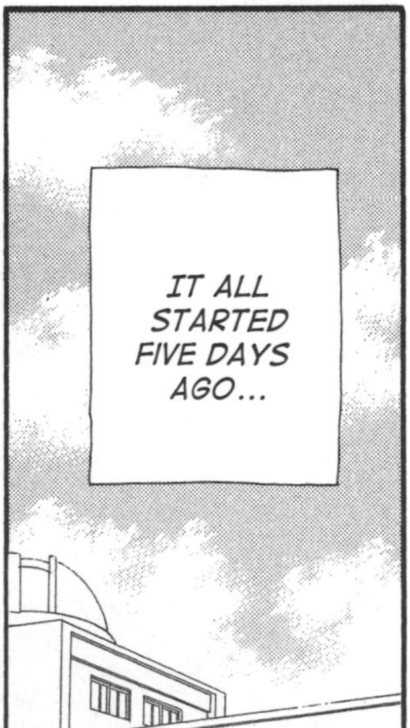
IT ALL STARTED FIVE DAYS AGO...

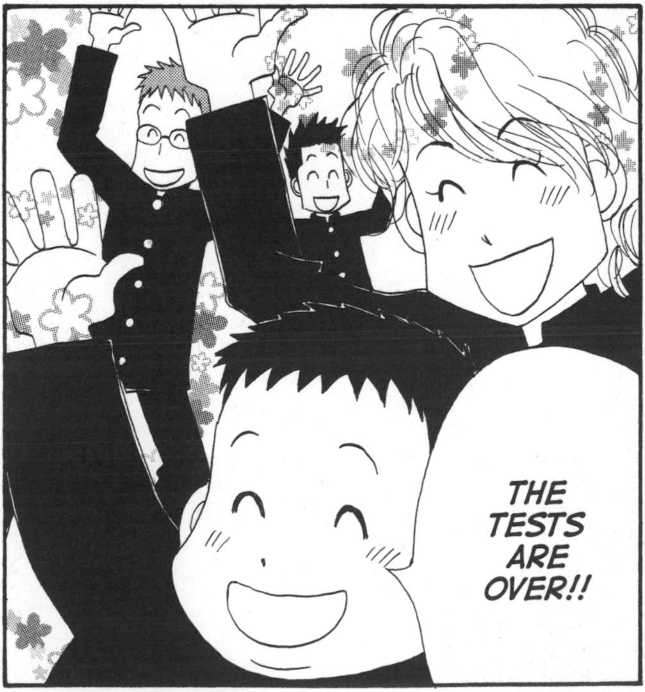
THE TESTS ARE OVER!!

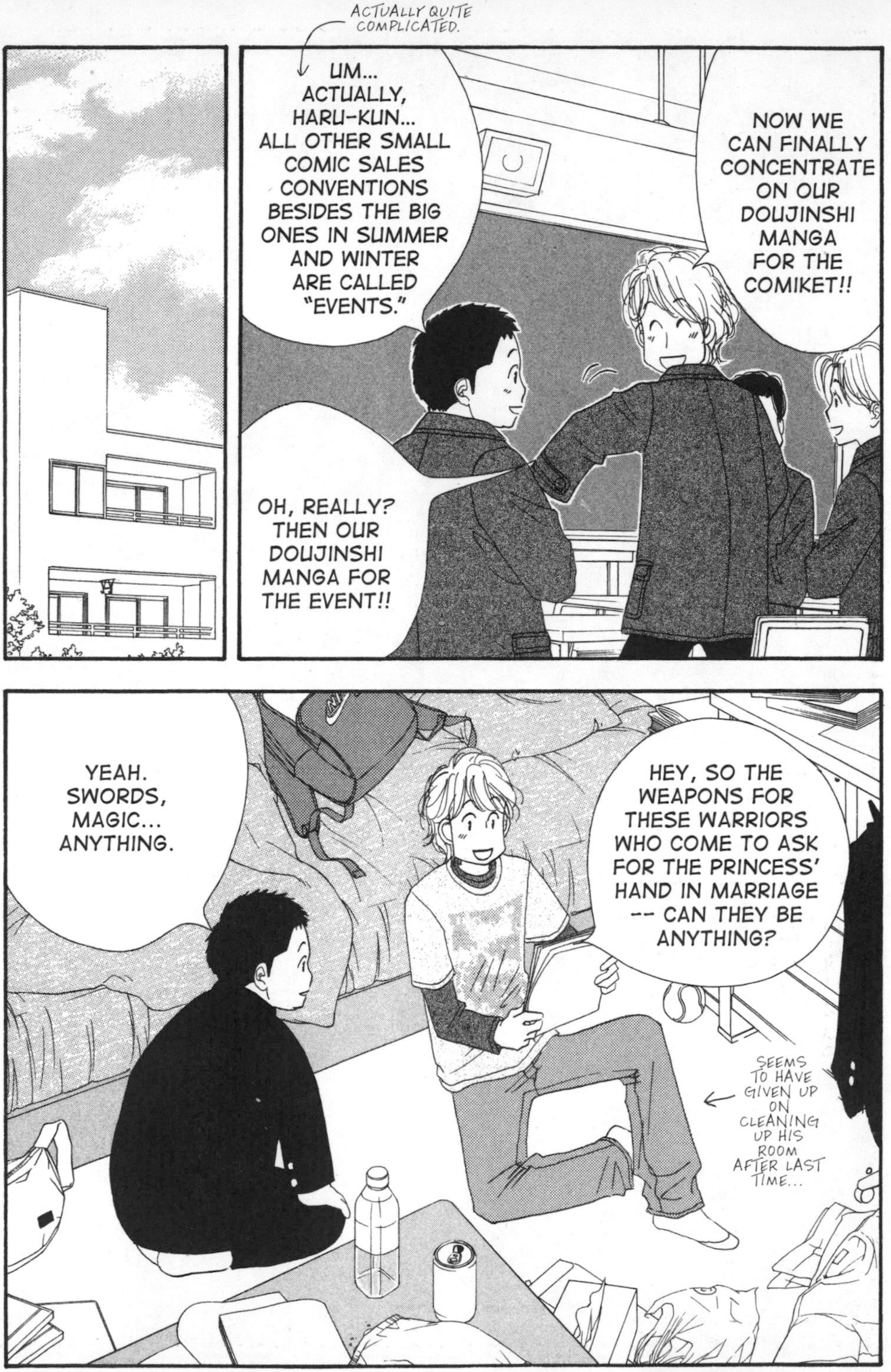
NOW WE CAN FINALLY CONCENTRATE ON OUR DOUJINSHI MANGA FOR THE COMIKET!!
ACTUALLY QUITE COMPLICATED.
UM... ACTUALLY, HARU-KUN... ALL OTHER SMALL COMIC SALES CONVENTIONS BESIDES THE BIG ONES IN SUMMER AND WINTER ARE CALLED "EVENTS."
OH, REALLY? THEN OUR DOUJINSHI MANGA FOR THE EVENT!!
HEY, SO THE WEAPONS FOR THESE WARRIORS WHO COME TO ASK FOR THE PRINCESS' HAND IN MARRIAGE -- CAN THEY BE ANYTHING?
YEAH. SWORDS, MAGIC... ANYTHING.
SEEMS TO HAVE GIVEN UP ON CLEANING UP HIS ROOM AFTER LAST TIME...

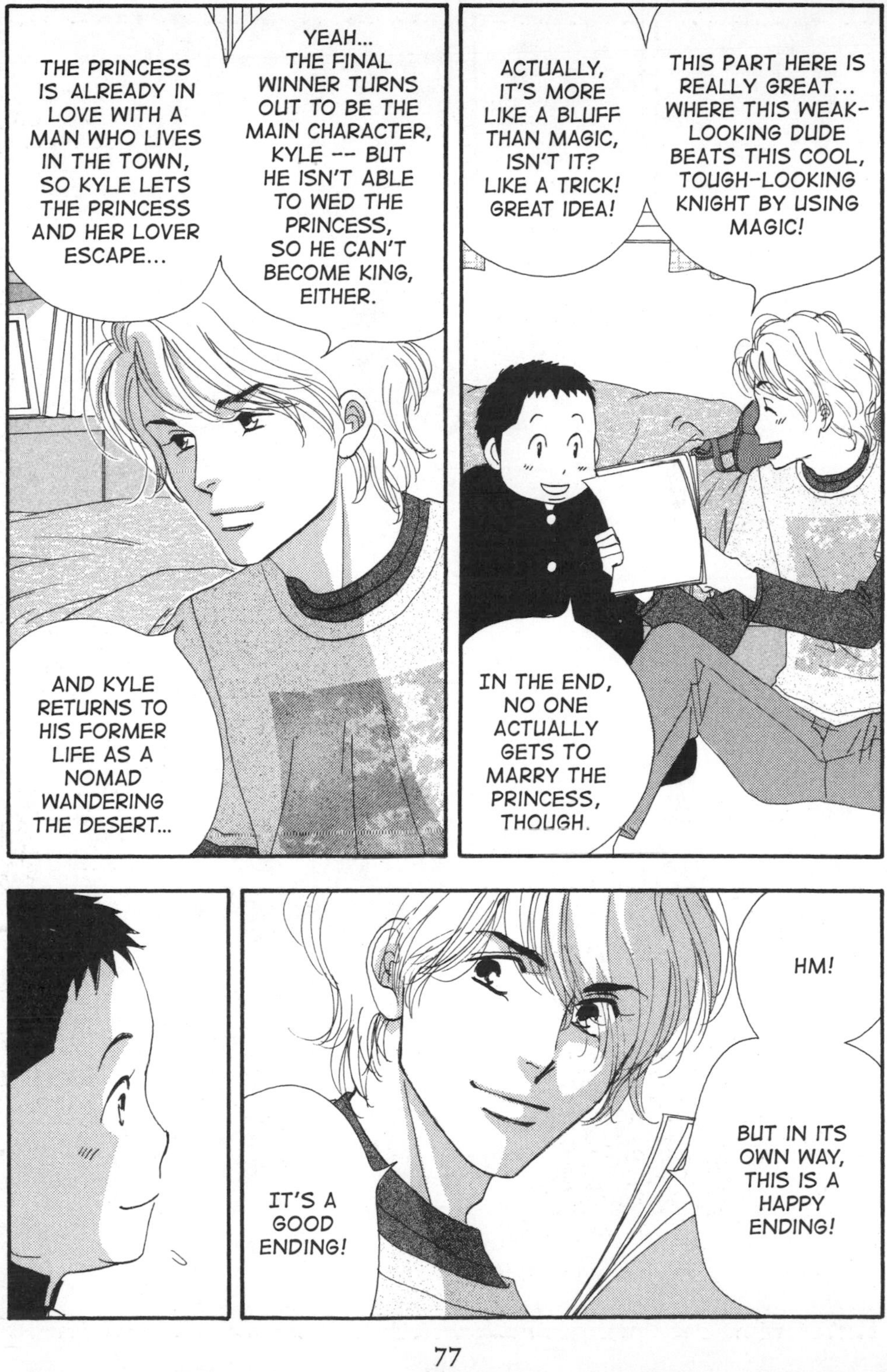
THIS PART HERE IS REALLY GREAT... WHERE THIS WEAK-LOOKING DUDE BEATS THIS COOL, TOUGH-LOOKING KNIGHT BY USING MAGIC!
ACTUALLY, IT'S MORE LIKE A BLUFF THAN MAGIC, ISN'T IT? LIKE A TRICK! GREAT IDEA!
IN THE END, NO ONE ACTUALLY GETS TO MARRY THE PRINCESS, THOUGH.
YEAH... THE FINAL WINNER TURNS OUT TO BE THE MAIN CHARACTER, KYLE -- BUT HE ISN'T ABLE TO WED THE PRINCESS, SO HE CAN'T BECOME KING, EITHER.
THE PRINCESS IS ALREADY IN LOVE WITH A MAN WHO LIVES IN THE TOWN, SO KYLE LETS THE PRINCESS AND HER LOVER ESCAPE...
AND KYLE RETURNS TO HIS FORMER LIFE AS A NOMAD WANDERING THE DESERT...
HM!
BUT IN ITS OWN WAY, THIS IS A HAPPY ENDING!
IT'S A GOOD ENDING!

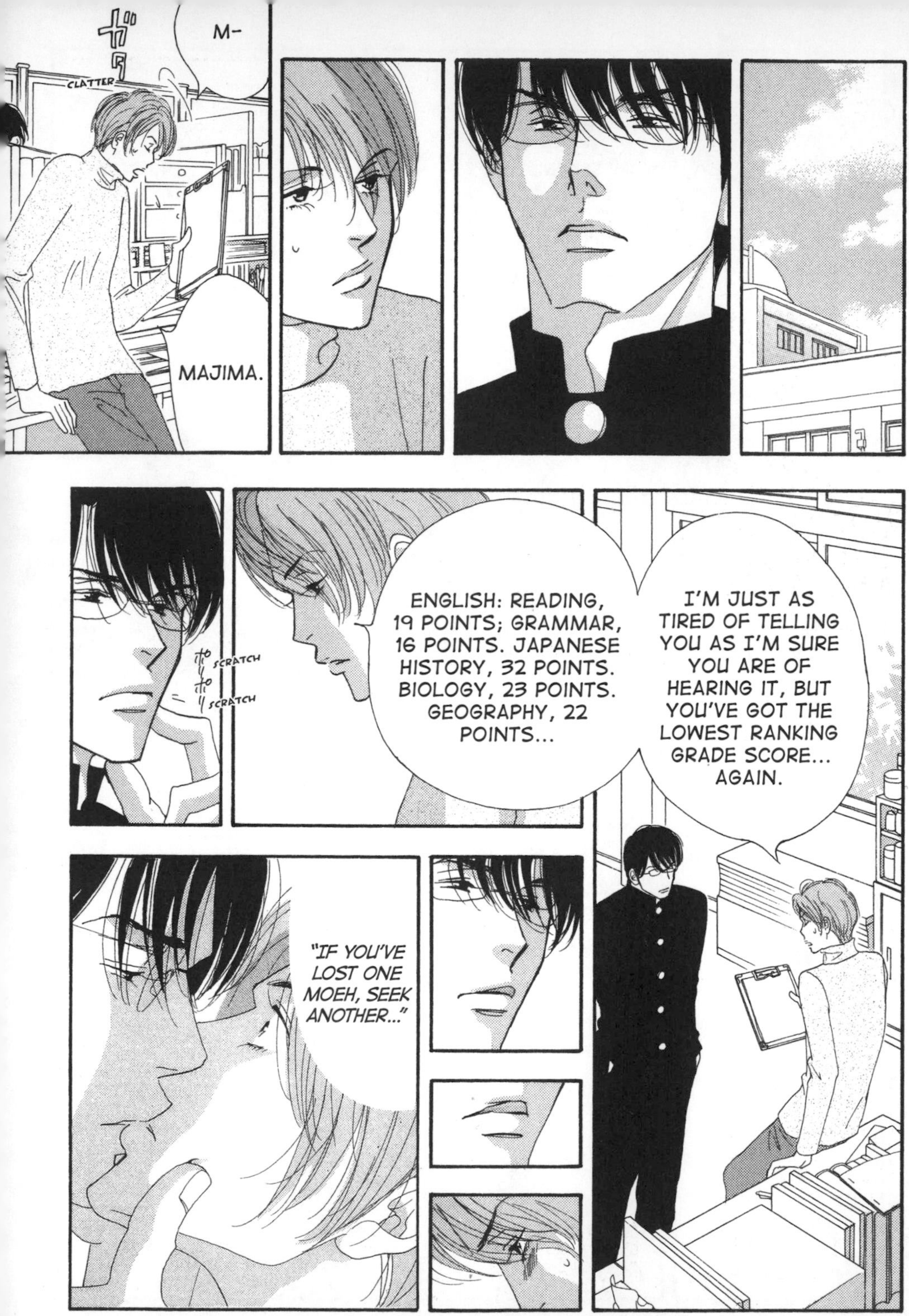
M-
CLATTER
MAJIMA.
I'M JUST AS TIRED OF TELLING YOU AS I'M SURE YOU ARE OF HEARING IT, BUT YOU'VE GOT THE LOWEST RANKING GRADE SCORE... AGAIN.
ENGLISH: READING, 19 POINTS; GRAMMAR, 16 POINTS. JAPANESE HISTORY, 32 POINTS. BIOLOGY, 23 POINTS. GEOGRAPHY, 22 POINTS...
SCRATCH
SCRATCH
"IF YOU'VE LOST ONE MOEH, SEEK ANOTHER..."

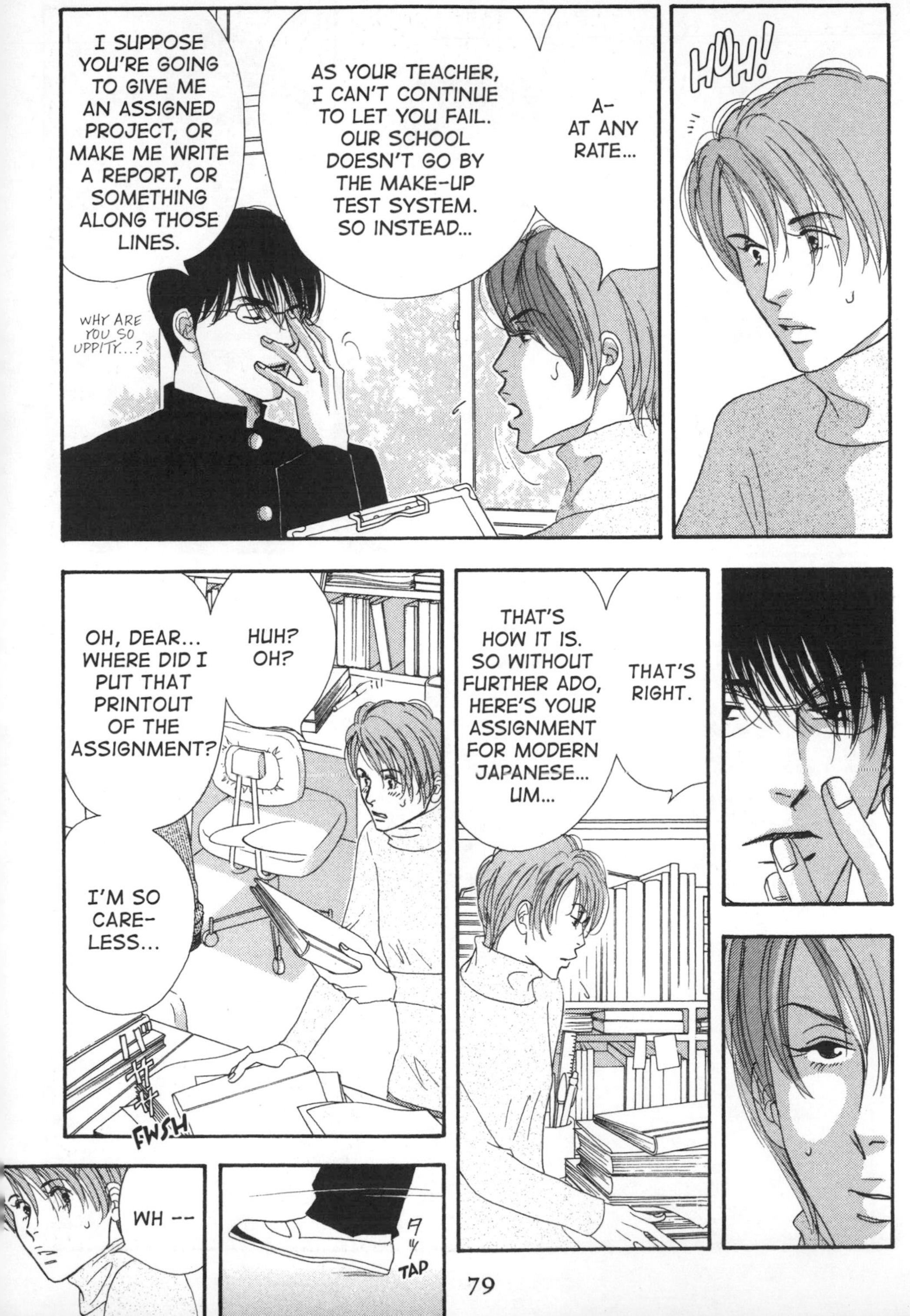
HUH!
A-
AT ANY RATE...
AS YOUR TEACHER, I CAN'T CONTINUE TO LET YOU FAIL. OUR SCHOOL DOESN'T GO BY THE MAKE-UP TEST SYSTEM. SO INSTEAD...
I SUPPOSE YOU'RE GOING TO GIVE ME AN ASSIGNED PROJECT, OR MAKE ME WRITE A REPORT, OR SOMETHING ALONG THOSE LINES.
WHY ARE YOU SO UPPITY...?
THAT'S RIGHT.
THAT'S HOW IT IS. SO WITHOUT FURTHER ADO, HERE'S YOUR ASSIGNMENT FOR MODERN JAPANESE... UM...
HUH? OH?
OH, DEAR... WHERE DID I PUT THAT PRINTOUT OF THE ASSIGNMENT?
I'M SO CARE-LESS...
FWSH
TAP
WH --

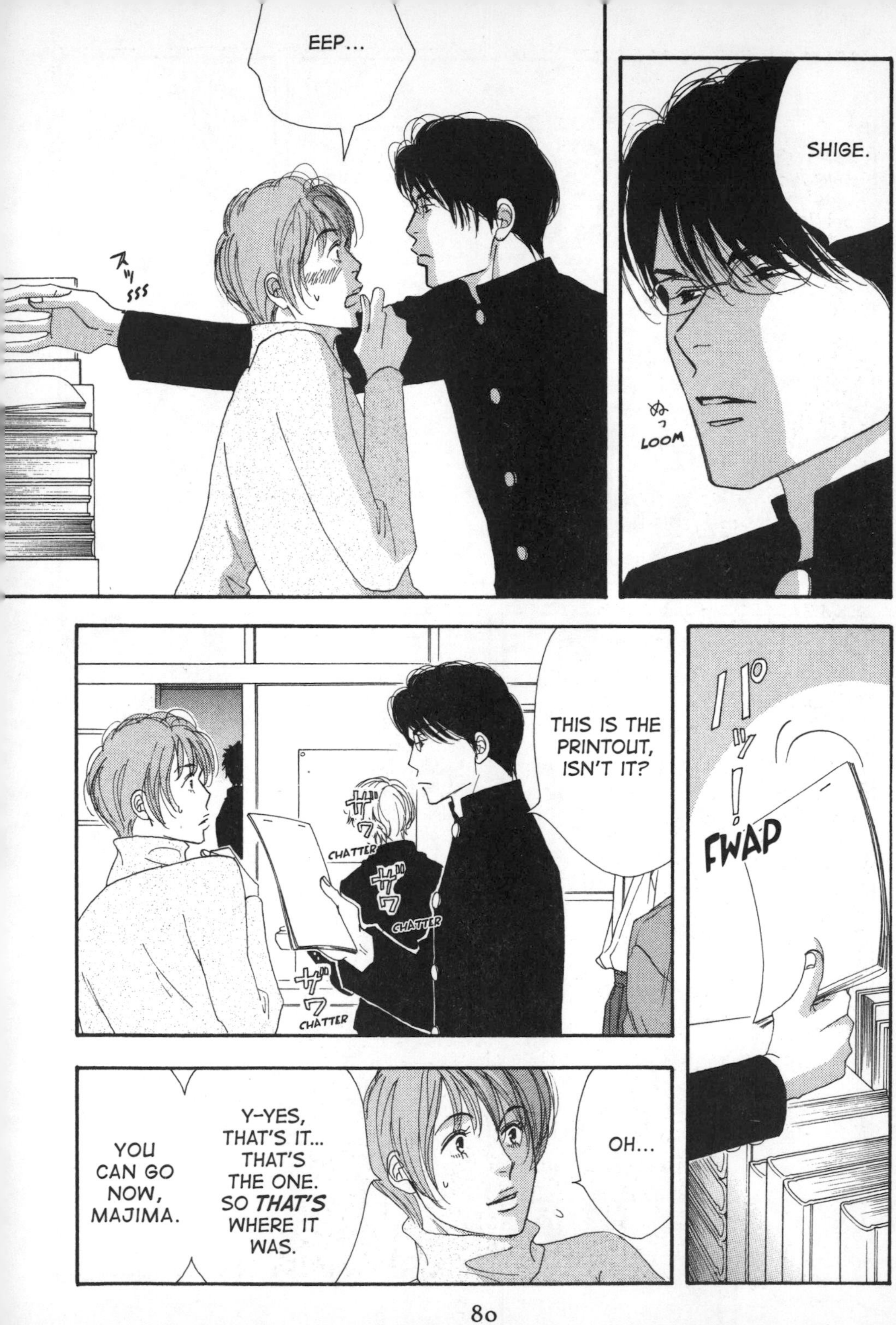
SHIGE.
ぬっ
LOOM
EEP...
スッ
SSS
パッ!
FWAP
THIS IS THE PRINTOUT, ISN'T IT?
ザワ
CHATTER
ザワ
CHATTER
ザワ
CHATTER
OH...
Y-YES, THAT'S IT... THAT'S THE ONE. SO ***THAT'S*** WHERE IT WAS.
YOU CAN GO NOW, MAJIMA.

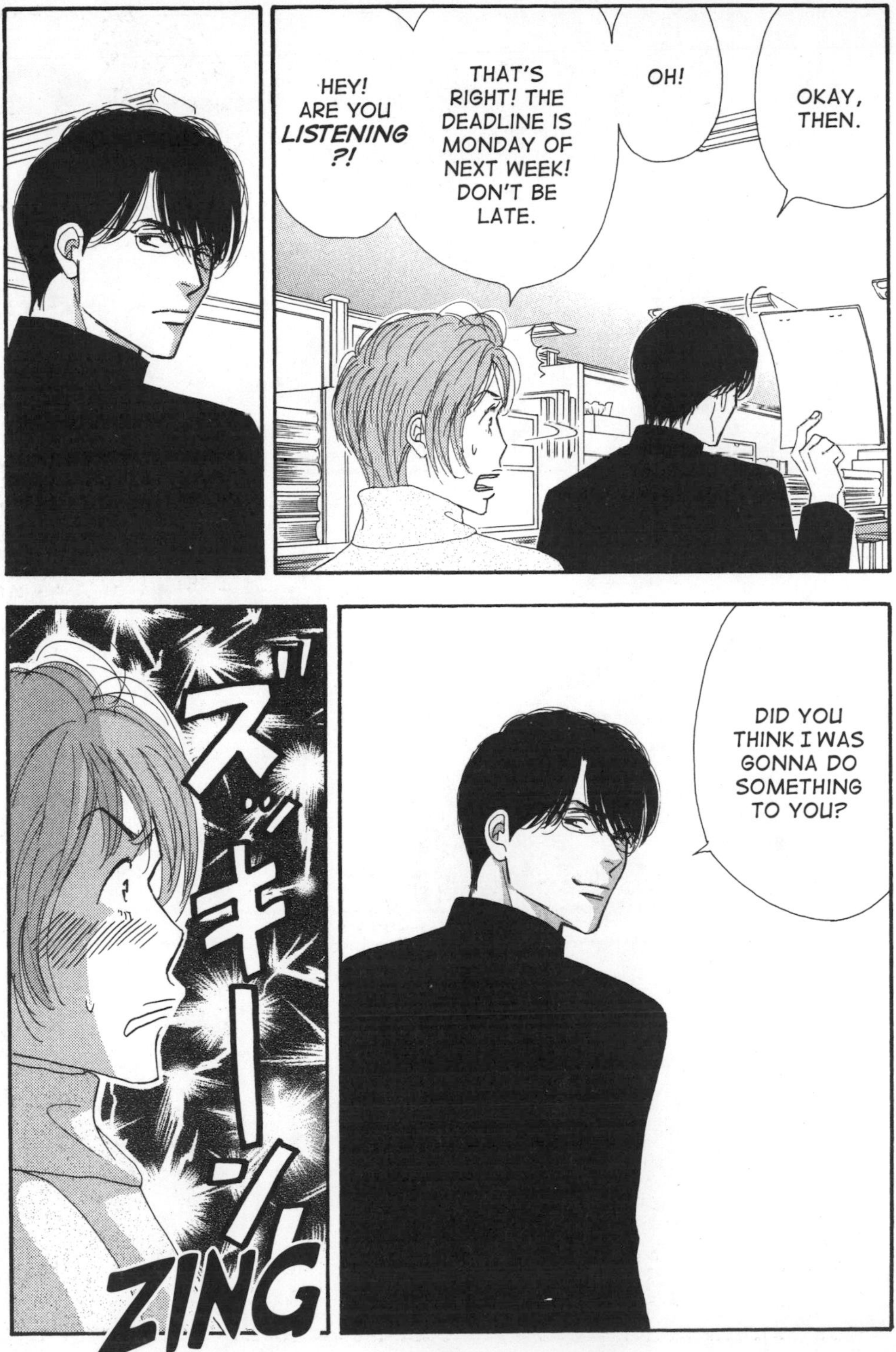
OKAY, THEN.
OH!
THAT'S RIGHT! THE DEADLINE IS MONDAY OF NEXT WEEK! DON'T BE LATE.
HEY! ARE YOU *LISTENING* ?!
DID YOU THINK I WAS GONNA DO SOMETHING TO YOU?
ズキーン
ZING

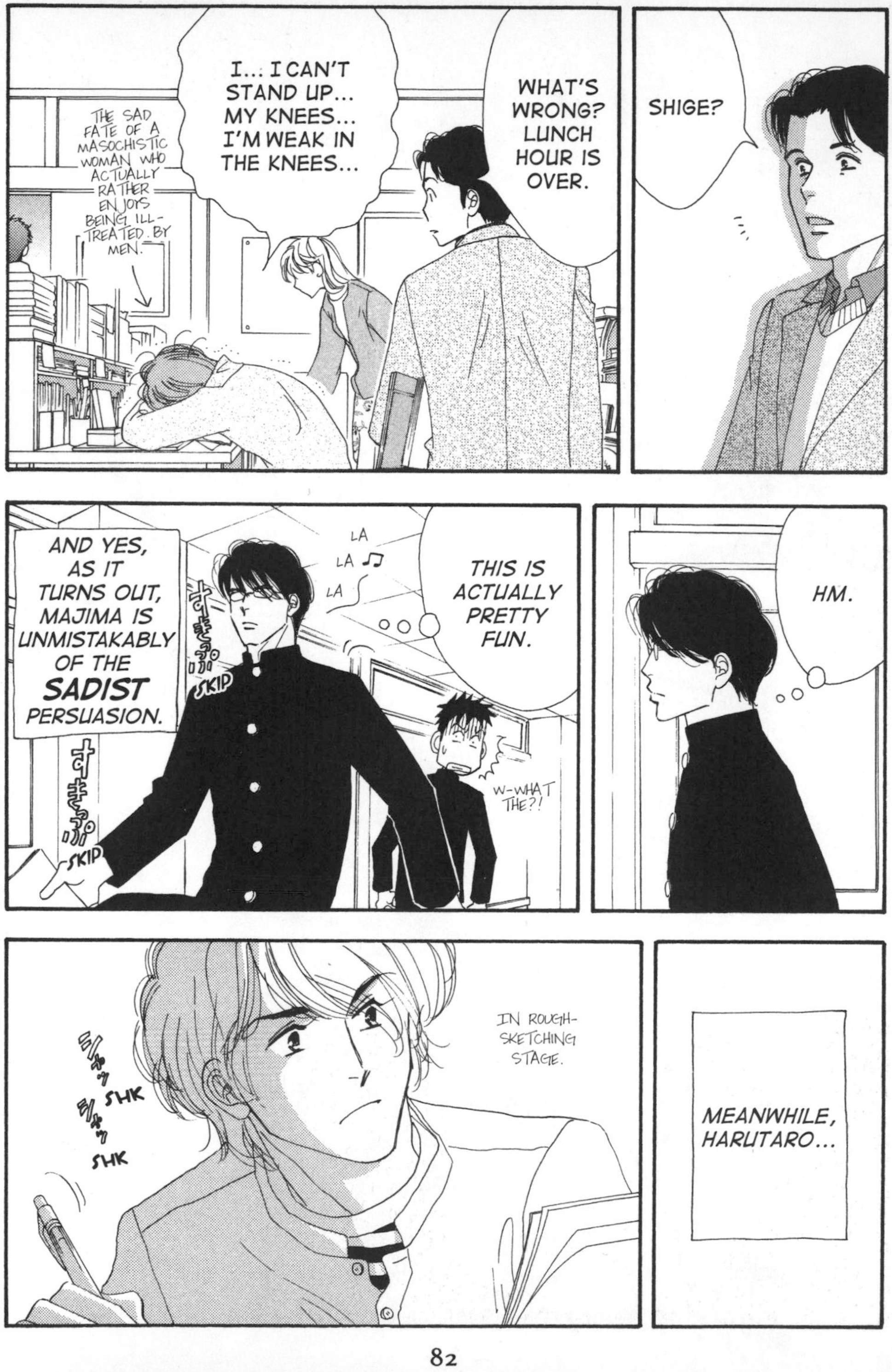
SHIGE?
WHAT'S WRONG? LUNCH HOUR IS OVER.
I... I CAN'T STAND UP... MY KNEES... I'M WEAK IN THE KNEES...
THE SAD FATE OF A MASOCHISTIC WOMAN WHO ACTUALLY RATHER ENJOYS BEING ILL-TREATED BY MEN.
HM.
THIS IS ACTUALLY PRETTY FUN.
LA LA ♫ LA
W-WHAT THE?!
SKIP
AND YES, AS IT TURNS OUT, MAJIMA IS UNMISTAKABLY OF THE SADIST PERSUASION.
SKIP
MEANWHILE, HARUTARO...
IN ROUGH-SKETCHING STAGE.
SHK
SHK

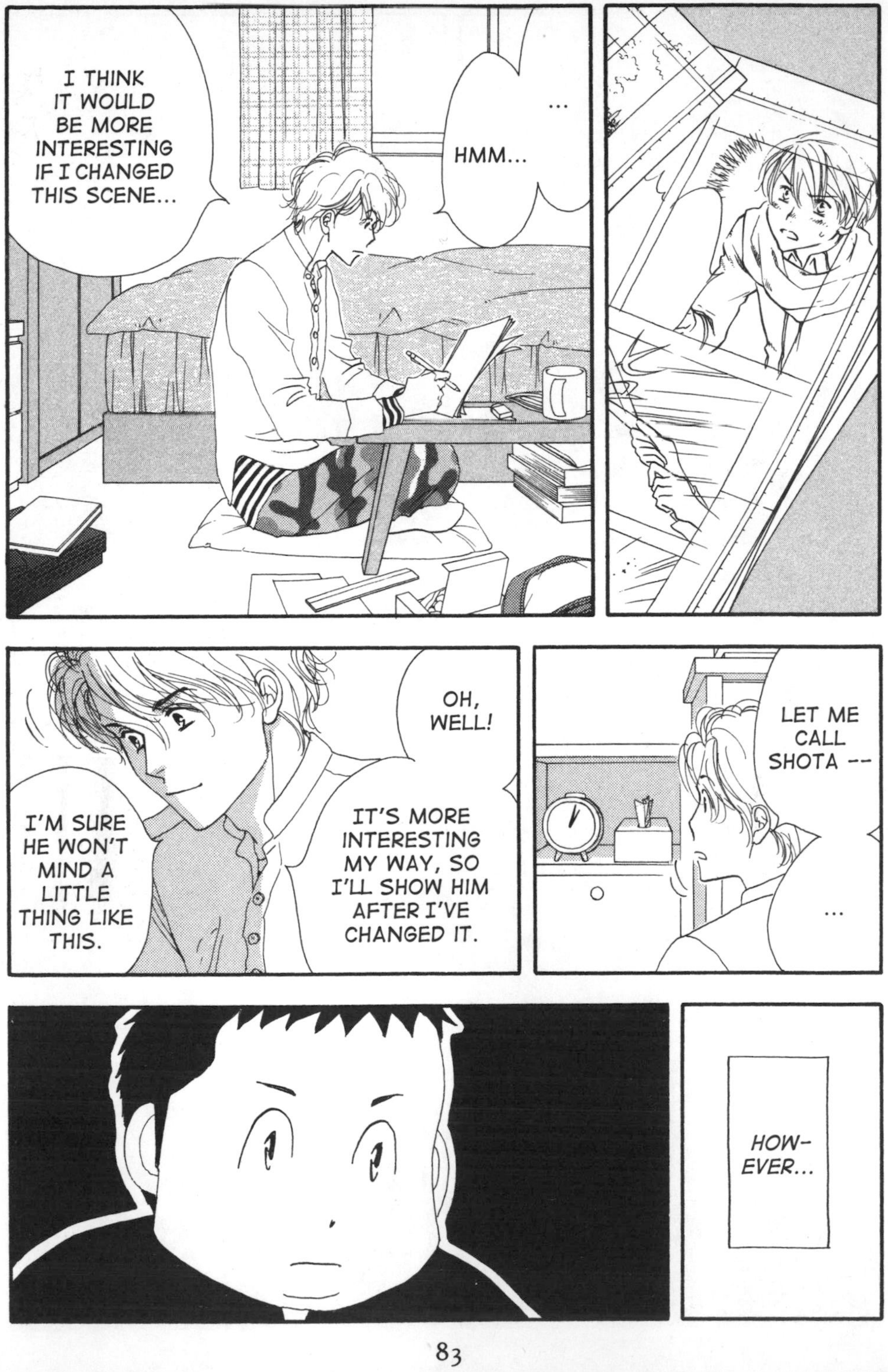
... HMM...
I THINK IT WOULD BE MORE INTERESTING IF I CHANGED THIS SCENE...
LET ME CALL SHOTA --
...
OH, WELL!
IT'S MORE INTERESTING MY WAY, SO I'LL SHOW HIM AFTER I'VE CHANGED IT.
I'M SURE HE WON'T MIND A LITTLE THING LIKE THIS.
HOW-EVER...

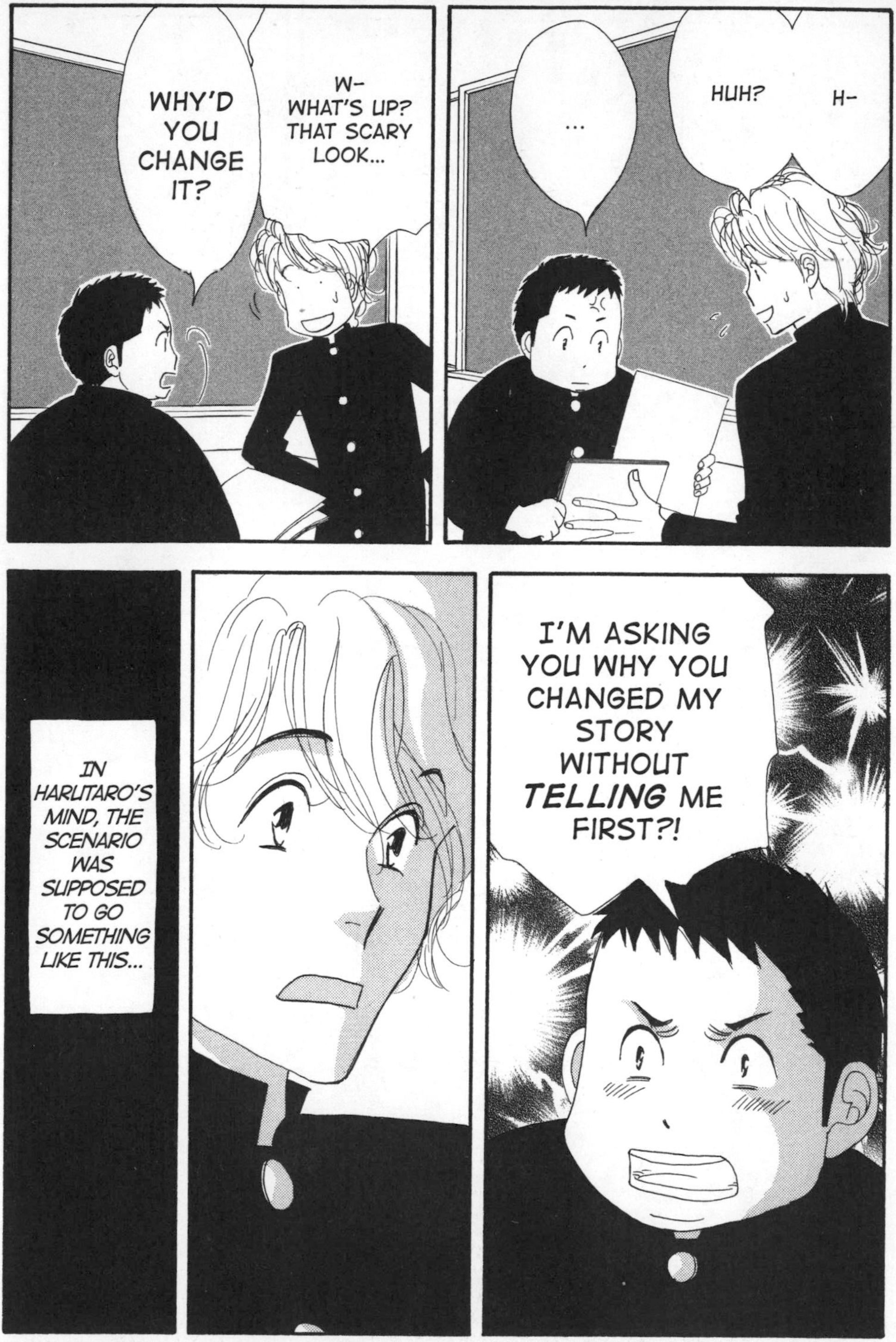
H-
HUH?
...
W- WHAT'S UP? THAT SCARY LOOK...
WHY'D YOU CHANGE IT?
I'M ASKING YOU WHY YOU CHANGED MY STORY WITHOUT *TELLING* ME FIRST?!
IN HARUTARO'S MIND, THE SCENARIO WAS SUPPOSED TO GO SOMETHING LIKE THIS...

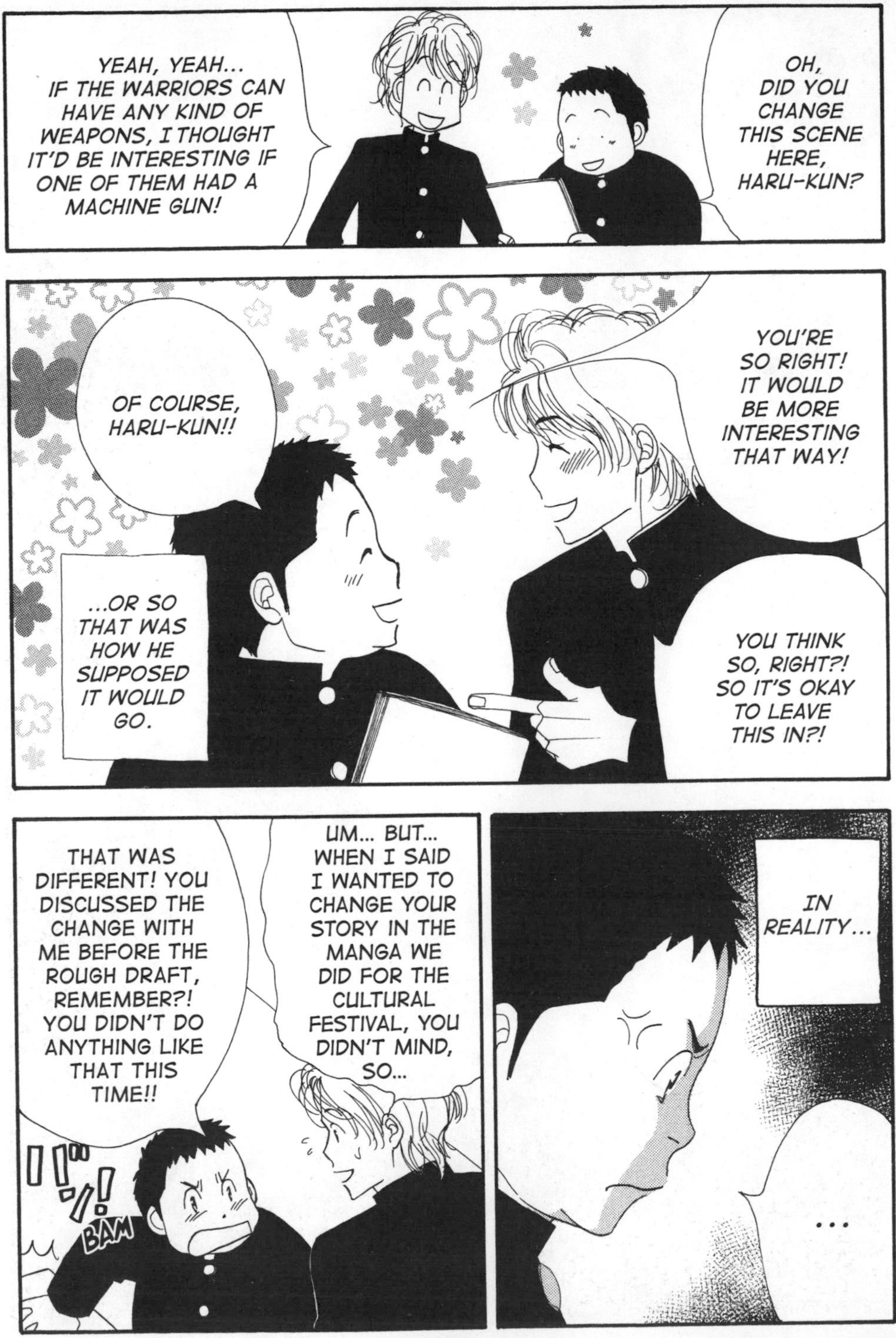
OH, DID YOU CHANGE THIS SCENE HERE, HARU-KUN?
YEAH, YEAH... IF THE WARRIORS CAN HAVE ANY KIND OF WEAPONS, I THOUGHT IT'D BE INTERESTING IF ONE OF THEM HAD A MACHINE GUN!
YOU'RE SO RIGHT! IT WOULD BE MORE INTERESTING THAT WAY!
YOU THINK SO, RIGHT?! SO IT'S OKAY TO LEAVE THIS IN?!
OF COURSE, HARU-KUN!!
...OR SO THAT WAS HOW HE SUPPOSED IT WOULD GO.
IN REALITY...
...
UM... BUT... WHEN I SAID I WANTED TO CHANGE YOUR STORY IN THE MANGA WE DID FOR THE CULTURAL FESTIVAL, YOU DIDN'T MIND, SO...
THAT WAS DIFFERENT! YOU DISCUSSED THE CHANGE WITH ME BEFORE THE ROUGH DRAFT, REMEMBER?! YOU DIDN'T DO ANYTHING LIKE THAT THIS TIME!!
BAM

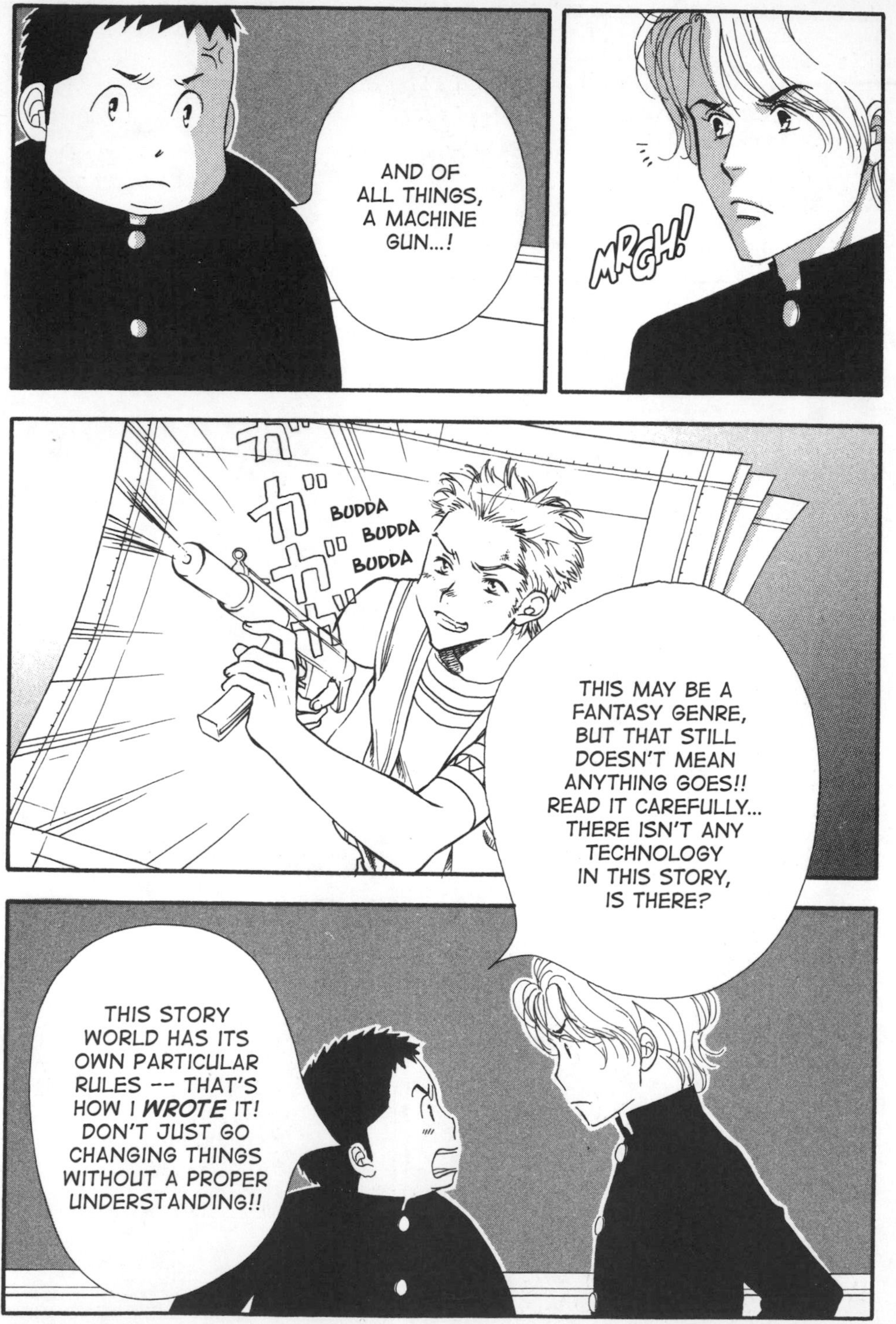
MRGH!
AND OF ALL THINGS, A MACHINE GUN...!
BUDDA BUDDA BUDDA
THIS MAY BE A FANTASY GENRE, BUT THAT STILL DOESN'T MEAN ANYTHING GOES!! READ IT CAREFULLY... THERE ISN'T ANY TECHNOLOGY IN THIS STORY, IS THERE?
THIS STORY WORLD HAS ITS OWN PARTICULAR RULES -- THAT'S HOW I WROTE IT! DON'T JUST GO CHANGING THINGS WITHOUT A PROPER UNDERSTANDING!!

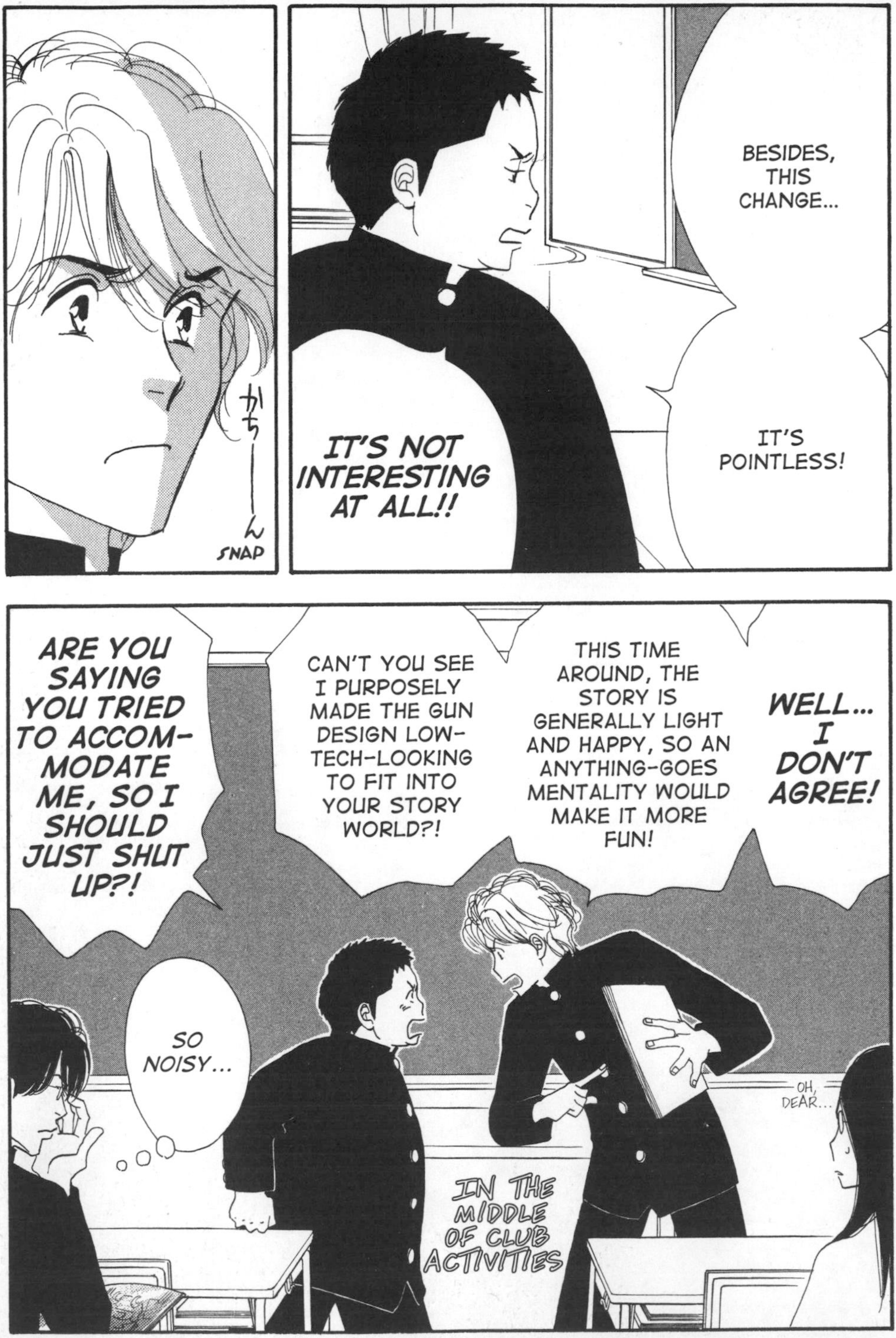
BESIDES, THIS CHANGE...
IT'S POINTLESS!
IT'S NOT INTERESTING AT ALL!!
かちーん
SNAP
WELL... I DON'T AGREE!
THIS TIME AROUND, THE STORY IS GENERALLY LIGHT AND HAPPY, SO AN ANYTHING-GOES MENTALITY WOULD MAKE IT MORE FUN!
CAN'T YOU SEE I PURPOSELY MADE THE GUN DESIGN LOW-TECH-LOOKING TO FIT INTO YOUR STORY WORLD?!
ARE YOU SAYING YOU TRIED TO ACCOMMODATE ME, SO I SHOULD JUST SHUT UP?!
OH, DEAR...
SO NOISY...
IN THE MIDDLE OF CLUB ACTIVITIES

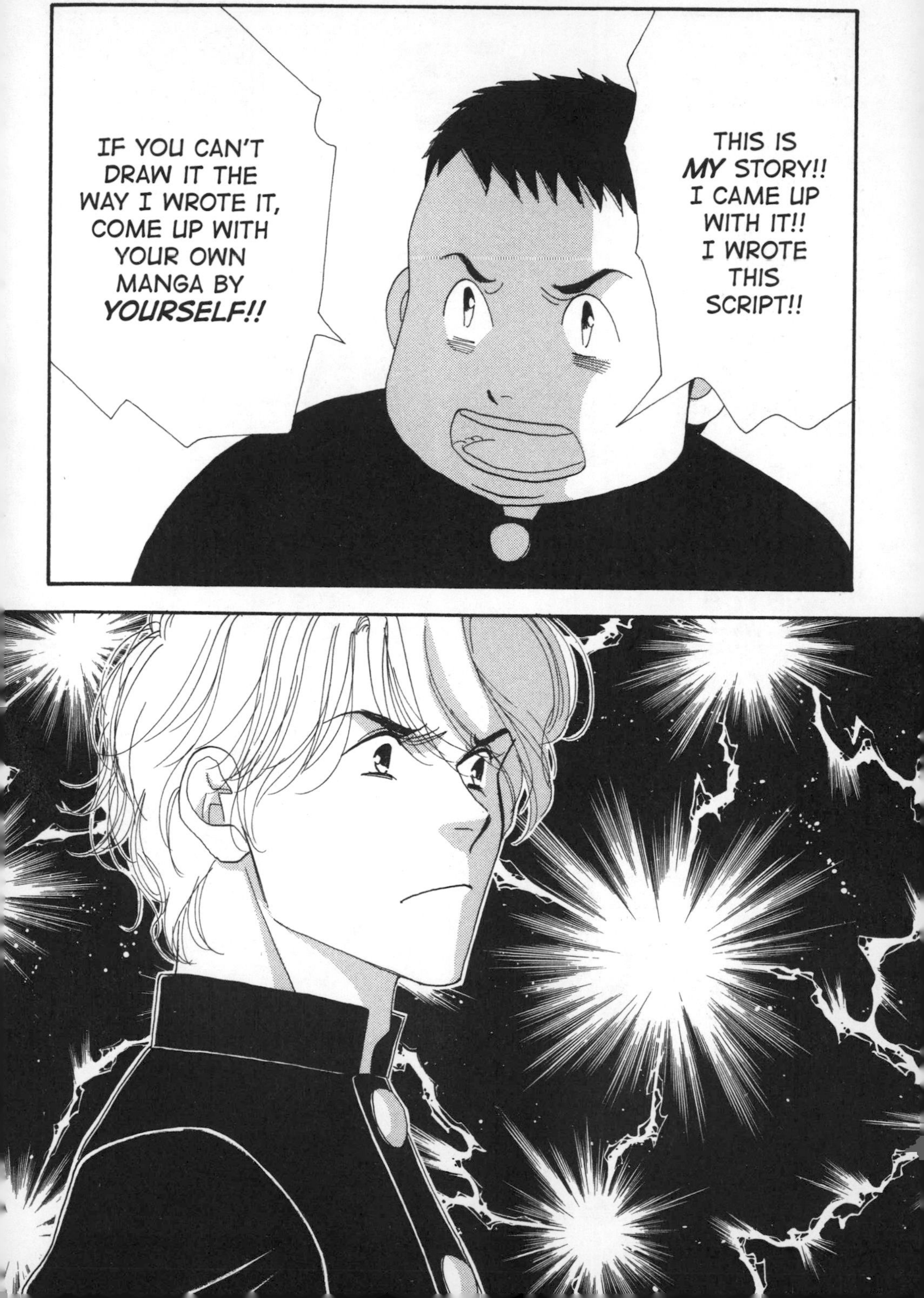
THIS IS *MY* STORY!! I CAME UP WITH IT!! I WROTE THIS SCRIPT!!
IF YOU CAN'T DRAW IT THE WAY I WROTE IT, COME UP WITH YOUR OWN MANGA BY *YOURSELF!!*

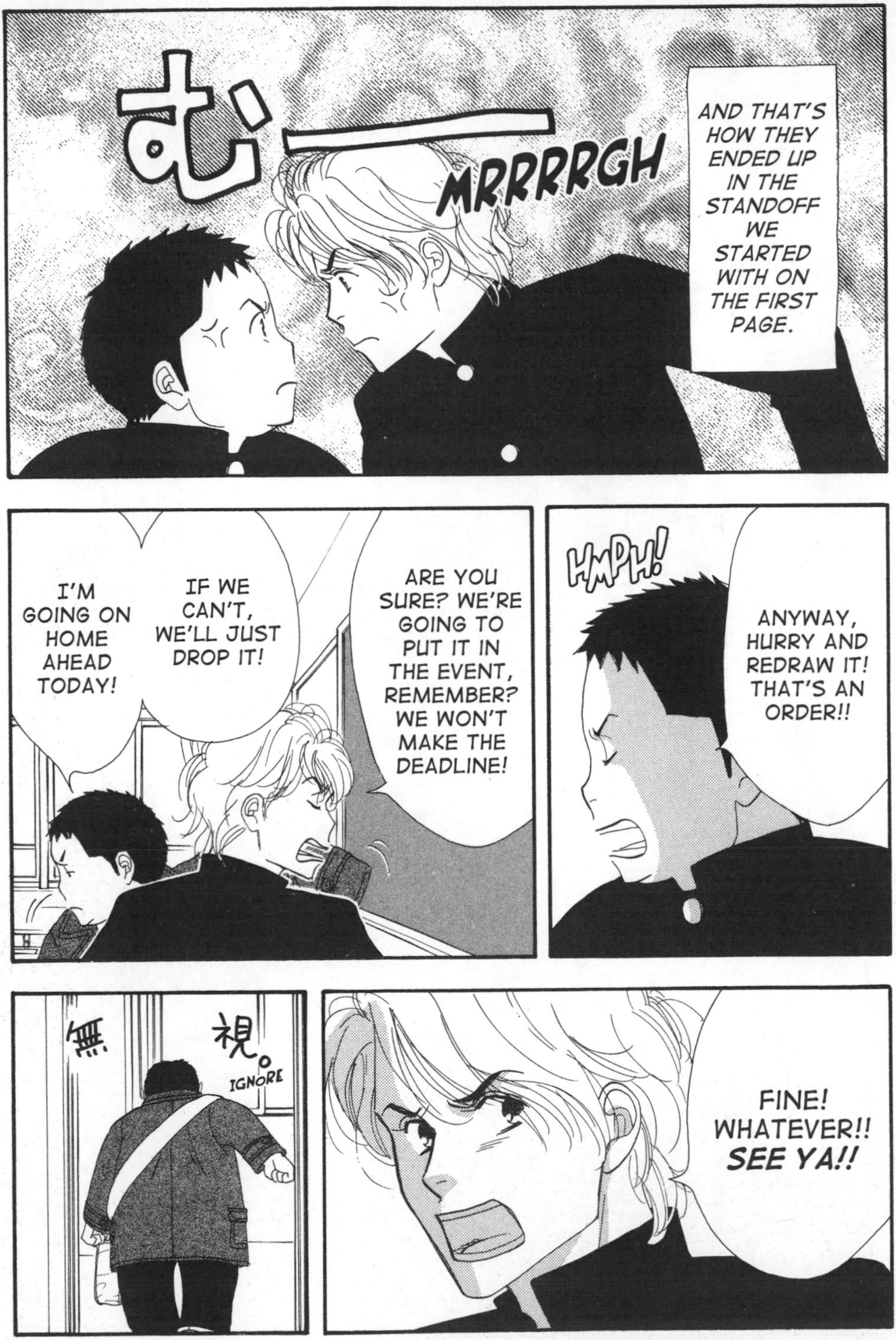
AND THAT'S HOW THEY ENDED UP IN THE STANDOFF WE STARTED WITH ON THE FIRST PAGE.
むー
MRRRRGH
HMPH!
ANYWAY, HURRY AND REDRAW IT! THAT'S AN ORDER!!
ARE YOU SURE? WE'RE GOING TO PUT IT IN THE EVENT, REMEMBER? WE WON'T MAKE THE DEADLINE!
IF WE CAN'T, WE'LL JUST DROP IT!
I'M GOING ON HOME AHEAD TODAY!
FINE! WHATEVER!! SEE YA!!
無視。
IGNORE

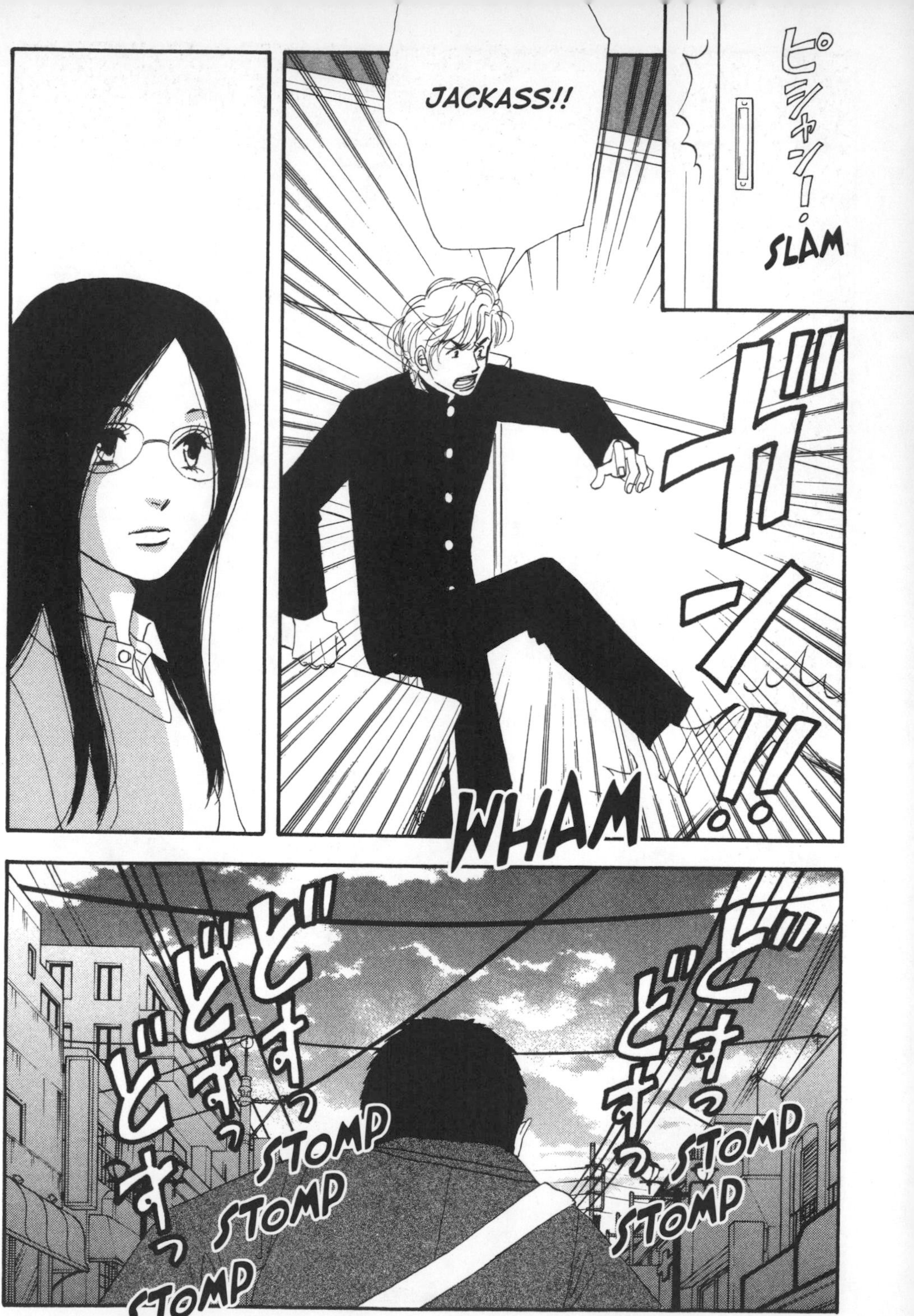

ピシャン!
SLAM
JACKASS!!
ガン!!
WHAM
どすっ
どすっ
STOMP
STOMP
どすっ
どすっ
どすっ
STOMP
STOMP
STOMP

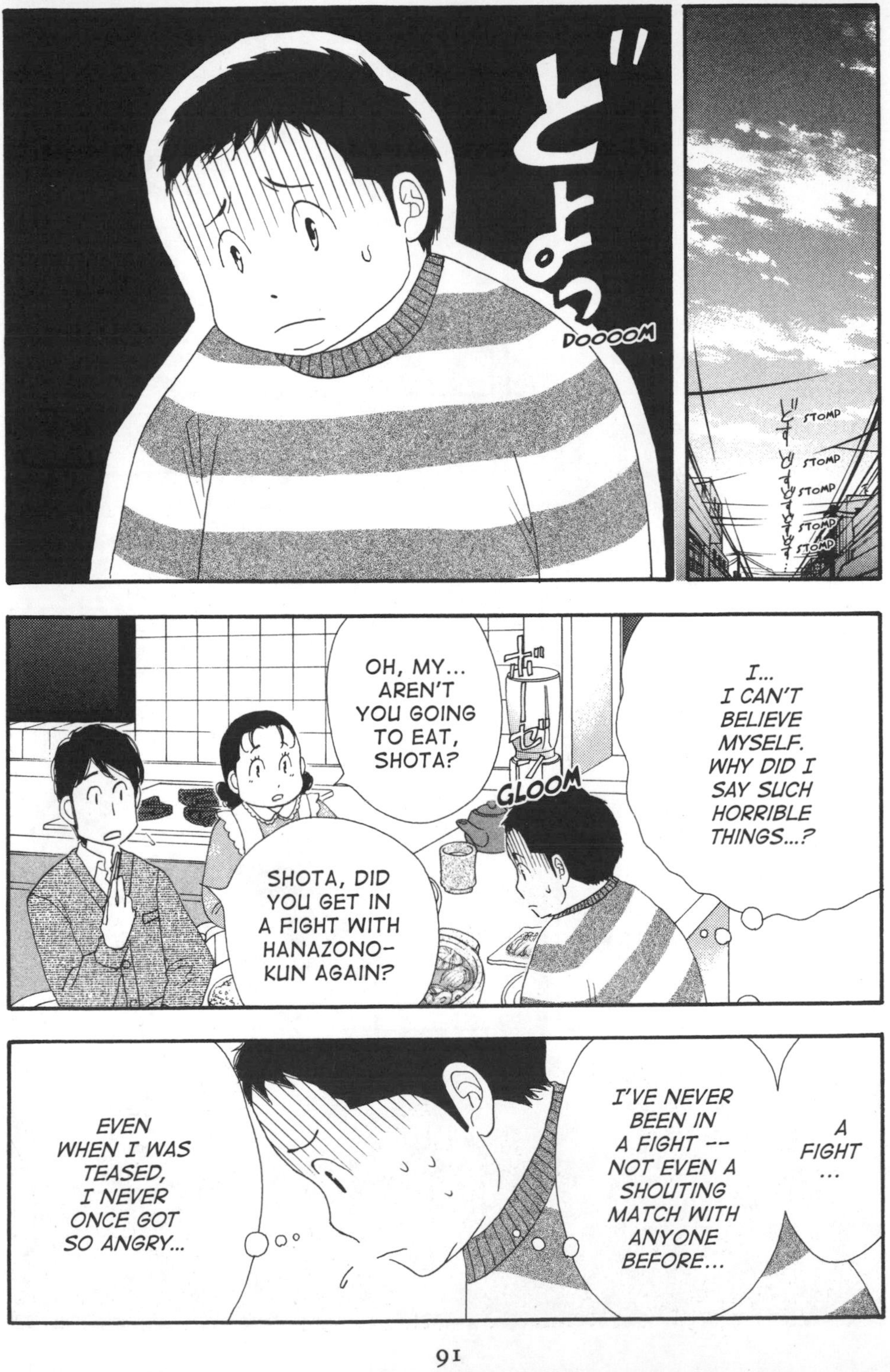
STOMP
STOMP
STOMP
STOMP
STOMP
どよっ
DOOOOM
I... I CAN'T BELIEVE MYSELF. WHY DID I SAY SUCH HORRIBLE THINGS...?
OH, MY... AREN'T YOU GOING TO EAT, SHOTA?
GLOOM
SHOTA, DID YOU GET IN A FIGHT WITH HANAZONO-KUN AGAIN?
A FIGHT ...
I'VE NEVER BEEN IN A FIGHT -- NOT EVEN A SHOUTING MATCH WITH ANYONE BEFORE...
EVEN WHEN I WAS TEASED, I NEVER ONCE GOT SO ANGRY...

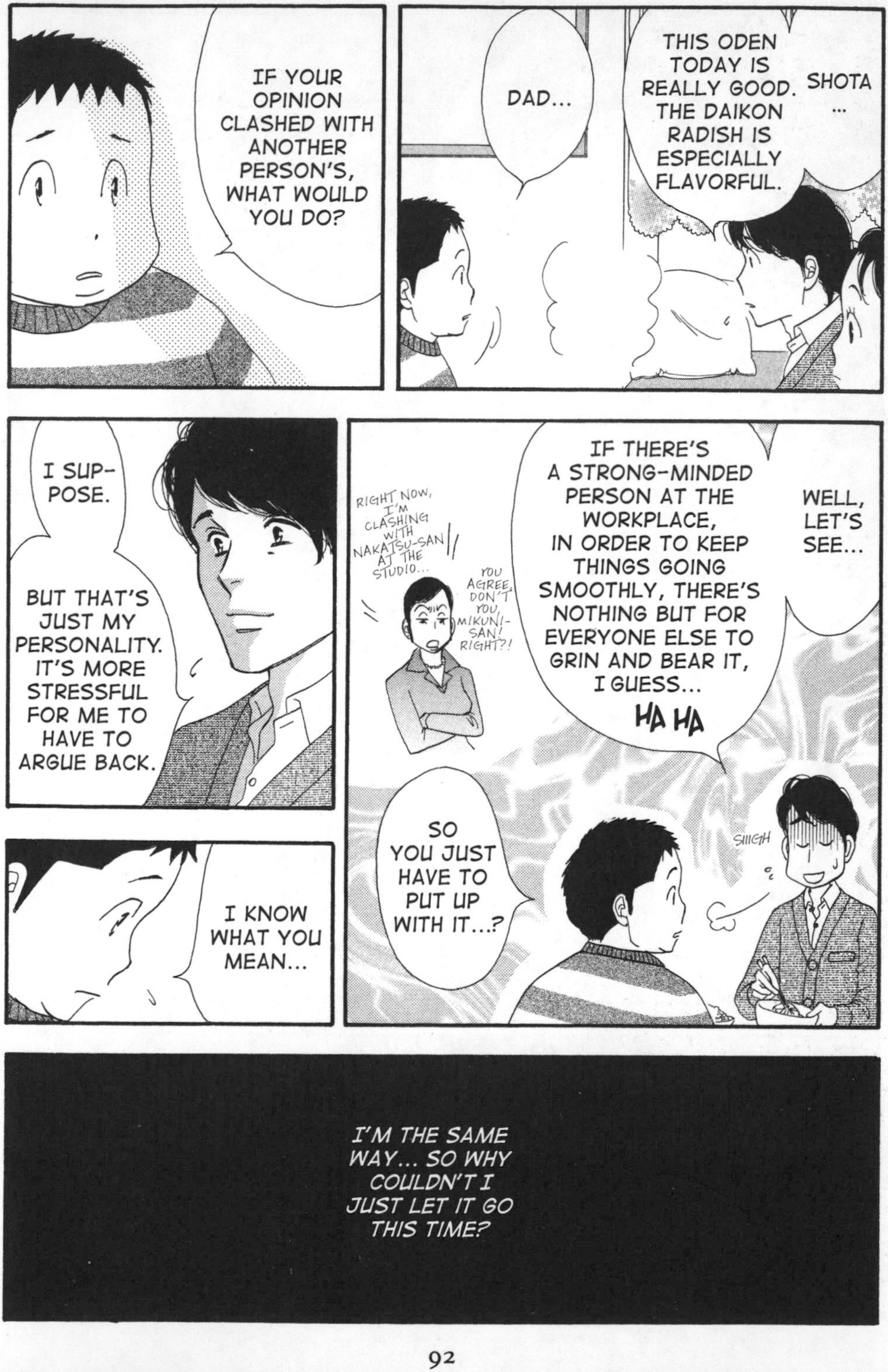
SHOTA ...
THIS ODEN TODAY IS REALLY GOOD. THE DAIKON RADISH IS ESPECIALLY FLAVORFUL.
DAD...
IF YOUR OPINION CLASHED WITH ANOTHER PERSON'S, WHAT WOULD YOU DO?
WELL, LET'S SEE...
IF THERE'S A STRONG-MINDED PERSON AT THE WORKPLACE, IN ORDER TO KEEP THINGS GOING SMOOTHLY, THERE'S NOTHING BUT FOR EVERYONE ELSE TO GRIN AND BEAR IT, I GUESS...
HA HA
RIGHT NOW, I'M CLASHING WITH NAKATSU-SAN AT THE STUDIO...
YOU AGREE, DON'T YOU, MIKUNI-SAN! RIGHT?!
SIIGH
SO YOU JUST HAVE TO PUT UP WITH IT...?
I SUP-POSE.
BUT THAT'S JUST MY PERSONALITY. IT'S MORE STRESSFUL FOR ME TO HAVE TO ARGUE BACK.
I KNOW WHAT YOU MEAN...
I'M THE SAME WAY... SO WHY COULDN'T I JUST LET IT GO THIS TIME?

IT'S EGO.
IT'S THE EGO AND PRIDE OF AN ARTIST, A CREATOR. NO MATTER HOW CLOSE THEY ARE AS FRIENDS, IT'S JUST ONE THING THEY COULDN'T COMPROMISE ON.
CREAK
WITHIN ALL OF US, THERE'S A CERTAIN LINE THAT CANNOT BE CROSSED...
THAT'S WHY I WORK ALONE...
SOLO...
IT MAY BE LONELY, BUT AT LEAST I'M FREE.

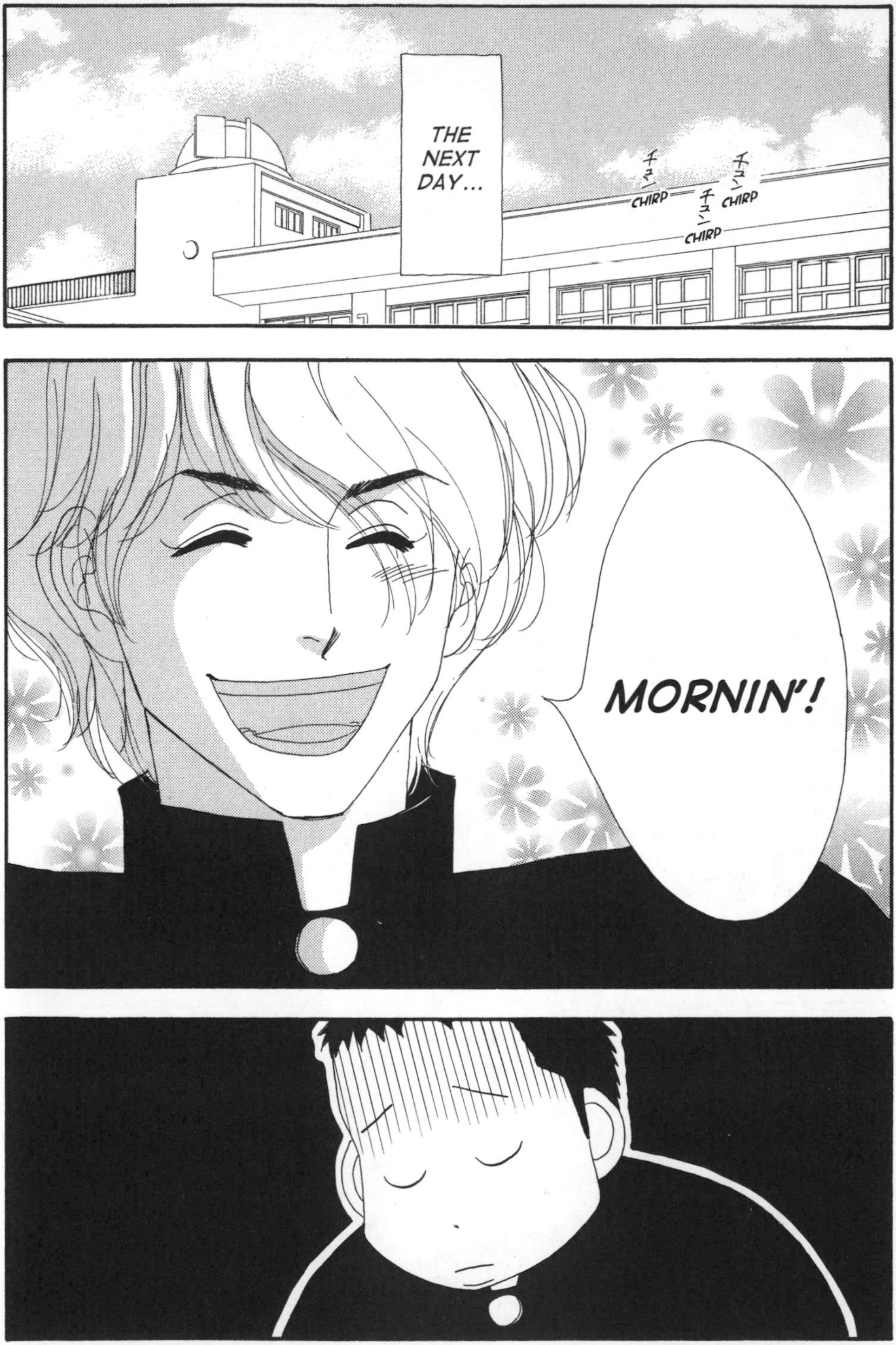
THE NEXT DAY...
CHIRP
CHIRP
CHIRP
MORNIN'!

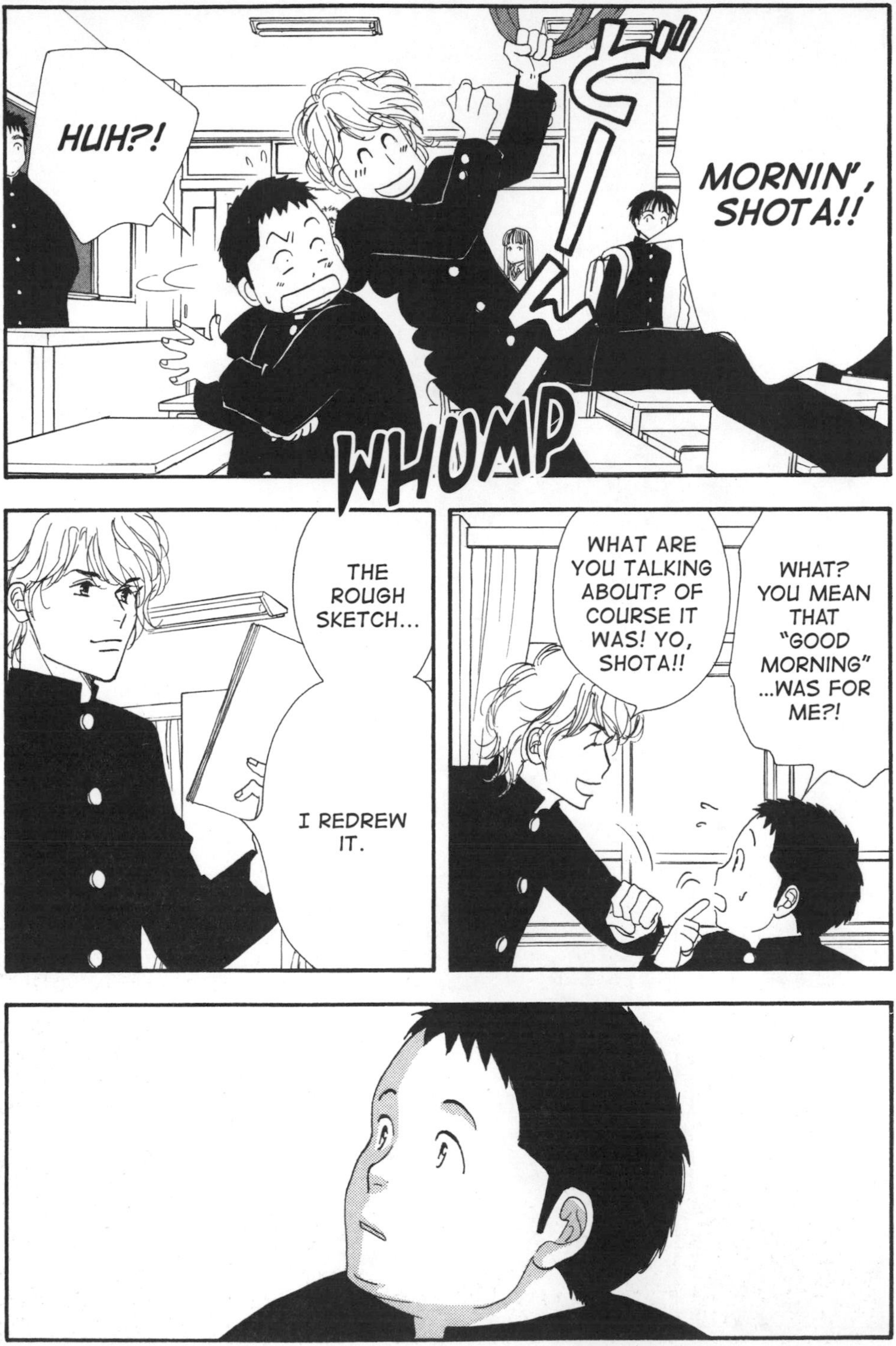
MORNIN', SHOTA!!
HUH?!
WHUMP
WHAT? YOU MEAN THAT "GOOD MORNING" ...WAS FOR ME?!
WHAT ARE YOU TALKING ABOUT? OF COURSE IT WAS! YO, SHOTA!!
THE ROUGH SKETCH...
I REDREW IT.

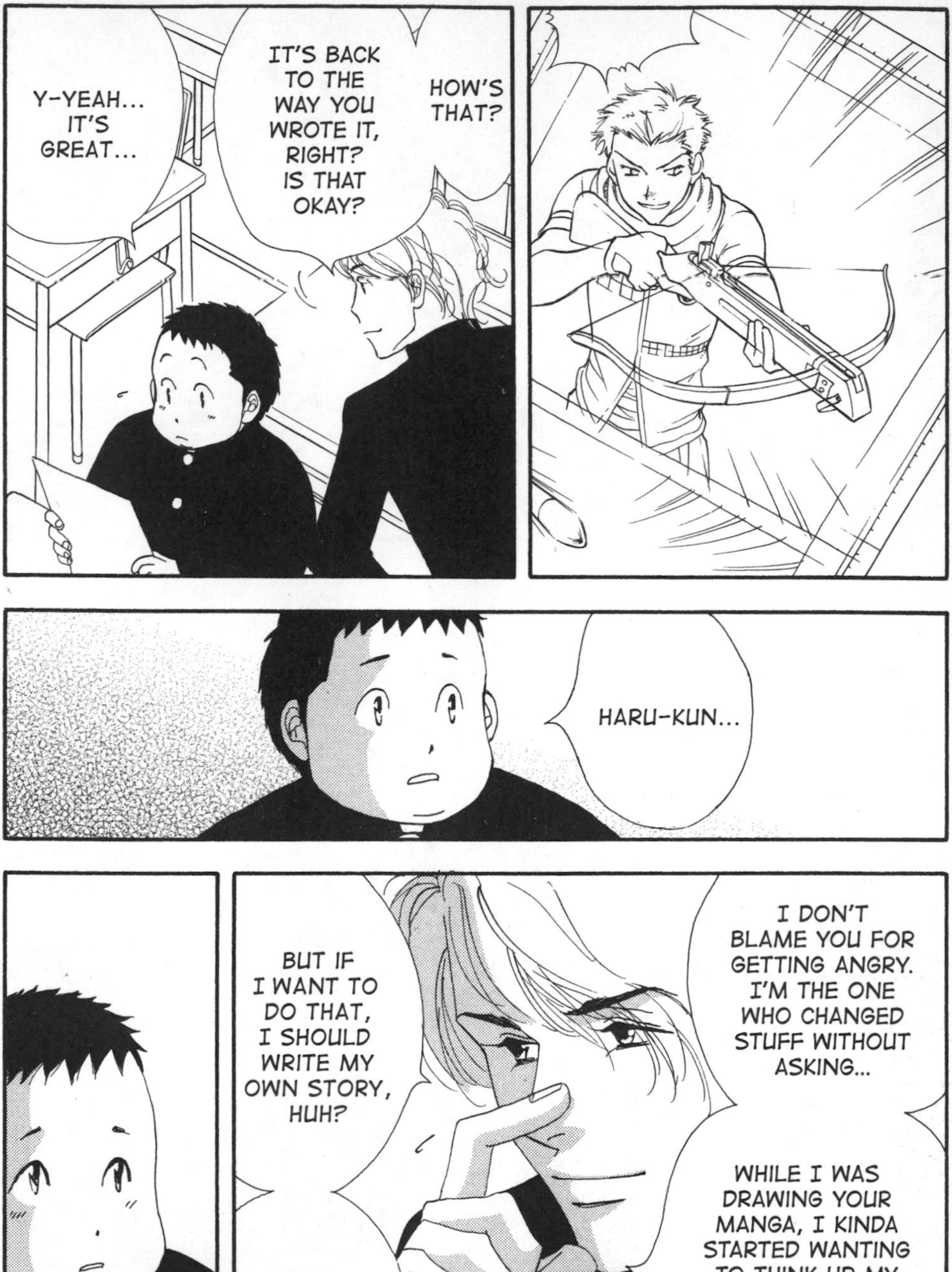
HOW'S THAT?
IT'S BACK TO THE WAY YOU WROTE IT, RIGHT? IS THAT OKAY?
Y-YEAH... IT'S GREAT...
HARU-KUN...
I DON'T BLAME YOU FOR GETTING ANGRY. I'M THE ONE WHO CHANGED STUFF WITHOUT ASKING...
WHILE I WAS DRAWING YOUR MANGA, I KINDA STARTED WANTING TO THINK UP MY OWN STUFF, TOO... THAT'S PROBABLY WHY I MESSED WITH YOUR WORK.
BUT IF I WANT TO DO THAT, I SHOULD WRITE MY OWN STORY, HUH?
SORRY.

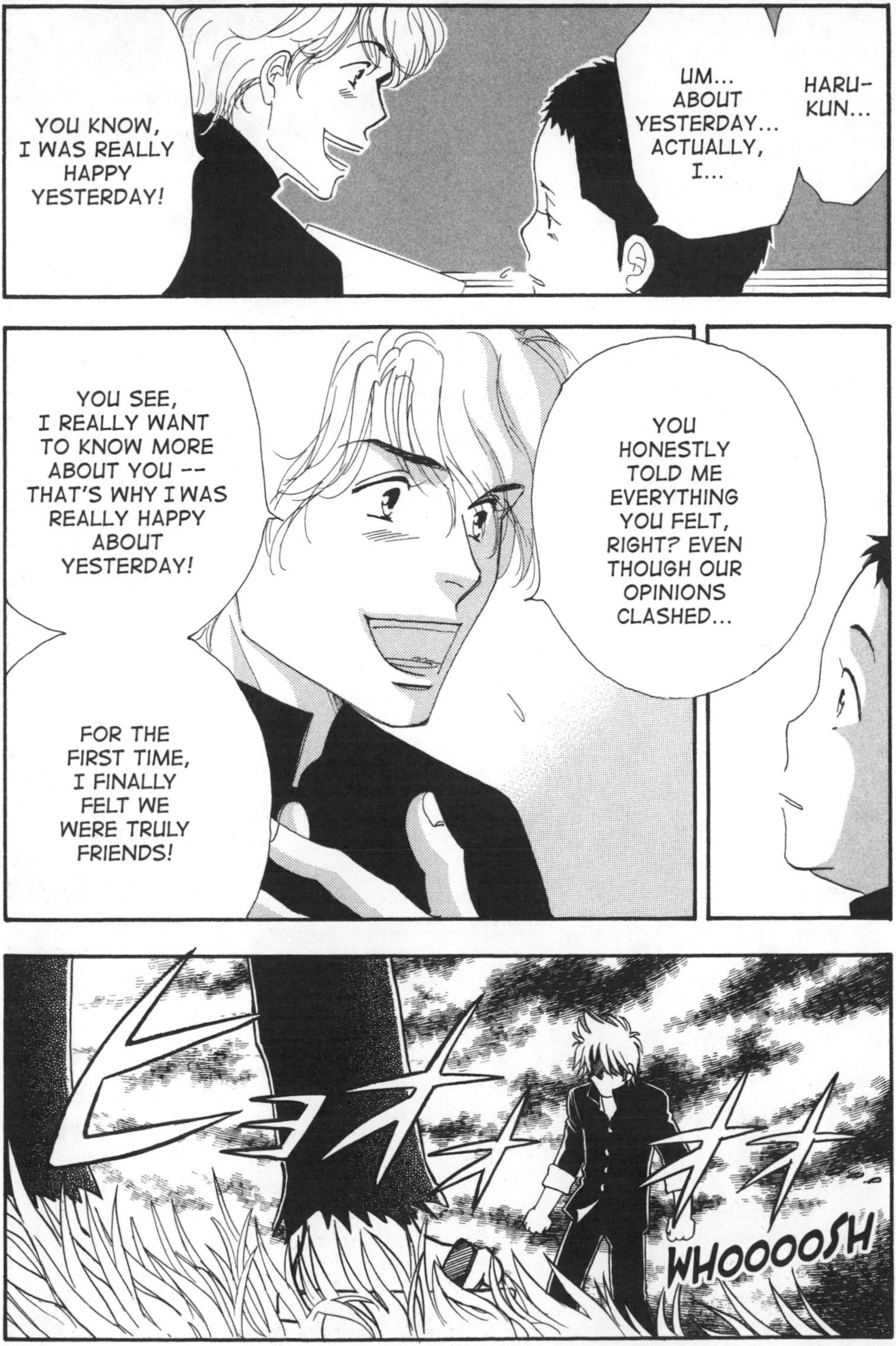
HARU-KUN...
UM... ABOUT YESTERDAY... ACTUALLY, I...
YOU KNOW, I WAS REALLY HAPPY YESTERDAY!
YOU HONESTLY TOLD ME EVERYTHING YOU FELT, RIGHT? EVEN THOUGH OUR OPINIONS CLASHED...
YOU SEE, I REALLY WANT TO KNOW MORE ABOUT YOU -- THAT'S WHY I WAS REALLY HAPPY ABOUT YESTERDAY!
FOR THE FIRST TIME, I FINALLY FELT WE WERE TRULY FRIENDS!
WHOOOOSH

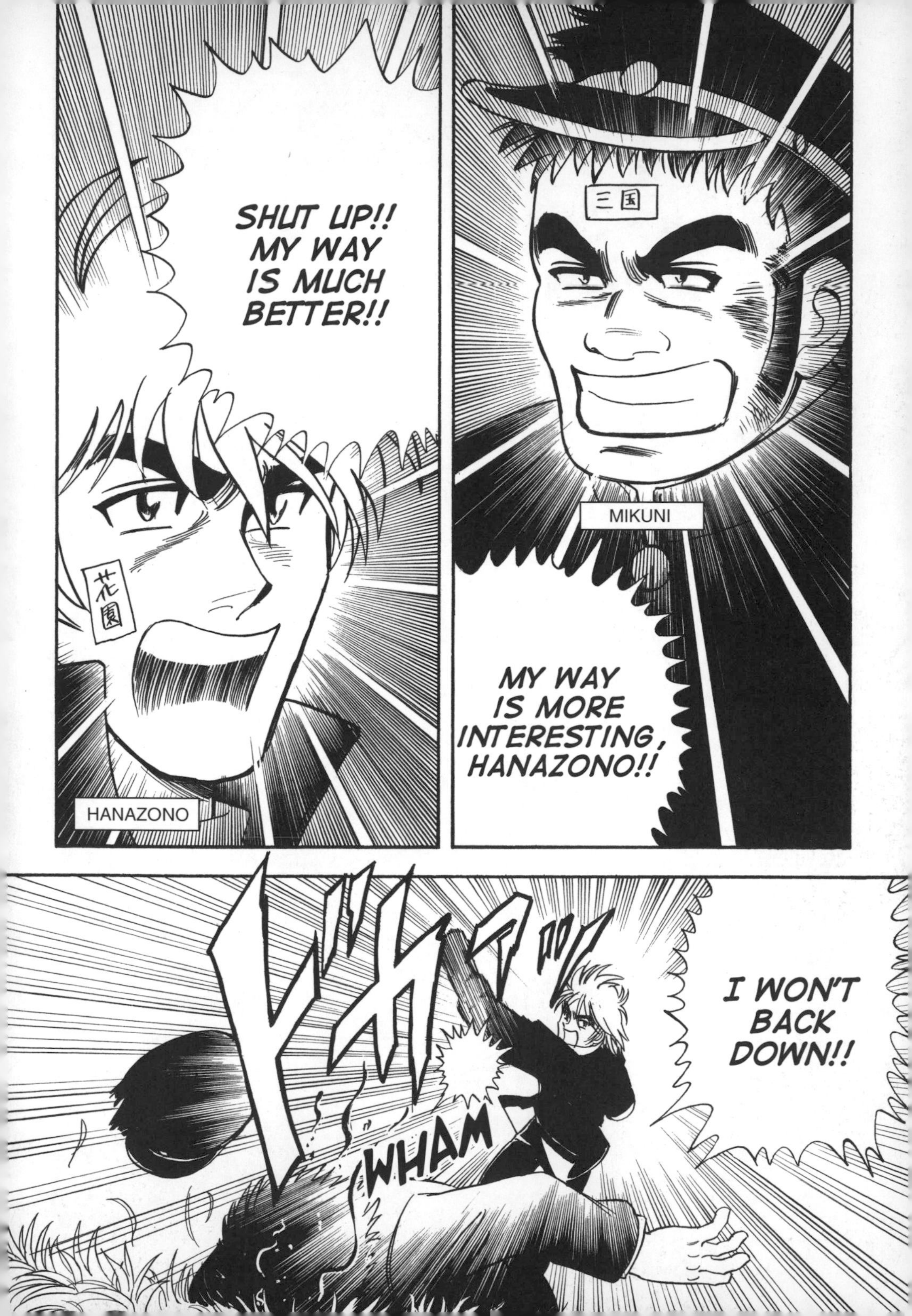
三国
MIKUNI
MY WAY IS MORE INTERESTING, HANAZONO!!
SHUT UP!! MY WAY IS MUCH BETTER!!
花園
HANAZONO
I WON'T BACK DOWN!!
WHAM

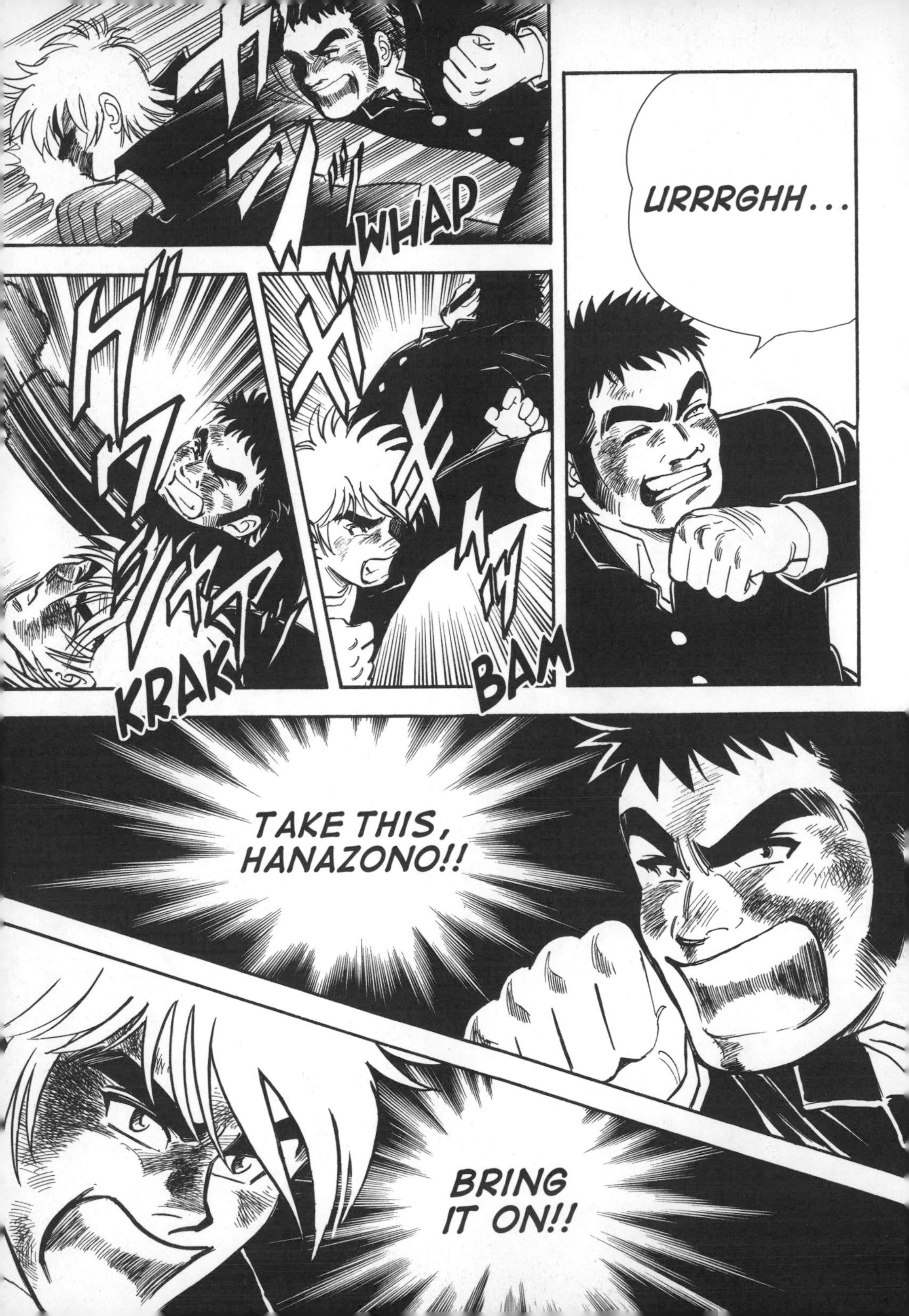
URRRGHH...
WHAP
BAM
KRAK
TAKE THIS, HANAZONO!!
BRING IT ON!!

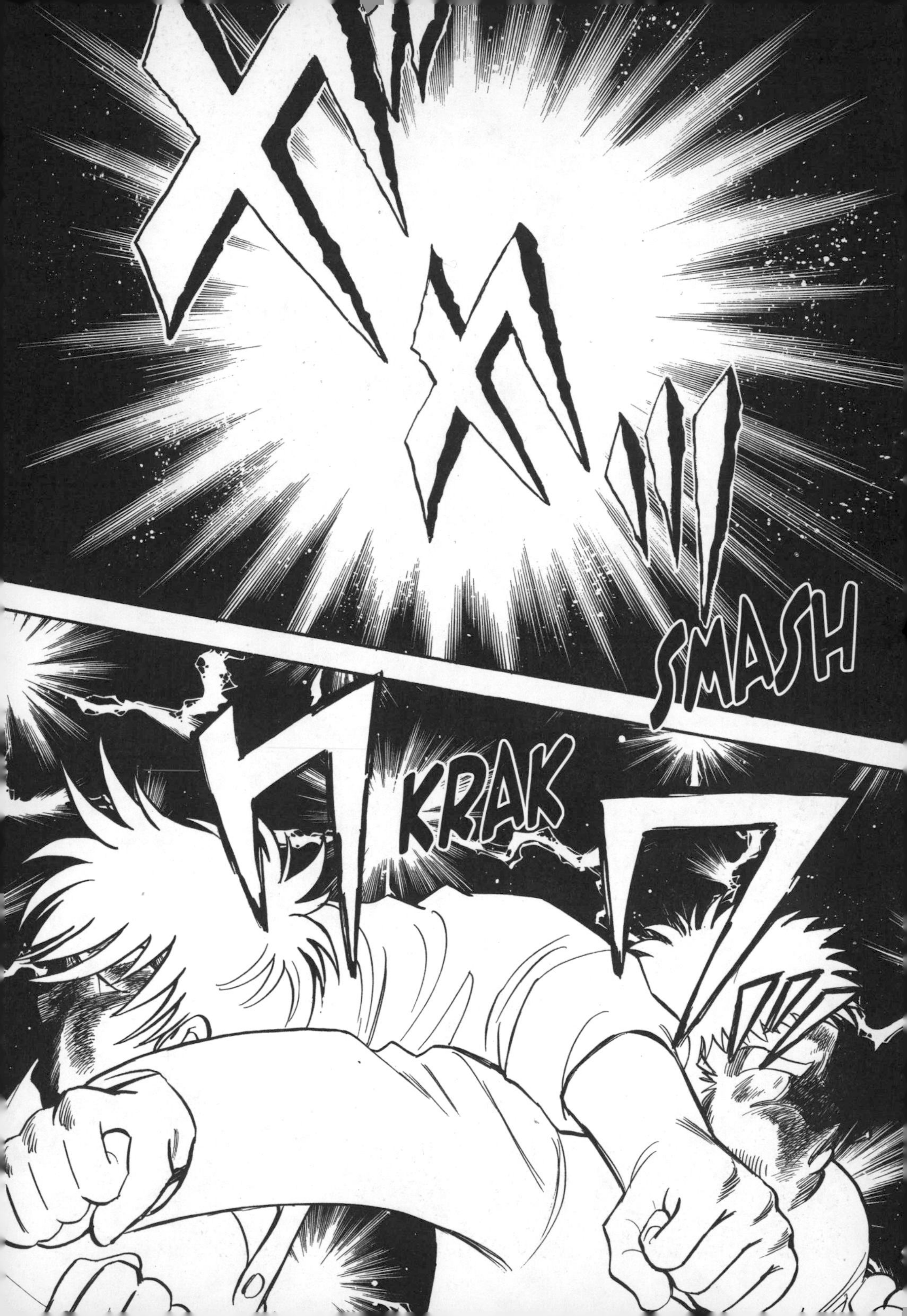
SMASH
KRAK

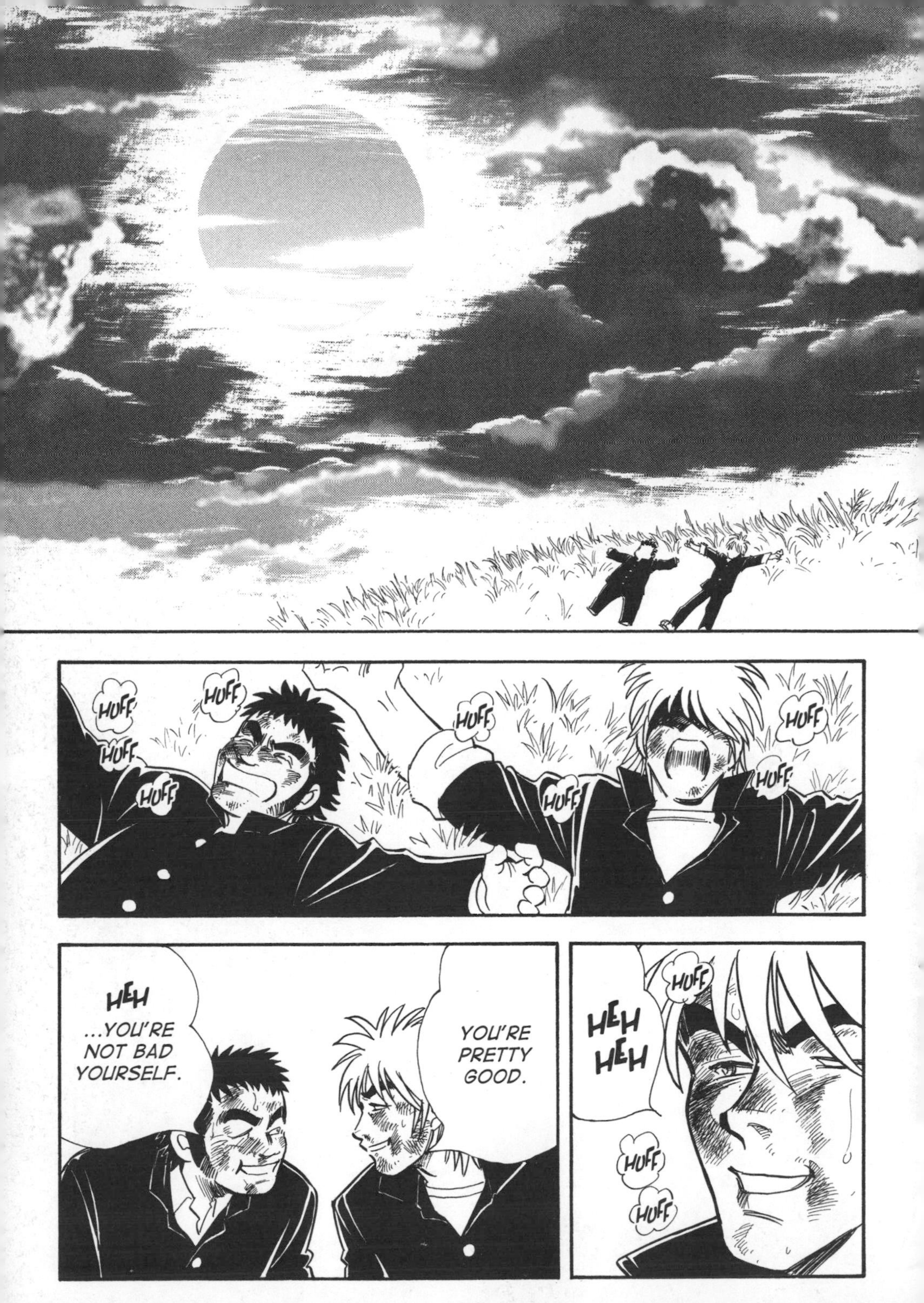
HUFF
HUFF
HUFF
HUFF
HUFF
HUFF
HUFF
HUFF
HUFF
HEH HEH
HUFF
HUFF
YOU'RE PRETTY GOOD.
HEH
...YOU'RE NOT BAD YOURSELF.

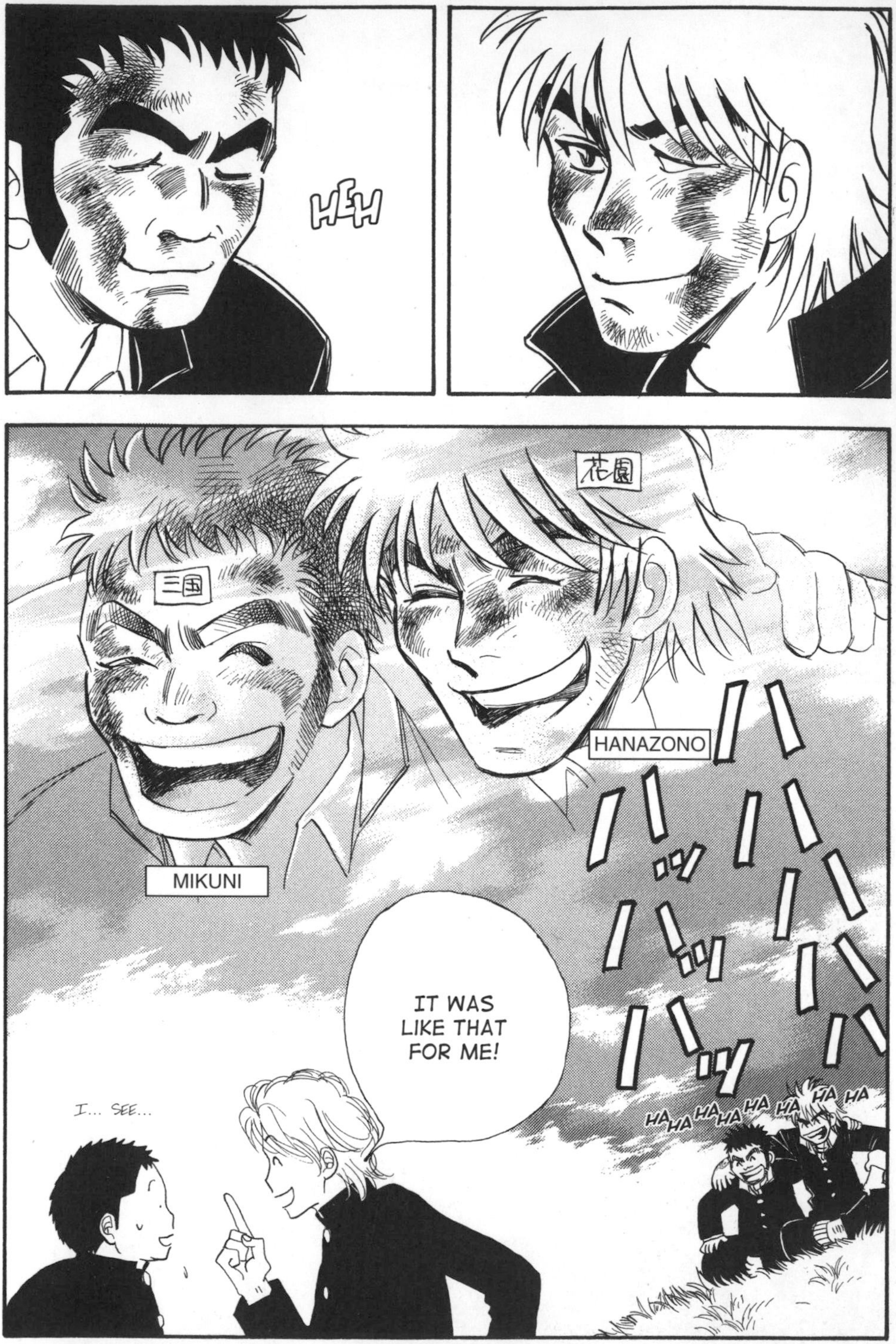
HEH
花園
三国
HANAZONO
MIKUNI
ハハハハハ
ハッハッハッ
IT WAS LIKE THAT FOR ME!
HA HA HA HA HA HA HA HA
I... SEE...

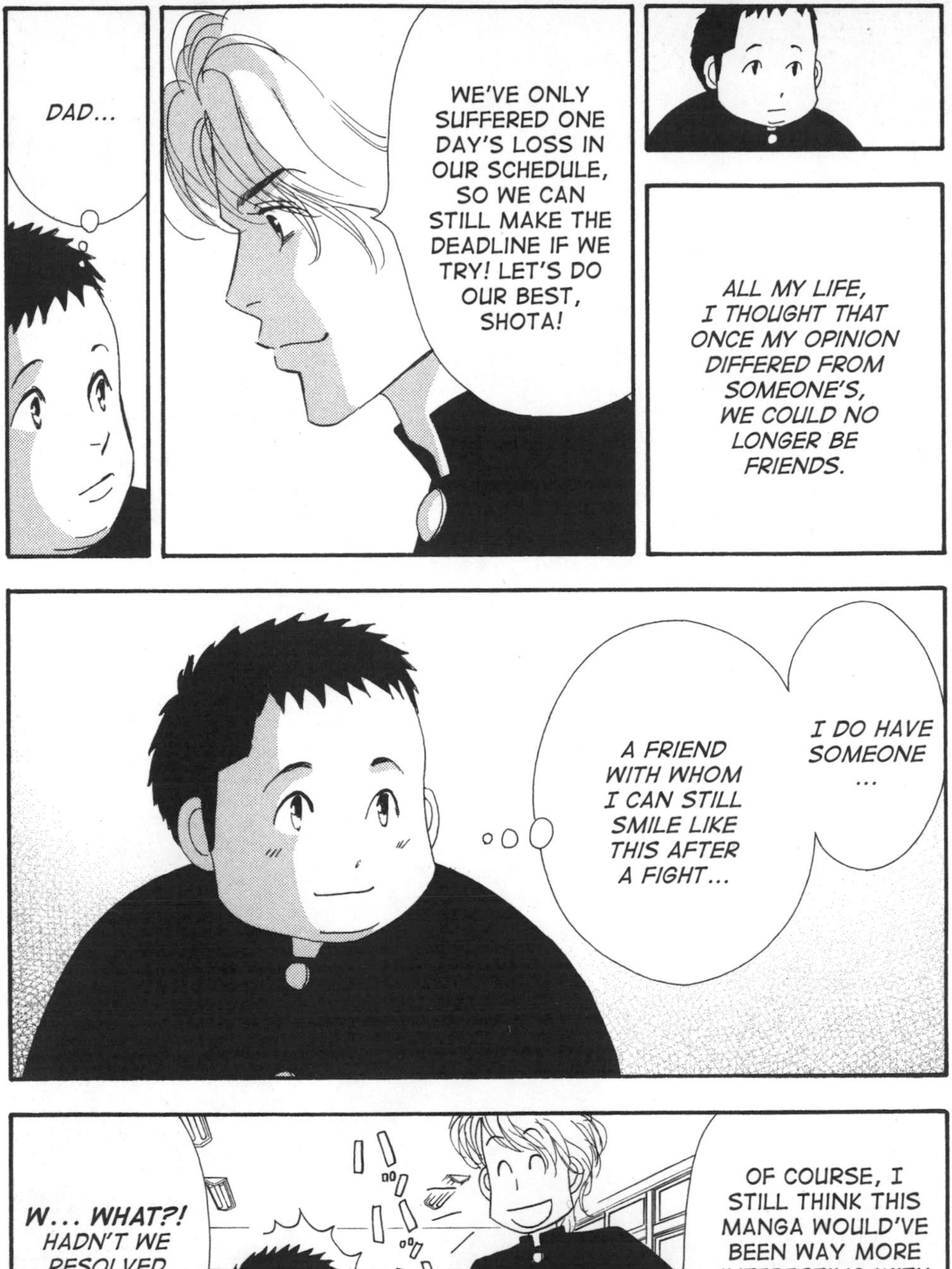
ALL MY LIFE, I THOUGHT THAT ONCE MY OPINION DIFFERED FROM SOMEONE'S, WE COULD NO LONGER BE FRIENDS.
WE'VE ONLY SUFFERED ONE DAY'S LOSS IN OUR SCHEDULE, SO WE CAN STILL MAKE THE DEADLINE IF WE TRY! LET'S DO OUR BEST, SHOTA!
DAD...
I DO HAVE SOMEONE ...
A FRIEND WITH WHOM I CAN STILL SMILE LIKE THIS AFTER A FIGHT...
OF COURSE, I STILL THINK THIS MANGA WOULD'VE BEEN WAY MORE INTERESTING WITH MY MACHINE GUN STILL IN IT, THOUGH!
HA HA HA
W... WHAT?! HADN'T WE RESOLVED THAT ISSUE?!

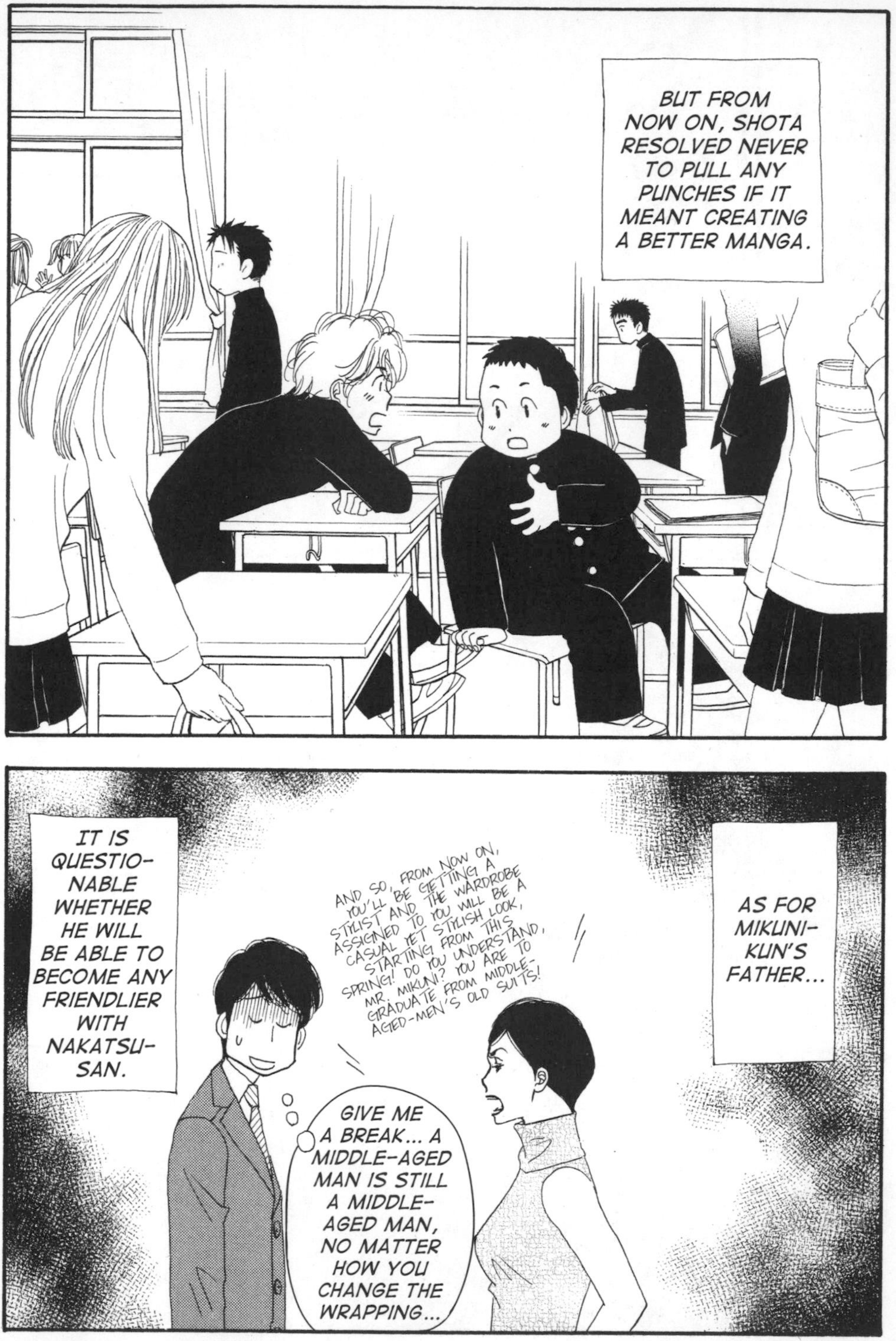
BUT FROM NOW ON, SHOTA RESOLVED NEVER TO PULL ANY PUNCHES IF IT MEANT CREATING A BETTER MANGA.
AS FOR MIKUNI-KUN'S FATHER...
AND SO, FROM NOW ON, YOU'LL BE GETTING A STYLIST AND THE WARDROBE ASSIGNED TO YOU WILL BE A CASUAL YET STYLISH LOOK, STARTING FROM THIS SPRING! DO YOU UNDERSTAND, MR. MIKUNI? YOU ARE TO GRADUATE FROM MIDDLE-AGED-MEN'S OLD SUITS!
GIVE ME A BREAK... A MIDDLE-AGED MAN IS STILL A MIDDLE-AGED MAN, NO MATTER HOW YOU CHANGE THE WRAPPING...
IT IS QUESTIONABLE WHETHER HE WILL BE ABLE TO BECOME ANY FRIENDLIER WITH NAKATSU-SAN.

#13 PART 1

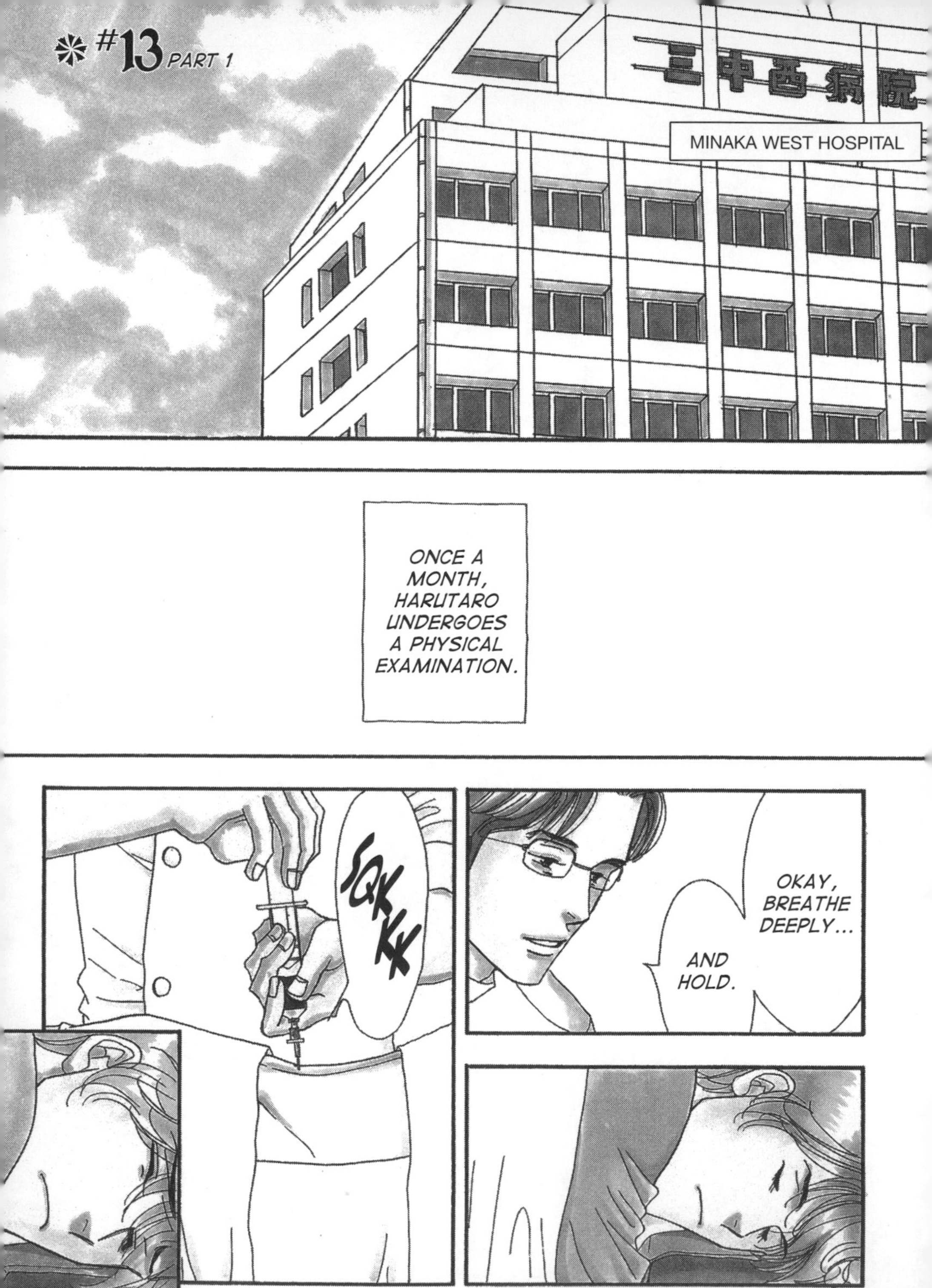
MINAKA WEST HOSPITAL
ONCE A MONTH, HARUTARO UNDERGOES A PHYSICAL EXAMINATION.
OKAY, BREATHE DEEPLY...
AND HOLD.
SQKKK

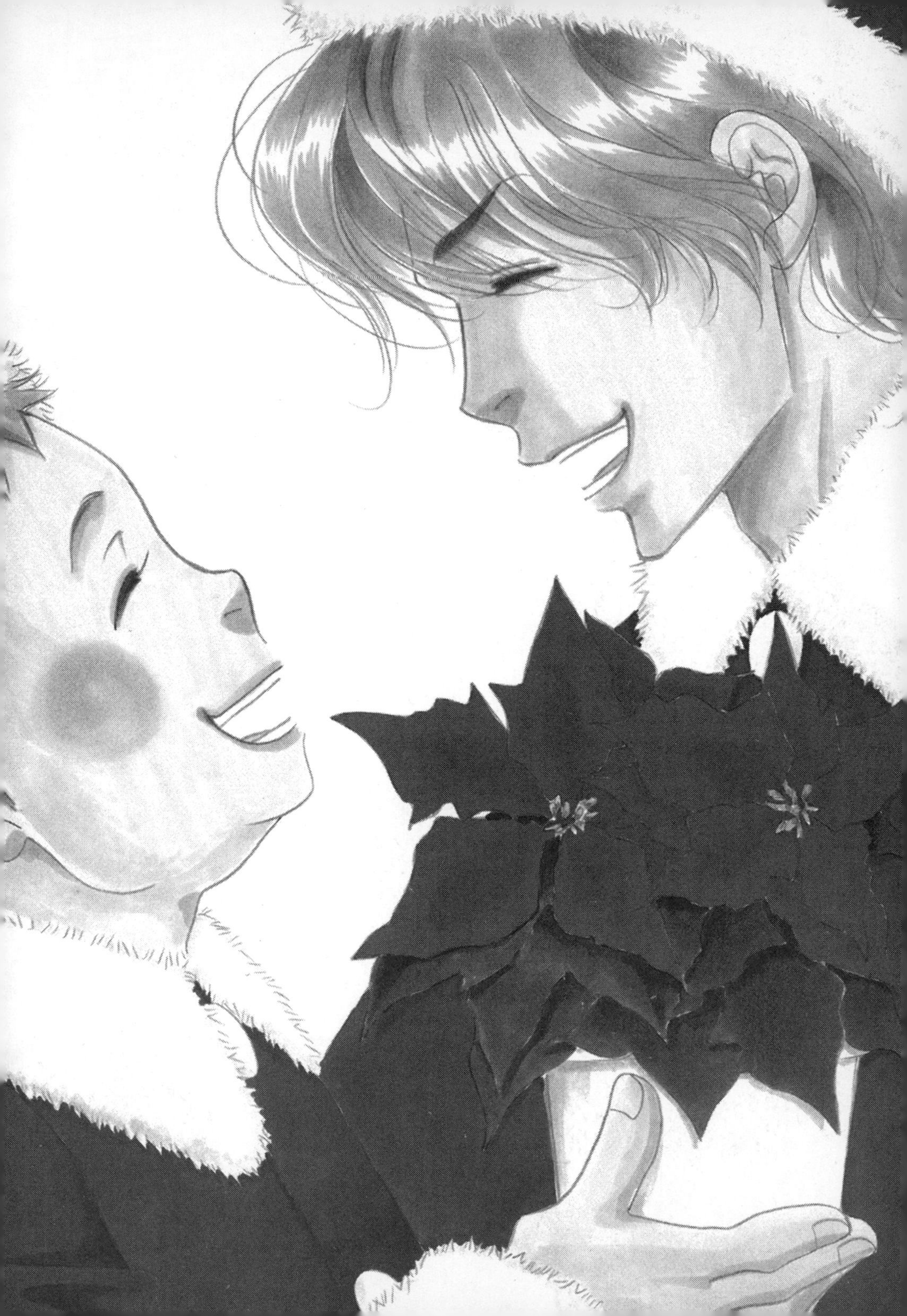

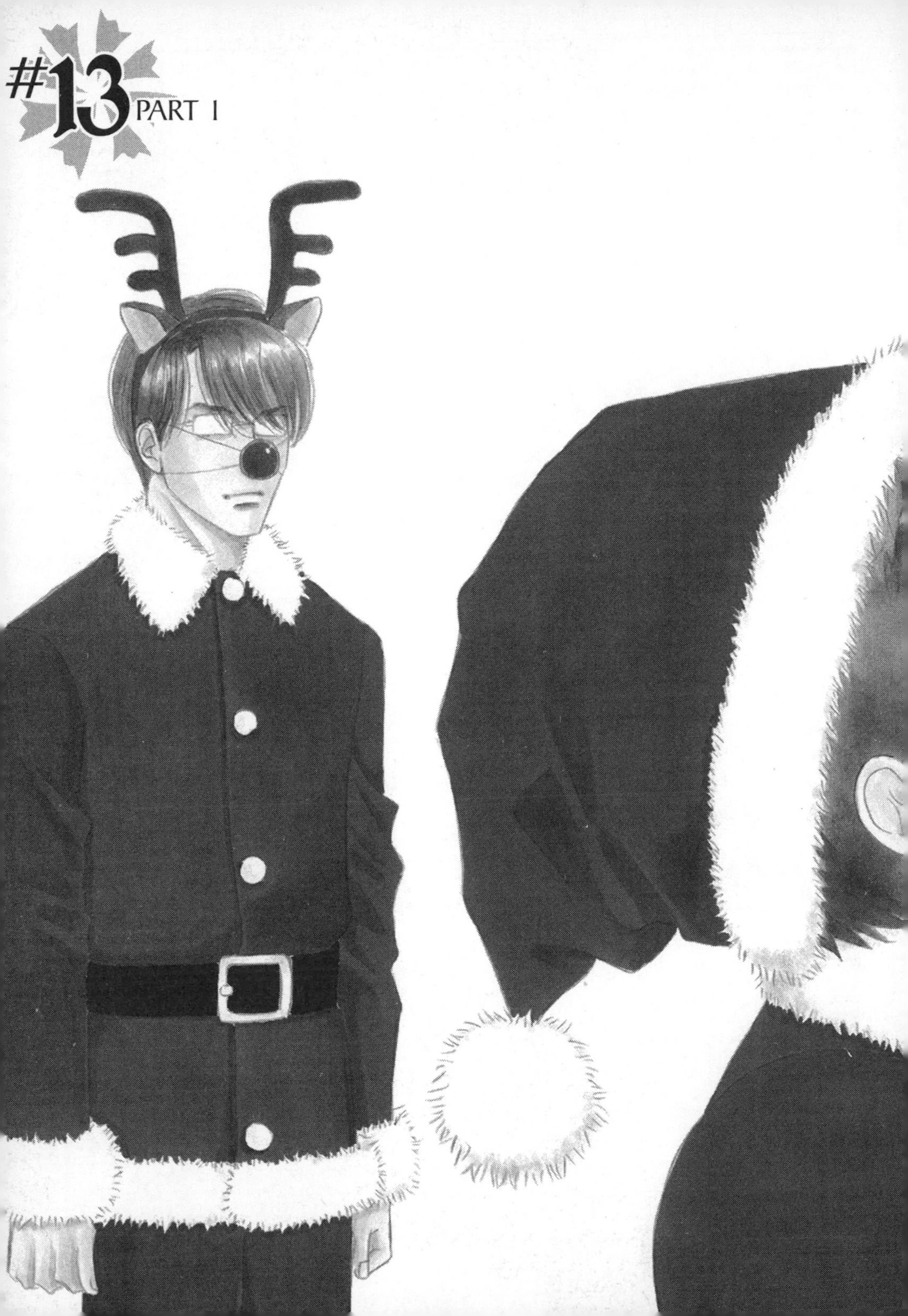
#13 PART 1

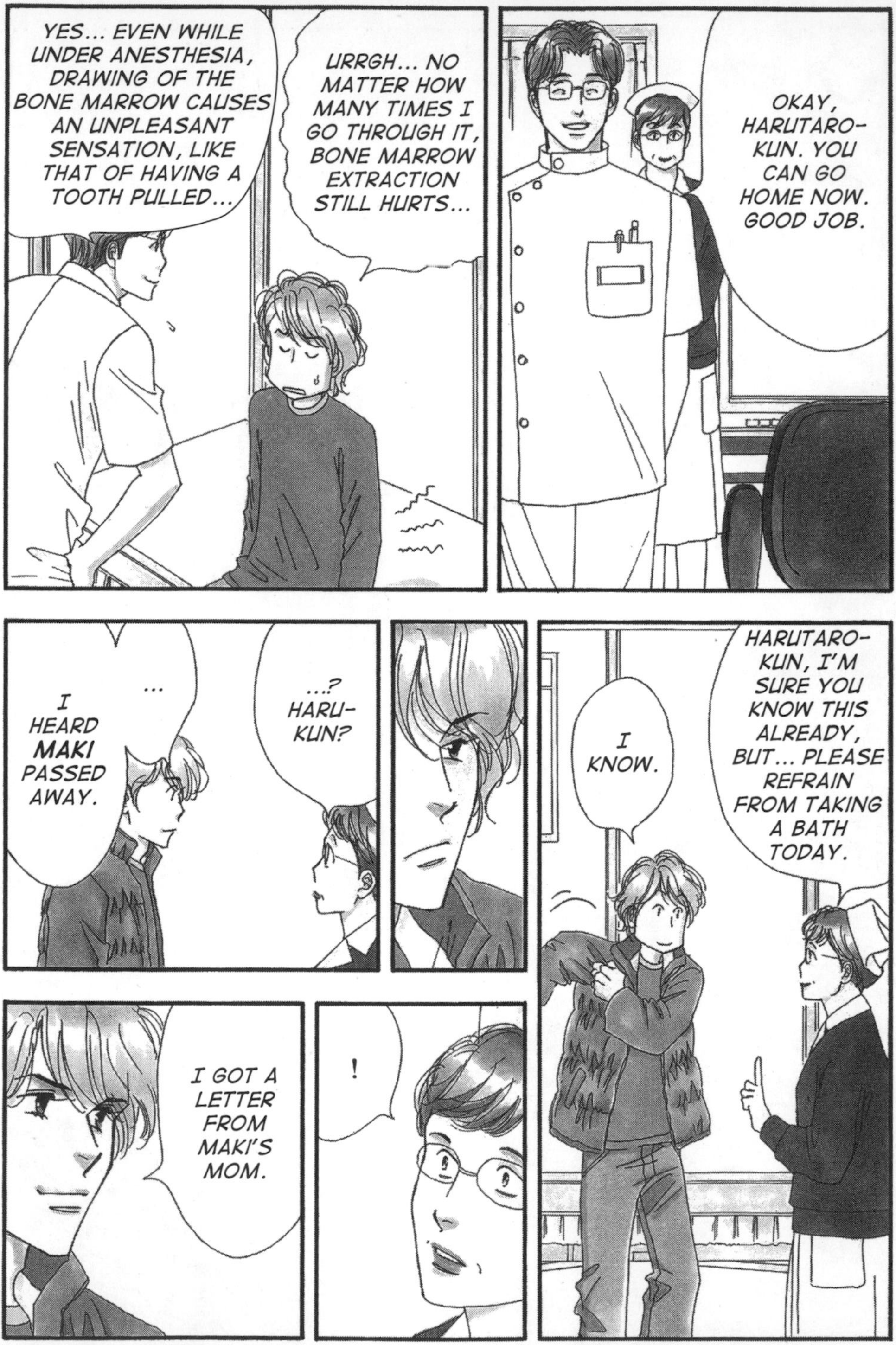
OKAY, HARUTARO-KUN. YOU CAN GO HOME NOW. GOOD JOB.
URRGH... NO MATTER HOW MANY TIMES I GO THROUGH IT, BONE MARROW EXTRACTION STILL HURTS...
YES... EVEN WHILE UNDER ANESTHESIA, DRAWING OF THE BONE MARROW CAUSES AN UNPLEASANT SENSATION, LIKE THAT OF HAVING A TOOTH PULLED...
HARUTARO-KUN, I'M SURE YOU KNOW THIS ALREADY, BUT... PLEASE REFRAIN FROM TAKING A BATH TODAY.
I KNOW.
...? HARU-KUN?
...
I HEARD **MAKI** PASSED AWAY.
!
I GOT A LETTER FROM MAKI'S MOM.

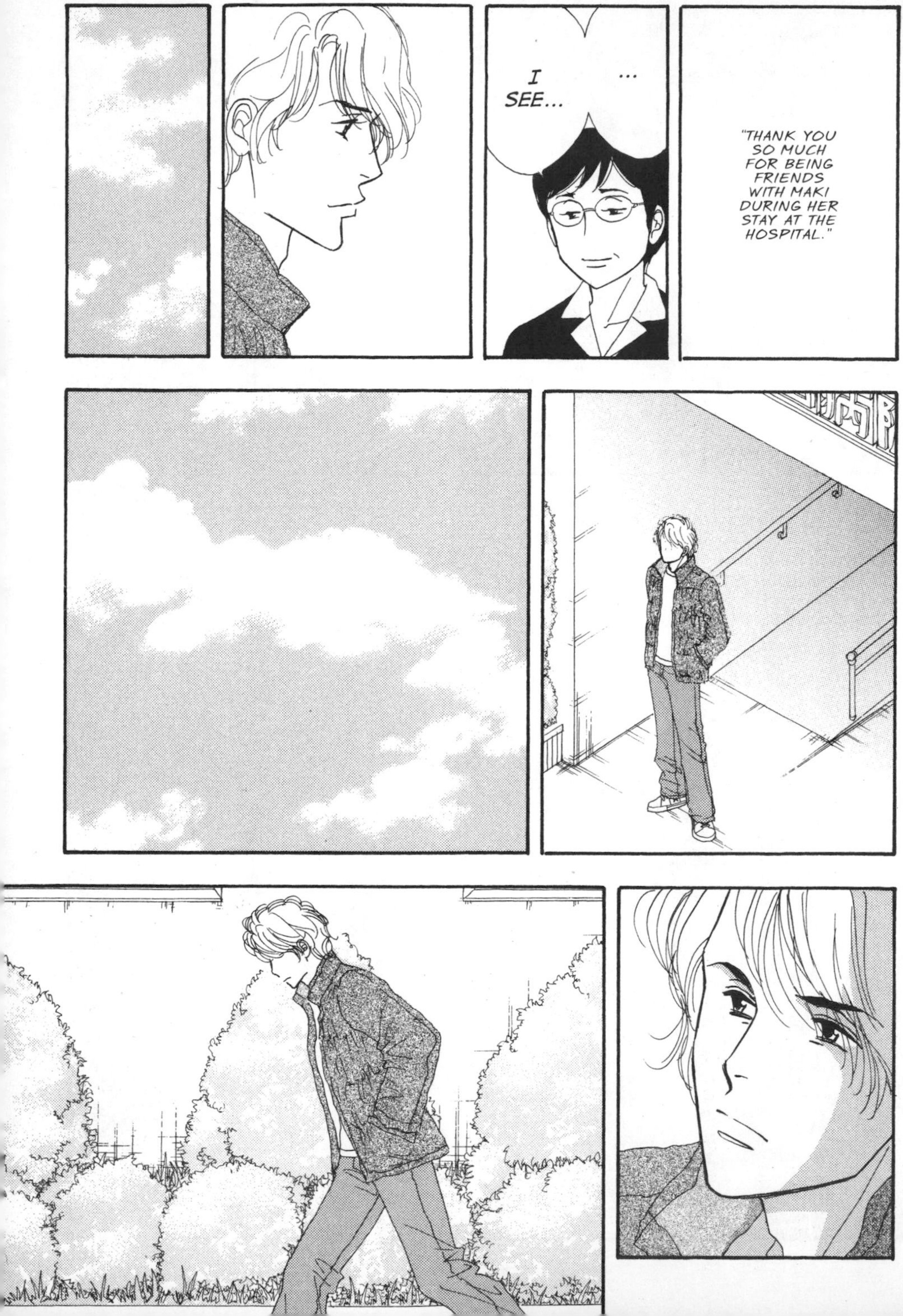
"THANK YOU SO MUCH FOR BEING FRIENDS WITH MAKI DURING HER STAY AT THE HOSPITAL."
...
I SEE...

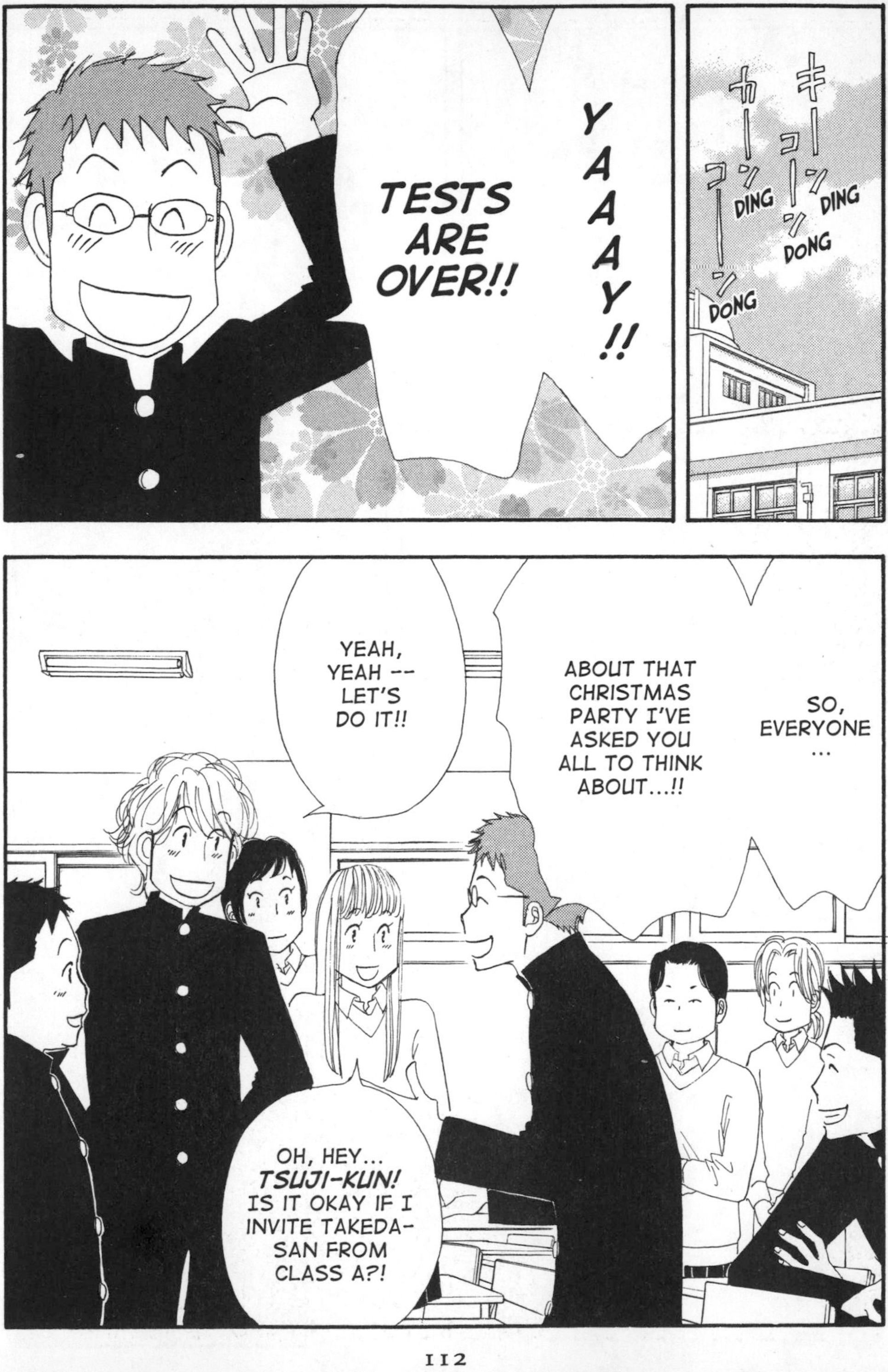

キーンコーン
DING DONG
カーンコーン
DING DONG
YAAAAY!!
TESTS ARE OVER!!
SO, EVERYONE ...
ABOUT THAT CHRISTMAS PARTY I'VE ASKED YOU ALL TO THINK ABOUT...!!
YEAH, YEAH -- LET'S DO IT!!
OH, HEY... TSUJI-KUN! IS IT OKAY IF I INVITE TAKEDA-SAN FROM CLASS A?!

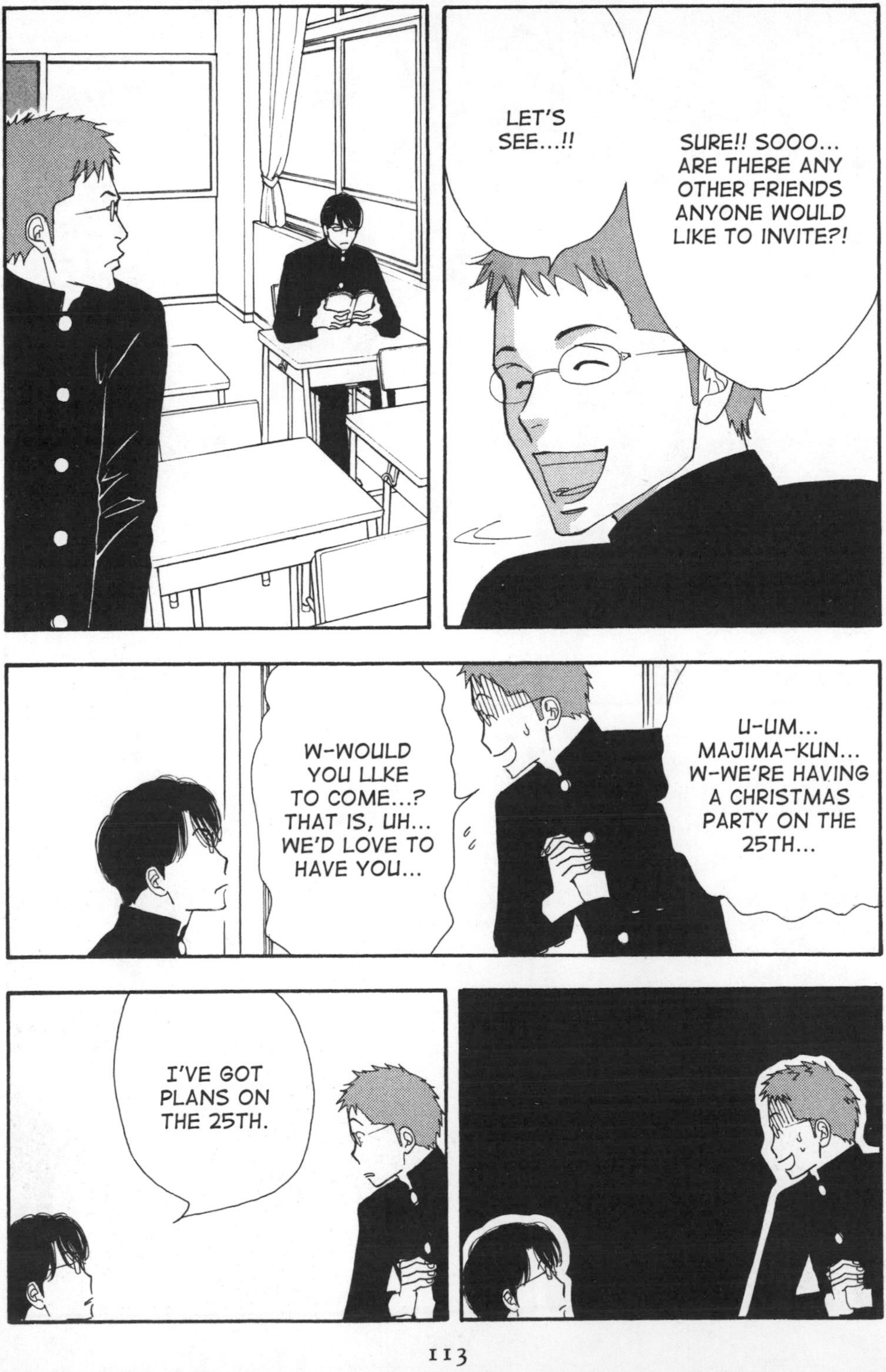
SURE!! SOOO... ARE THERE ANY OTHER FRIENDS ANYONE WOULD LIKE TO INVITE?!
LET'S SEE...!!
U-UM... MAJIMA-KUN... W-WE'RE HAVING A CHRISTMAS PARTY ON THE 25TH...
W-WOULD YOU LLKE TO COME...? THAT IS, UH... WE'D LOVE TO HAVE YOU...
I'VE GOT PLANS ON THE 25TH.

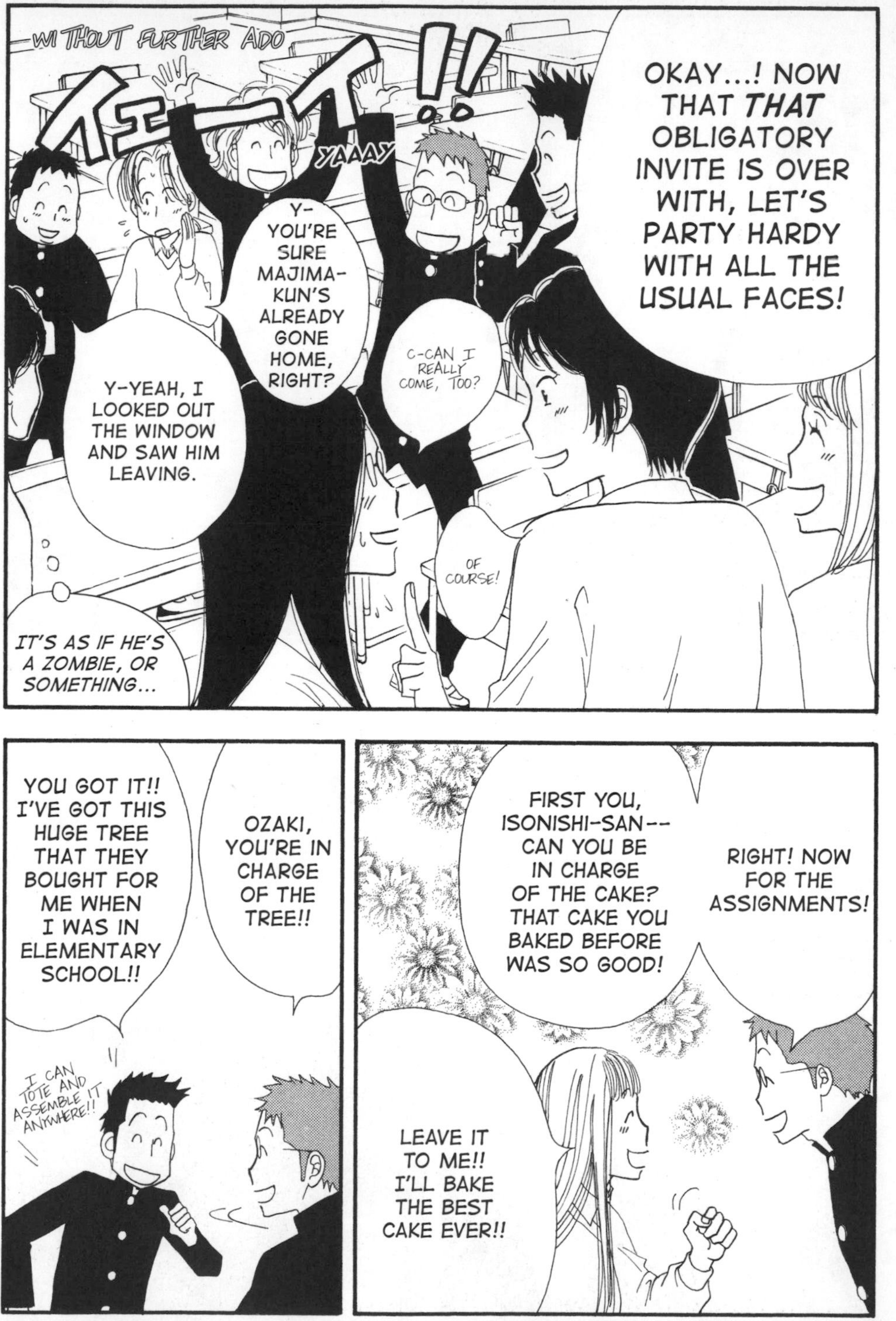

WITHOUT FURTHER ADO
OKAY...! NOW THAT *THAT* OBLIGATORY INVITE IS OVER WITH, LET'S PARTY HARDY WITH ALL THE USUAL FACES!
イェーイ!!
YAAAY
Y-YOU'RE SURE MAJIMA-KUN'S ALREADY GONE HOME, RIGHT?
Y-YEAH, I LOOKED OUT THE WINDOW AND SAW HIM LEAVING.
C-CAN I REALLY COME, TOO?
OF COURSE!
IT'S AS IF HE'S A ZOMBIE, OR SOMETHING...
RIGHT! NOW FOR THE ASSIGNMENTS!
FIRST YOU, ISONISHI-SAN-- CAN YOU BE IN CHARGE OF THE CAKE? THAT CAKE YOU BAKED BEFORE WAS SO GOOD!
LEAVE IT TO ME!! I'LL BAKE THE BEST CAKE EVER!!
OZAKI, YOU'RE IN CHARGE OF THE TREE!!
YOU GOT IT!! I'VE GOT THIS HUGE TREE THAT THEY BOUGHT FOR ME WHEN I WAS IN ELEMENTARY SCHOOL!!
I CAN TOTE AND ASSEMBLE IT ANYWHERE!!

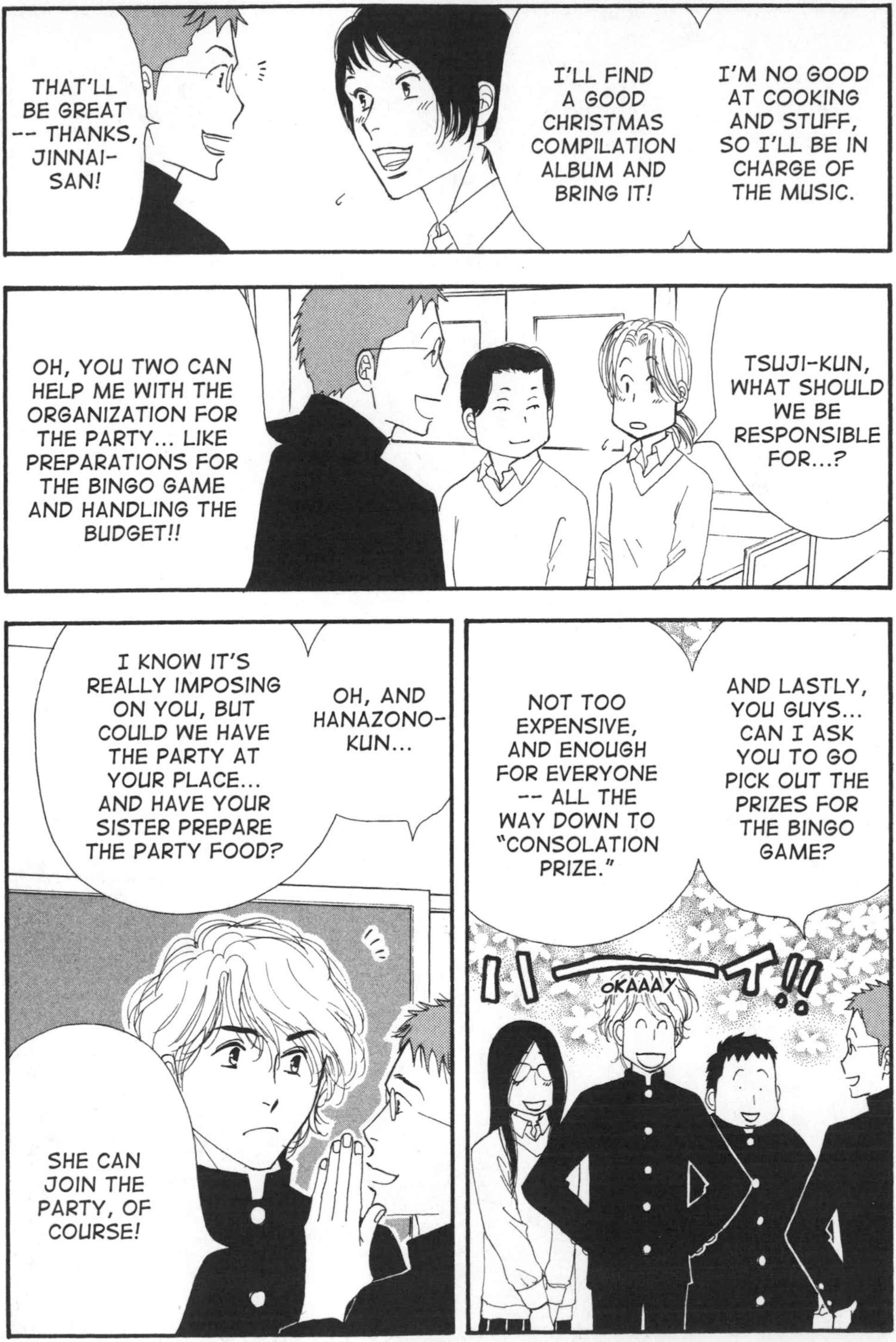
I'M NO GOOD AT COOKING AND STUFF, SO I'LL BE IN CHARGE OF THE MUSIC.
I'LL FIND A GOOD CHRISTMAS COMPILATION ALBUM AND BRING IT!
THAT'LL BE GREAT -- THANKS, JINNAI-SAN!
TSUJI-KUN, WHAT SHOULD WE BE RESPONSIBLE FOR...?
OH, YOU TWO CAN HELP ME WITH THE ORGANIZATION FOR THE PARTY... LIKE PREPARATIONS FOR THE BINGO GAME AND HANDLING THE BUDGET!!
AND LASTLY, YOU GUYS... CAN I ASK YOU TO GO PICK OUT THE PRIZES FOR THE BINGO GAME?
NOT TOO EXPENSIVE, AND ENOUGH FOR EVERYONE -- ALL THE WAY DOWN TO "CONSOLATION PRIZE."
OKAAAY
OH, AND HANAZONO-KUN...
I KNOW IT'S REALLY IMPOSING ON YOU, BUT COULD WE HAVE THE PARTY AT YOUR PLACE... AND HAVE YOUR SISTER PREPARE THE PARTY FOOD?
SHE CAN JOIN THE PARTY, OF COURSE!

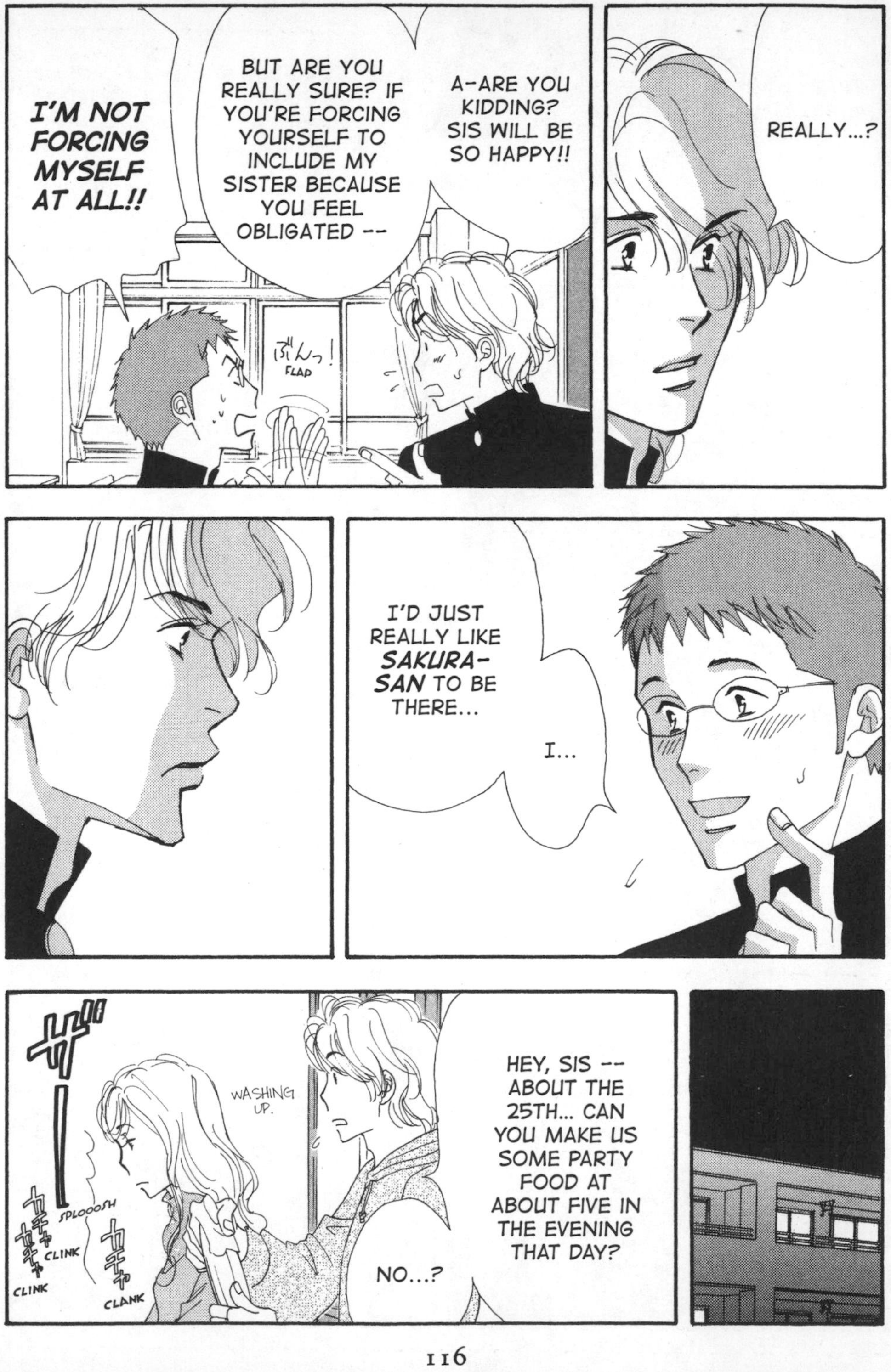
REALLY...?
A-ARE YOU KIDDING? SIS WILL BE SO HAPPY!!
BUT ARE YOU REALLY SURE? IF YOU'RE FORCING YOURSELF TO INCLUDE MY SISTER BECAUSE YOU FEEL OBLIGATED --
I'M NOT FORCING MYSELF AT ALL!!
ぶんっ!
FLAP
I...
I'D JUST REALLY LIKE SAKURA-SAN TO BE THERE...
HEY, SIS -- ABOUT THE 25TH... CAN YOU MAKE US SOME PARTY FOOD AT ABOUT FIVE IN THE EVENING THAT DAY?
NO...?
WASHING UP.
SPLOOOSH
カチャ
CLANK
カチャ
CLINK
カチャ
CLINK

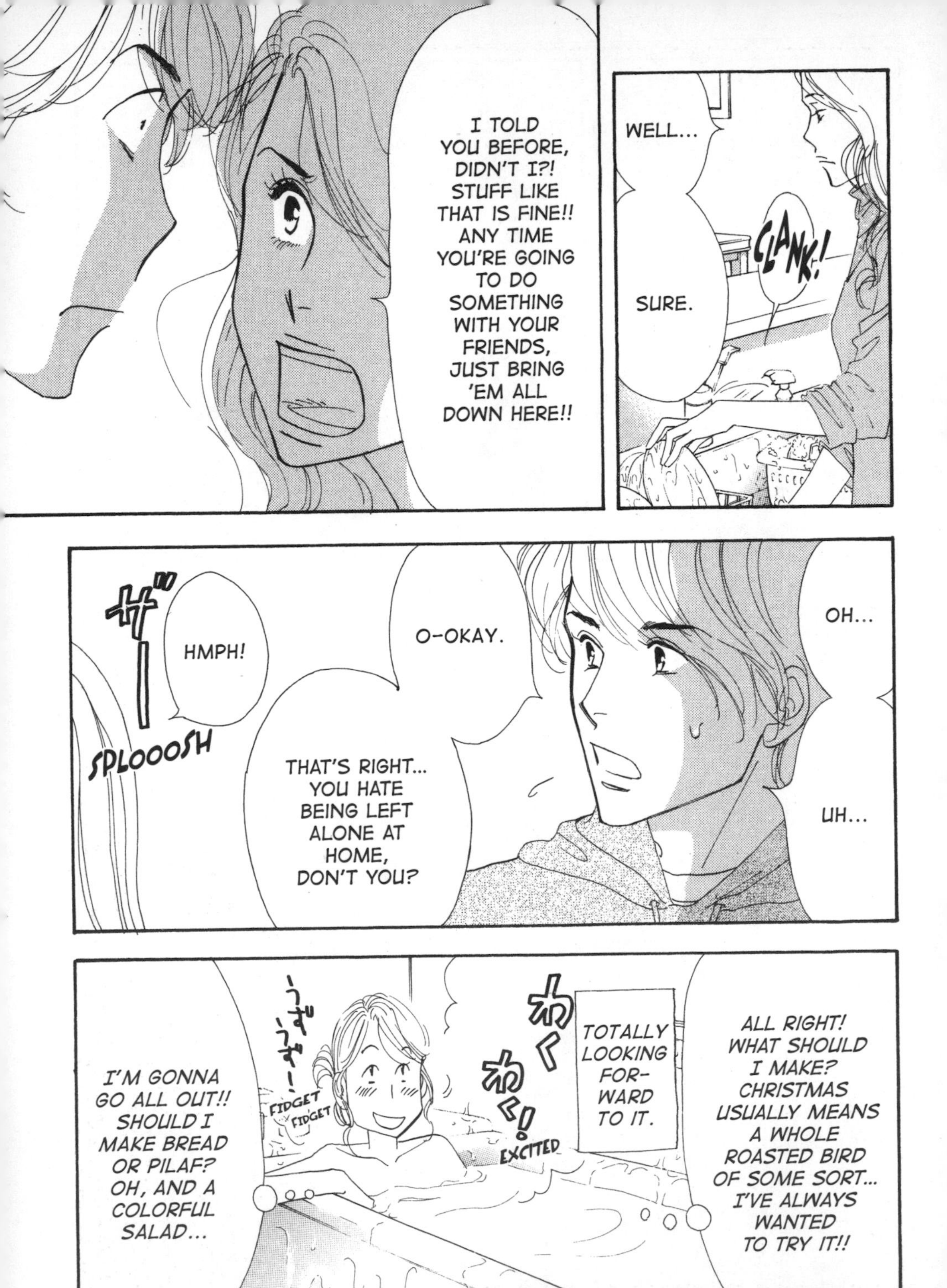
WELL...
SURE.
CLANK!
I TOLD YOU BEFORE, DIDN'T I?! STUFF LIKE THAT IS FINE!! ANY TIME YOU'RE GOING TO DO SOMETHING WITH YOUR FRIENDS, JUST BRING 'EM ALL DOWN HERE!!
OH...
UH...
O-OKAY.
THAT'S RIGHT... YOU HATE BEING LEFT ALONE AT HOME, DON'T YOU?
HMPH!
ザー
SPLOOOSH
ALL RIGHT! WHAT SHOULD I MAKE? CHRISTMAS USUALLY MEANS A WHOLE ROASTED BIRD OF SOME SORT... I'VE ALWAYS WANTED TO TRY IT!!
TOTALLY LOOKING FOR-WARD TO IT.
わくわく!
EXCITED
うずうず!
FIDGET FIDGET
I'M GONNA GO ALL OUT!! SHOULD I MAKE BREAD OR PILAF? OH, AND A COLORFUL SALAD...

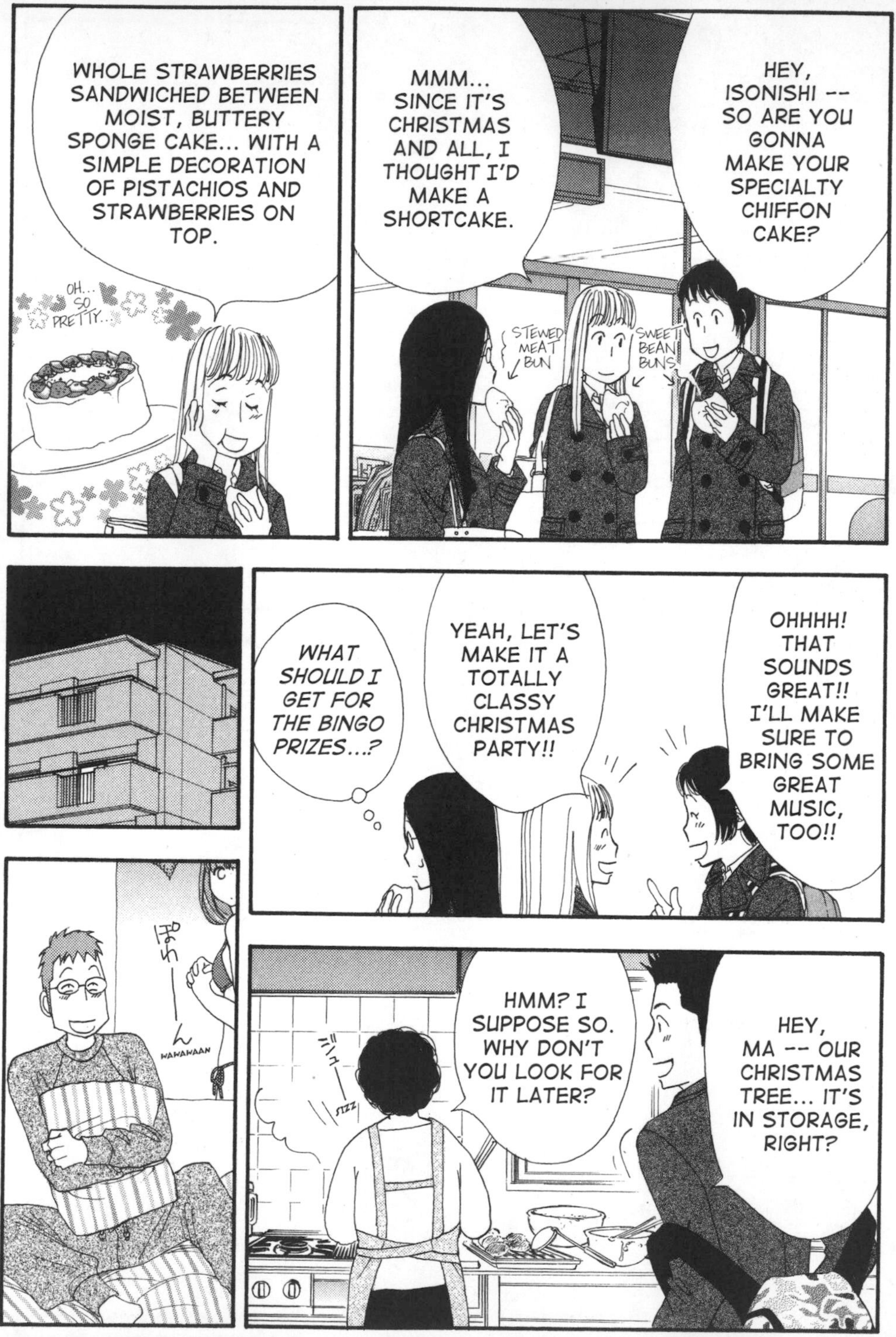
HEY, ISONISHI -- SO ARE YOU GONNA MAKE YOUR SPECIALTY CHIFFON CAKE?
MMM... SINCE IT'S CHRISTMAS AND ALL, I THOUGHT I'D MAKE A SHORTCAKE.
SWEET BEAN BUNS
STEWED MEAT BUN
WHOLE STRAWBERRIES SANDWICHED BETWEEN MOIST, BUTTERY SPONGE CAKE... WITH A SIMPLE DECORATION OF PISTACHIOS AND STRAWBERRIES ON TOP.
OH... SO PRETTY...
OHHHH! THAT SOUNDS GREAT!! I'LL MAKE SURE TO BRING SOME GREAT MUSIC, TOO!!
YEAH, LET'S MAKE IT A TOTALLY CLASSY CHRISTMAS PARTY!!
WHAT SHOULD I GET FOR THE BINGO PRIZES...?
HEY, MA -- OUR CHRISTMAS TREE... IT'S IN STORAGE, RIGHT?
HMM? I SUPPOSE SO. WHY DON'T YOU LOOK FOR IT LATER?
SIZZ
WAWAWAAN

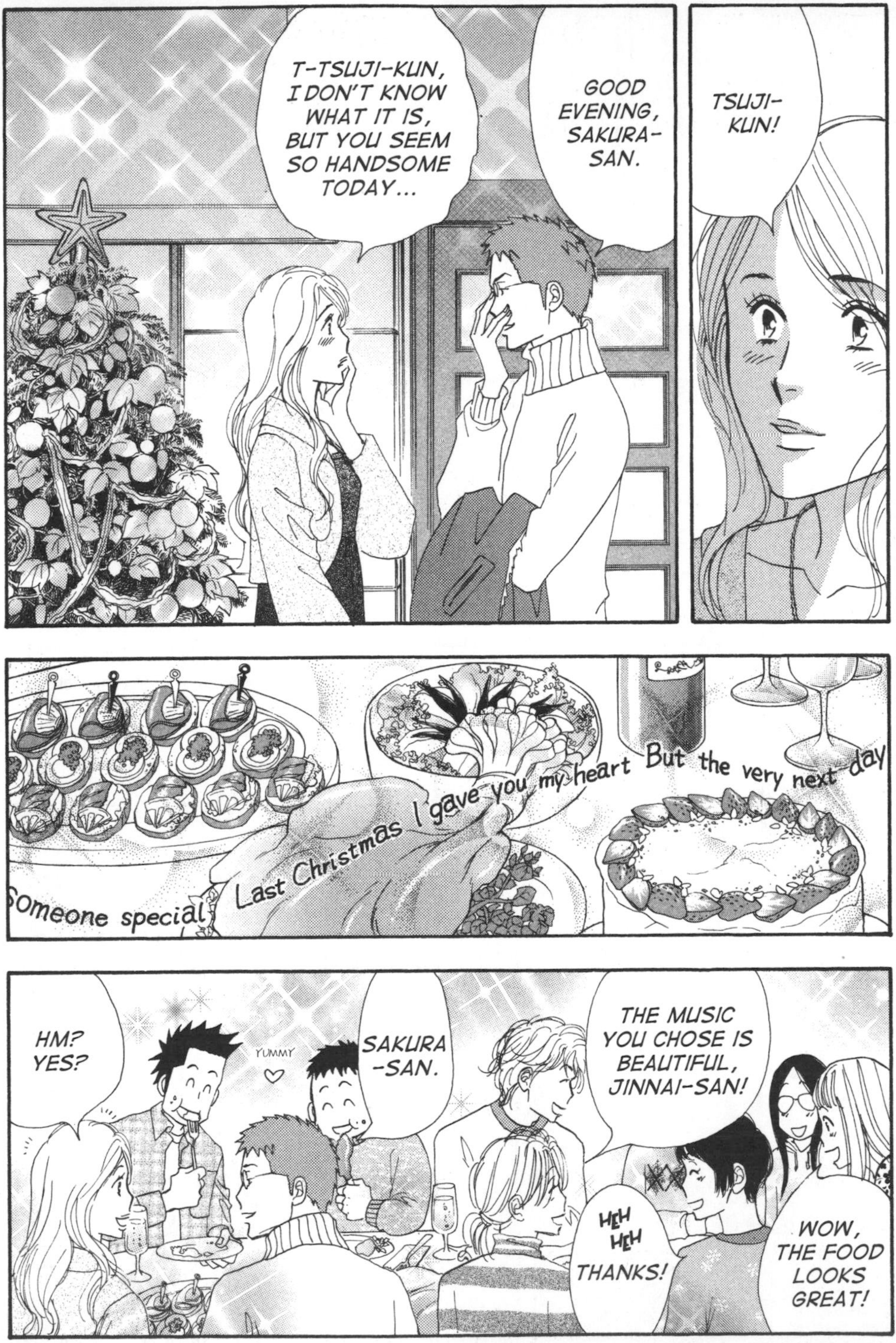
TSUJI-KUN!
GOOD EVENING, SAKURA-SAN.
T-TSUJI-KUN, I DON'T KNOW WHAT IT IS, BUT YOU SEEM SO HANDSOME TODAY...
Last Christmas I gave you my heart But the very next day
Someone special
THE MUSIC YOU CHOSE IS BEAUTIFUL, JINNAI-SAN!
WOW, THE FOOD LOOKS GREAT!
HEH HEH
THANKS!
SAKURA-SAN.
YUMMY
HM? YES?

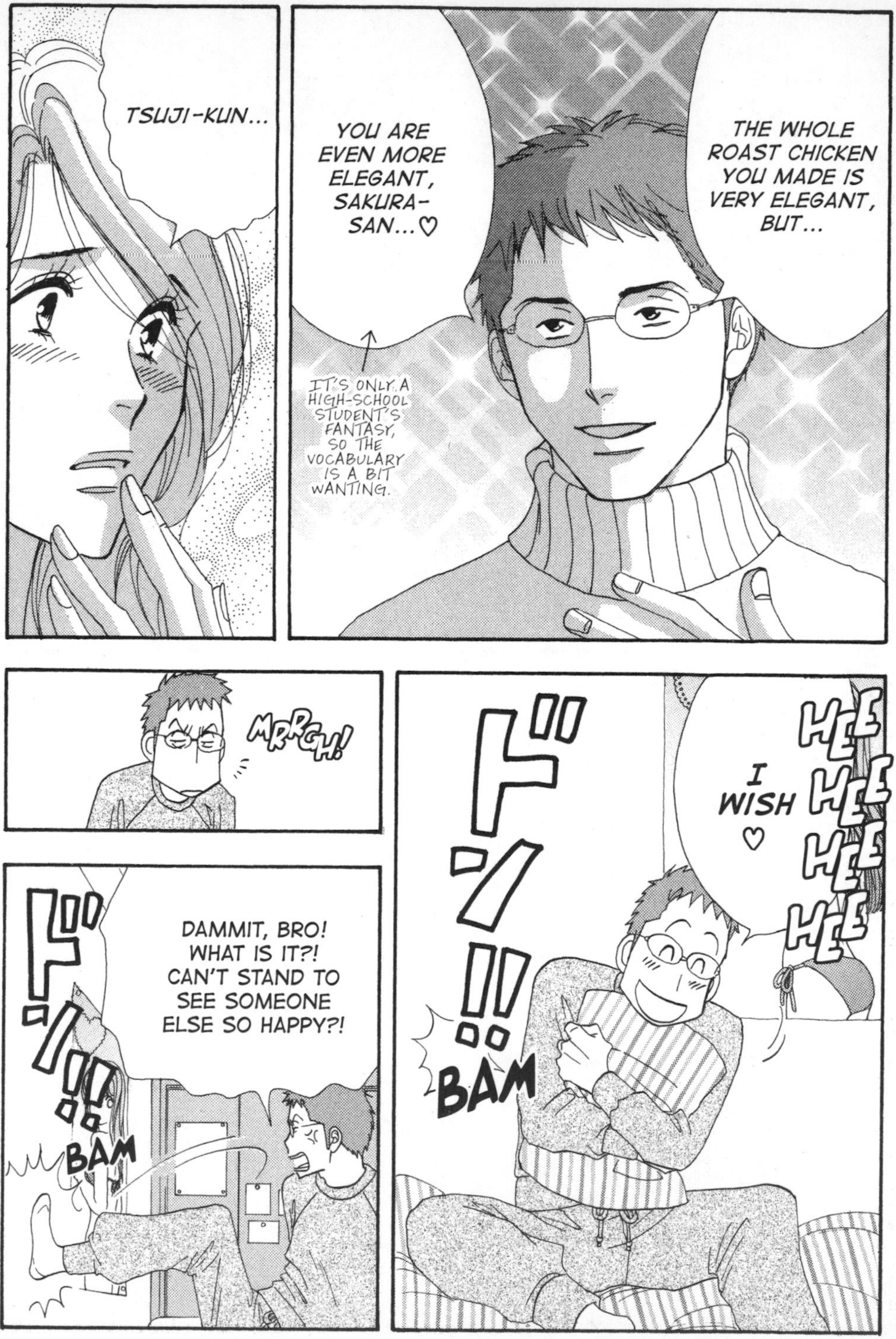
THE WHOLE ROAST CHICKEN YOU MADE IS VERY ELEGANT, BUT...
YOU ARE EVEN MORE ELEGANT, SAKURA-SAN...♡
IT'S ONLY A HIGH-SCHOOL STUDENT'S FANTASY, SO THE VOCABULARY IS A BIT WANTING.
TSUJI-KUN...
HEE HEE HEE HEE HEE
I WISH ♡
ドン!!
BAM
MRRGH!
ドン!!
BAM
DAMMIT, BRO! WHAT IS IT?! CAN'T STAND TO SEE SOMEONE ELSE SO HAPPY?!

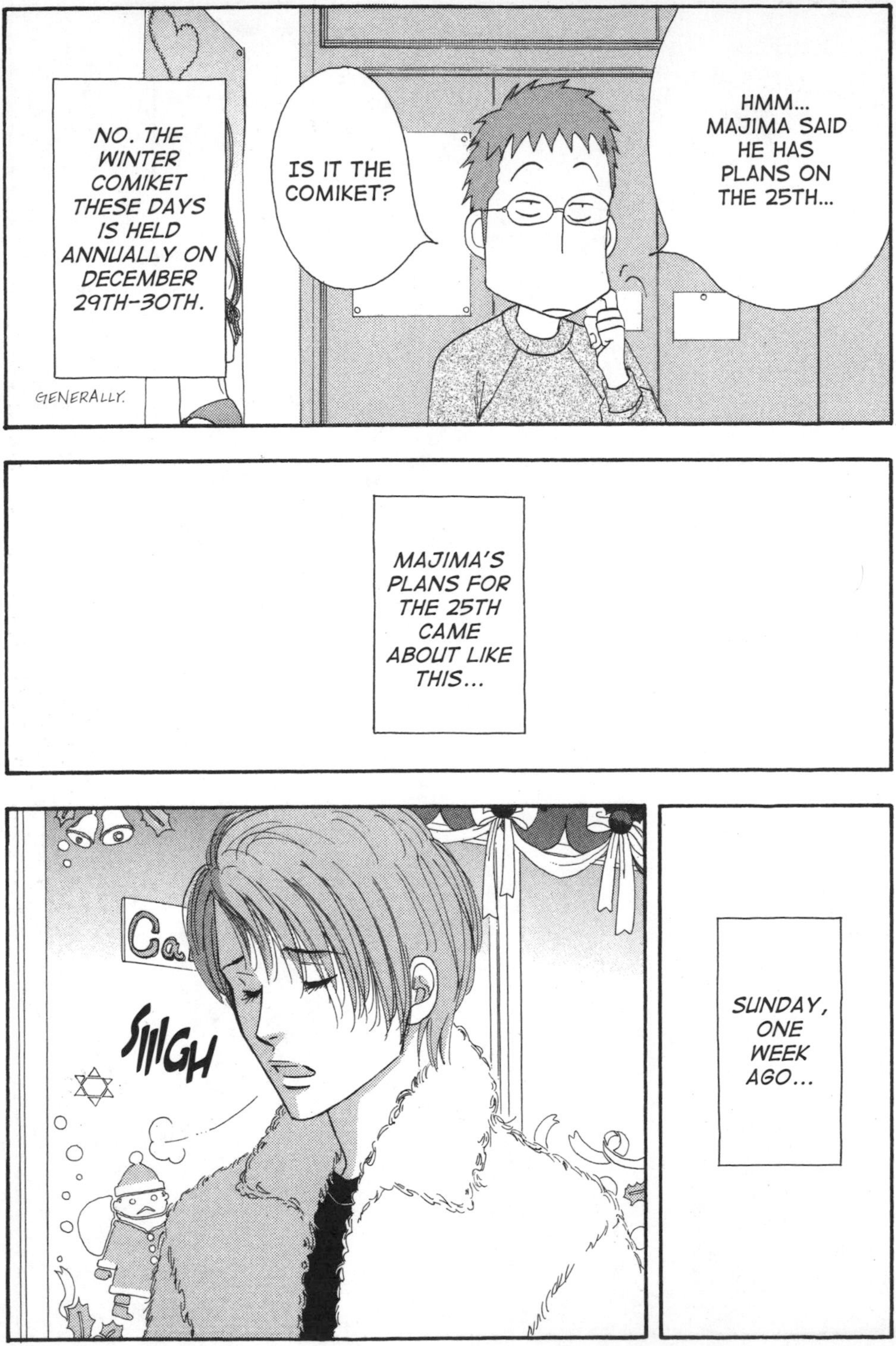
HMM... MAJIMA SAID HE HAS PLANS ON THE 25TH...
IS IT THE COMIKET?
NO. THE WINTER COMIKET THESE DAYS IS HELD ANNUALLY ON DECEMBER 29TH-30TH.
GENERALLY.
MAJIMA'S PLANS FOR THE 25TH CAME ABOUT LIKE THIS...
SUNDAY, ONE WEEK AGO...
SIIIGH

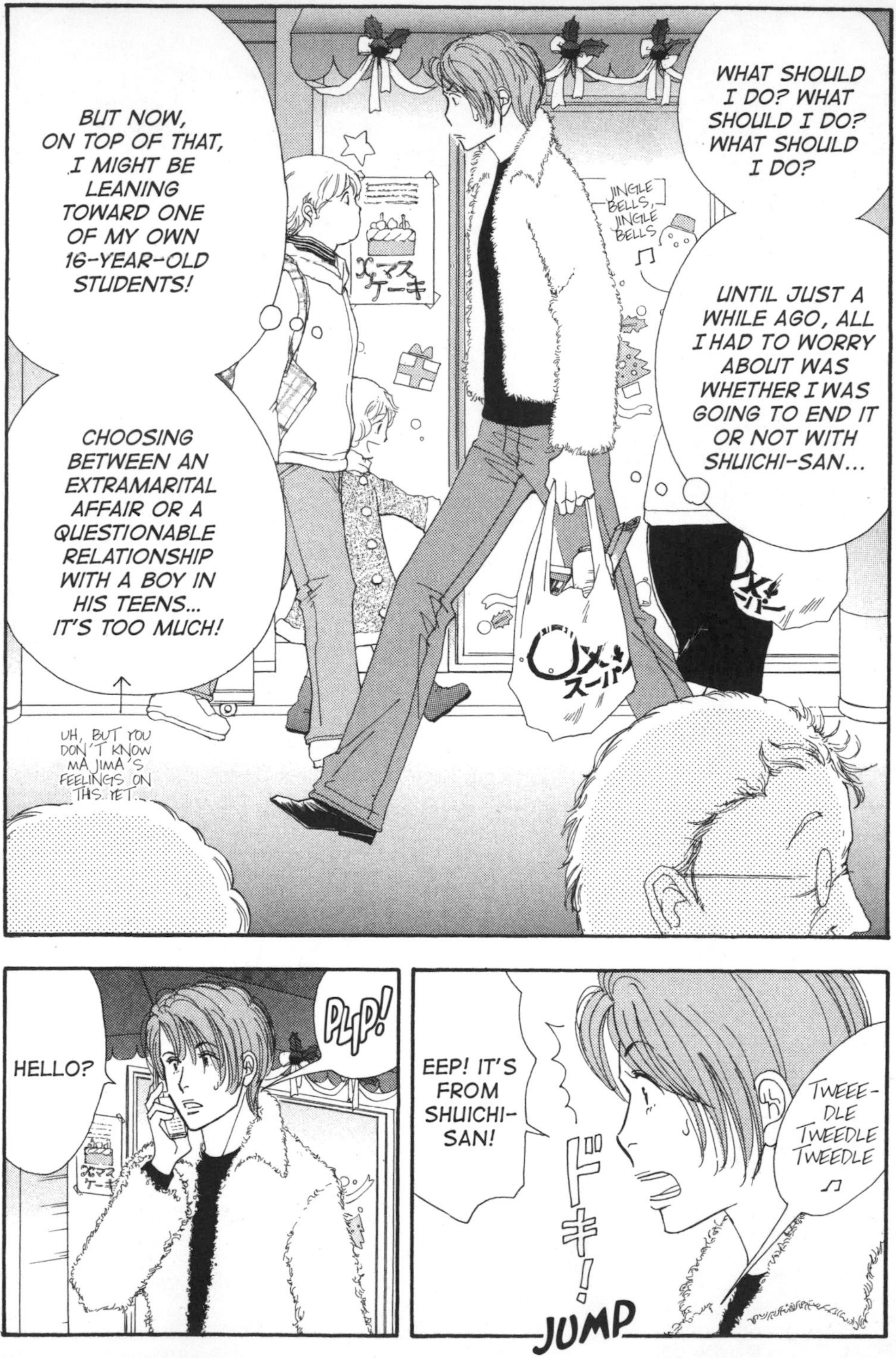
WHAT SHOULD I DO? WHAT SHOULD I DO? WHAT SHOULD I DO?
UNTIL JUST A WHILE AGO, ALL I HAD TO WORRY ABOUT WAS WHETHER I WAS GOING TO END IT OR NOT WITH SHUICHI-SAN...
JINGLE BELLS, JINGLE BELLS ♫
Xマス ケーキ
BUT NOW, ON TOP OF THAT, I MIGHT BE LEANING TOWARD ONE OF MY OWN 16-YEAR-OLD STUDENTS!
CHOOSING BETWEEN AN EXTRAMARITAL AFFAIR OR A QUESTIONABLE RELATIONSHIP WITH A BOY IN HIS TEENS... IT'S TOO MUCH!
UH, BUT YOU DON'T KNOW MAJIMA'S FEELINGS ON THIS YET...
TWEEEDLE TWEEDLE TWEEDLE ♫
EEP! IT'S FROM SHUICHI-SAN!
ドキ!
JUMP
PLIP!
HELLO?

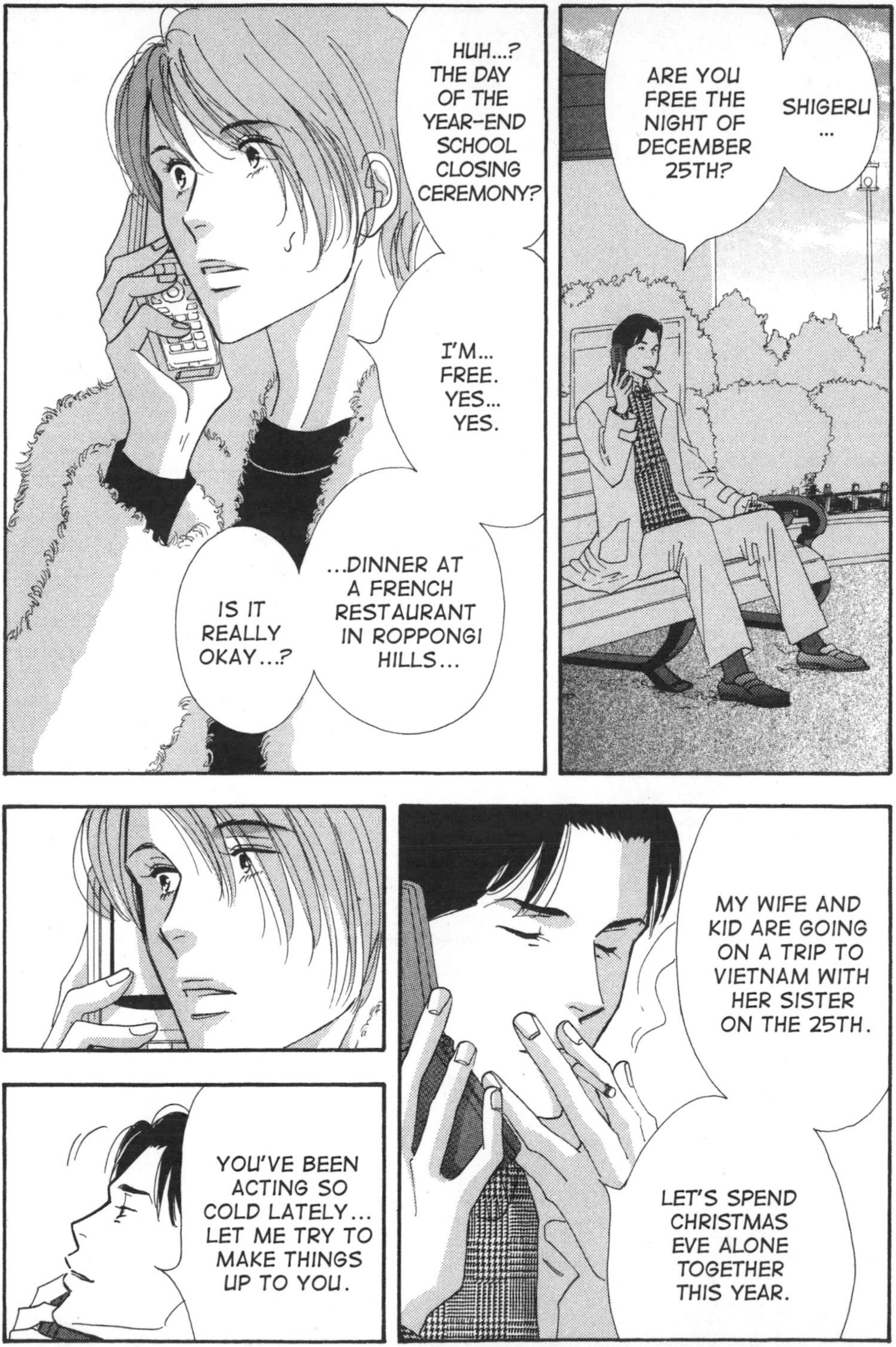
SHIGERU ...
ARE YOU FREE THE NIGHT OF DECEMBER 25TH?
HUH...? THE DAY OF THE YEAR-END SCHOOL CLOSING CEREMONY?
I'M... FREE. YES... YES.
...DINNER AT A FRENCH RESTAURANT IN ROPPONGI HILLS...
IS IT REALLY OKAY...?
MY WIFE AND KID ARE GOING ON A TRIP TO VIETNAM WITH HER SISTER ON THE 25TH.
LET'S SPEND CHRISTMAS EVE ALONE TOGETHER THIS YEAR.
YOU'VE BEEN ACTING SO COLD LATELY... LET ME TRY TO MAKE THINGS UP TO YOU.

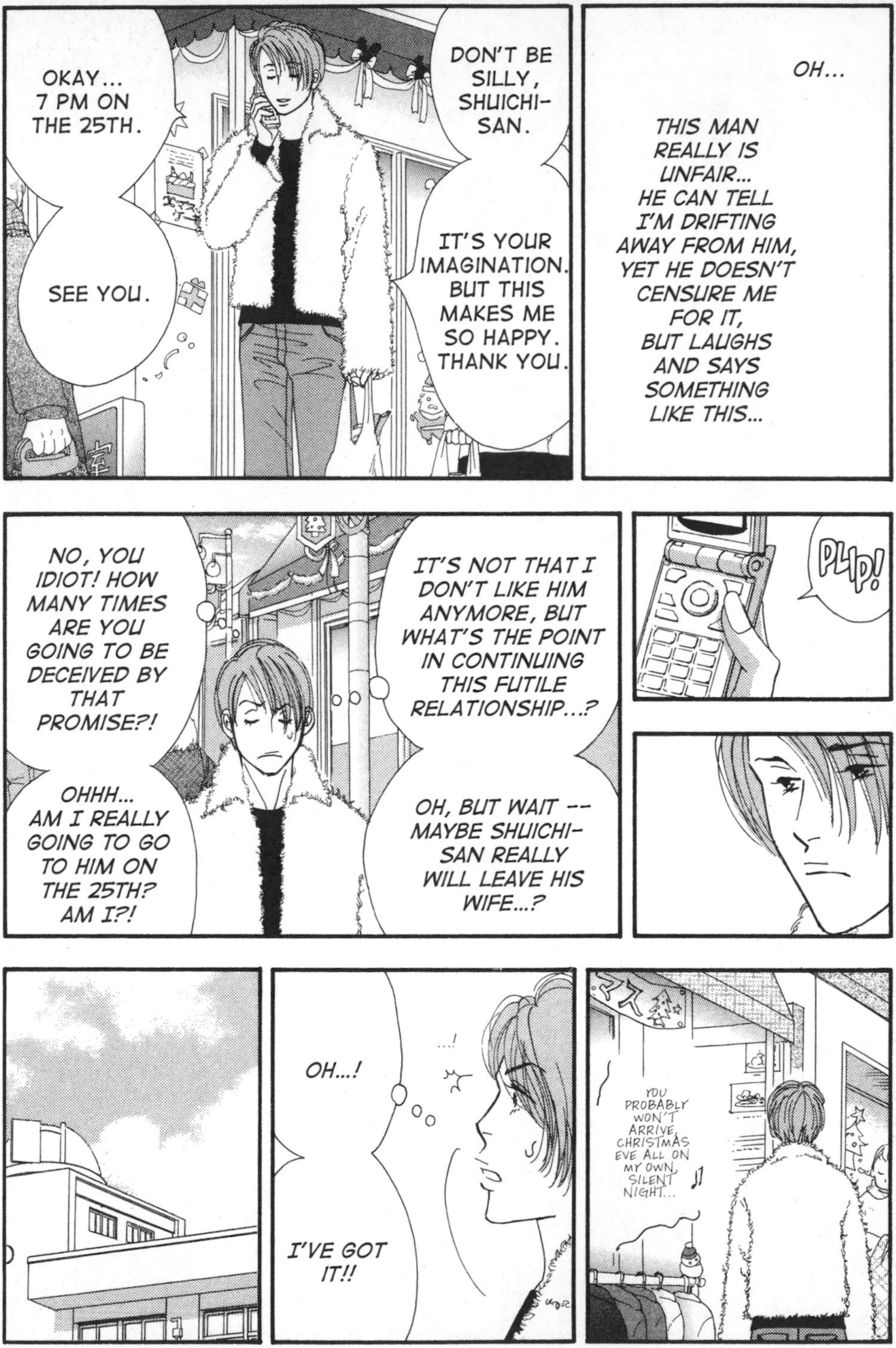
OH...
THIS MAN REALLY IS UNFAIR... HE CAN TELL I'M DRIFTING AWAY FROM HIM, YET HE DOESN'T CENSURE ME FOR IT, BUT LAUGHS AND SAYS SOMETHING LIKE THIS...
DON'T BE SILLY, SHUICHI-SAN.
IT'S YOUR IMAGINATION. BUT THIS MAKES ME SO HAPPY. THANK YOU.
OKAY... 7 PM ON THE 25TH.
SEE YOU.
PLIP!
IT'S NOT THAT I DON'T LIKE HIM ANYMORE, BUT WHAT'S THE POINT IN CONTINUING THIS FUTILE RELATIONSHIP...?
OH, BUT WAIT -- MAYBE SHUICHI-SAN REALLY WILL LEAVE HIS WIFE...?
NO, YOU IDIOT! HOW MANY TIMES ARE YOU GOING TO BE DECEIVED BY THAT PROMISE?!
OHHH... AM I REALLY GOING TO GO TO HIM ON THE 25TH? AM I?!
YOU PROBABLY WON'T ARRIVE, CHRISTMAS EVE ALL ON MY OWN, SILENT NIGHT...
...!
OH...!
I'VE GOT IT!!

WHY HERE AND NOT THE FACULTY LOUNGE?
JUST BECAUSE.
DECEMBER 25TH -- HAVE YOU GOT PLANS?
NO.
TH... THEN GO OUT TO DINNER WITH ME!!
HUH?!
O-ON THE MID-TERMS THIS TIME... YOU DIDN'T HAVE ANY RED MARKS, RIGHT? SO THIS IS YOUR REWARD.
I STUDIED BECAUSE I WOULDN'T BE ABLE TO GET TO THE WINTER COMIKET IF I HAD TO TAKE YEAR-END MAKE-UP LESSONS.
A- ANYWAY !!
YOU CAN EAT ANYTHING YOU WANT... SUSHI, GRILLED BEEF -- MY TREAT!
OKAY? IT'S NOT A BAD DEAL, IS IT?!

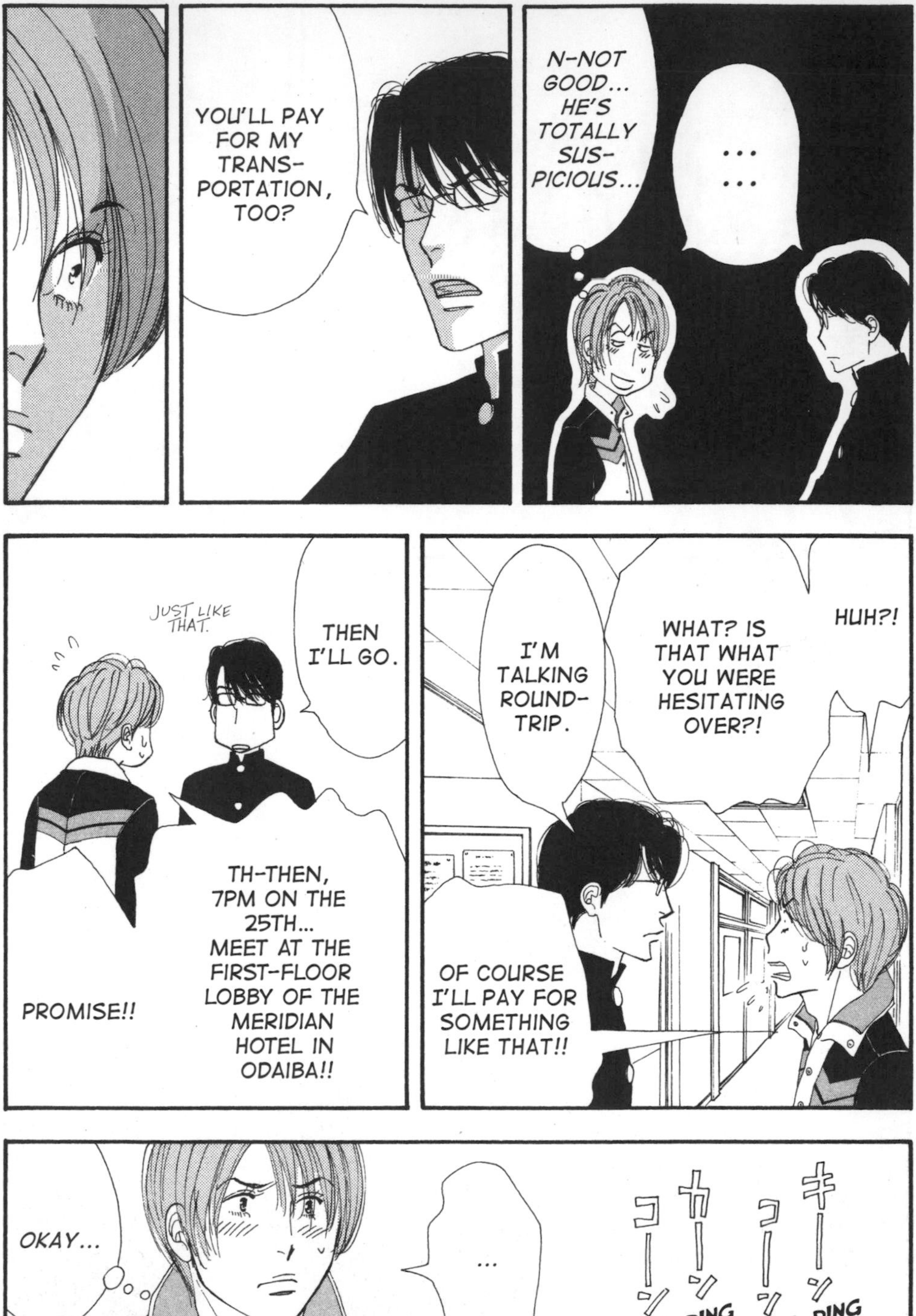
. . .
. . .
N-NOT GOOD... HE'S TOTALLY SUS-PICIOUS...
YOU'LL PAY FOR MY TRANS-PORTATION, TOO?
HUH?!
WHAT? IS THAT WHAT YOU WERE HESITATING OVER?!
I'M TALKING ROUND-TRIP.
OF COURSE I'LL PAY FOR SOMETHING LIKE THAT!!
THEN I'LL GO.
JUST LIKE THAT.
TH-THEN, 7PM ON THE 25TH... MEET AT THE FIRST-FLOOR LOBBY OF THE MERIDIAN HOTEL IN ODAIBA!!
PROMISE!!
キーンコーン
DING DONG
カーンコーン
DING DONG
...
OKAY...

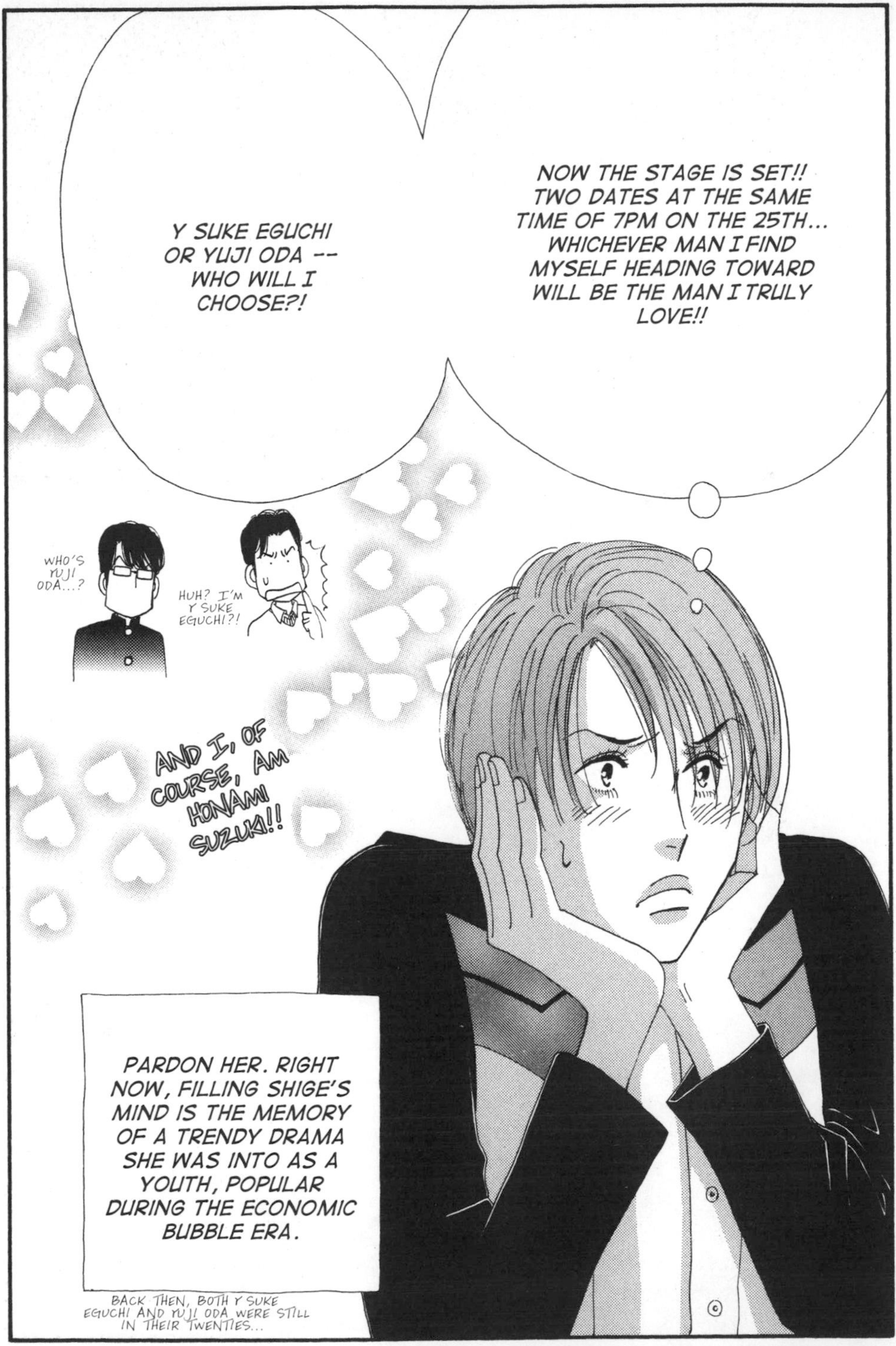
NOW THE STAGE IS SET!! TWO DATES AT THE SAME TIME OF 7PM ON THE 25TH... WHICHEVER MAN I FIND MYSELF HEADING TOWARD WILL BE THE MAN I TRULY LOVE!!
Y SUKE EGUCHI OR YUJI ODA -- WHO WILL I CHOOSE?!
HUH? I'M Y SUKE EGUCHI?!
WHO'S YUJI ODA...?
AND I, OF COURSE, AM HONAMI SUZUKI!!
PARDON HER. RIGHT NOW, FILLING SHIGE'S MIND IS THE MEMORY OF A TRENDY DRAMA SHE WAS INTO AS A YOUTH, POPULAR DURING THE ECONOMIC BUBBLE ERA.
BACK THEN, BOTH Y SUKE EGUCHI AND YUJI ODA WERE STILL IN THEIR TWENTIES...

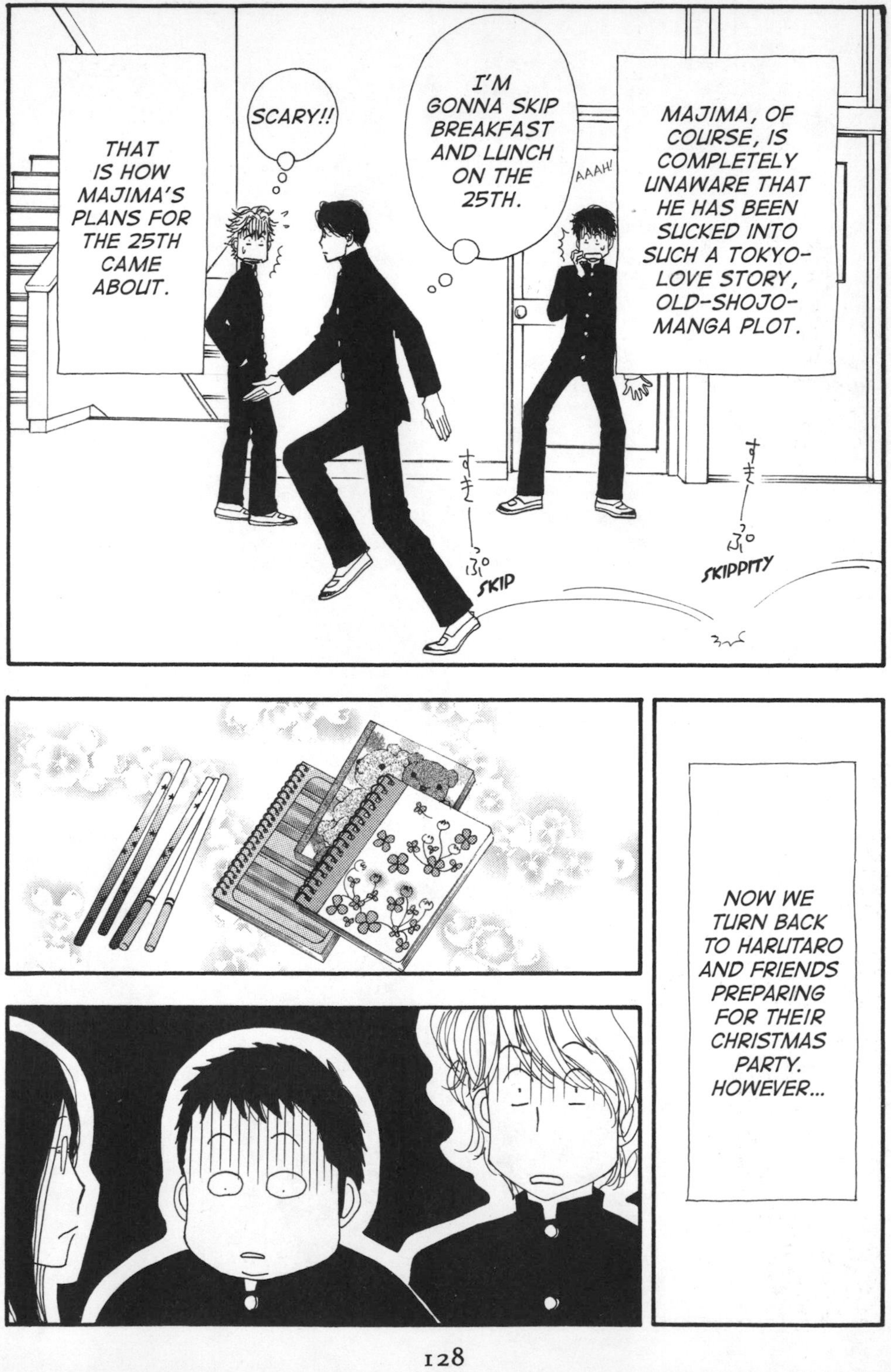
MAJIMA, OF COURSE, IS COMPLETELY UNAWARE THAT HE HAS BEEN SUCKED INTO SUCH A TOKYO-LOVE STORY, OLD-SHOJO-MANGA PLOT.
AAAH!
I'M GONNA SKIP BREAKFAST AND LUNCH ON THE 25TH.
SCARY!!
THAT IS HOW MAJIMA'S PLANS FOR THE 25TH CAME ABOUT.
すきーぷ
SKIPPITY
すきーぷ
SKIP
NOW WE TURN BACK TO HARUTARO AND FRIENDS PREPARING FOR THEIR CHRISTMAS PARTY. HOWEVER...

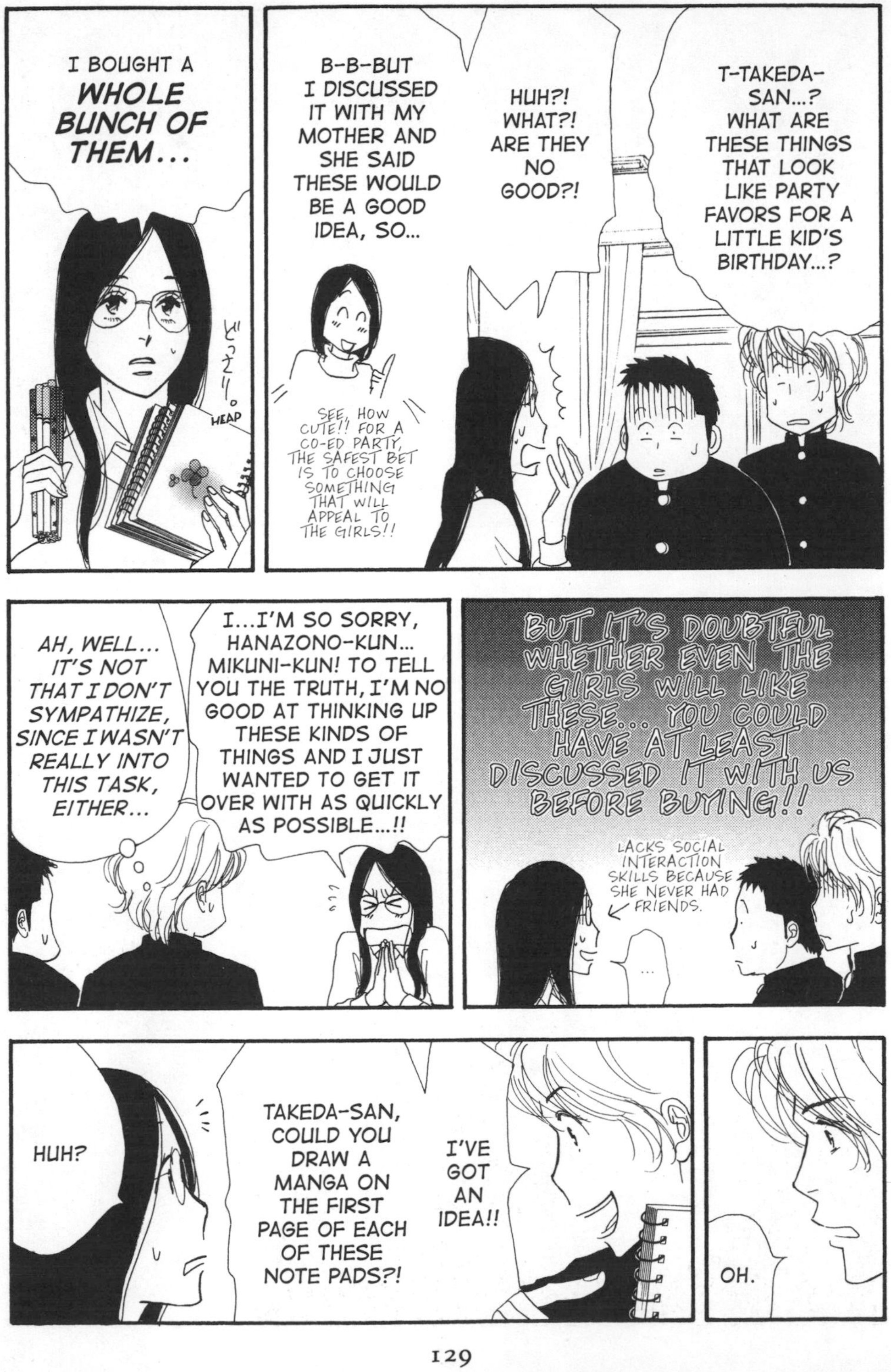
T-TAKEDA-SAN...? WHAT ARE THESE THINGS THAT LOOK LIKE PARTY FAVORS FOR A LITTLE KID'S BIRTHDAY...?
HUH?! WHAT?! ARE THEY NO GOOD?!
B-B-BUT I DISCUSSED IT WITH MY MOTHER AND SHE SAID THESE WOULD BE A GOOD IDEA, SO...
SEE, HOW CUTE!! FOR A CO-ED PARTY, THE SAFEST BET IS TO CHOOSE SOMETHING THAT WILL APPEAL TO THE GIRLS!!
I BOUGHT A WHOLE BUNCH OF THEM...
どっさり。
HEAP
BUT IT'S DOUBTFUL WHETHER EVEN THE GIRLS WILL LIKE THESE... YOU COULD HAVE AT LEAST DISCUSSED IT WITH US BEFORE BUYING!!
LACKS SOCIAL INTERACTION SKILLS BECAUSE SHE NEVER HAD FRIENDS.
...
I...I'M SO SORRY, HANAZONO-KUN... MIKUNI-KUN! TO TELL YOU THE TRUTH, I'M NO GOOD AT THINKING UP THESE KINDS OF THINGS AND I JUST WANTED TO GET IT OVER WITH AS QUICKLY AS POSSIBLE...!!
AH, WELL... IT'S NOT THAT I DON'T SYMPATHIZE, SINCE I WASN'T REALLY INTO THIS TASK, EITHER...
OH.
I'VE GOT AN IDEA!!
TAKEDA-SAN, COULD YOU DRAW A MANGA ON THE FIRST PAGE OF EACH OF THESE NOTE PADS?!
HUH?

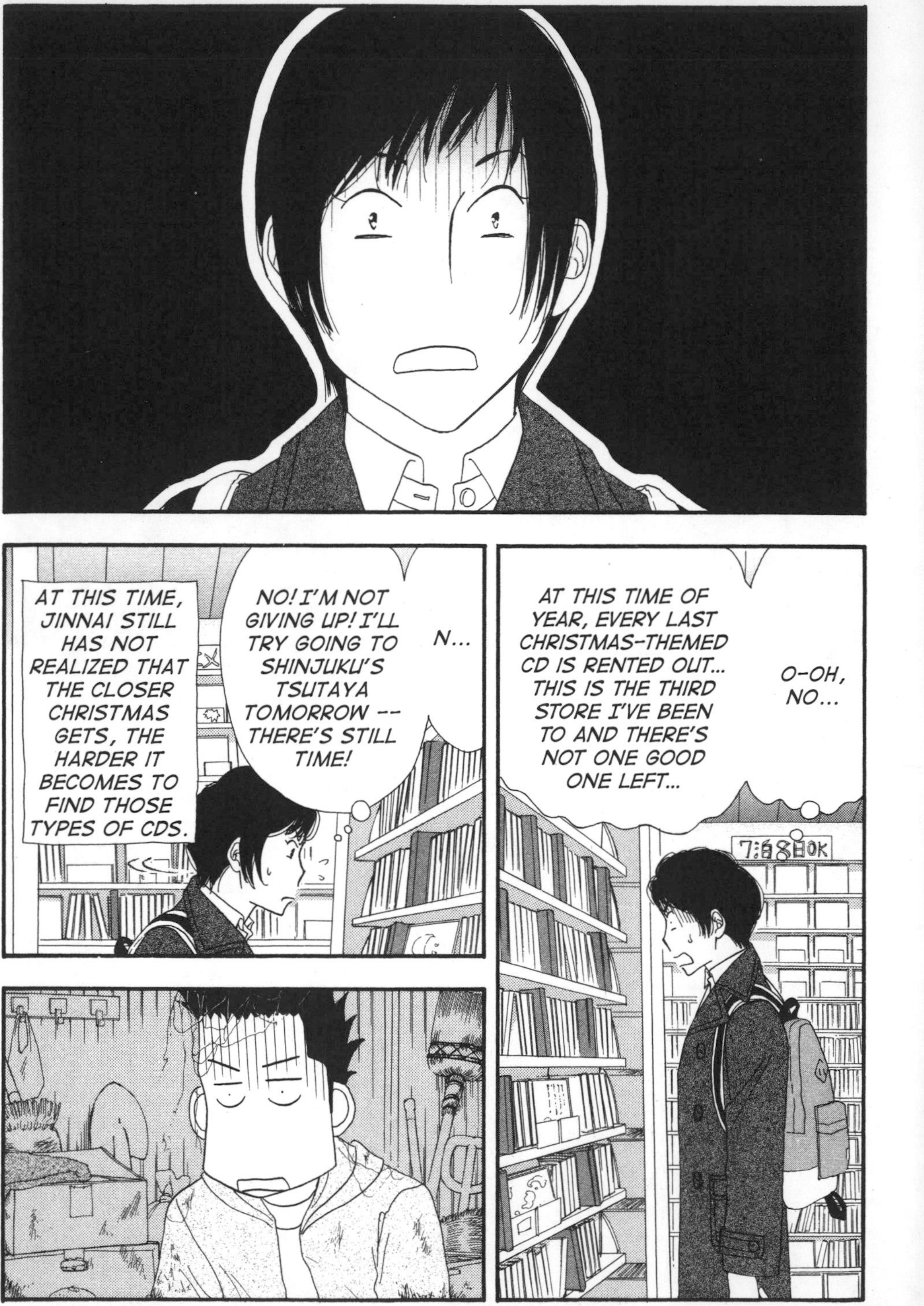
O-OH, NO...
AT THIS TIME OF YEAR, EVERY LAST CHRISTMAS-THEMED CD IS RENTED OUT... THIS IS THE THIRD STORE I'VE BEEN TO AND THERE'S NOT ONE GOOD ONE LEFT...
N...
NO! I'M NOT GIVING UP! I'LL TRY GOING TO SHINJUKU'S TSUTAYA TOMORROW -- THERE'S STILL TIME!
AT THIS TIME, JINNAI STILL HAS NOT REALIZED THAT THE CLOSER CHRISTMAS GETS, THE HARDER IT BECOMES TO FIND THOSE TYPES OF CDS.

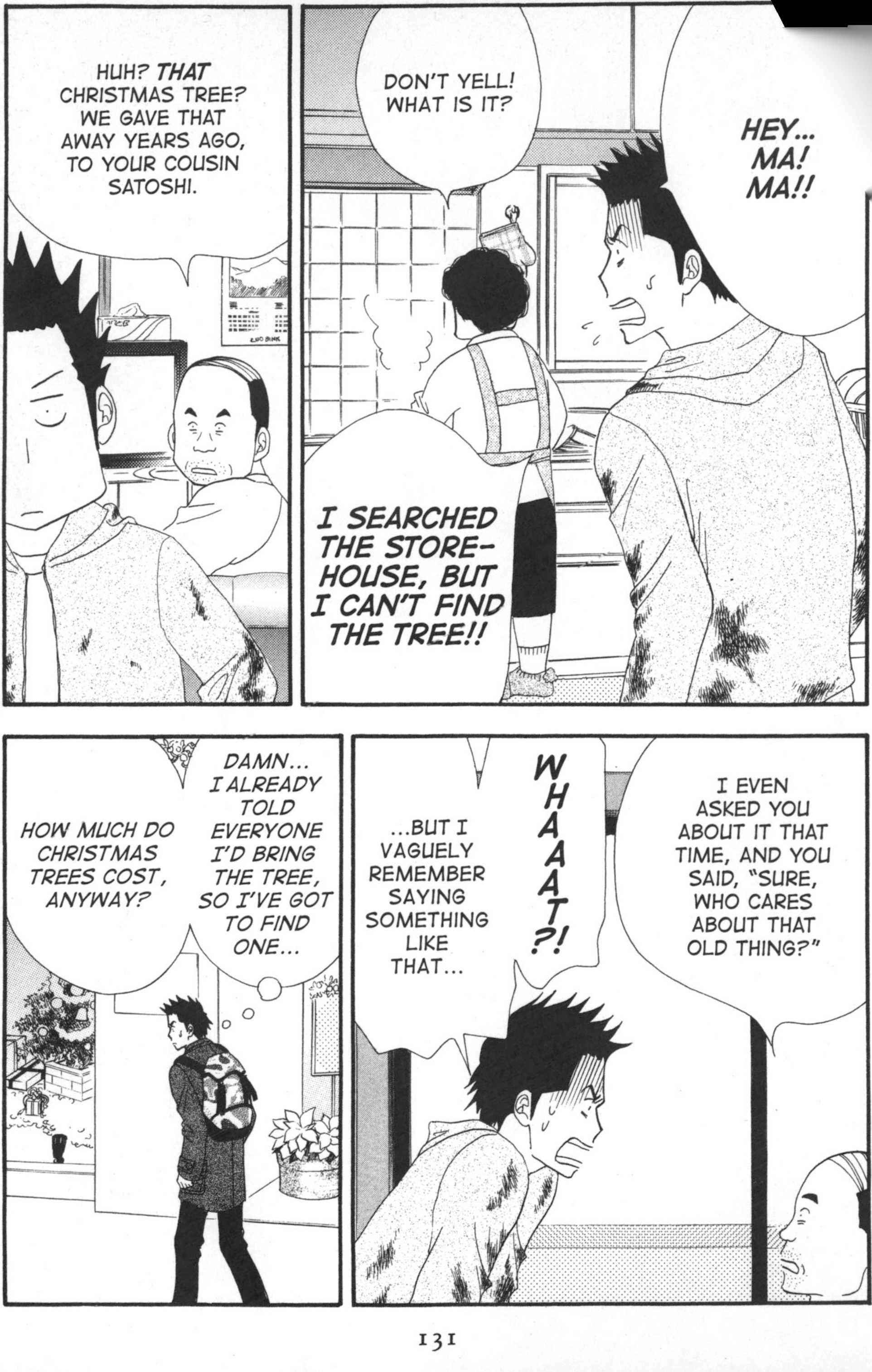
HEY... MA! MA!!
DON'T YELL! WHAT IS IT?
I SEARCHED THE STORE-HOUSE, BUT I CAN'T FIND THE TREE!!
HUH? *THAT* CHRISTMAS TREE? WE GAVE THAT AWAY YEARS AGO, TO YOUR COUSIN SATOSHI.
I EVEN ASKED YOU ABOUT IT THAT TIME, AND YOU SAID, "SURE, WHO CARES ABOUT THAT OLD THING?"
WHAAAT?!
...BUT I VAGUELY REMEMBER SAYING SOMETHING LIKE THAT...
DAMN... I ALREADY TOLD EVERYONE I'D BRING THE TREE, SO I'VE GOT TO FIND ONE...
HOW MUCH DO CHRISTMAS TREES COST, ANYWAY?

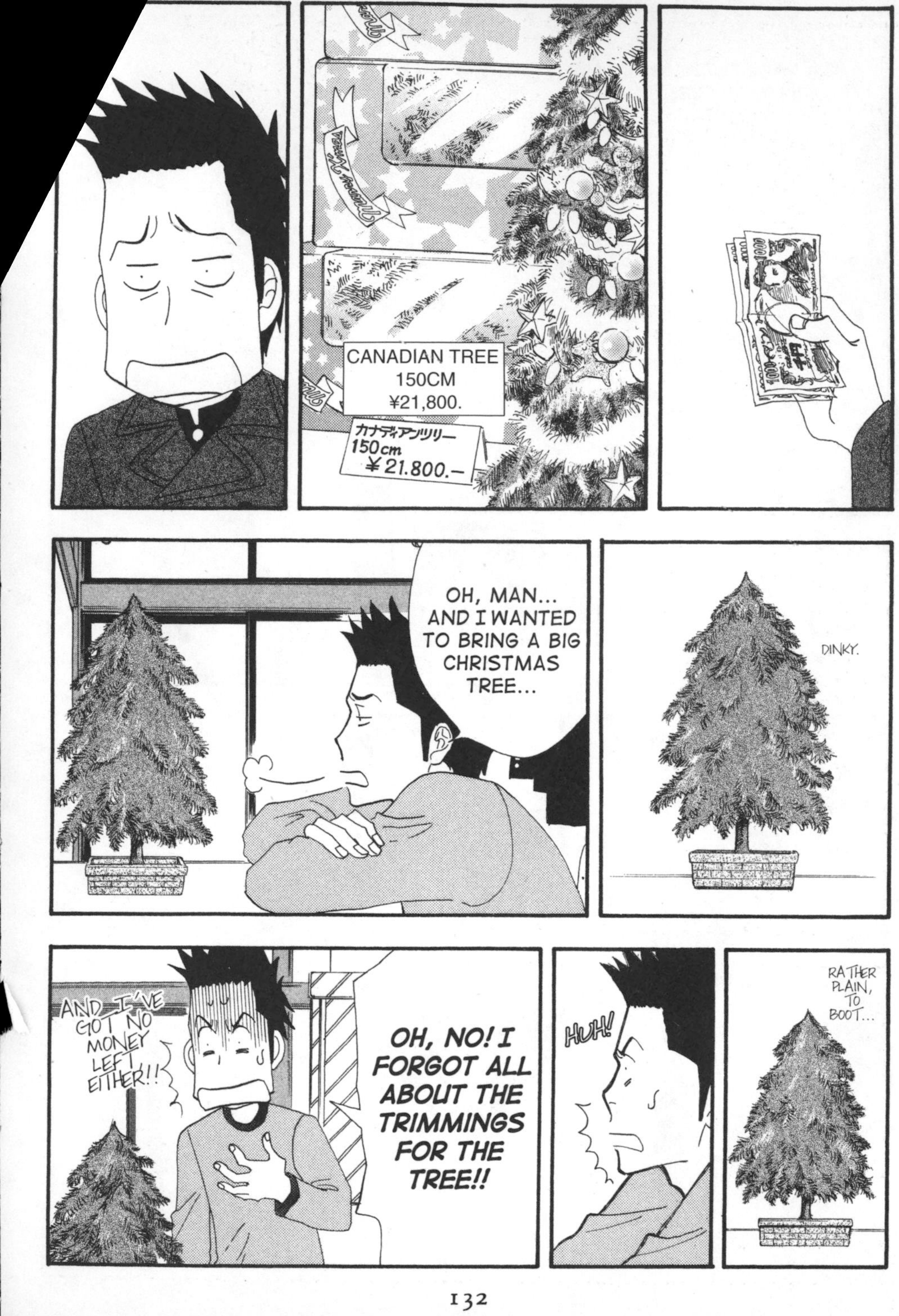
CANADIAN TREE
150CM
¥21,800.
カナディアンツリー
150cm
¥21.800.–
DINKY.
OH, MAN... AND I WANTED TO BRING A BIG CHRISTMAS TREE...
RATHER PLAIN, TO BOOT...
HUH!
OH, NO! I FORGOT ALL ABOUT THE TRIMMINGS FOR THE TREE!!
AND I'VE GOT NO MONEY LEFT EITHER!!

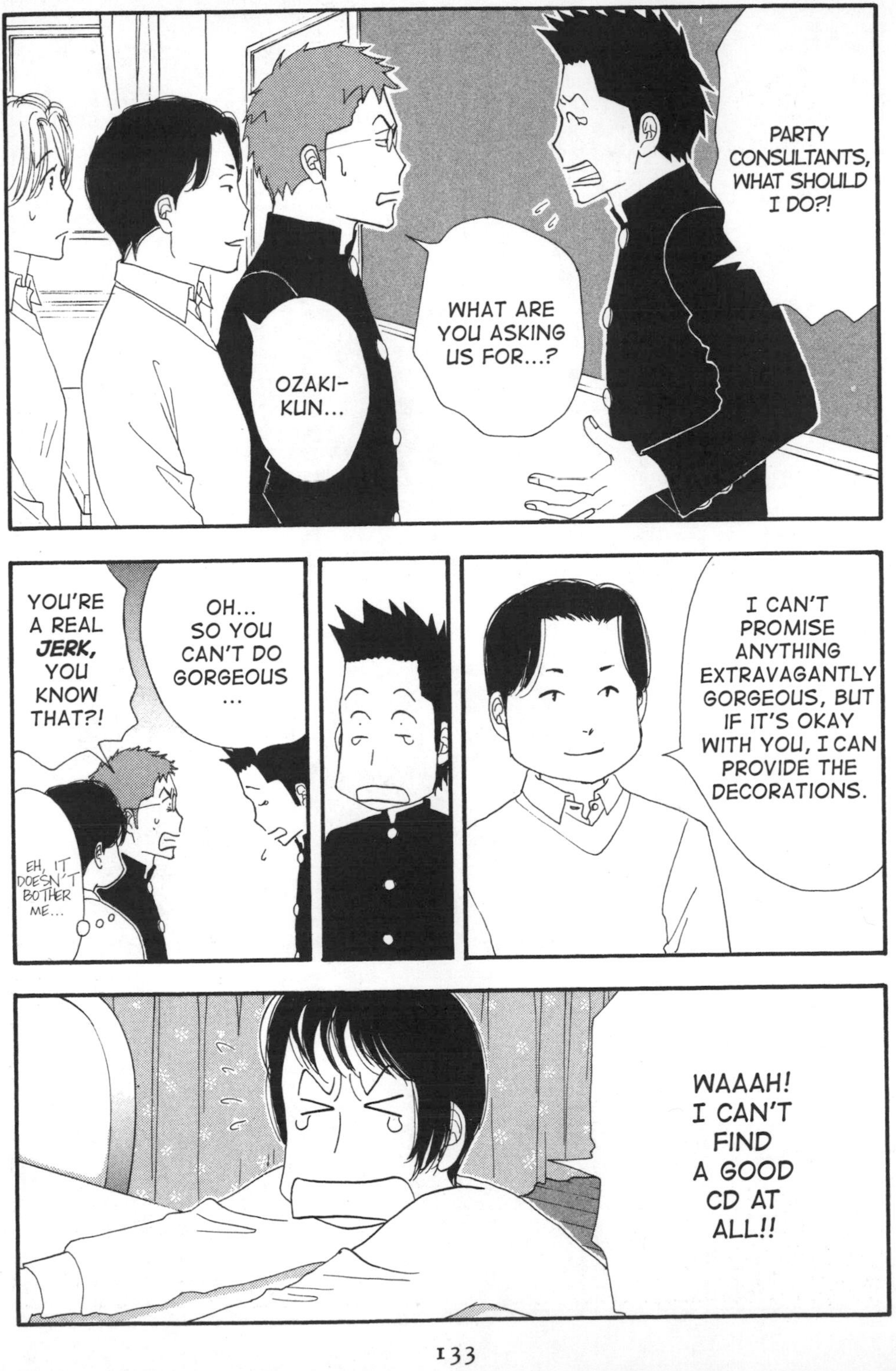
PARTY CONSULTANTS, WHAT SHOULD I DO?!
WHAT ARE YOU ASKING US FOR...?
OZAKI-KUN...
I CAN'T PROMISE ANYTHING EXTRAVAGANTLY GORGEOUS, BUT IF IT'S OKAY WITH YOU, I CAN PROVIDE THE DECORATIONS.
OH... SO YOU CAN'T DO GORGEOUS ...
YOU'RE A REAL **JERK,** YOU KNOW THAT?!
EH, IT DOESN'T BOTHER ME...
WAAAH! I CAN'T FIND A GOOD CD AT ALL!!

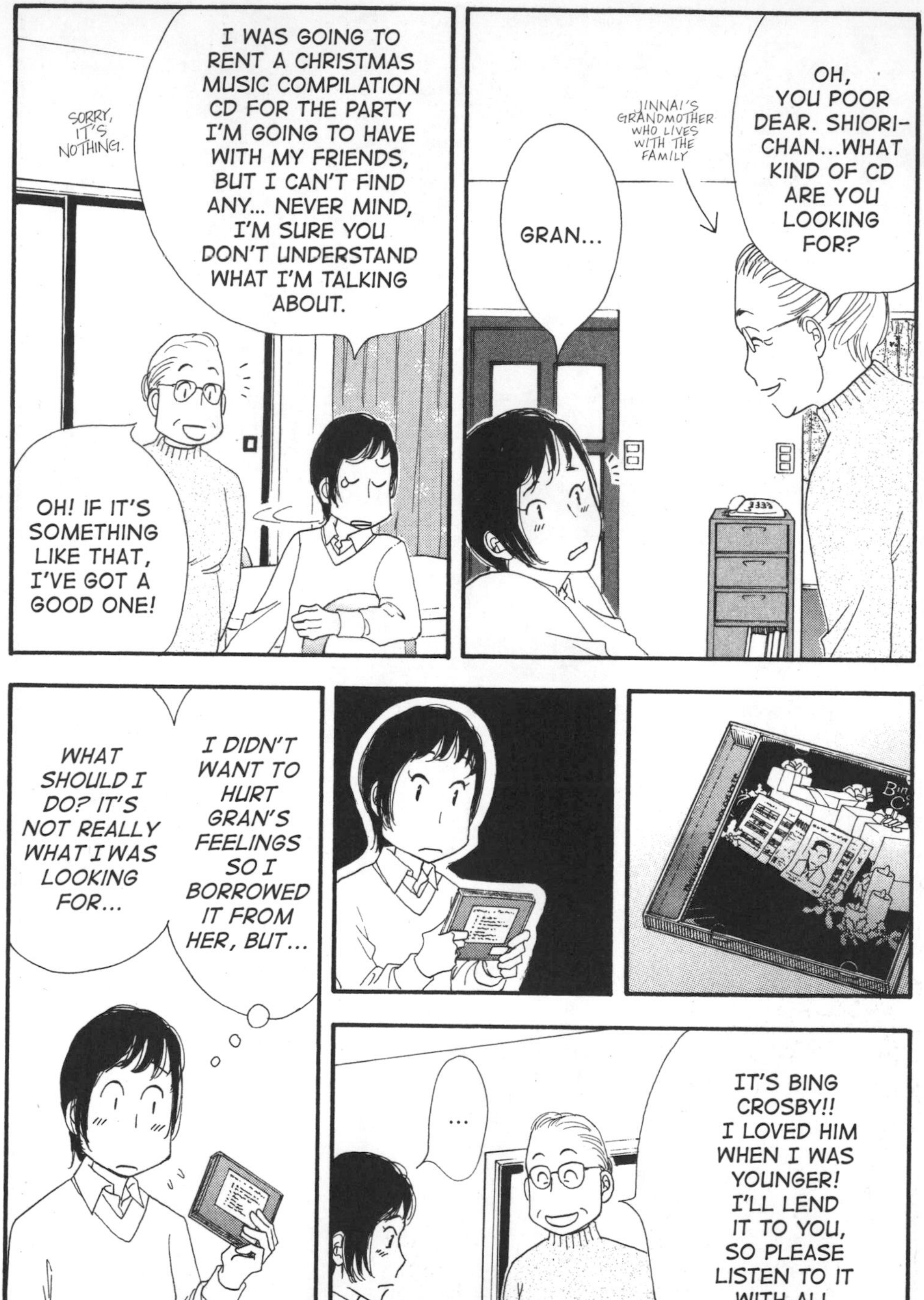
OH, YOU POOR DEAR. SHIORI-CHAN...WHAT KIND OF CD ARE YOU LOOKING FOR?
JINNAI'S GRANDMOTHER WHO LIVES WITH THE FAMILY
GRAN...
I WAS GOING TO RENT A CHRISTMAS MUSIC COMPILATION CD FOR THE PARTY I'M GOING TO HAVE WITH MY FRIENDS, BUT I CAN'T FIND ANY... NEVER MIND, I'M SURE YOU DON'T UNDERSTAND WHAT I'M TALKING ABOUT.
SORRY, IT'S NOTHING.
OH! IF IT'S SOMETHING LIKE THAT, I'VE GOT A GOOD ONE!
IT'S BING CROSBY!! I LOVED HIM WHEN I WAS YOUNGER! I'LL LEND IT TO YOU, SO PLEASE LISTEN TO IT WITH ALL YOUR FRIENDS.
...
I DIDN'T WANT TO HURT GRAN'S FEELINGS SO I BORROWED IT FROM HER, BUT...
WHAT SHOULD I DO? IT'S NOT REALLY WHAT I WAS LOOKING FOR...

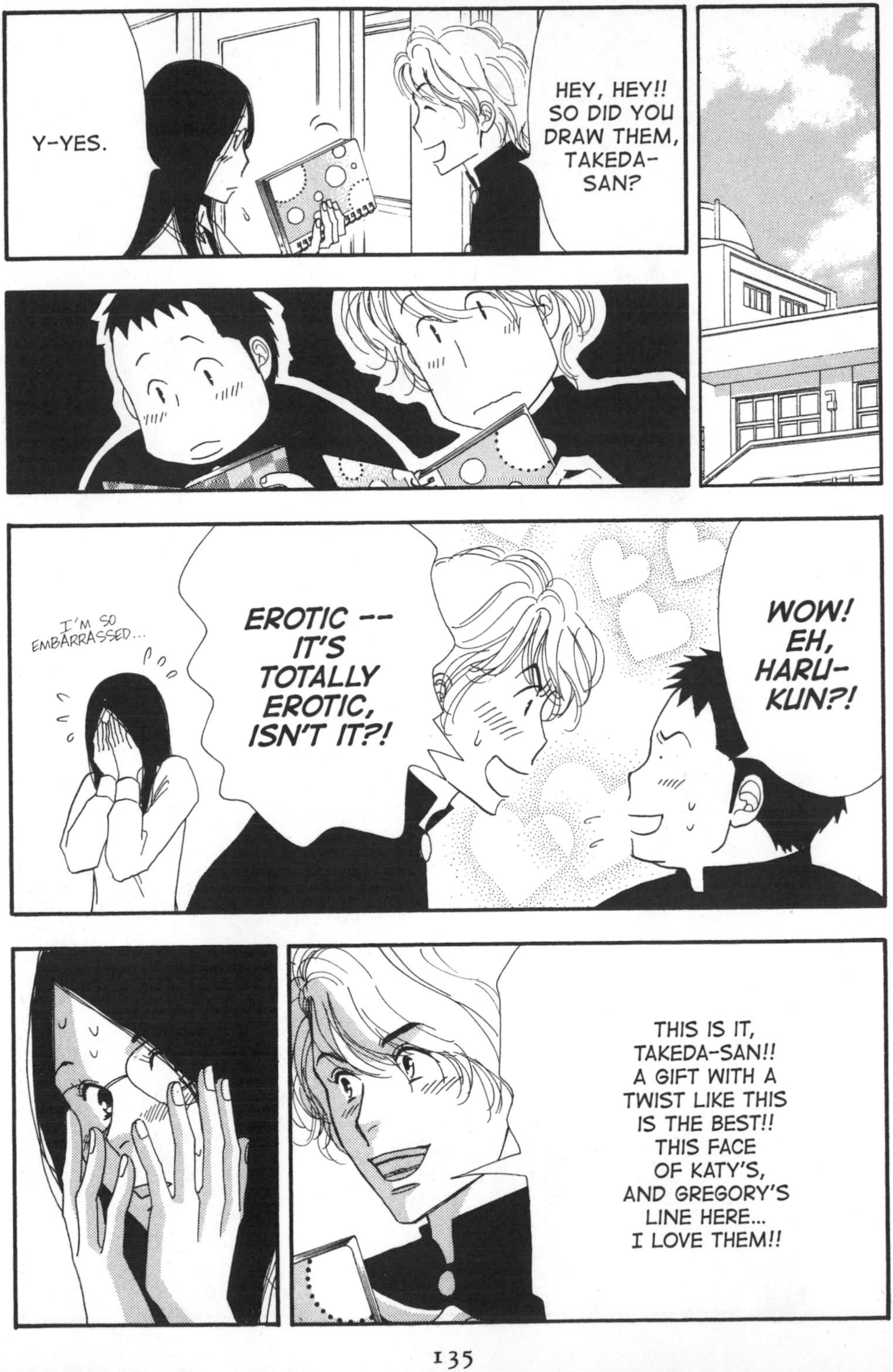
HEY, HEY!! SO DID YOU DRAW THEM, TAKEDA-SAN?
Y-YES.
WOW! EH, HARU-KUN?!
EROTIC -- IT'S TOTALLY EROTIC, ISN'T IT?!
I'M SO EMBARRASSED...
THIS IS IT, TAKEDA-SAN!! A GIFT WITH A TWIST LIKE THIS IS THE BEST!! THIS FACE OF KATY'S, AND GREGORY'S LINE HERE... I LOVE THEM!!

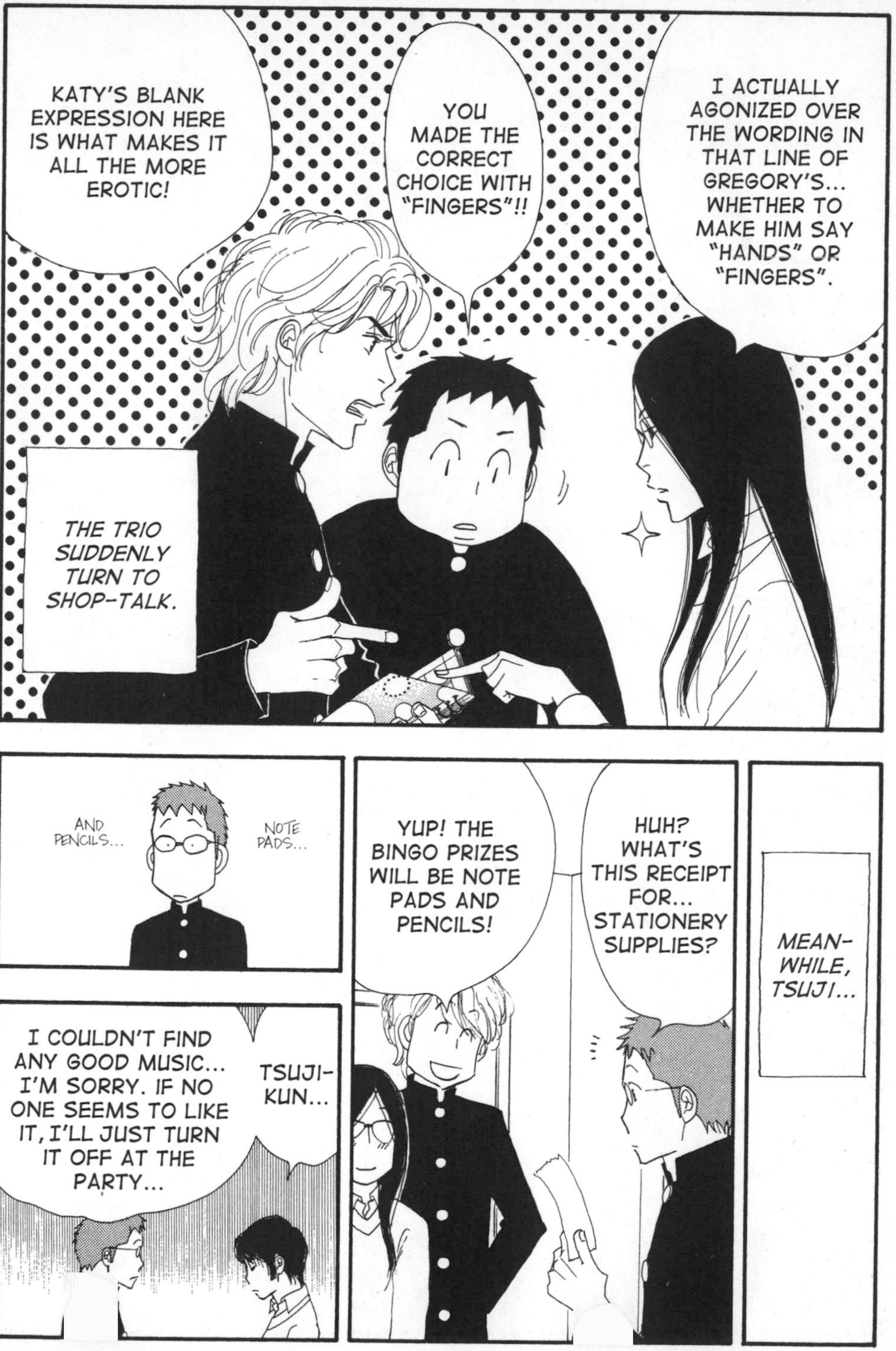
I ACTUALLY AGONIZED OVER THE WORDING IN THAT LINE OF GREGORY'S... WHETHER TO MAKE HIM SAY "HANDS" OR "FINGERS".
YOU MADE THE CORRECT CHOICE WITH "FINGERS"!!
KATY'S BLANK EXPRESSION HERE IS WHAT MAKES IT ALL THE MORE EROTIC!
THE TRIO SUDDENLY TURN TO SHOP-TALK.
MEAN-WHILE, TSUJI...
HUH? WHAT'S THIS RECEIPT FOR... STATIONERY SUPPLIES?
YUP! THE BINGO PRIZES WILL BE NOTE PADS AND PENCILS!
NOTE PADS...
AND PENCILS...
TSUJI-KUN...
I COULDN'T FIND ANY GOOD MUSIC... I'M SORRY. IF NO ONE SEEMS TO LIKE IT, I'LL JUST TURN IT OFF AT THE PARTY...

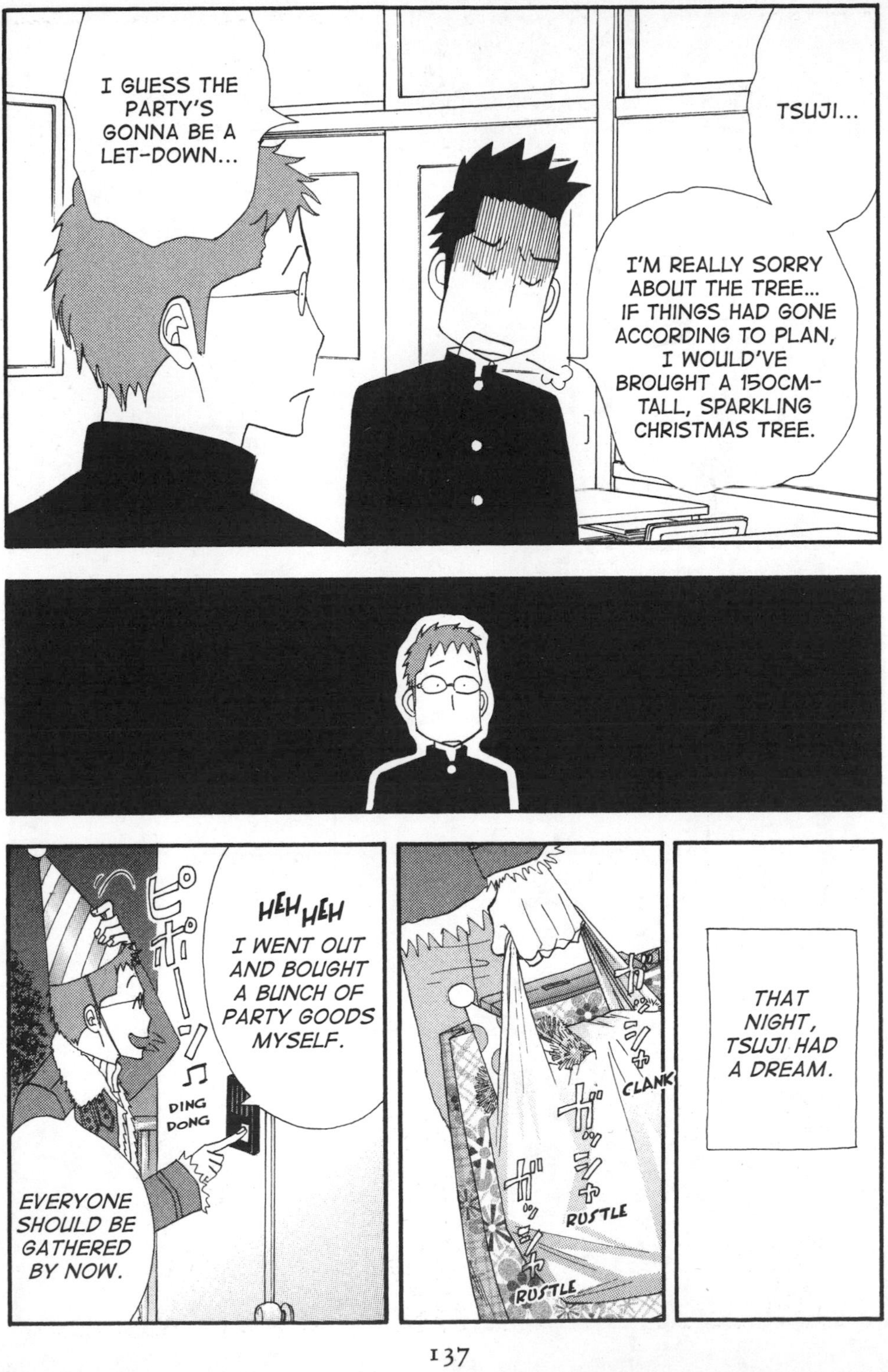
TSUJI...
I'M REALLY SORRY ABOUT THE TREE... IF THINGS HAD GONE ACCORDING TO PLAN, I WOULD'VE BROUGHT A 150CM-TALL, SPARKLING CHRISTMAS TREE.
I GUESS THE PARTY'S GONNA BE A LET-DOWN...
THAT NIGHT, TSUJI HAD A DREAM.
CLANK
RUSTLE
RUSTLE
HEH HEH
I WENT OUT AND BOUGHT A BUNCH OF PARTY GOODS MYSELF.
DING DONG
EVERYONE SHOULD BE GATHERED BY NOW.

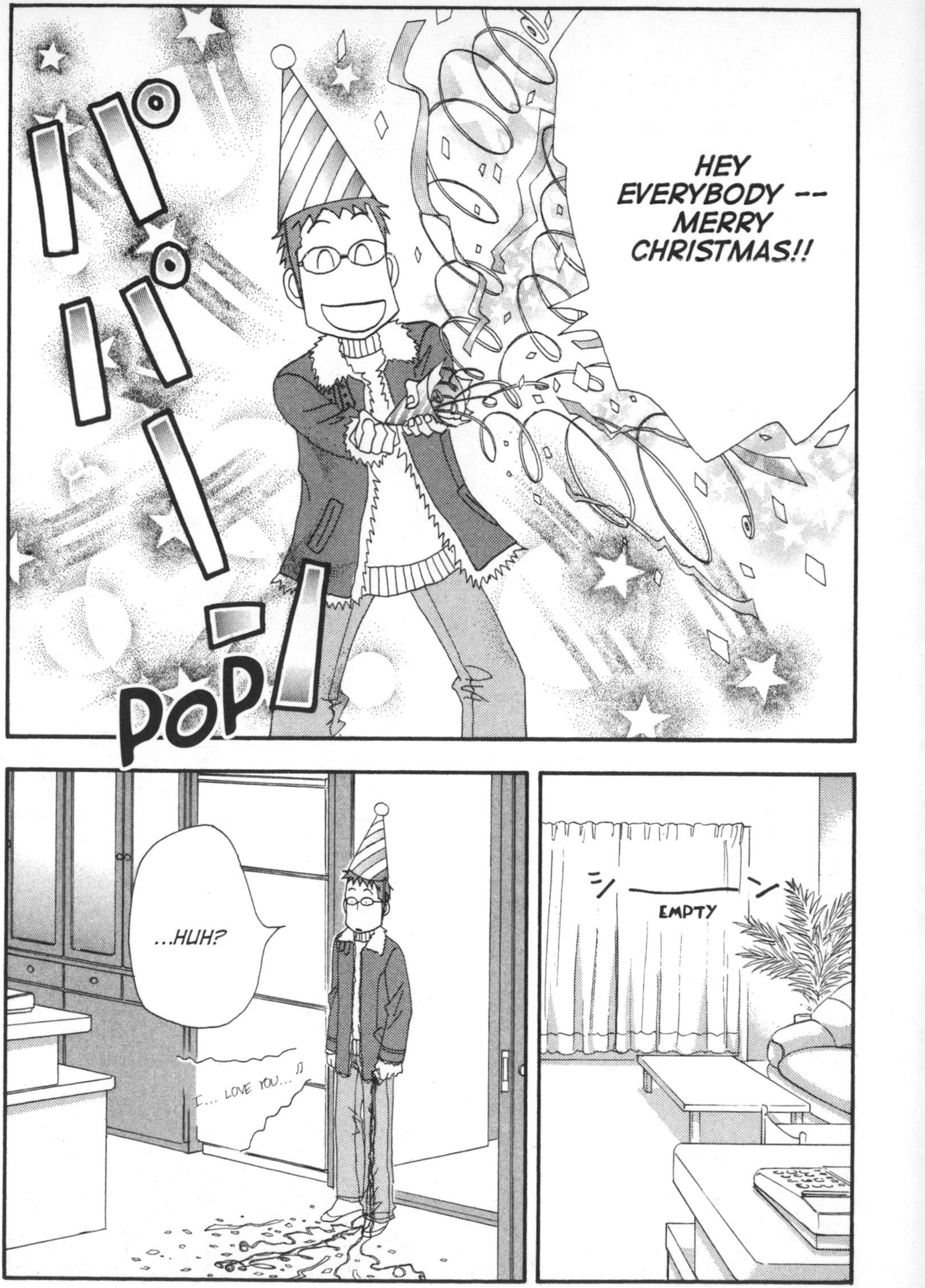
HEY EVERYBODY -- MERRY CHRISTMAS!!
POP
EMPTY
...HUH?
I... LOVE YOU... ♫

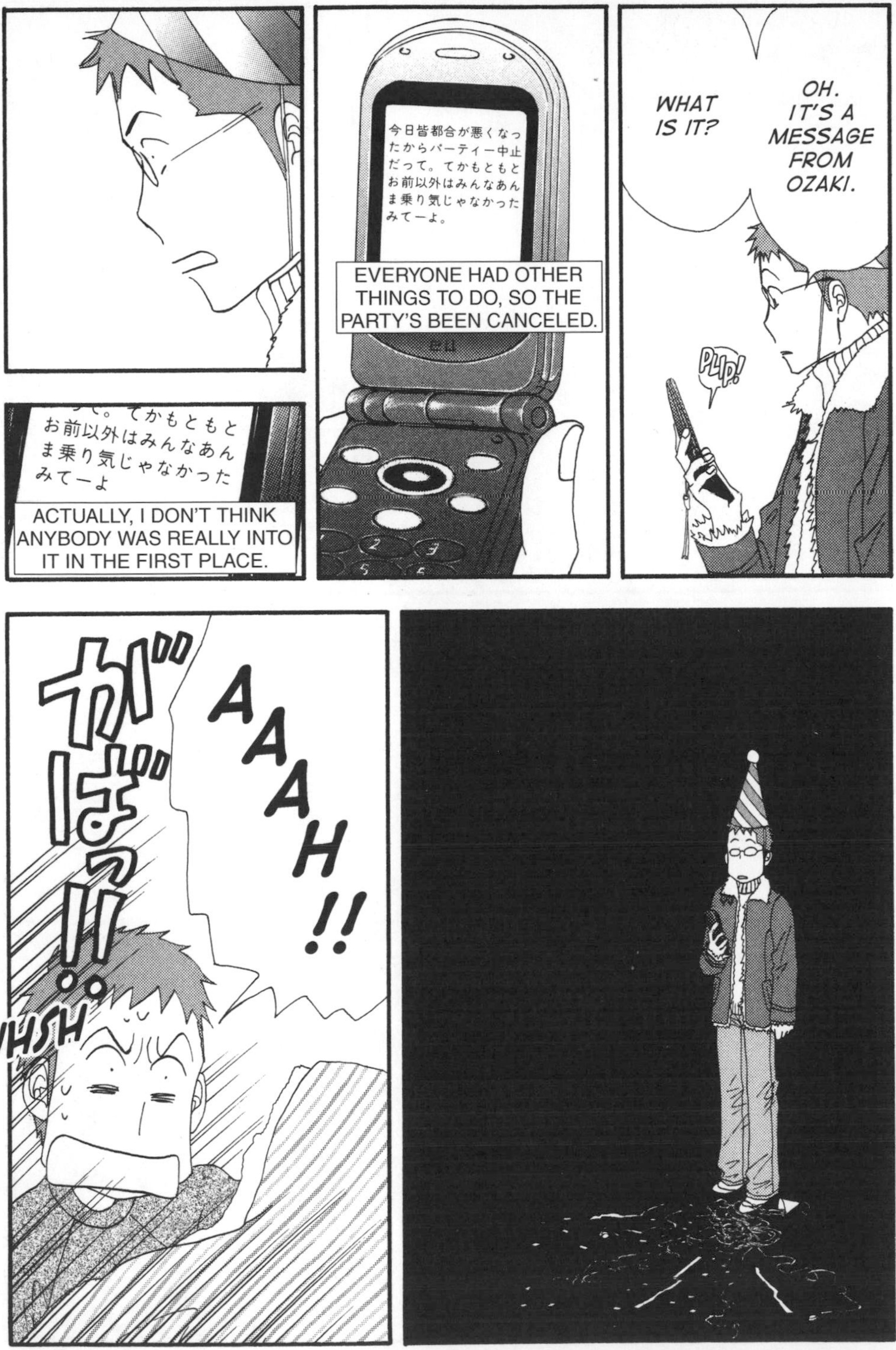
OH. IT'S A MESSAGE FROM OZAKI.
WHAT IS IT?
PLIP!
今日皆都合が悪くなったからパーティー中止だって。てかもともとお前以外はみんなあんま乗り気じゃなかったみてーよ。
EVERYONE HAD OTHER THINGS TO DO, SO THE PARTY'S BEEN CANCELED.
お前以外はみんなあんま乗り気じゃなかったみてーよ
ACTUALLY, I DON'T THINK ANYBODY WAS REALLY INTO IT IN THE FIRST PLACE.
がばっ!!
AAAAH!!
WHSH

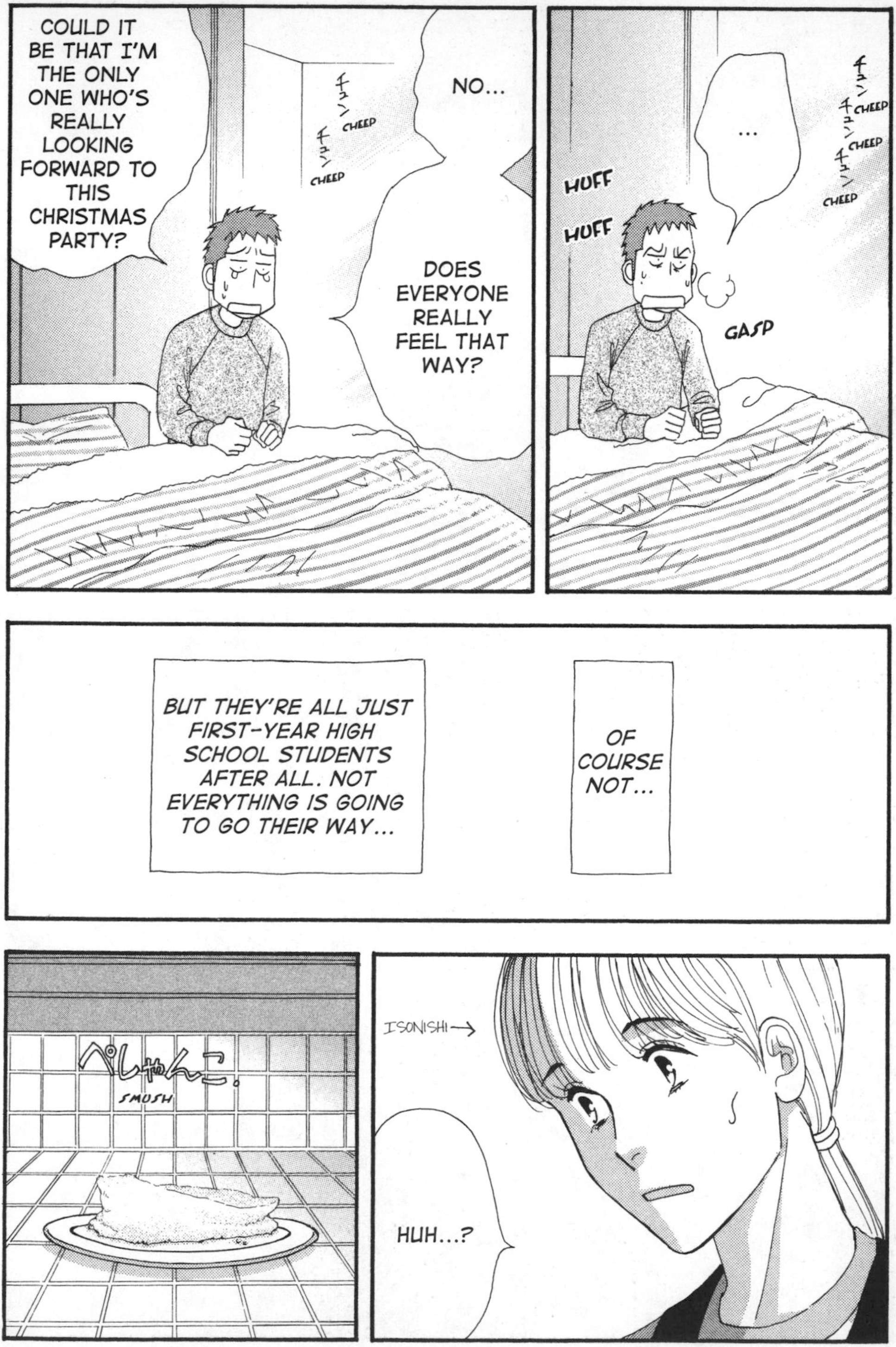
...
HUFF
HUFF
GASP
チュン CHEEP
チュン CHEEP
チュン CHEEP
COULD IT BE THAT I'M THE ONLY ONE WHO'S REALLY LOOKING FORWARD TO THIS CHRISTMAS PARTY?
NO...
チュン CHEEP
チュン CHEEP
DOES EVERYONE REALLY FEEL THAT WAY?
OF COURSE NOT...
BUT THEY'RE ALL JUST FIRST-YEAR HIGH SCHOOL STUDENTS AFTER ALL. NOT EVERYTHING IS GOING TO GO THEIR WAY...
ISONISHI→
HUH...?
ぺしゃんこ。
SMUSH

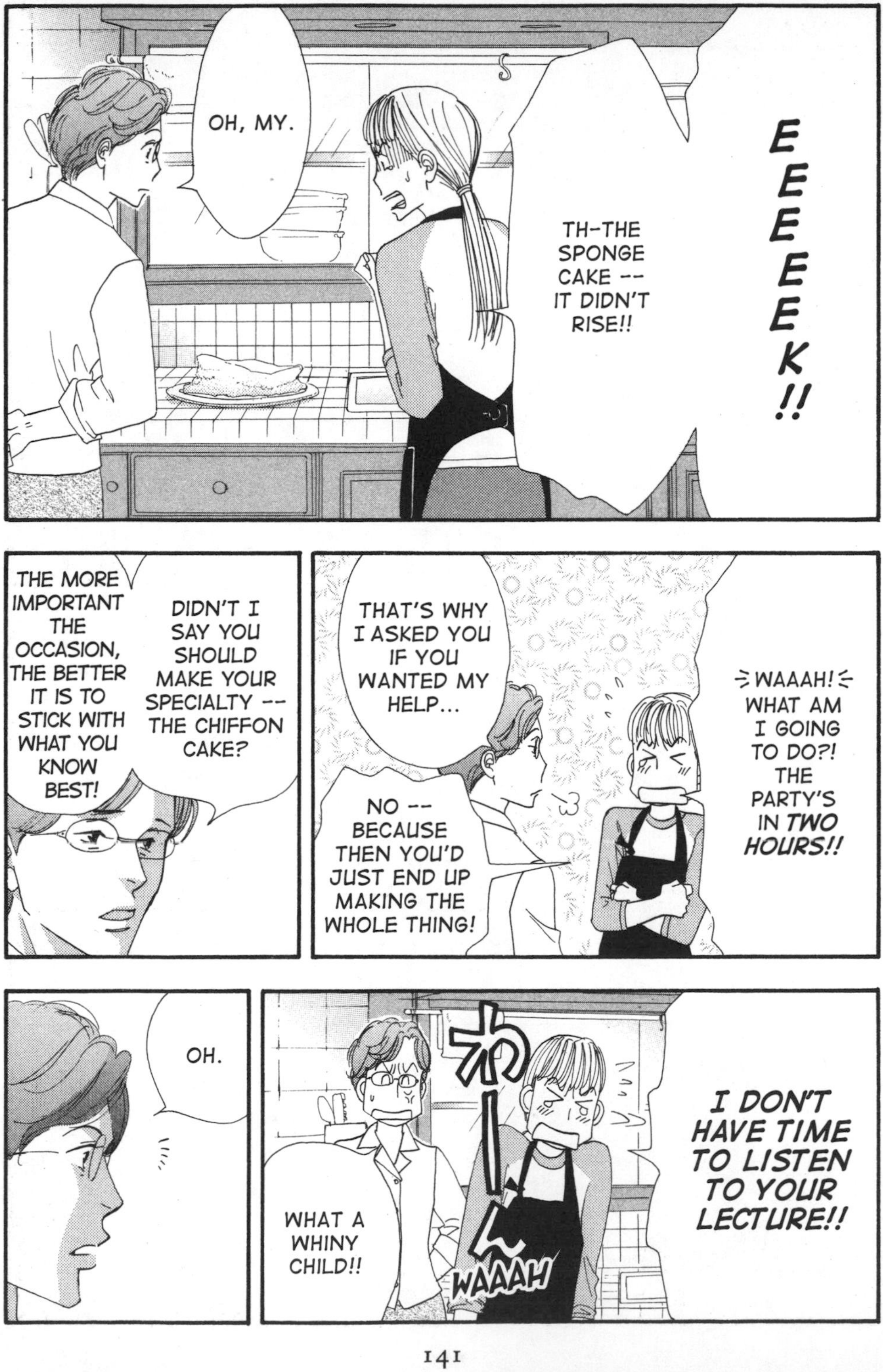
EEEEEK!!
TH-THE SPONGE CAKE -- IT DIDN'T RISE!!
OH, MY.
WAAAH! WHAT AM I GOING TO DO?! THE PARTY'S IN TWO HOURS!!
THAT'S WHY I ASKED YOU IF YOU WANTED MY HELP...
NO -- BECAUSE THEN YOU'D JUST END UP MAKING THE WHOLE THING!
DIDN'T I SAY YOU SHOULD MAKE YOUR SPECIALTY -- THE CHIFFON CAKE?
THE MORE IMPORTANT THE OCCASION, THE BETTER IT IS TO STICK WITH WHAT YOU KNOW BEST!
I DON'T HAVE TIME TO LISTEN TO YOUR LECTURE!!
わーん
WAAAH
WHAT A WHINY CHILD!!
OH.

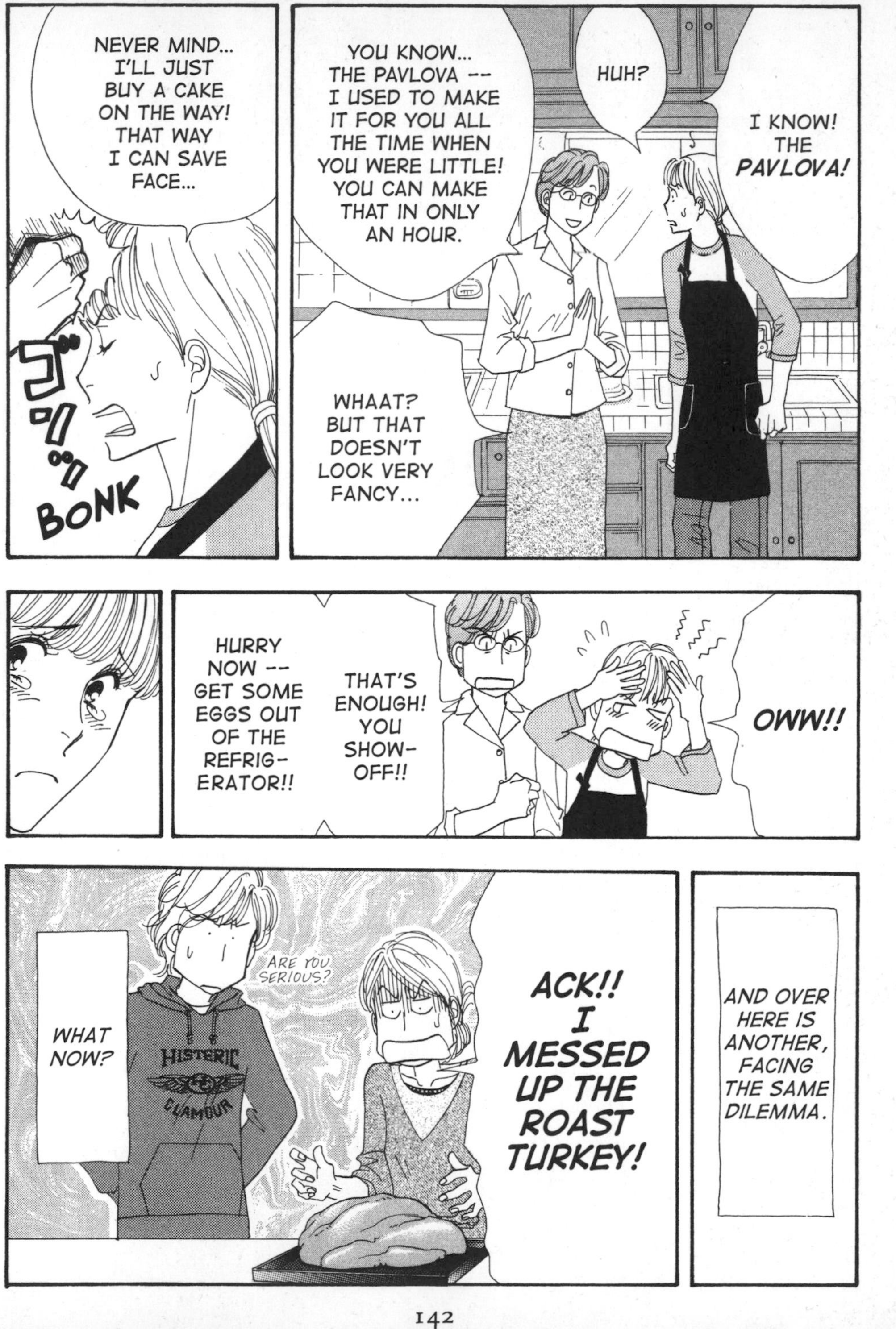
I KNOW! THE PAVLOVA!
HUH?
YOU KNOW... THE PAVLOVA -- I USED TO MAKE IT FOR YOU ALL THE TIME WHEN YOU WERE LITTLE! YOU CAN MAKE THAT IN ONLY AN HOUR.
WHAAT? BUT THAT DOESN'T LOOK VERY FANCY...
NEVER MIND... I'LL JUST BUY A CAKE ON THE WAY! THAT WAY I CAN SAVE FACE...
BONK
OWW!!
THAT'S ENOUGH! YOU SHOW-OFF!!
HURRY NOW -- GET SOME EGGS OUT OF THE REFRIG-ERATOR!!
AND OVER HERE IS ANOTHER, FACING THE SAME DILEMMA.
ACK!! I MESSED UP THE ROAST TURKEY!
ARE YOU SERIOUS?
WHAT NOW?

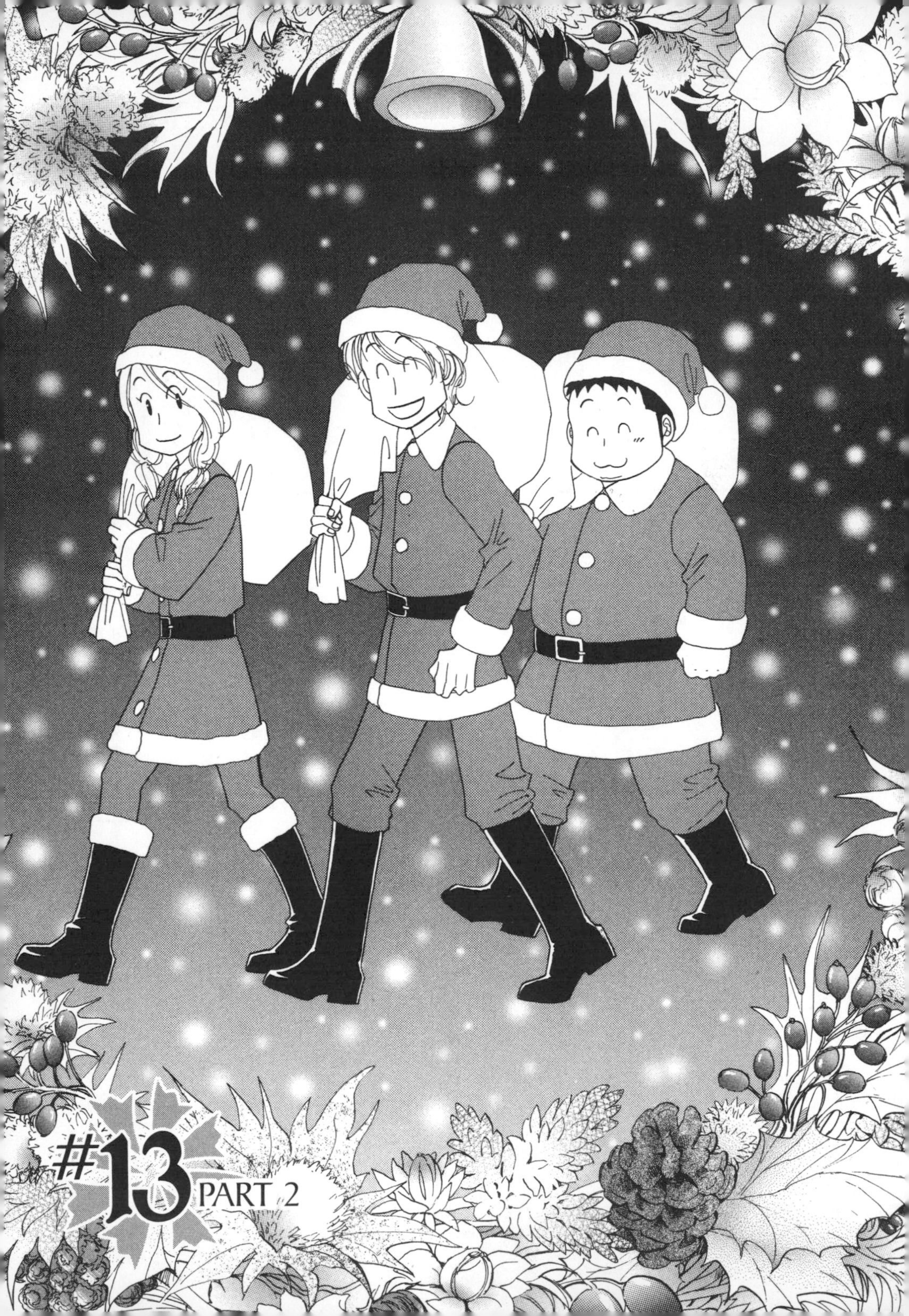
#13 PART 2

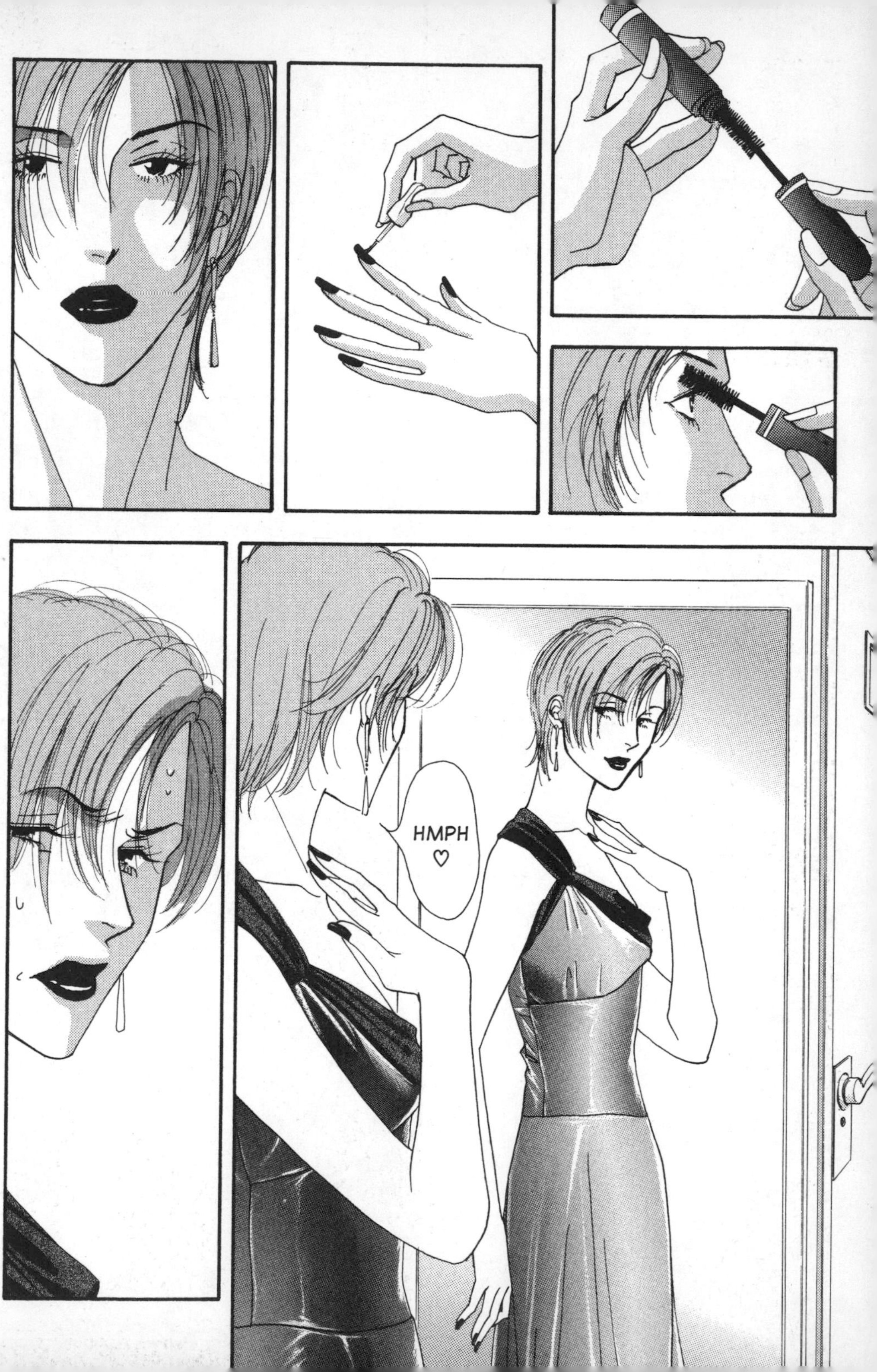
HMPH ♡

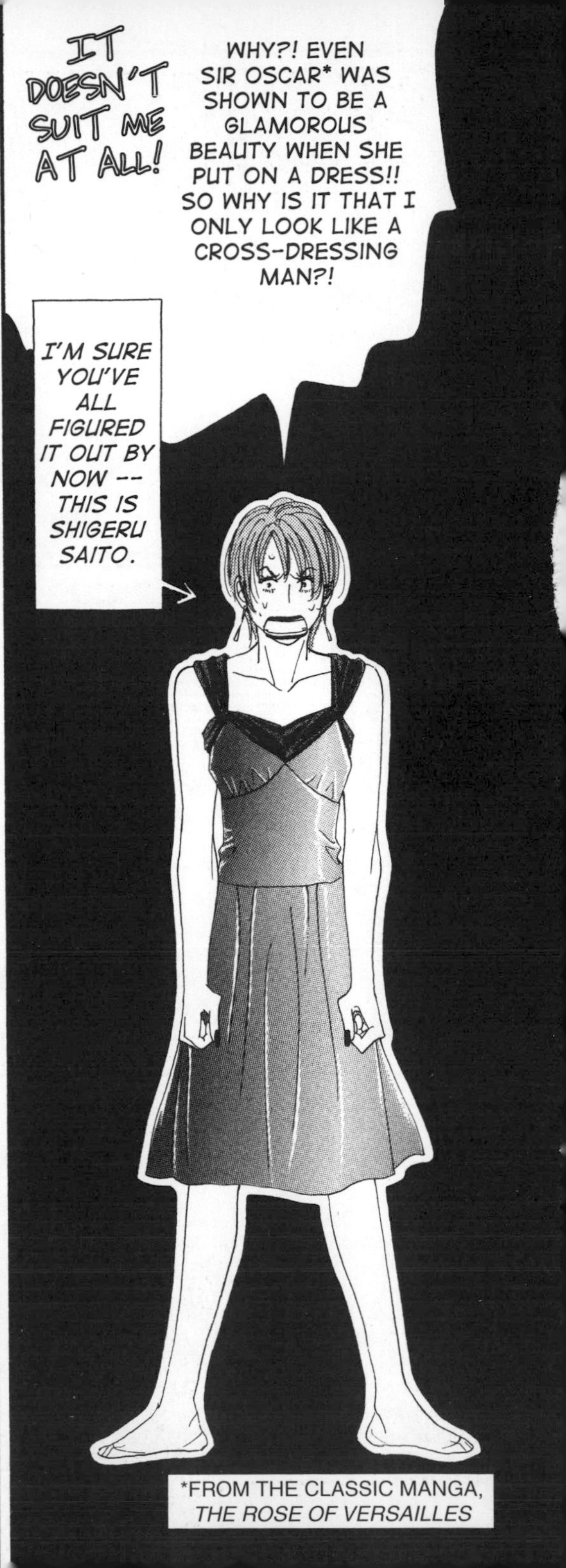
WHY?! EVEN SIR OSCAR* WAS SHOWN TO BE A GLAMOROUS BEAUTY WHEN SHE PUT ON A DRESS!! SO WHY IS IT THAT I ONLY LOOK LIKE A CROSS-DRESSING MAN?!
IT DOESN'T SUIT ME AT ALL!
I'M SURE YOU'VE ALL FIGURED IT OUT BY NOW -- THIS IS SHIGERU SAITO.

*FROM THE CLASSIC MANGA, *THE ROSE OF VERSAILLES*

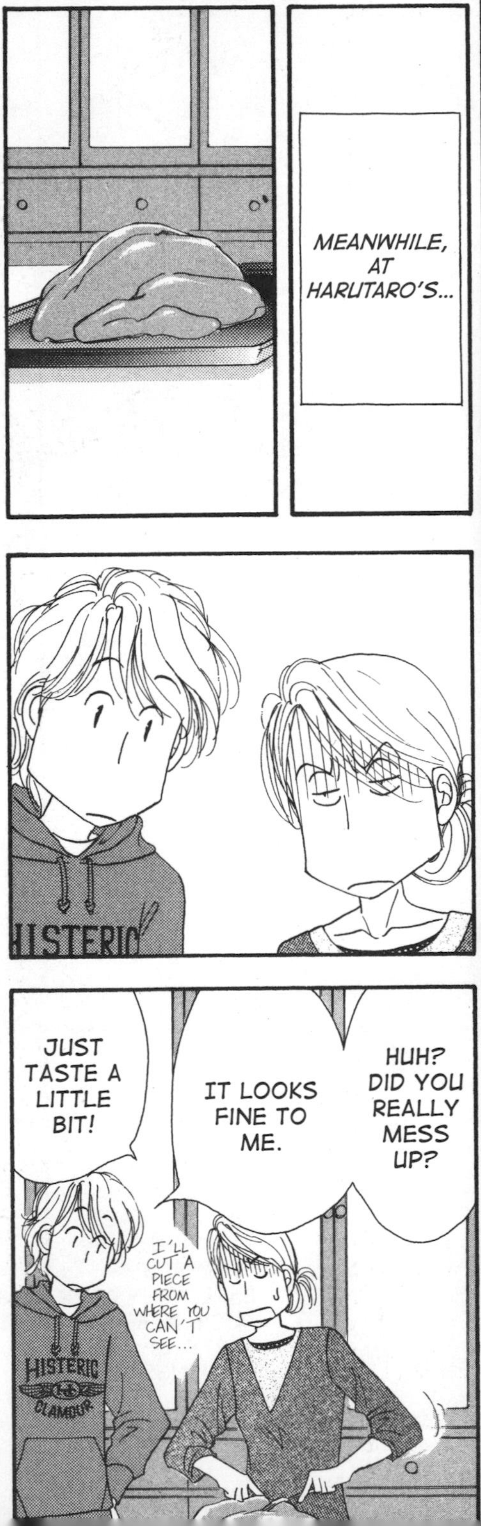
MEANWHILE, AT HARUTARO'S...
HISTERIC
HUH? DID YOU REALLY MESS UP?
IT LOOKS FINE TO ME.
JUST TASTE A LITTLE BIT!
I'LL CUT A PIECE FROM WHERE YOU CAN'T SEE...
HISTERIC GLAMOUR

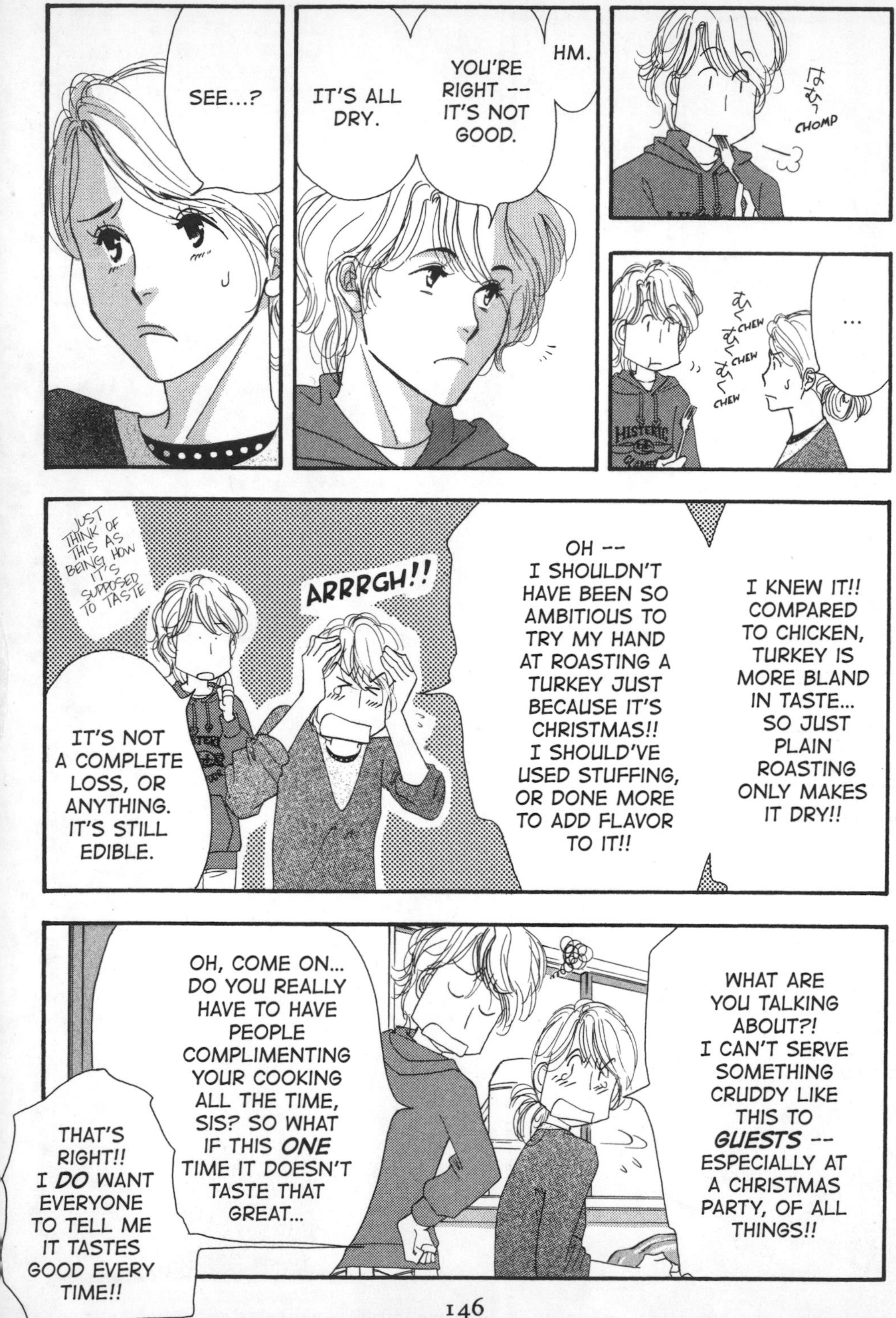
CHOMP
CHEW
CHEW
CHEW
...
HM.
YOU'RE RIGHT -- IT'S NOT GOOD.
IT'S ALL DRY.
SEE...?
I KNEW IT!! COMPARED TO CHICKEN, TURKEY IS MORE BLAND IN TASTE... SO JUST PLAIN ROASTING ONLY MAKES IT DRY!!
OH -- I SHOULDN'T HAVE BEEN SO AMBITIOUS TO TRY MY HAND AT ROASTING A TURKEY JUST BECAUSE IT'S CHRISTMAS!! I SHOULD'VE USED STUFFING, OR DONE MORE TO ADD FLAVOR TO IT!!
ARRRGH!!
JUST THINK OF THIS AS BEING HOW IT'S SUPPOSED TO TASTE
IT'S NOT A COMPLETE LOSS, OR ANYTHING. IT'S STILL EDIBLE.
WHAT ARE YOU TALKING ABOUT?! I CAN'T SERVE SOMETHING CRUDDY LIKE THIS TO GUESTS -- ESPECIALLY AT A CHRISTMAS PARTY, OF ALL THINGS!!
OH, COME ON... DO YOU REALLY HAVE TO HAVE PEOPLE COMPLIMENTING YOUR COOKING ALL THE TIME, SIS? SO WHAT IF THIS ONE TIME IT DOESN'T TASTE THAT GREAT...
THAT'S RIGHT!! I DO WANT EVERYONE TO TELL ME IT TASTES GOOD EVERY TIME!!

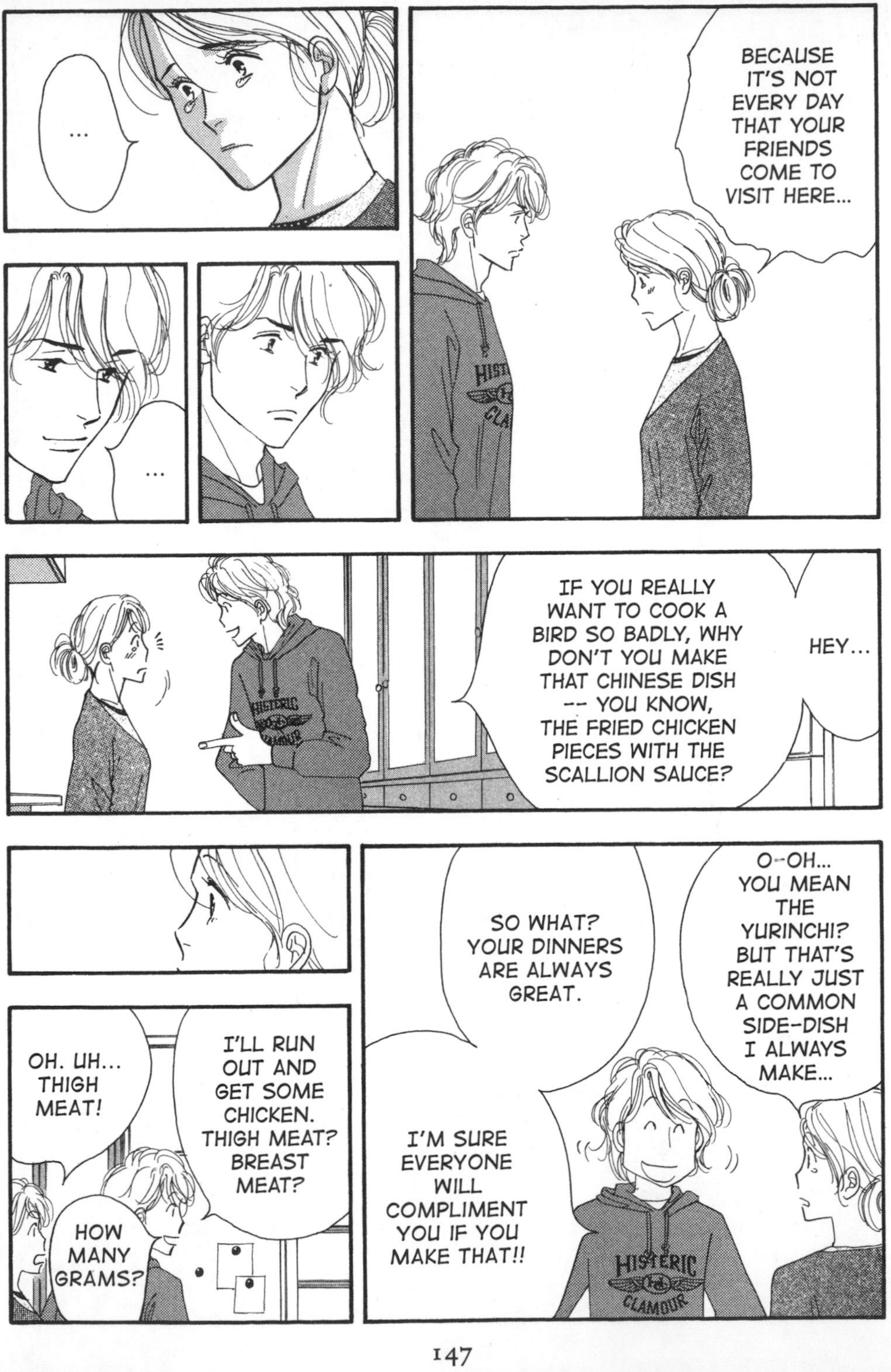
BECAUSE IT'S NOT EVERY DAY THAT YOUR FRIENDS COME TO VISIT HERE...
...
...
HEY...
IF YOU REALLY WANT TO COOK A BIRD SO BADLY, WHY DON'T YOU MAKE THAT CHINESE DISH -- YOU KNOW, THE FRIED CHICKEN PIECES WITH THE SCALLION SAUCE?
O-OH... YOU MEAN THE YURINCHI? BUT THAT'S REALLY JUST A COMMON SIDE-DISH I ALWAYS MAKE...
SO WHAT? YOUR DINNERS ARE ALWAYS GREAT.
I'M SURE EVERYONE WILL COMPLIMENT YOU IF YOU MAKE THAT!!
I'LL RUN OUT AND GET SOME CHICKEN. THIGH MEAT? BREAST MEAT?
OH. UH... THIGH MEAT!
HOW MANY GRAMS?

1.5KG!
I'LL JUST POP OUT.
HARUTA!
...THANK YOU!
NAH.
DON'T SWEAT IT. I KNOW HOW MUCH YOU'VE BEEN LOOKING FORWARD TO THIS CHRISTMAS PARTY.
ME, TOO...
"THIS PAST DECEMBER 2ND, MAKI PASSED ON INTO HEAVEN."
"HARUTARO-KUN, THANK YOU SO MUCH FOR BEING FRIENDS WITH MAKI DURING HER STAY AT THE HOSPITAL."
I KINDA HIT A DOWNER LATELY, SO I'VE BEEN LOOKING FORWARD TO HAVING FUN AT THIS PARTY...
ABOUT AS MUCH AS YOU HAVE, SIS.
バタン!
SLAM

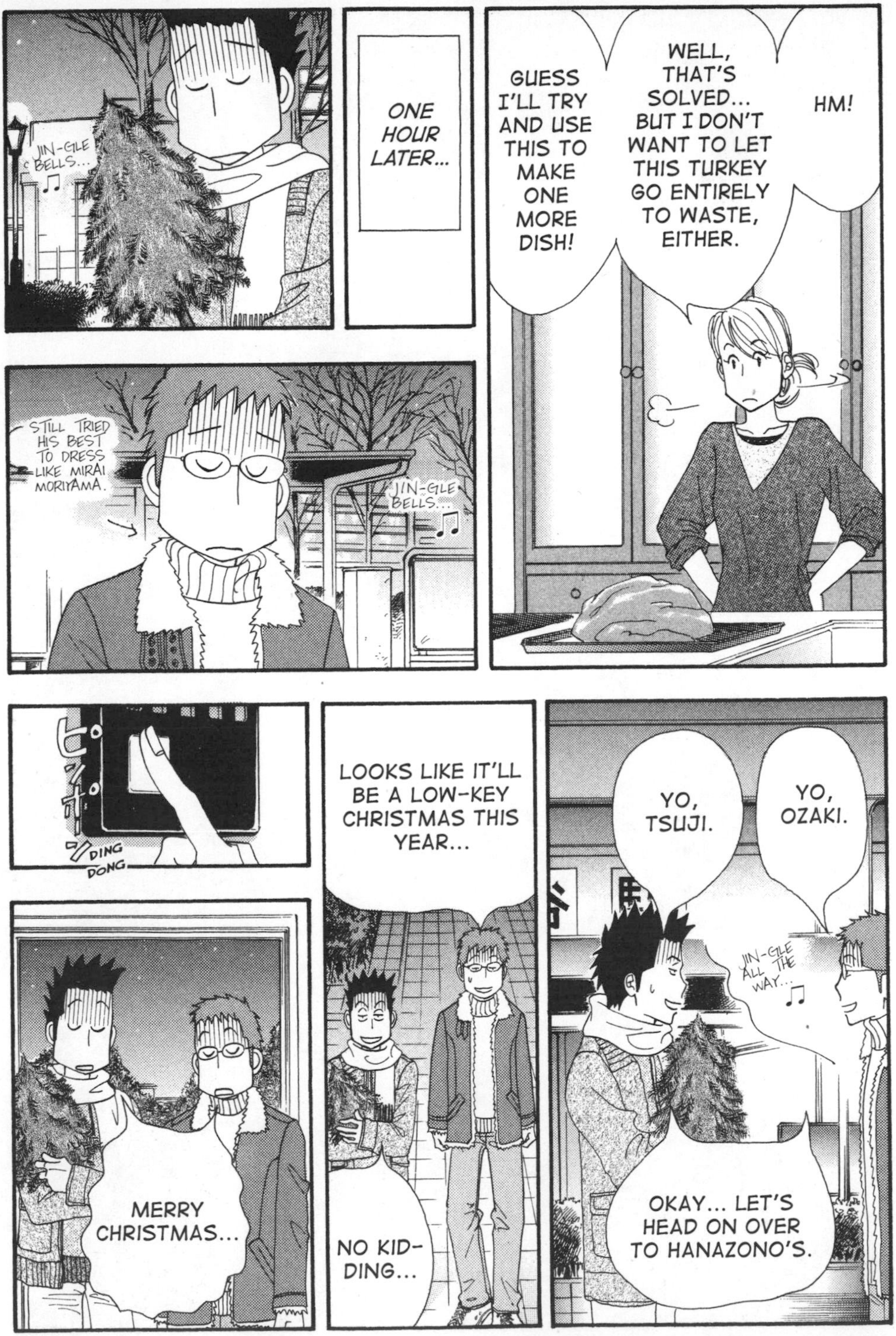
HM!
WELL, THAT'S SOLVED... BUT I DON'T WANT TO LET THIS TURKEY GO ENTIRELY TO WASTE, EITHER.
GUESS I'LL TRY AND USE THIS TO MAKE ONE MORE DISH!
ONE HOUR LATER...
JIN-GLE BELLS... ♫
JIN-GLE BELLS... ♫
STILL TRIED HIS BEST TO DRESS LIKE MIRAI MORIYAMA.
YO, OZAKI.
YO, TSUJI.
JIN-GLE ALL THE WAY... ♫
OKAY... LET'S HEAD ON OVER TO HANAZONO'S.
LOOKS LIKE IT'LL BE A LOW-KEY CHRISTMAS THIS YEAR...
NO KID-DING...
ピンポーン
DING DONG
MERRY CHRISTMAS...

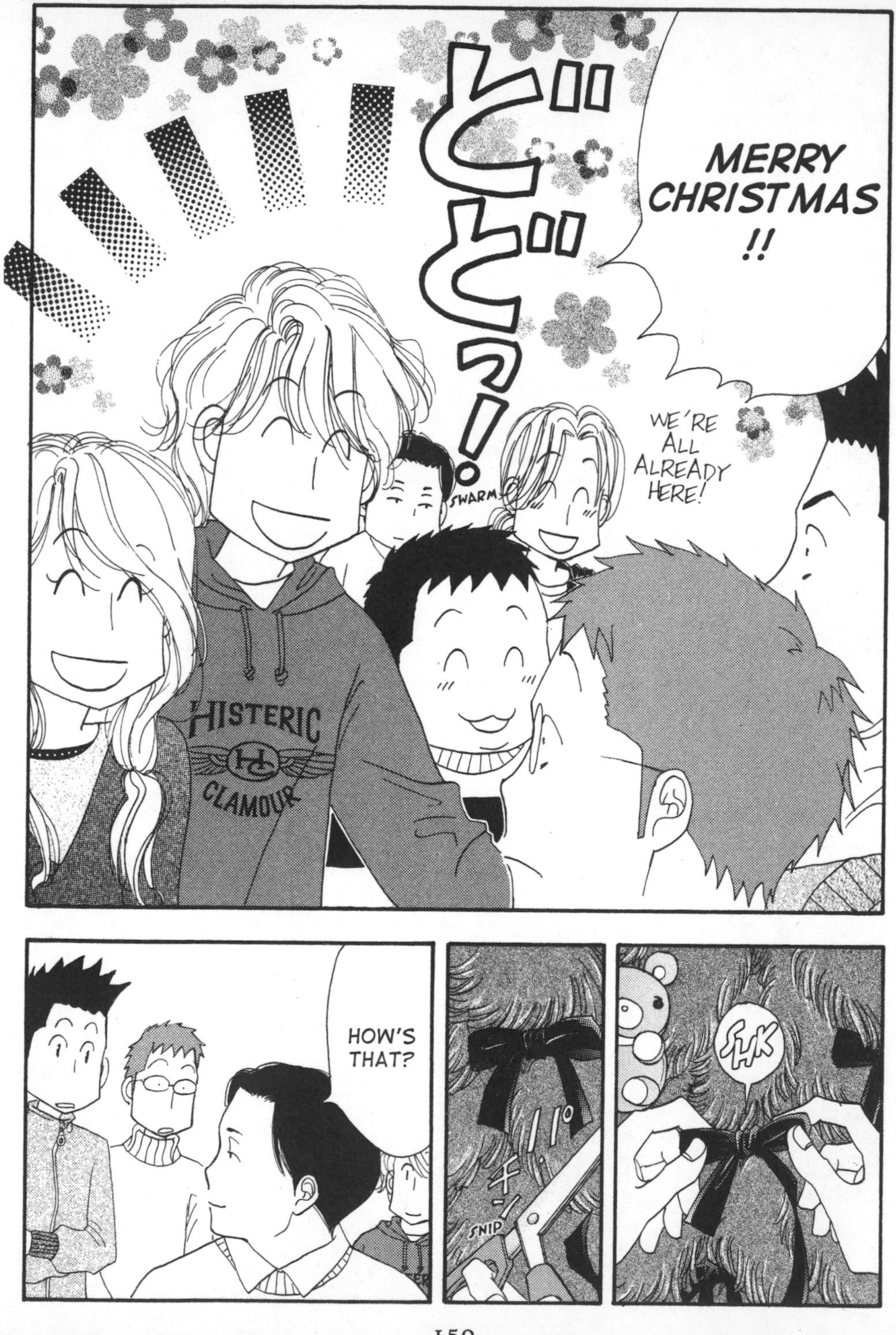
MERRY CHRISTMAS!!
どどっ!
WE'RE ALL ALREADY HERE!
SWARM
SHK
SNIP
HOW'S THAT?

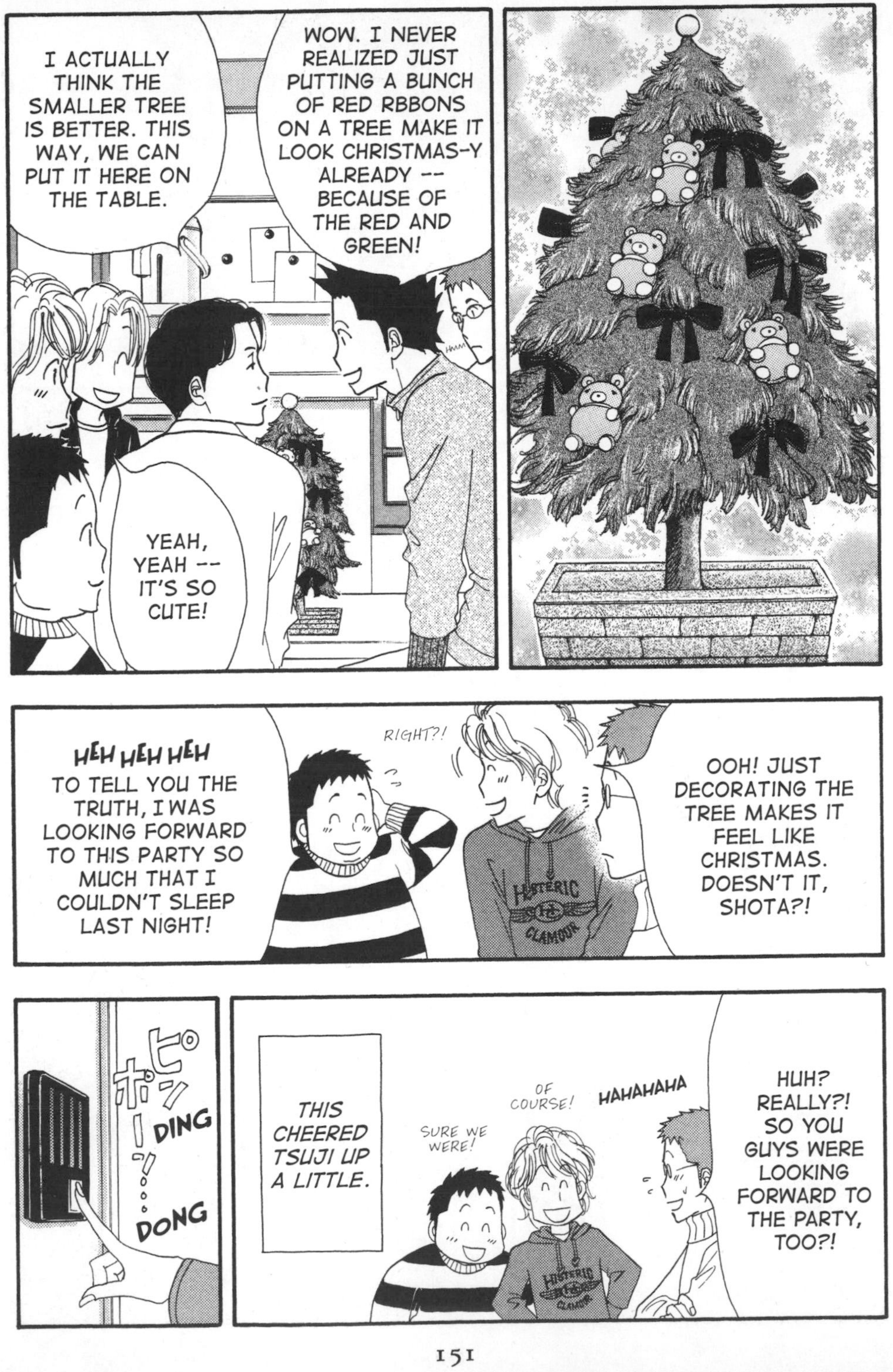
WOW. I NEVER REALIZED JUST PUTTING A BUNCH OF RED RBBONS ON A TREE MAKE IT LOOK CHRISTMAS-Y ALREADY -- BECAUSE OF THE RED AND GREEN!
I ACTUALLY THINK THE SMALLER TREE IS BETTER. THIS WAY, WE CAN PUT IT HERE ON THE TABLE.
YEAH, YEAH -- IT'S SO CUTE!
OOH! JUST DECORATING THE TREE MAKES IT FEEL LIKE CHRISTMAS. DOESN'T IT, SHOTA?!
RIGHT?!
HEH HEH HEH
TO TELL YOU THE TRUTH, I WAS LOOKING FORWARD TO THIS PARTY SO MUCH THAT I COULDN'T SLEEP LAST NIGHT!
HUH? REALLY?! SO YOU GUYS WERE LOOKING FORWARD TO THE PARTY, TOO?!
HAHAHAHA
OF COURSE!
SURE WE WERE!
THIS CHEERED TSUJI UP A LITTLE.
ピンポーン
DING
DONG

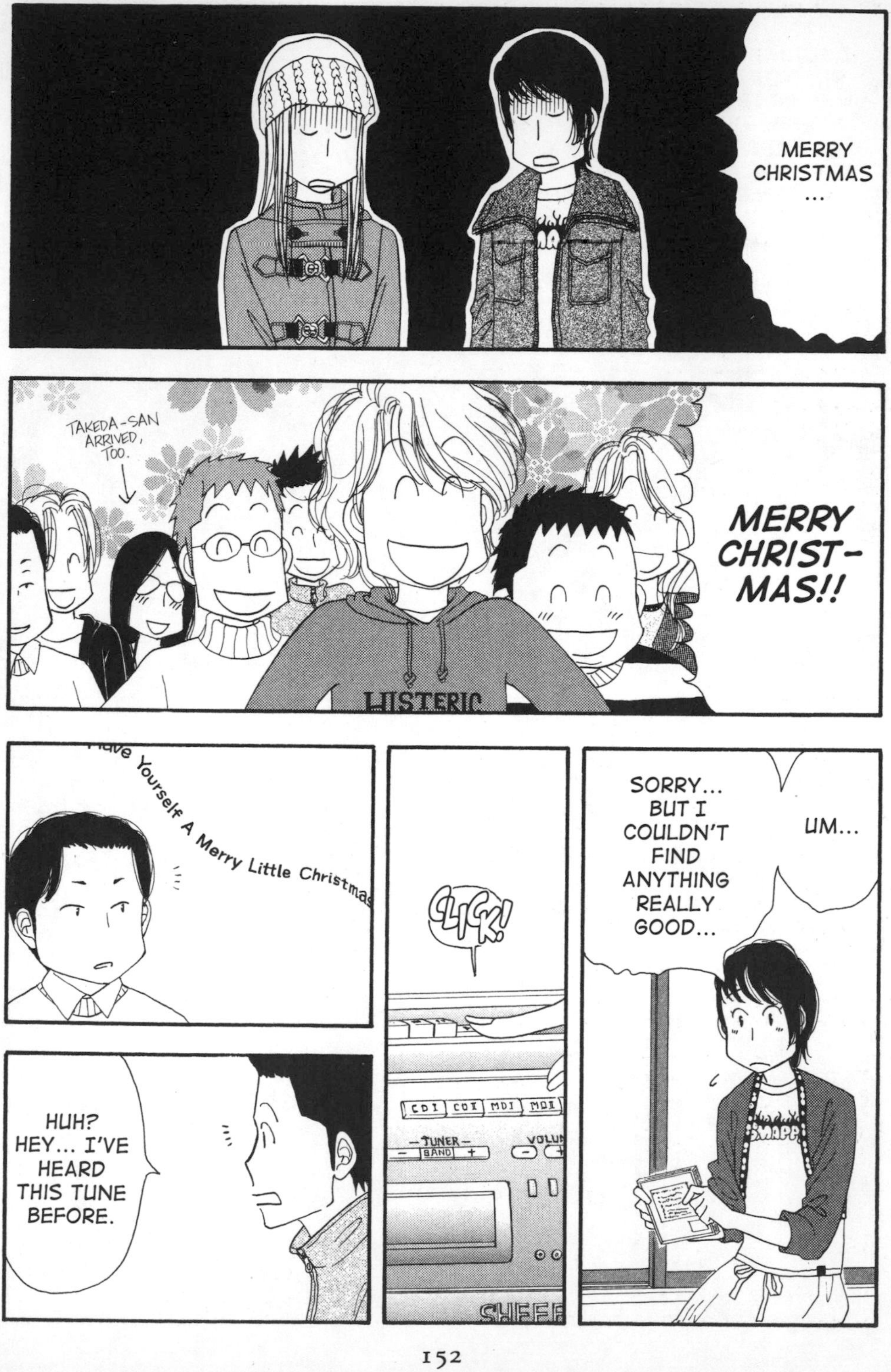
MERRY CHRISTMAS ...
MERRY CHRIST-MAS!!
TAKEDA-SAN ARRIVED, TOO.
UM...
SORRY... BUT I COULDN'T FIND ANYTHING REALLY GOOD...
CLICK!
ave Yourself A Merry Little Christmas
HUH? HEY... I'VE HEARD THIS TUNE BEFORE.

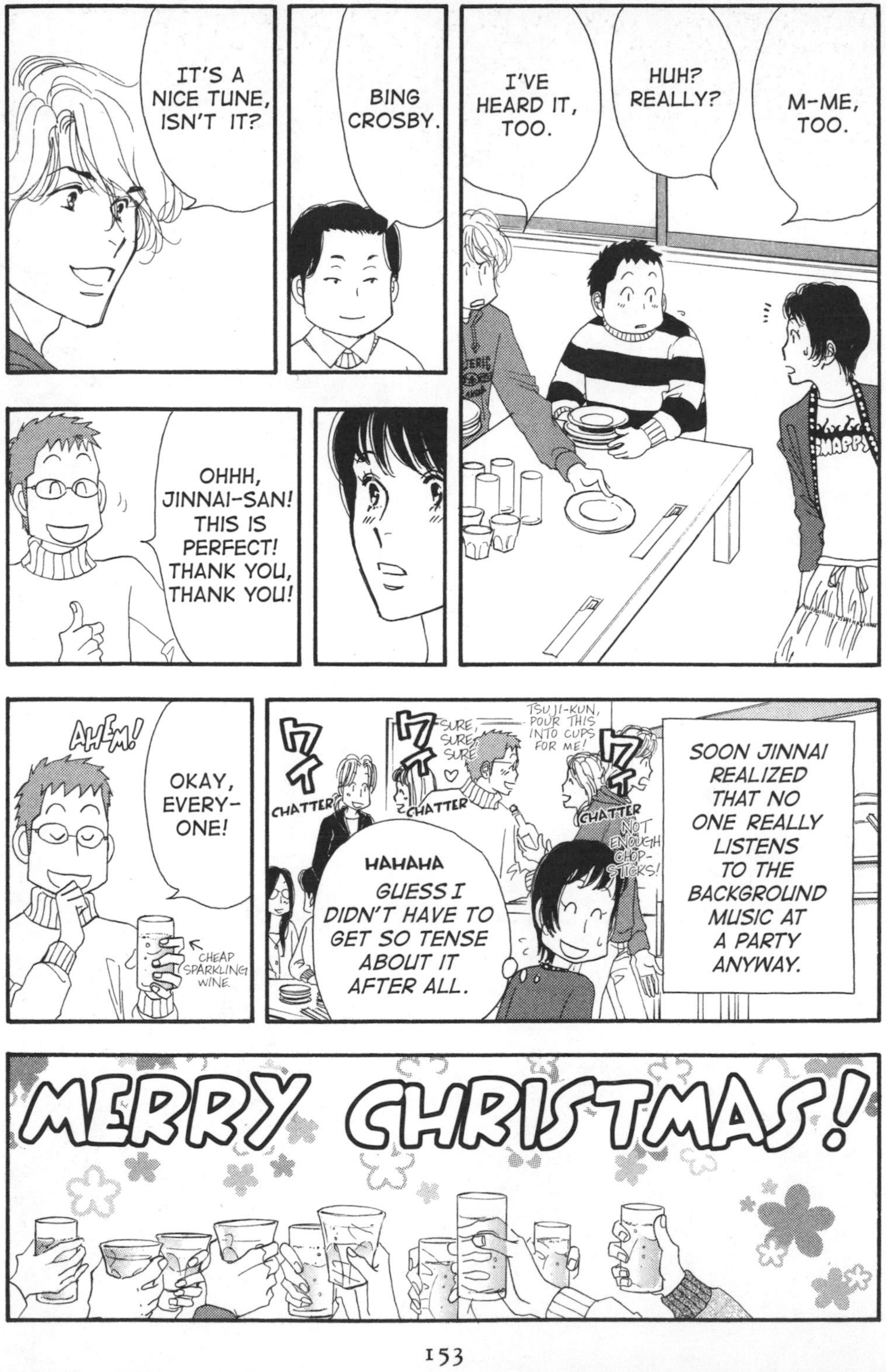
M-ME, TOO.
HUH? REALLY?
I'VE HEARD IT, TOO.
BING CROSBY.
IT'S A NICE TUNE, ISN'T IT?
OHHH, JINNAI-SAN! THIS IS PERFECT! THANK YOU, THANK YOU!
SOON JINNAI REALIZED THAT NO ONE REALLY LISTENS TO THE BACKGROUND MUSIC AT A PARTY ANYWAY.
TSUJI-KUN, POUR THIS INTO CUPS FOR ME!
CHATTER
NOT ENOUGH CHOP-STICKS!
SURE, SURE, SURE
CHATTER
CHATTER
HAHAHA GUESS I DIDN'T HAVE TO GET SO TENSE ABOUT IT AFTER ALL.
AHEM!
OKAY, EVERY-ONE!
CHEAP SPARKLING WINE.
MERRY CHRISTMAS!

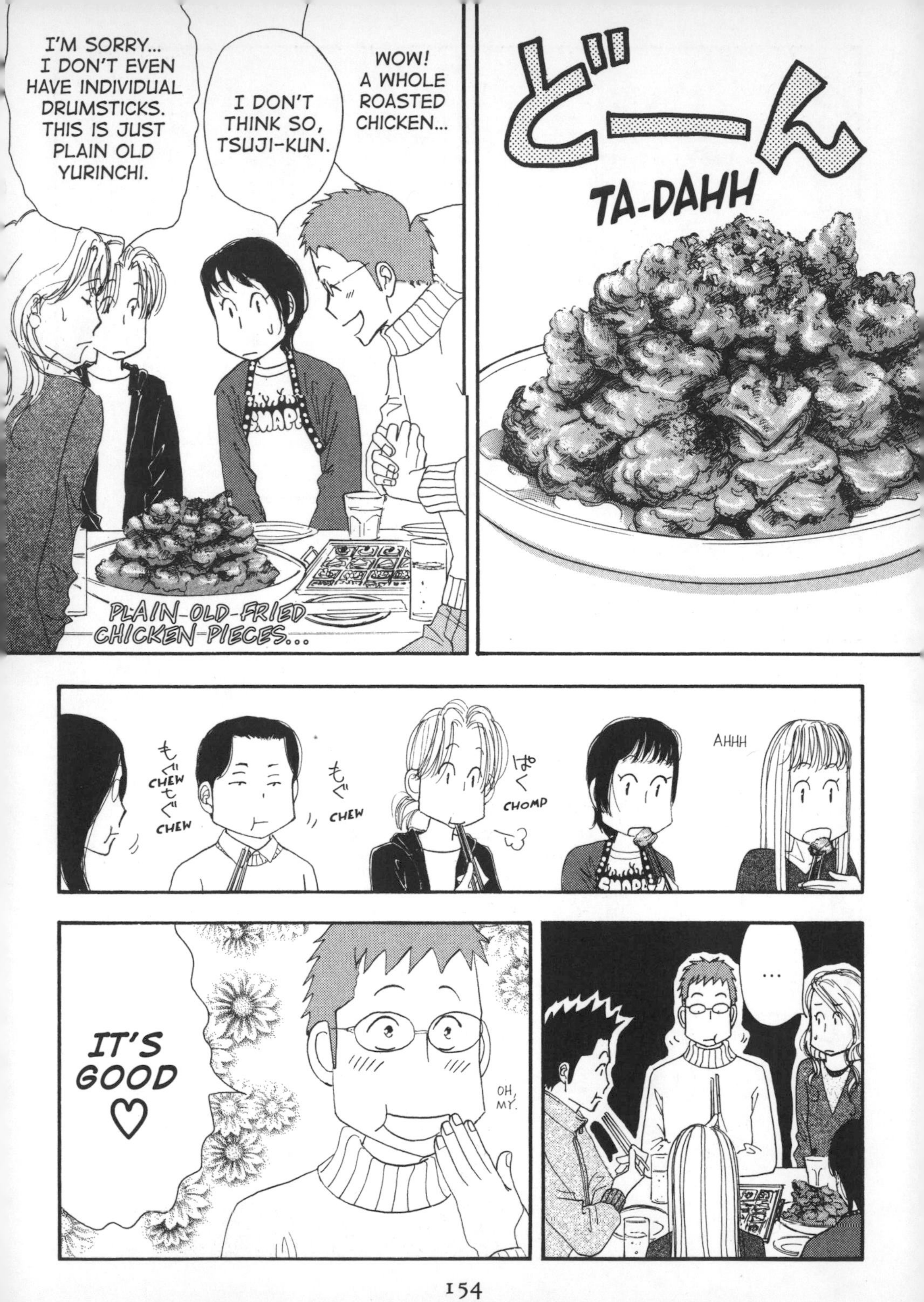
どーん
TA-DAHH
WOW! A WHOLE ROASTED CHICKEN...
I DON'T THINK SO, TSUJI-KUN.
I'M SORRY... I DON'T EVEN HAVE INDIVIDUAL DRUMSTICKS. THIS IS JUST PLAIN OLD YURINCHI.
PLAIN-OLD-FRIED CHICKEN-PIECES...
AHHH
ぱく
CHOMP
もぐ
CHEW
もぐもぐ
CHEW CHEW
...
OH, MY.
IT'S GOOD ♡

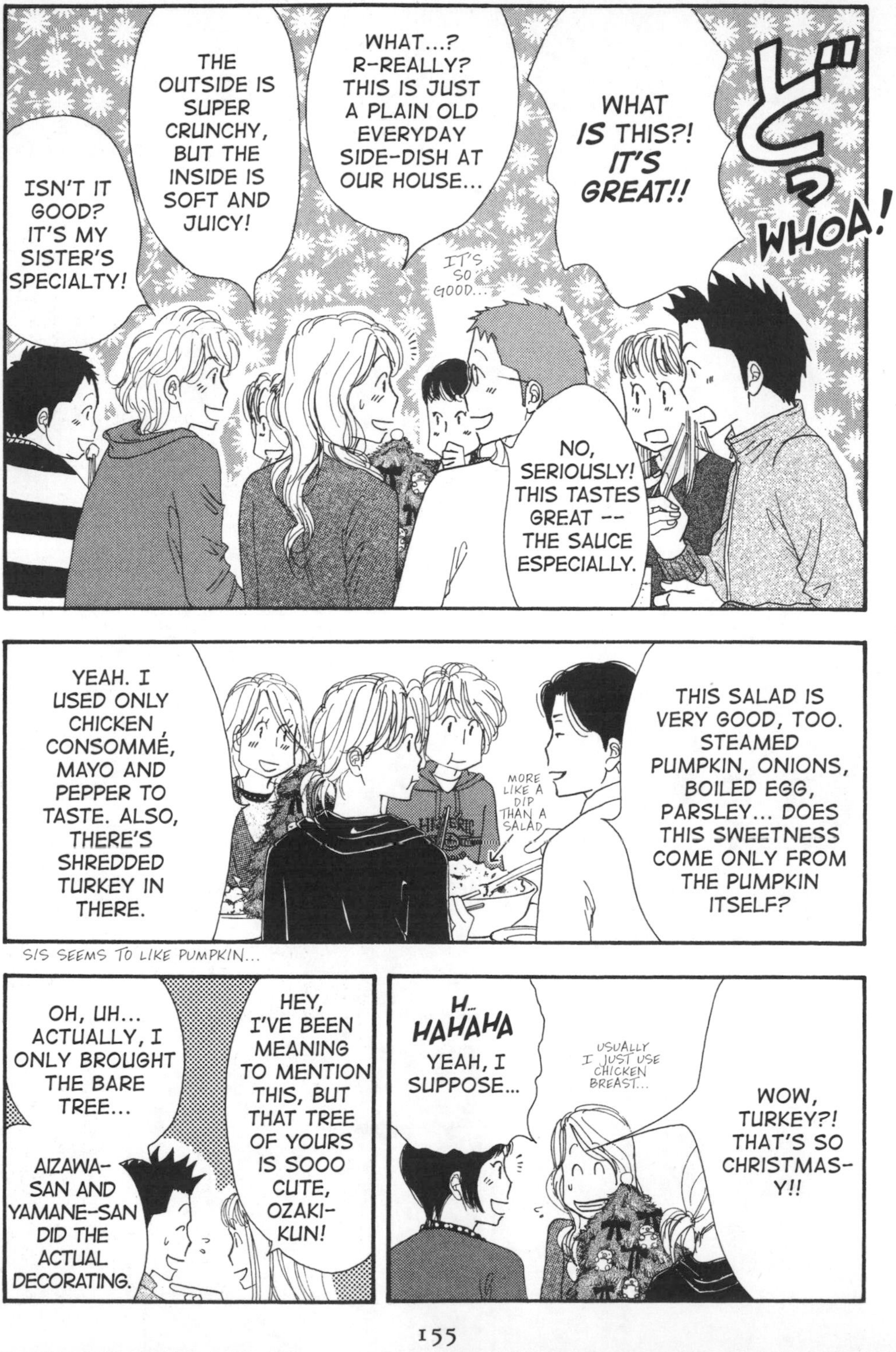
どっ WHOA!
WHAT IS THIS?! IT'S GREAT!!
NO, SERIOUSLY! THIS TASTES GREAT -- THE SAUCE ESPECIALLY.
WHAT...? R-REALLY? THIS IS JUST A PLAIN OLD EVERYDAY SIDE-DISH AT OUR HOUSE...
IT'S SO GOOD...
THE OUTSIDE IS SUPER CRUNCHY, BUT THE INSIDE IS SOFT AND JUICY!
ISN'T IT GOOD? IT'S MY SISTER'S SPECIALTY!
THIS SALAD IS VERY GOOD, TOO. STEAMED PUMPKIN, ONIONS, BOILED EGG, PARSLEY... DOES THIS SWEETNESS COME ONLY FROM THE PUMPKIN ITSELF?
MORE LIKE A DIP THAN A SALAD
YEAH. I USED ONLY CHICKEN CONSOMMÉ, MAYO AND PEPPER TO TASTE. ALSO, THERE'S SHREDDED TURKEY IN THERE.
SIS SEEMS TO LIKE PUMPKIN...
WOW, TURKEY?! THAT'S SO CHRISTMAS-Y!!
USUALLY I JUST USE CHICKEN BREAST...
H... HAHAHA
YEAH, I SUPPOSE...
HEY, I'VE BEEN MEANING TO MENTION THIS, BUT THAT TREE OF YOURS IS SOOO CUTE, OZAKI-KUN!
OH, UH... ACTUALLY, I ONLY BROUGHT THE BARE TREE...
AIZAWA-SAN AND YAMANE-SAN DID THE ACTUAL DECORATING.

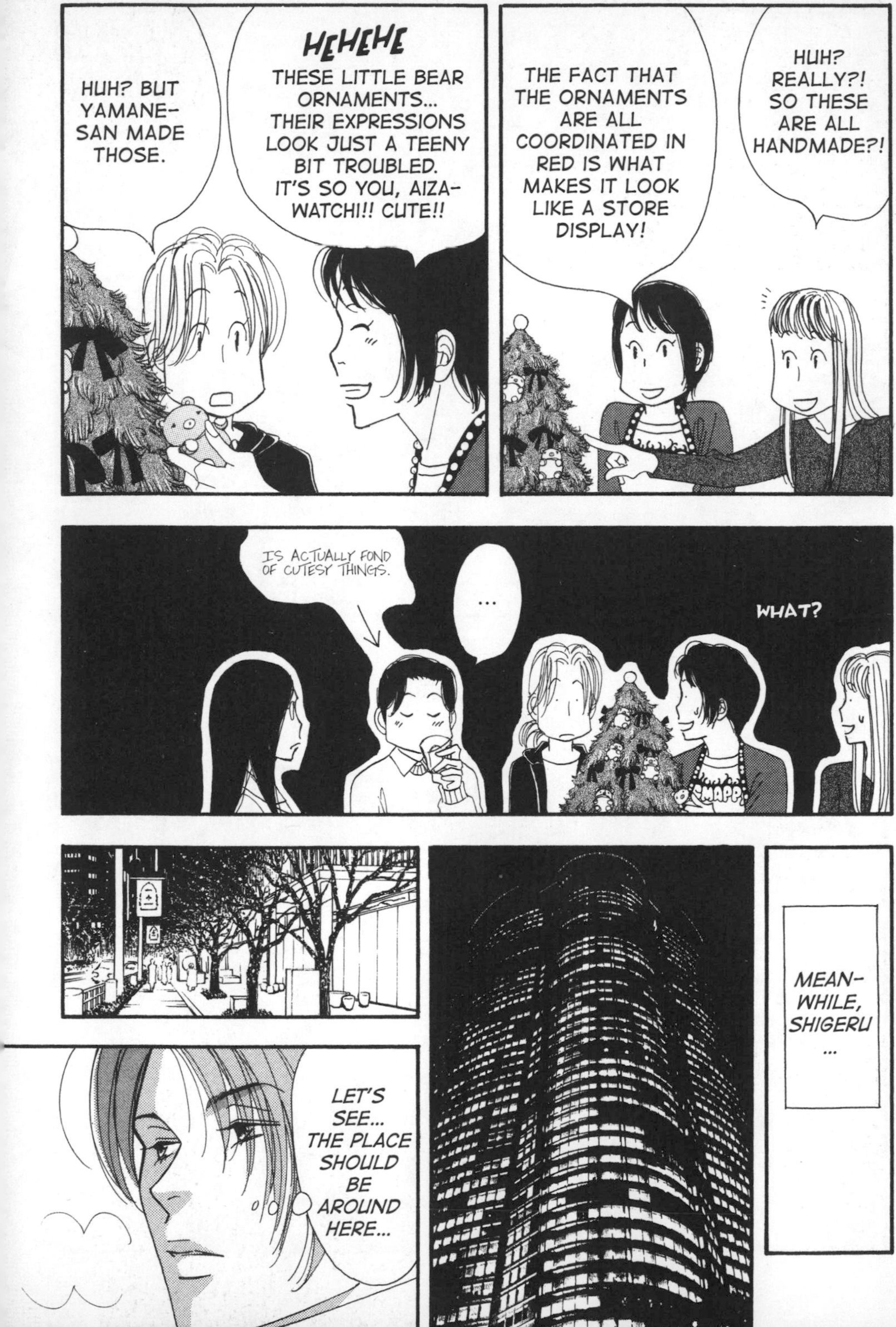
HUH? REALLY?! SO THESE ARE ALL HANDMADE?!
THE FACT THAT THE ORNAMENTS ARE ALL COORDINATED IN RED IS WHAT MAKES IT LOOK LIKE A STORE DISPLAY!
HEHEHE
THESE LITTLE BEAR ORNAMENTS... THEIR EXPRESSIONS LOOK JUST A TEENY BIT TROUBLED. IT'S SO YOU, AIZA-WATCHI!! CUTE!!
HUH? BUT YAMANE-SAN MADE THOSE.
WHAT?
...
IS ACTUALLY FOND OF CUTESY THINGS.
MEAN-WHILE, SHIGERU ...
LET'S SEE... THE PLACE SHOULD BE AROUND HERE...

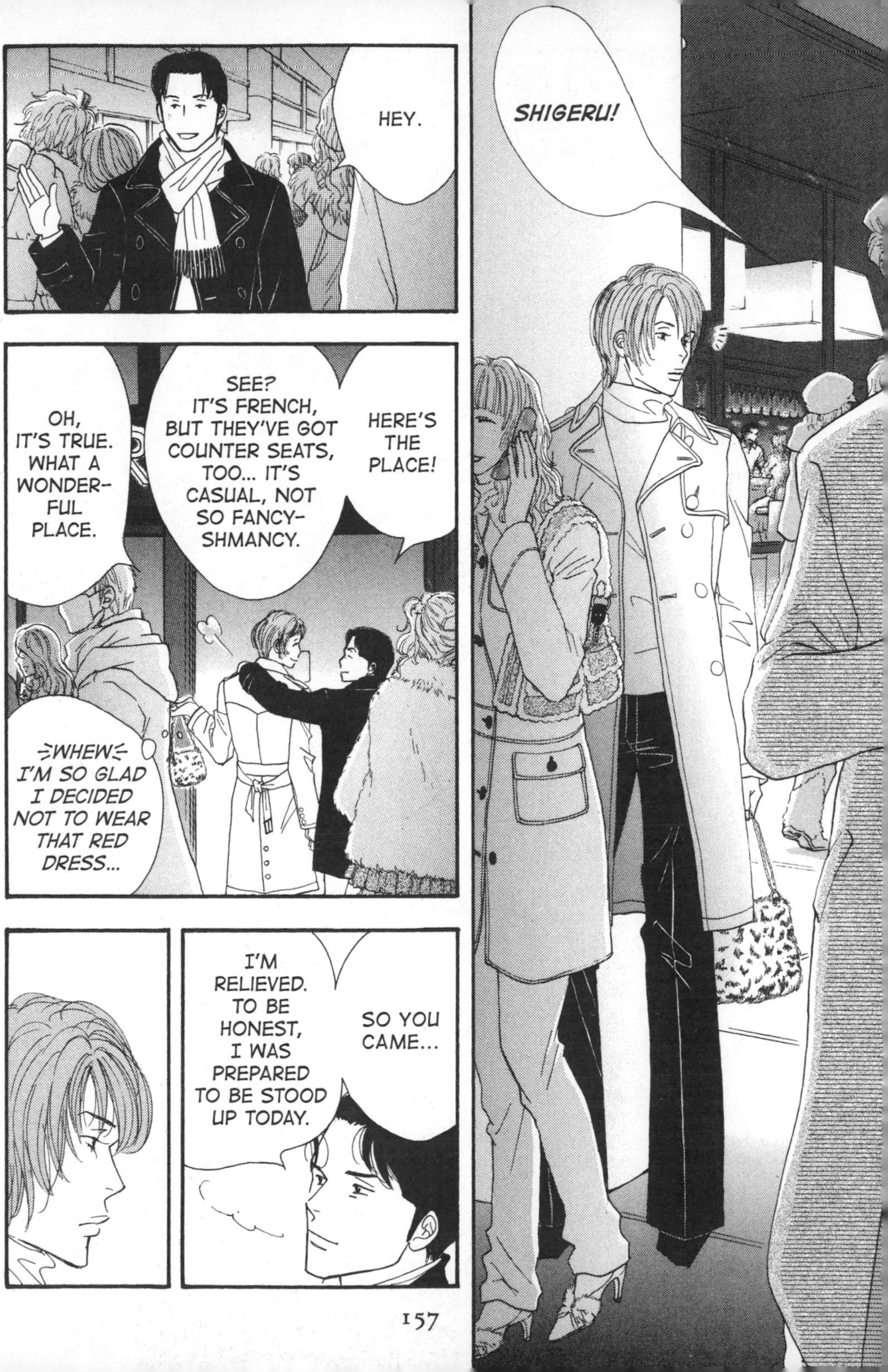

SHIGERU!
HEY.
HERE'S THE PLACE!
SEE? IT'S FRENCH, BUT THEY'VE GOT COUNTER SEATS, TOO... IT'S CASUAL, NOT SO FANCY-SHMANCY.
OH, IT'S TRUE. WHAT A WONDERFUL PLACE.
≠WHEW≠ I'M SO GLAD I DECIDED NOT TO WEAR THAT RED DRESS...
SO YOU CAME...
I'M RELIEVED. TO BE HONEST, I WAS PREPARED TO BE STOOD UP TODAY.

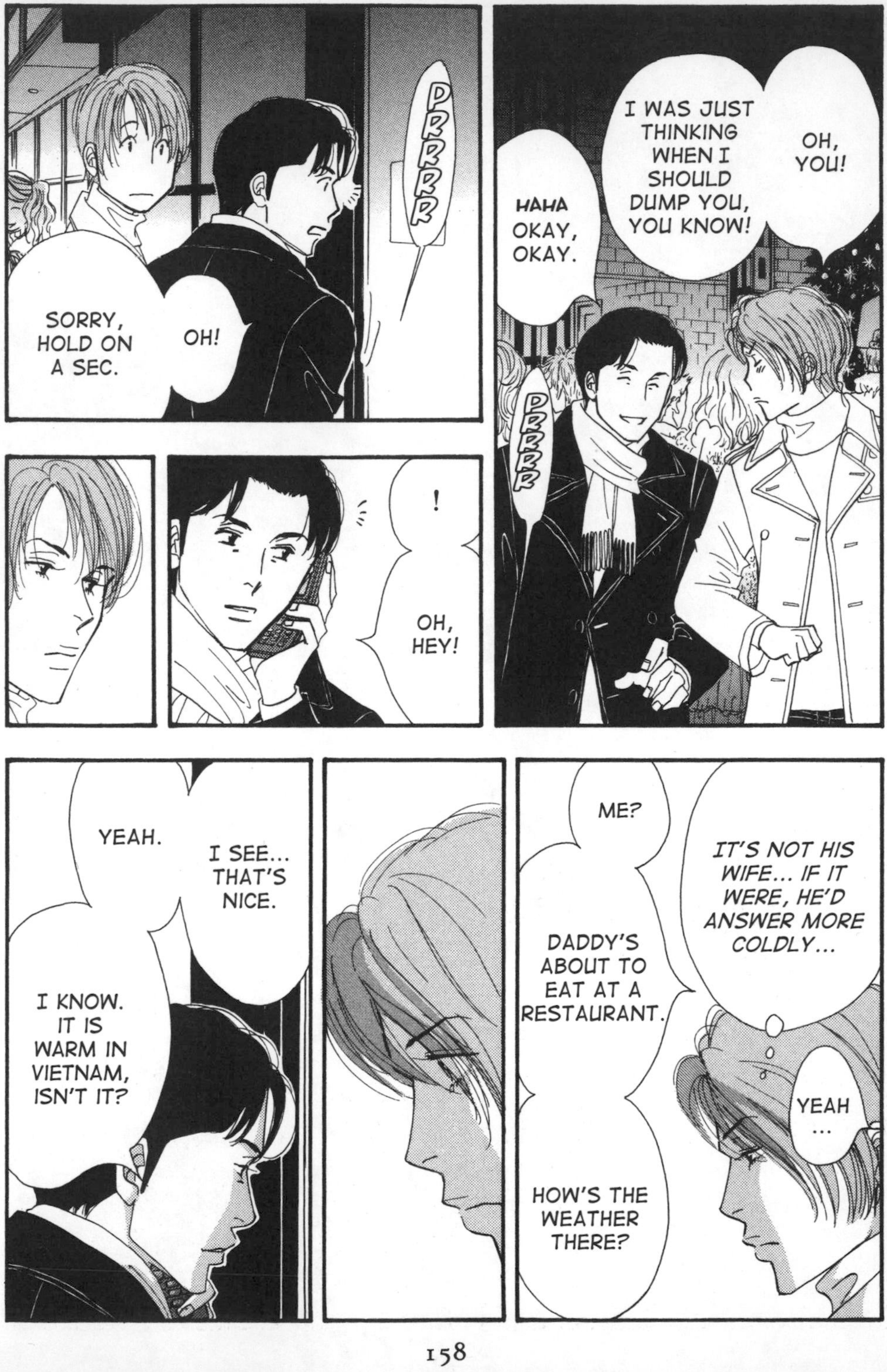
OH, YOU!
I WAS JUST THINKING WHEN I SHOULD DUMP YOU, YOU KNOW!
HAHA OKAY, OKAY.
PRRRR
PRRRR
OH!
SORRY, HOLD ON A SEC.
!
OH, HEY!
IT'S NOT HIS WIFE... IF IT WERE, HE'D ANSWER MORE COLDLY...
ME?
DADDY'S ABOUT TO EAT AT A RESTAURANT.
YEAH ...
HOW'S THE WEATHER THERE?
I SEE... THAT'S NICE.
YEAH.
I KNOW. IT IS WARM IN VIETNAM, ISN'T IT?

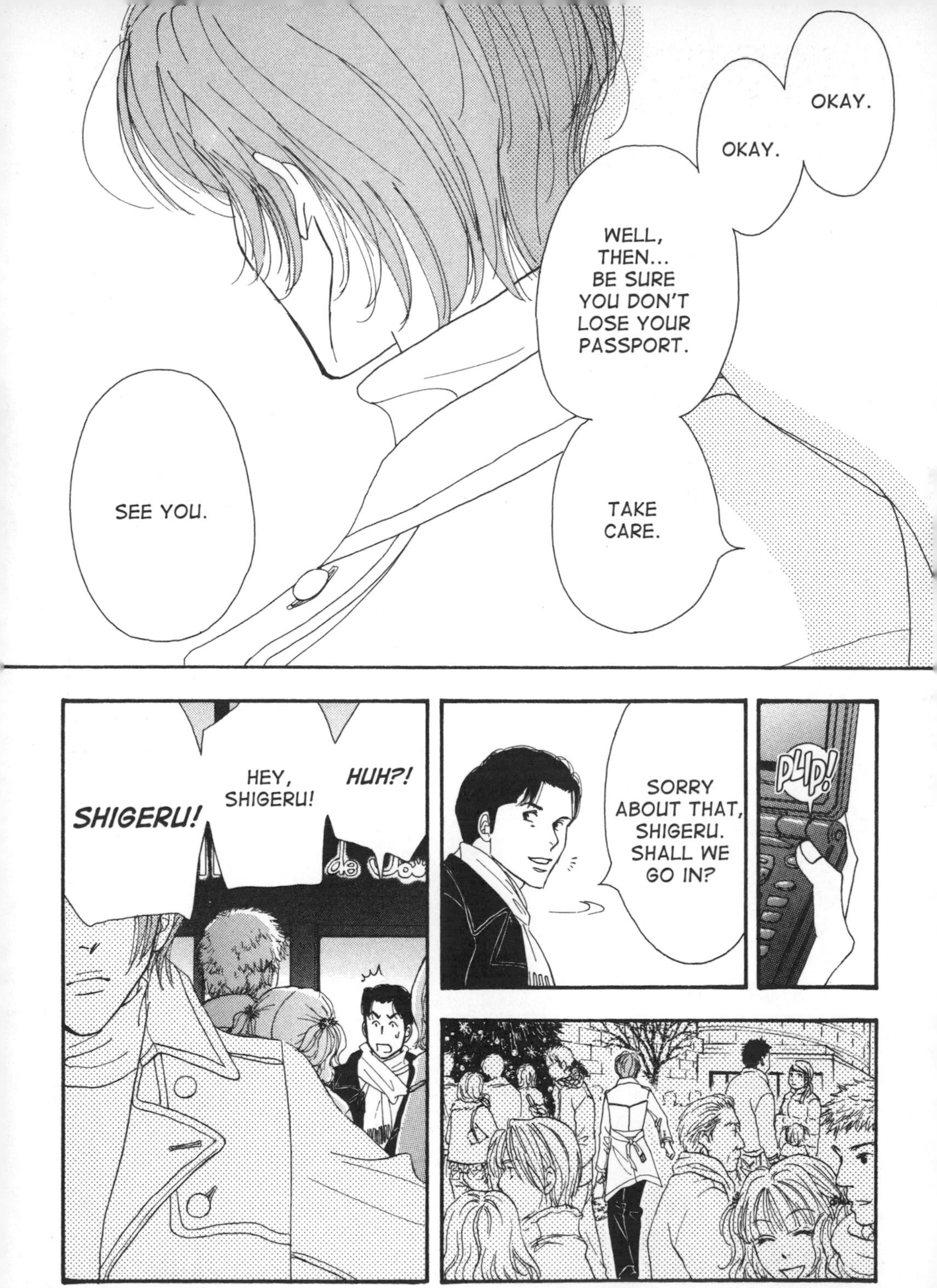
OKAY.
OKAY.
WELL, THEN... BE SURE YOU DON'T LOSE YOUR PASSPORT.
TAKE CARE.
SEE YOU.
PLIP!
SORRY ABOUT THAT, SHIGERU. SHALL WE GO IN?
HUH?!
HEY, SHIGERU!
SHIGERU!

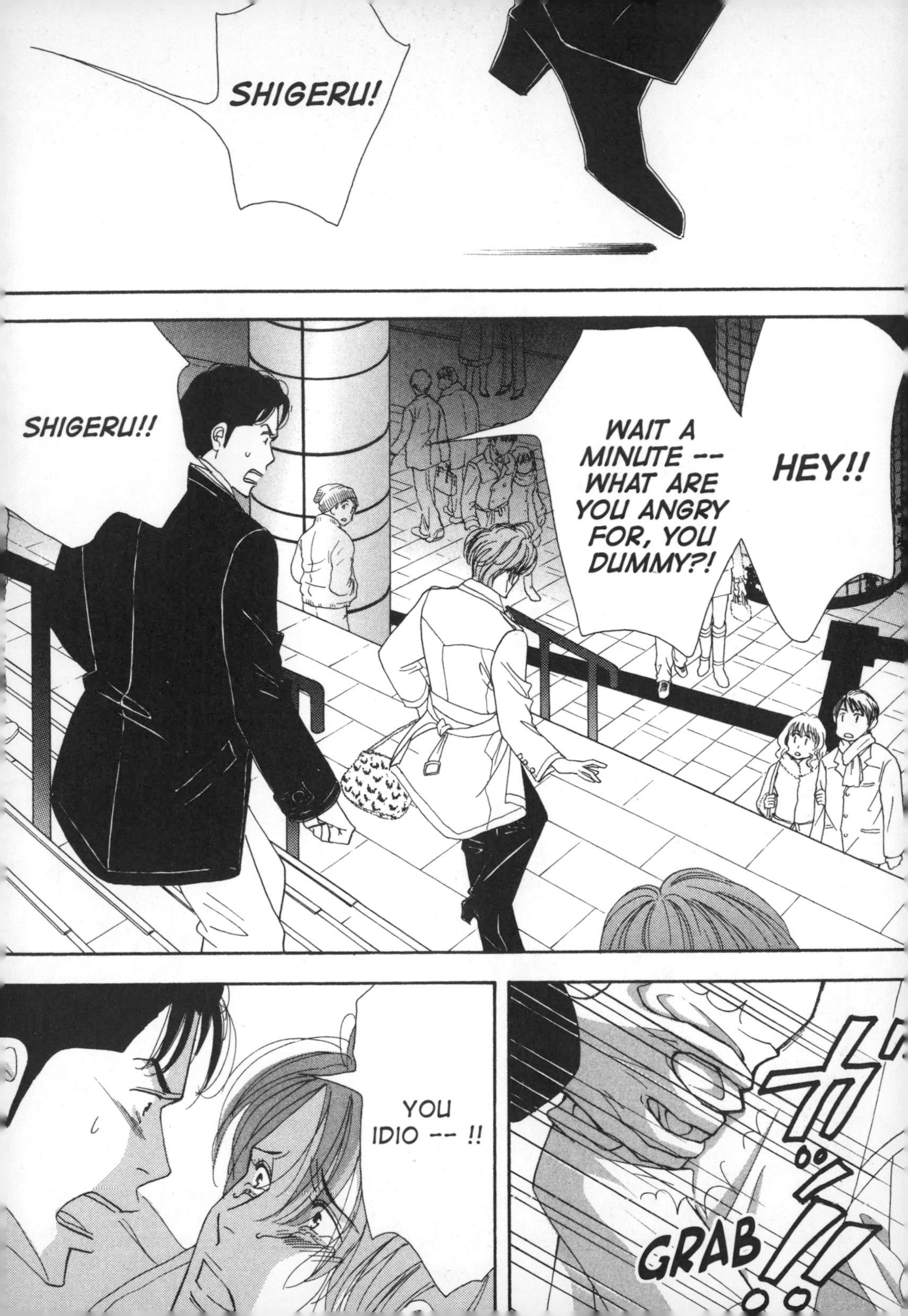
SHIGERU!
HEY!!
WAIT A MINUTE -- WHAT ARE YOU ANGRY FOR, YOU DUMMY?!
SHIGERU!!
GRAB!!
YOU IDIO -- !!

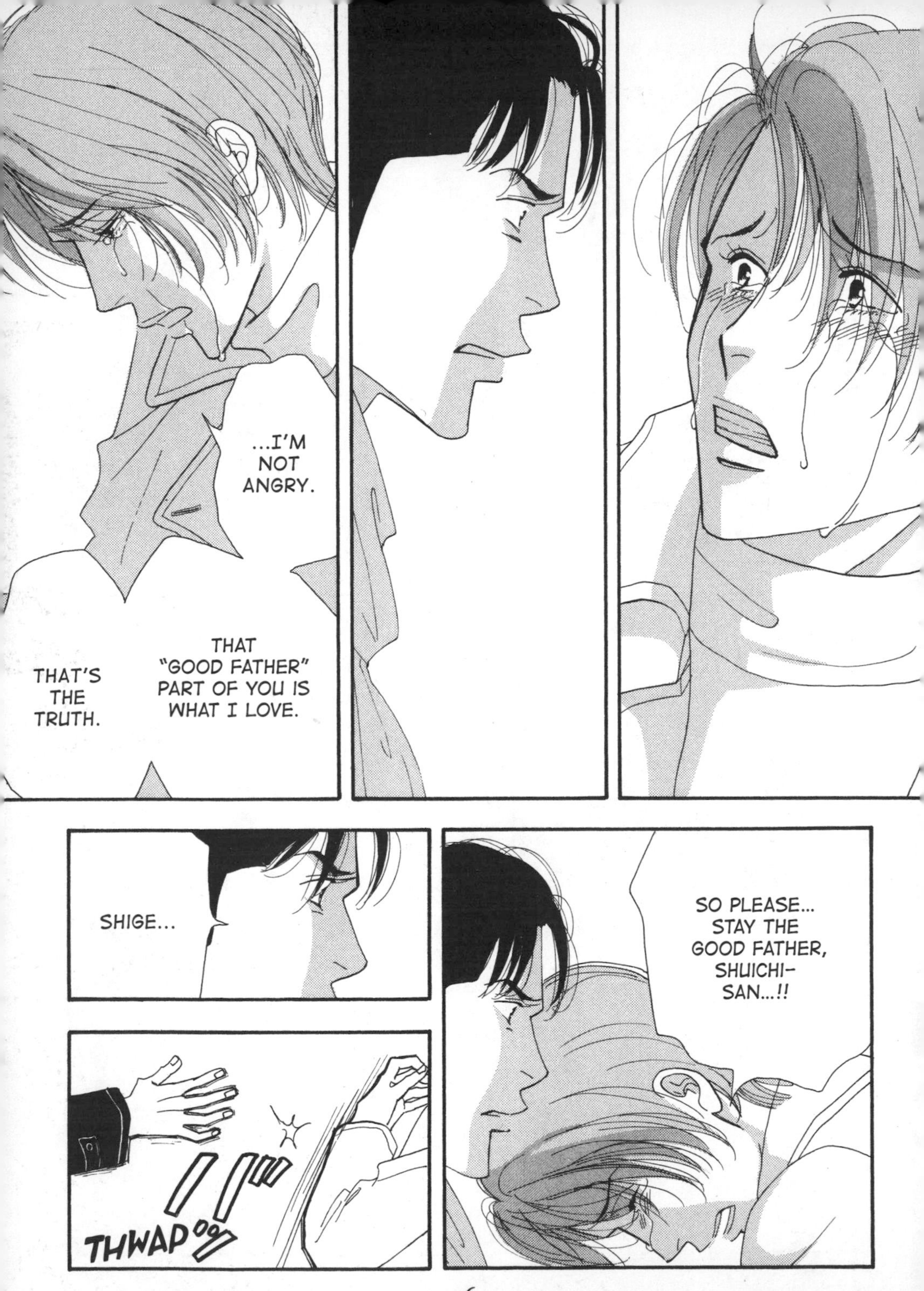
...I'M NOT ANGRY.
THAT "GOOD FATHER" PART OF YOU IS WHAT I LOVE.
THAT'S THE TRUTH.
SO PLEASE... STAY THE GOOD FATHER, SHUICHI-SAN...!!
SHIGE...
THWAP

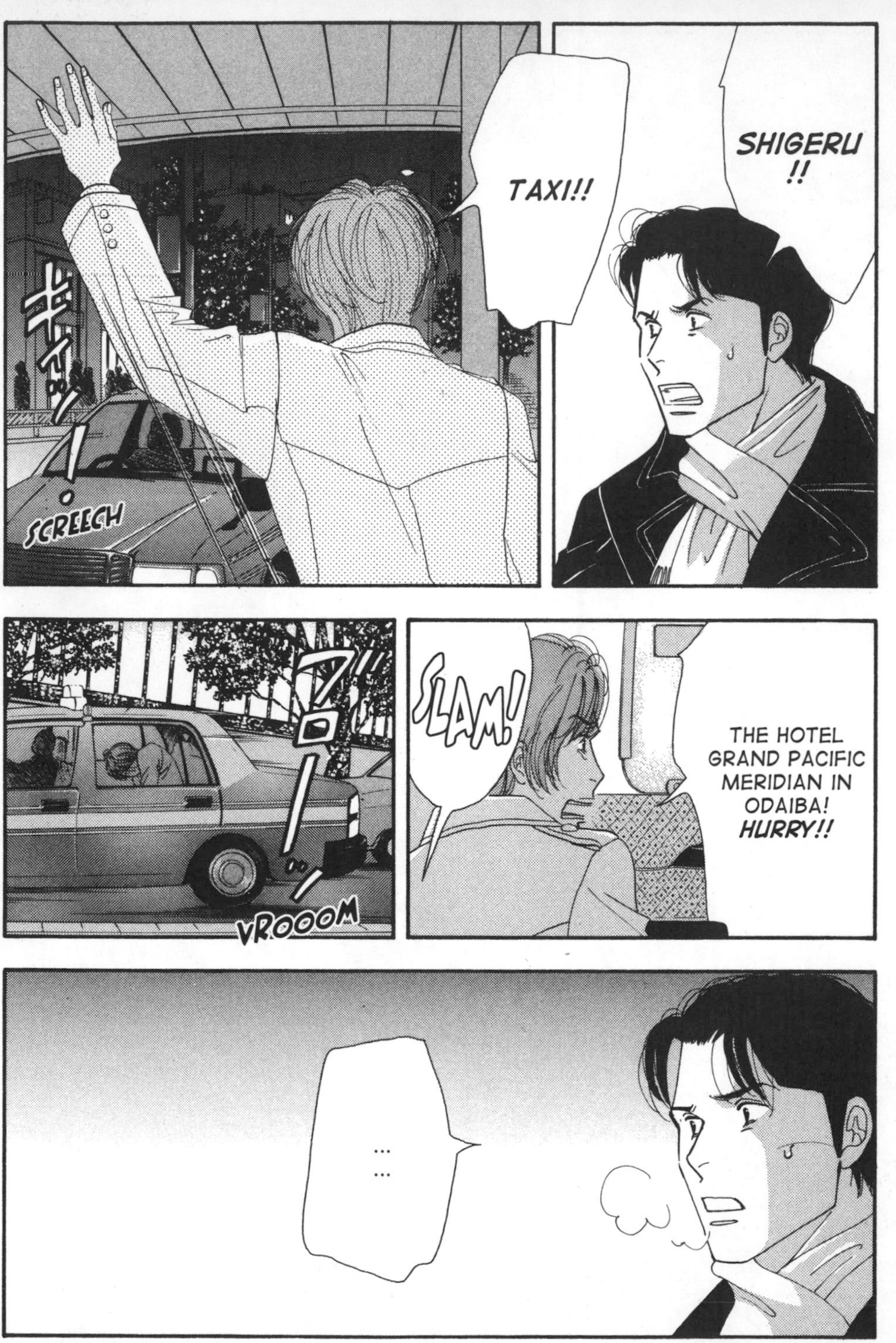
SHIGERU!!
TAXI!!
SCREECH
THE HOTEL GRAND PACIFIC MERIDIAN IN ODAIBA! HURRY!!
SLAM!
VROOOM
… …

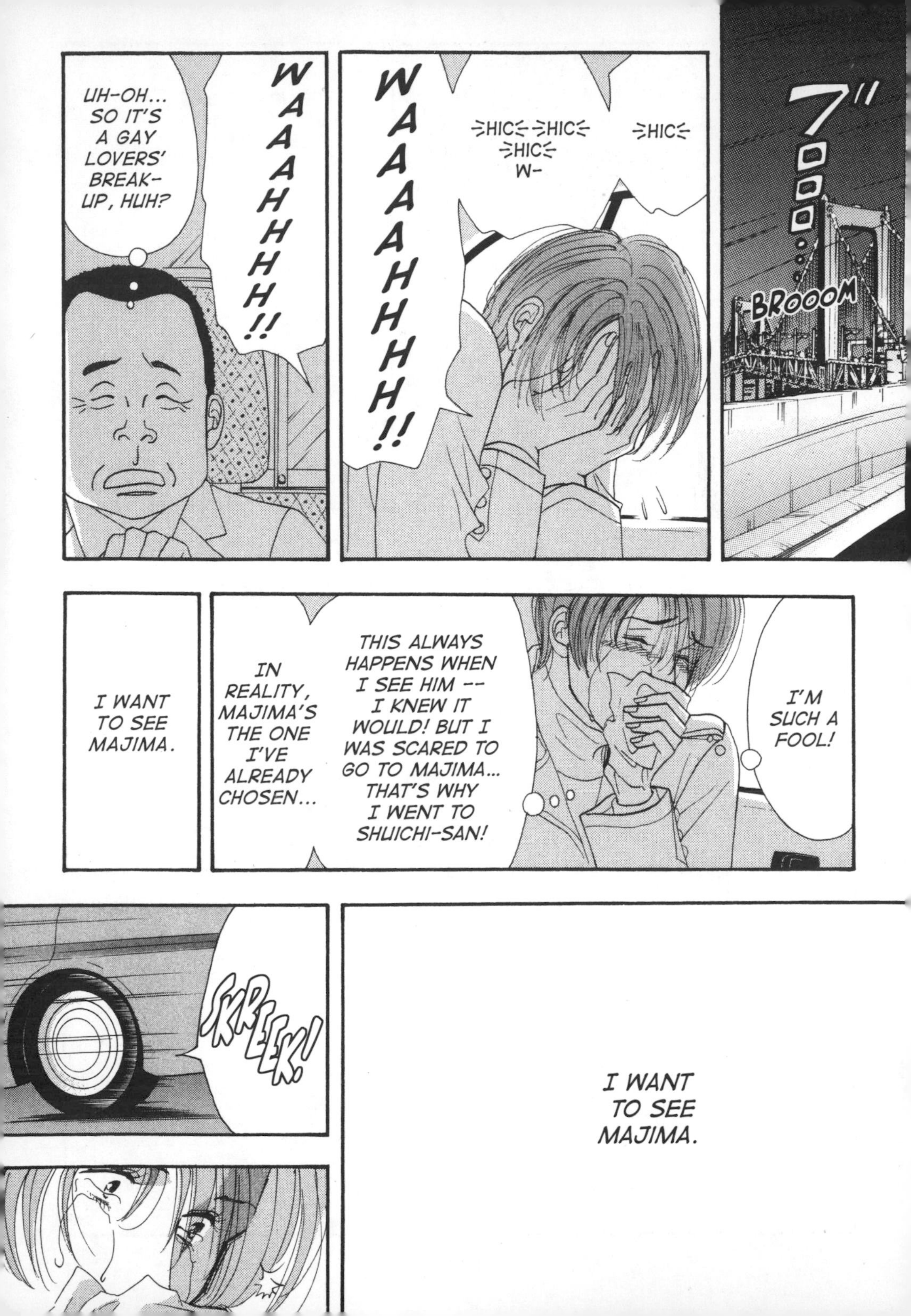
BROOOM
HIC
HIC HIC
HIC
W-
WAAAAAAHHHHHH!!
WAAAAHHHHH!!
UH-OH... SO IT'S A GAY LOVERS' BREAK-UP, HUH?
I'M SUCH A FOOL!
THIS ALWAYS HAPPENS WHEN I SEE HIM -- I KNEW IT WOULD! BUT I WAS SCARED TO GO TO MAJIMA... THAT'S WHY I WENT TO SHUICHI-SAN!
IN REALITY, MAJIMA'S THE ONE I'VE ALREADY CHOSEN...
I WANT TO SEE MAJIMA.
I WANT TO SEE MAJIMA.
SKREEEK!

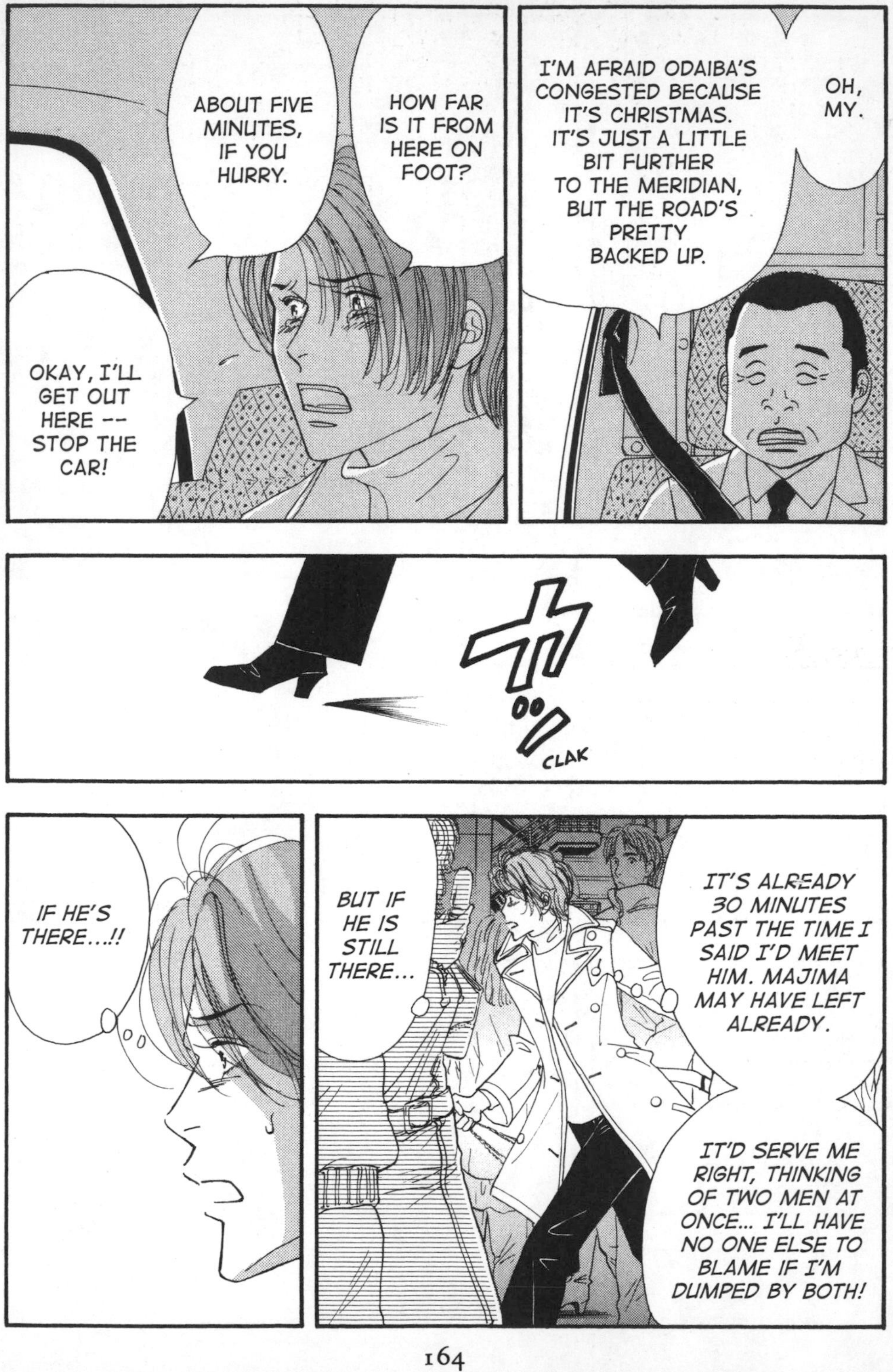
OH, MY.
I'M AFRAID ODAIBA'S CONGESTED BECAUSE IT'S CHRISTMAS. IT'S JUST A LITTLE BIT FURTHER TO THE MERIDIAN, BUT THE ROAD'S PRETTY BACKED UP.
HOW FAR IS IT FROM HERE ON FOOT?
ABOUT FIVE MINUTES, IF YOU HURRY.
OKAY, I'LL GET OUT HERE -- STOP THE CAR!
CLAK
IT'S ALREADY 30 MINUTES PAST THE TIME I SAID I'D MEET HIM. MAJIMA MAY HAVE LEFT ALREADY.
IT'D SERVE ME RIGHT, THINKING OF TWO MEN AT ONCE... I'LL HAVE NO ONE ELSE TO BLAME IF I'M DUMPED BY BOTH!
BUT IF HE IS STILL THERE...
IF HE'S THERE...!!

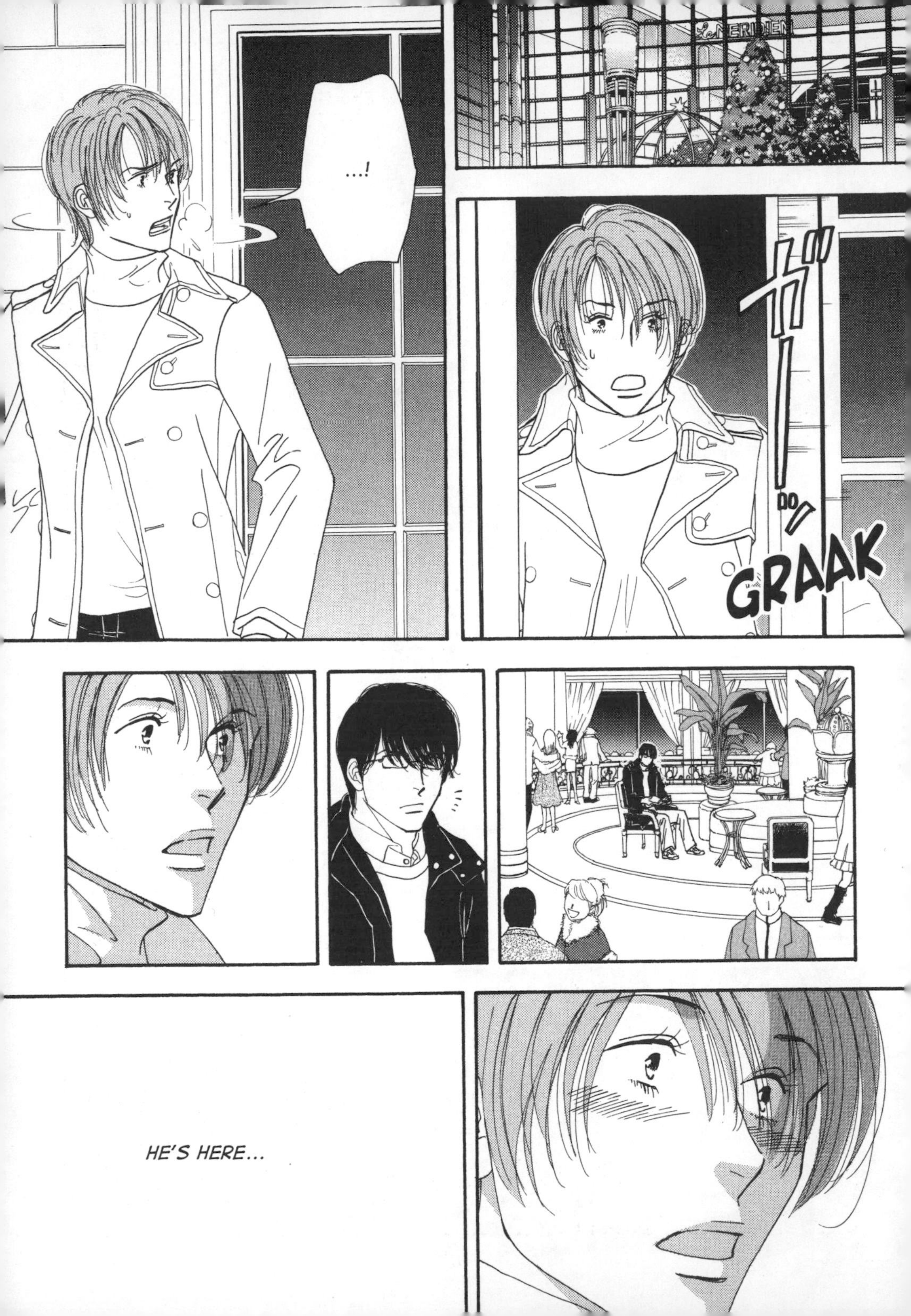
MERIDIEN
ガ
GRAAK
...!
HE'S HERE...

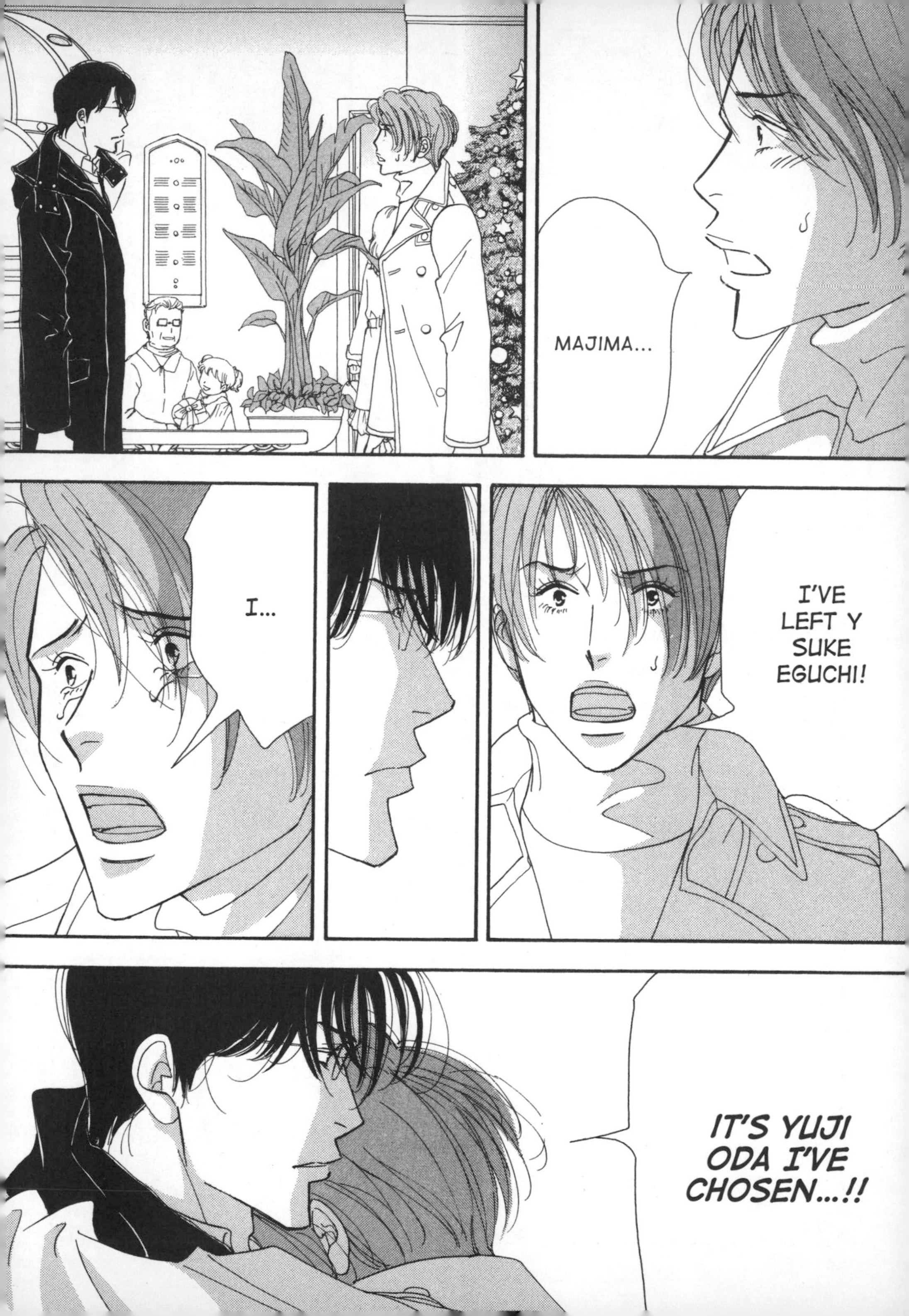
MAJIMA...
I'VE LEFT Y SUKE EGUCHI!
I...
IT'S YUJI ODA I'VE CHOSEN...!!

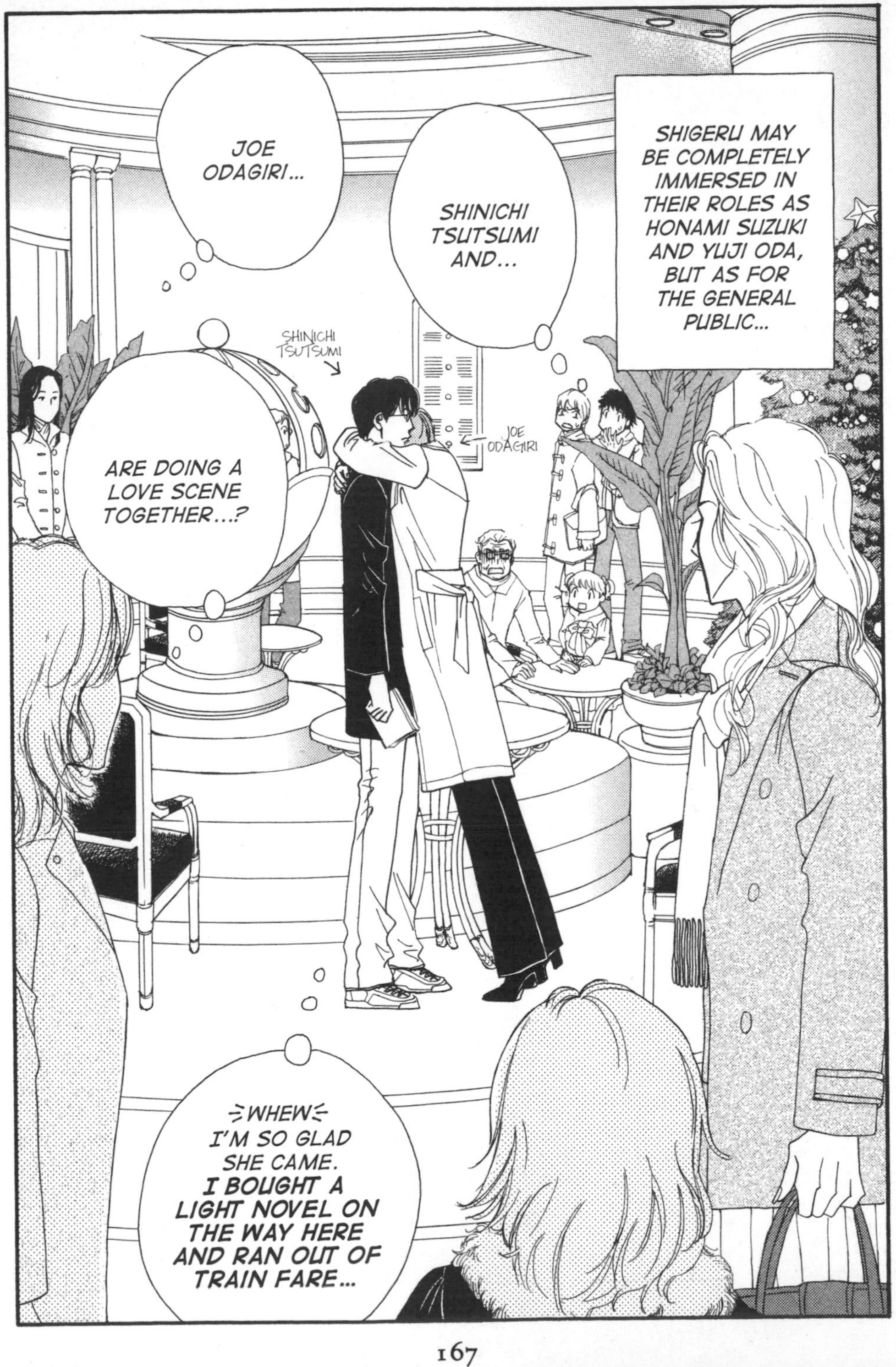
SHIGERU MAY BE COMPLETELY IMMERSED IN THEIR ROLES AS HONAMI SUZUKI AND YUJI ODA, BUT AS FOR THE GENERAL PUBLIC...
SHINICHI TSUTSUMI AND...
JOE ODAGIRI...
ARE DOING A LOVE SCENE TOGETHER...?
JOE ODAGIRI
SHINICHI TSUTSUMI
WHEW I'M SO GLAD SHE CAME. I BOUGHT A LIGHT NOVEL ON THE WAY HERE AND RAN OUT OF TRAIN FARE...

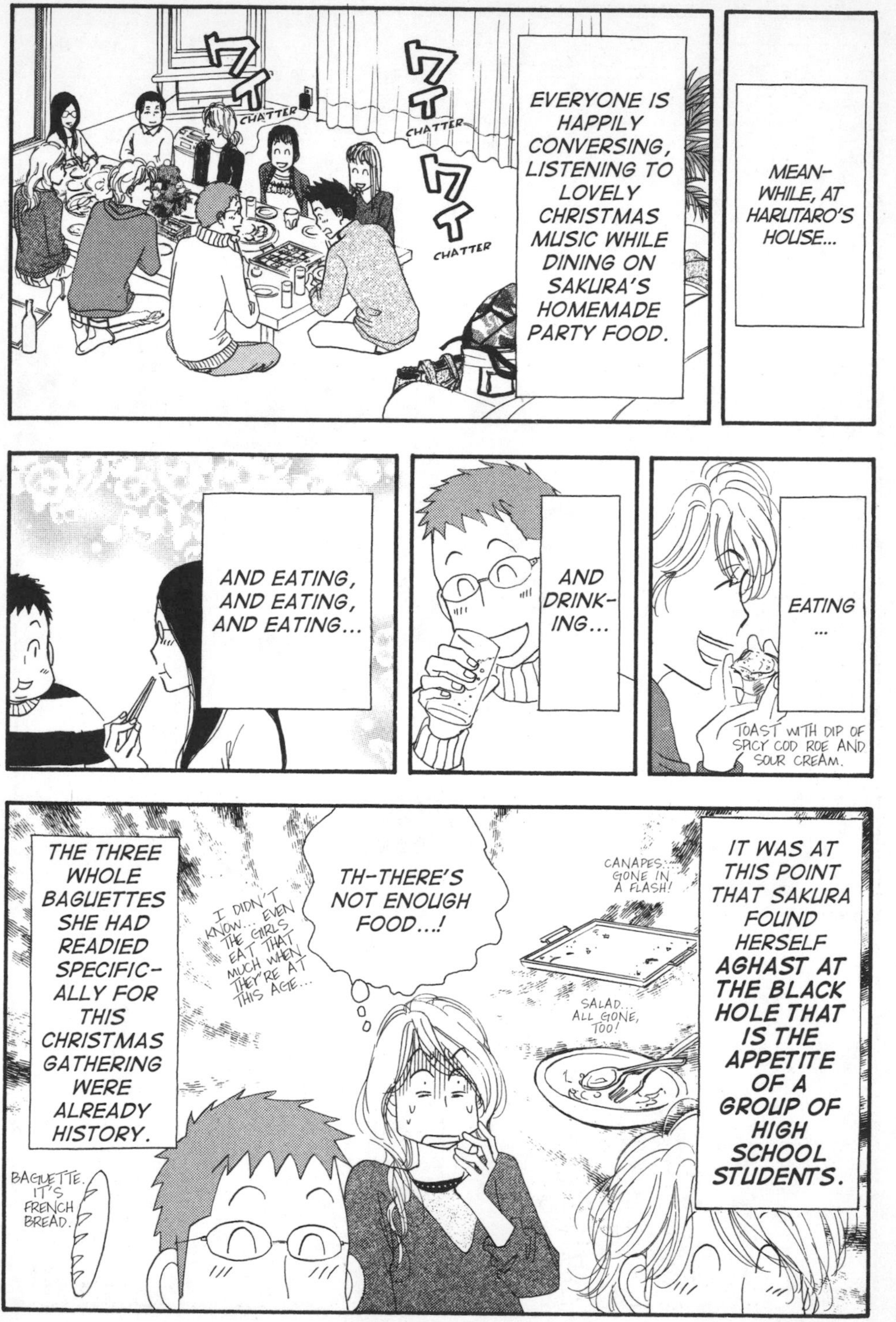
MEAN-WHILE, AT HARUTARO'S HOUSE...
EVERYONE IS HAPPILY CONVERSING, LISTENING TO LOVELY CHRISTMAS MUSIC WHILE DINING ON SAKURA'S HOMEMADE PARTY FOOD.
ワイ CHATTER
ワイ CHATTER
ワイ CHATTER
EATING ...
TOAST WITH DIP OF SPICY COD ROE AND SOUR CREAM.
AND DRINK-ING...
AND EATING, AND EATING, AND EATING...
IT WAS AT THIS POINT THAT SAKURA FOUND HERSELF AGHAST AT THE BLACK HOLE THAT IS THE APPETITE OF A GROUP OF HIGH SCHOOL STUDENTS.
CANAPES... GONE IN A FLASH!
SALAD... ALL GONE, TOO!
TH-THERE'S NOT ENOUGH FOOD...!
I DIDN'T KNOW... EVEN THE GIRLS EAT THAT MUCH WHEN THEY'RE AT THIS AGE...
THE THREE WHOLE BAGUETTES SHE HAD READIED SPECIFIC-ALLY FOR THIS CHRISTMAS GATHERING WERE ALREADY HISTORY.
BAGUETTE. IT'S FRENCH BREAD.

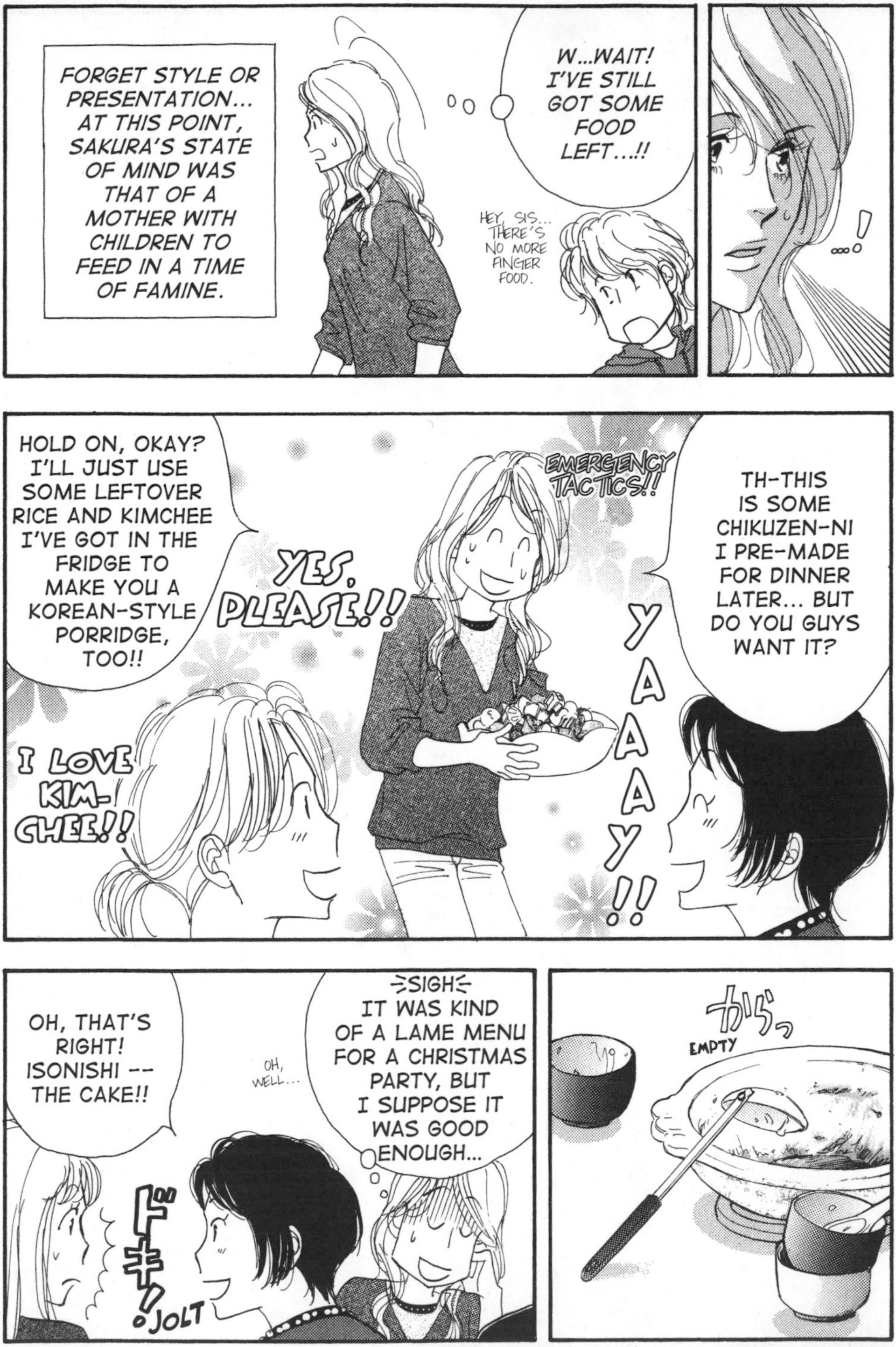
...!
W...WAIT! I'VE STILL GOT SOME FOOD LEFT...!!
HEY, SIS... THERE'S NO MORE FINGER FOOD.
FORGET STYLE OR PRESENTATION... AT THIS POINT, SAKURA'S STATE OF MIND WAS THAT OF A MOTHER WITH CHILDREN TO FEED IN A TIME OF FAMINE.
TH-THIS IS SOME CHIKUZEN-NI I PRE-MADE FOR DINNER LATER... BUT DO YOU GUYS WANT IT?
YAAAAY!!
EMERGENCY TACTICS!!
YES, PLEASE!!
HOLD ON, OKAY? I'LL JUST USE SOME LEFTOVER RICE AND KIMCHEE I'VE GOT IN THE FRIDGE TO MAKE YOU A KOREAN-STYLE PORRIDGE, TOO!!
I LOVE KIM-CHEE!!
からっ
EMPTY
SIGH
IT WAS KIND OF A LAME MENU FOR A CHRISTMAS PARTY, BUT I SUPPOSE IT WAS GOOD ENOUGH...
OH, WELL...
OH, THAT'S RIGHT! ISONISHI -- THE CAKE!!
ドキ!
JOLT

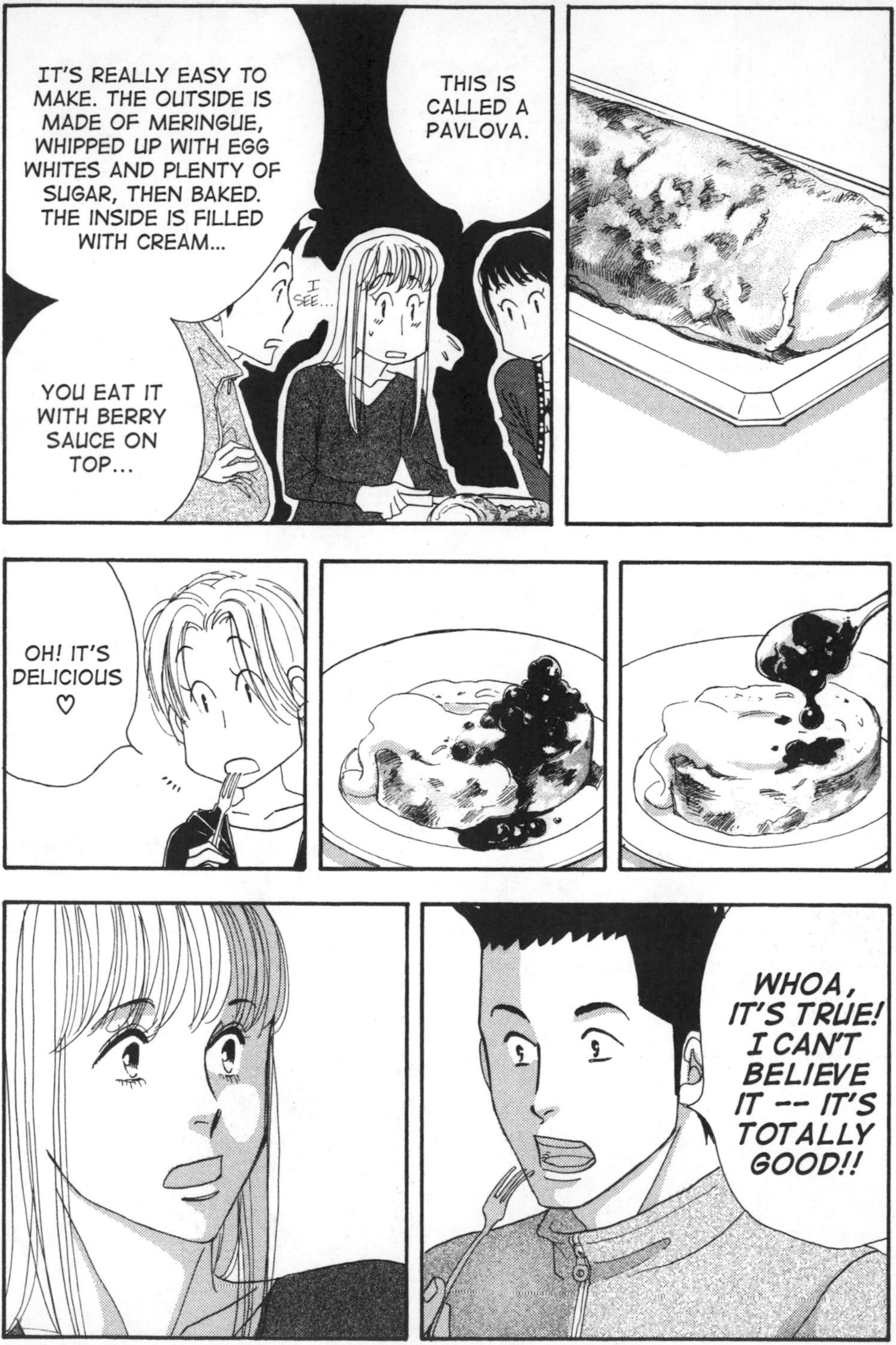
THIS IS CALLED A PAVLOVA.
IT'S REALLY EASY TO MAKE. THE OUTSIDE IS MADE OF MERINGUE, WHIPPED UP WITH EGG WHITES AND PLENTY OF SUGAR, THEN BAKED. THE INSIDE IS FILLED WITH CREAM...
I SEE...
YOU EAT IT WITH BERRY SAUCE ON TOP...
OH! IT'S DELICIOUS ♡
WHOA, IT'S TRUE! I CAN'T BELIEVE IT -- IT'S TOTALLY GOOD!!

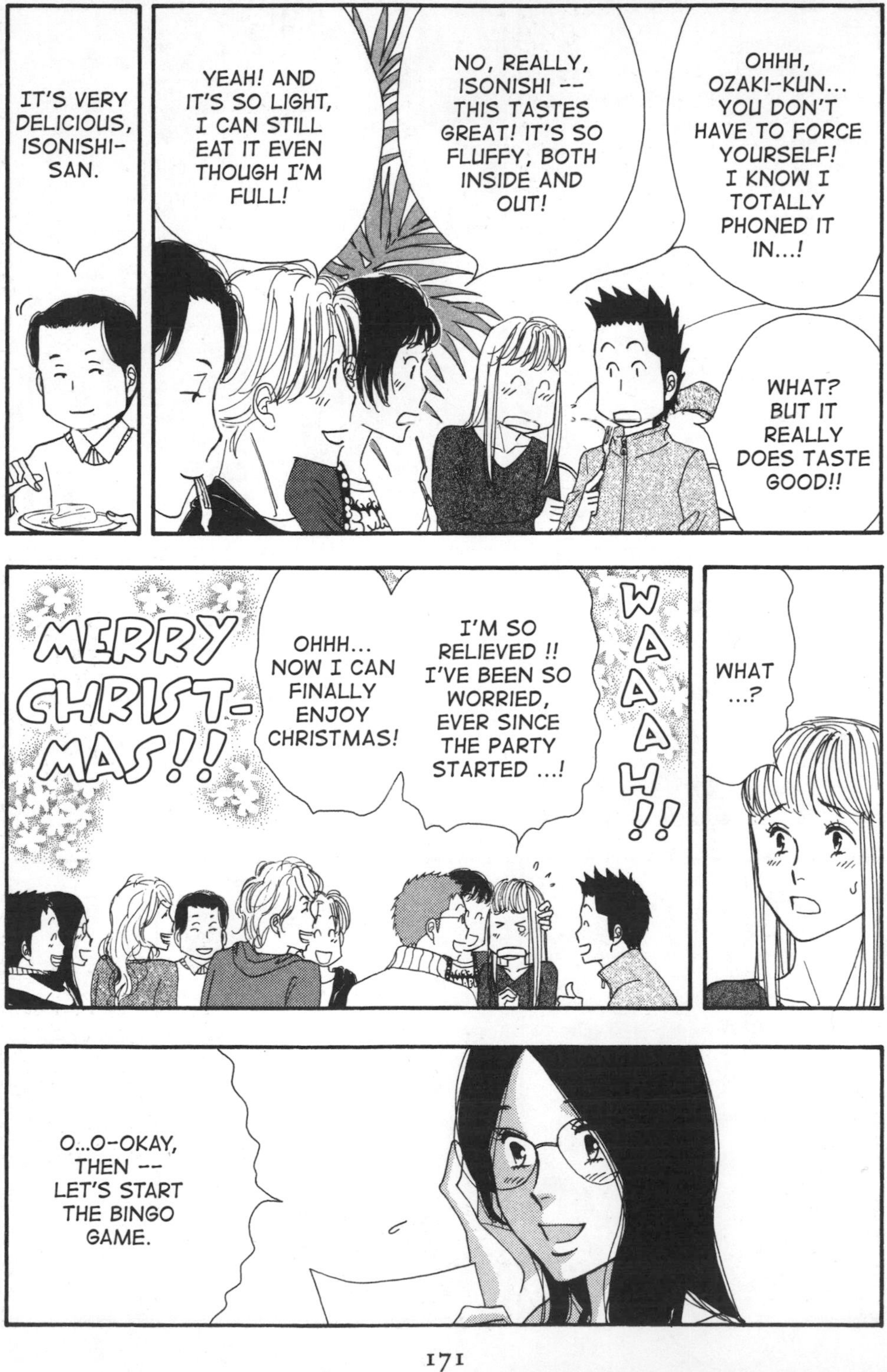
OHHH, OZAKI-KUN... YOU DON'T HAVE TO FORCE YOURSELF! I KNOW I TOTALLY PHONED IT IN...!
WHAT? BUT IT REALLY DOES TASTE GOOD!!
NO, REALLY, ISONISHI -- THIS TASTES GREAT! IT'S SO FLUFFY, BOTH INSIDE AND OUT!
YEAH! AND IT'S SO LIGHT, I CAN STILL EAT IT EVEN THOUGH I'M FULL!
IT'S VERY DELICIOUS, ISONISHI-SAN.
WHAT ...?
WAAAH!!
I'M SO RELIEVED !! I'VE BEEN SO WORRIED, EVER SINCE THE PARTY STARTED ...!
OHHH... NOW I CAN FINALLY ENJOY CHRISTMAS!
MERRY CHRIST-MAS!!
O...O-OKAY, THEN -- LET'S START THE BINGO GAME.

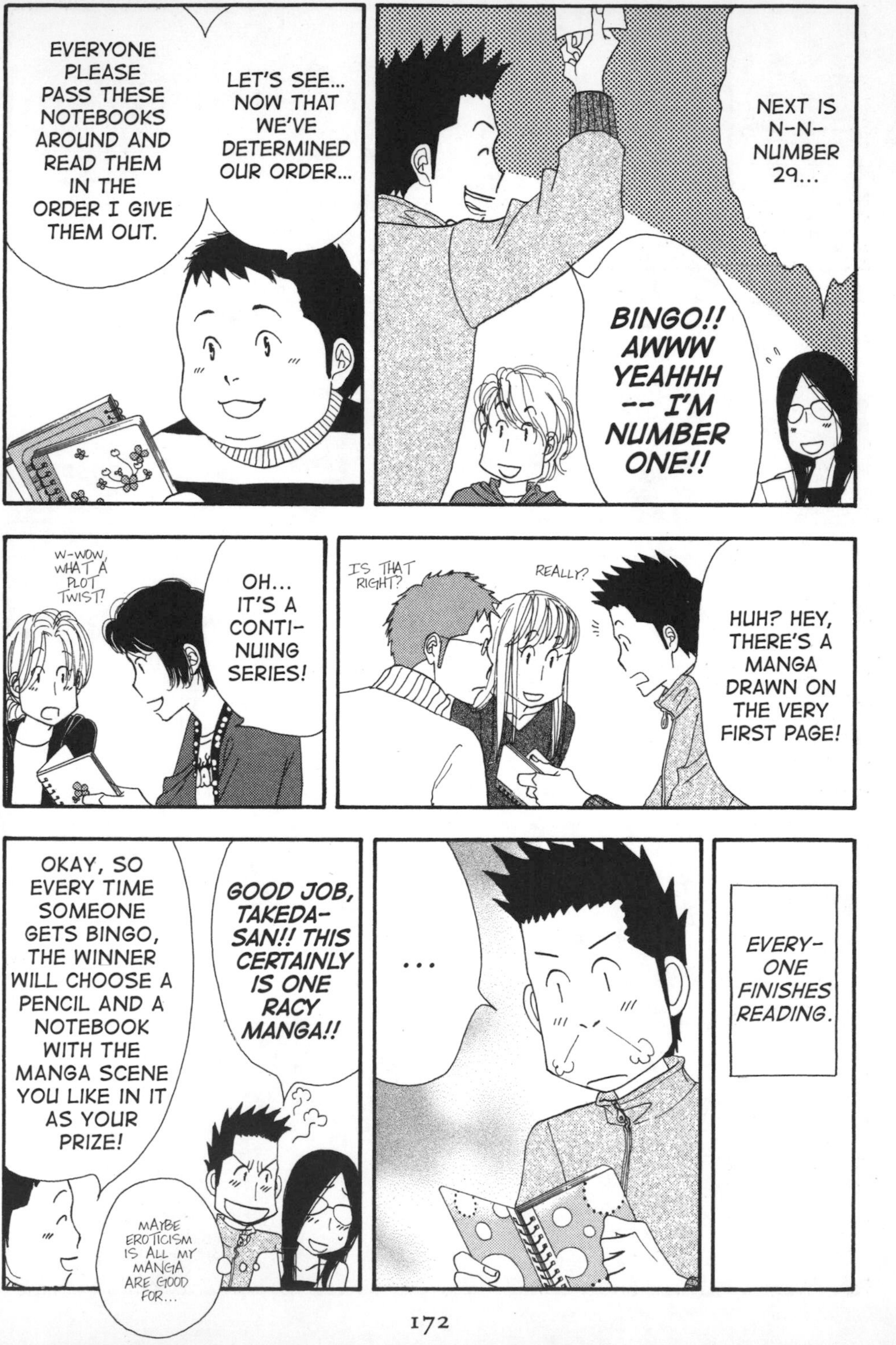
NEXT IS N-N-NUMBER 29...
BINGO!! AWWW YEAHHH -- I'M NUMBER ONE!!
LET'S SEE... NOW THAT WE'VE DETERMINED OUR ORDER...
EVERYONE PLEASE PASS THESE NOTEBOOKS AROUND AND READ THEM IN THE ORDER I GIVE THEM OUT.
HUH? HEY, THERE'S A MANGA DRAWN ON THE VERY FIRST PAGE!
REALLY?
IS THAT RIGHT?
OH... IT'S A CONTINUING SERIES!
W-WOW, WHAT A PLOT TWIST!
EVERYONE FINISHES READING.
...
GOOD JOB, TAKEDA-SAN!! THIS CERTAINLY IS ONE RACY MANGA!!
OKAY, SO EVERY TIME SOMEONE GETS BINGO, THE WINNER WILL CHOOSE A PENCIL AND A NOTEBOOK WITH THE MANGA SCENE YOU LIKE IN IT AS YOUR PRIZE!
MAYBE EROTICISM IS ALL MY MANGA ARE GOOD FOR...

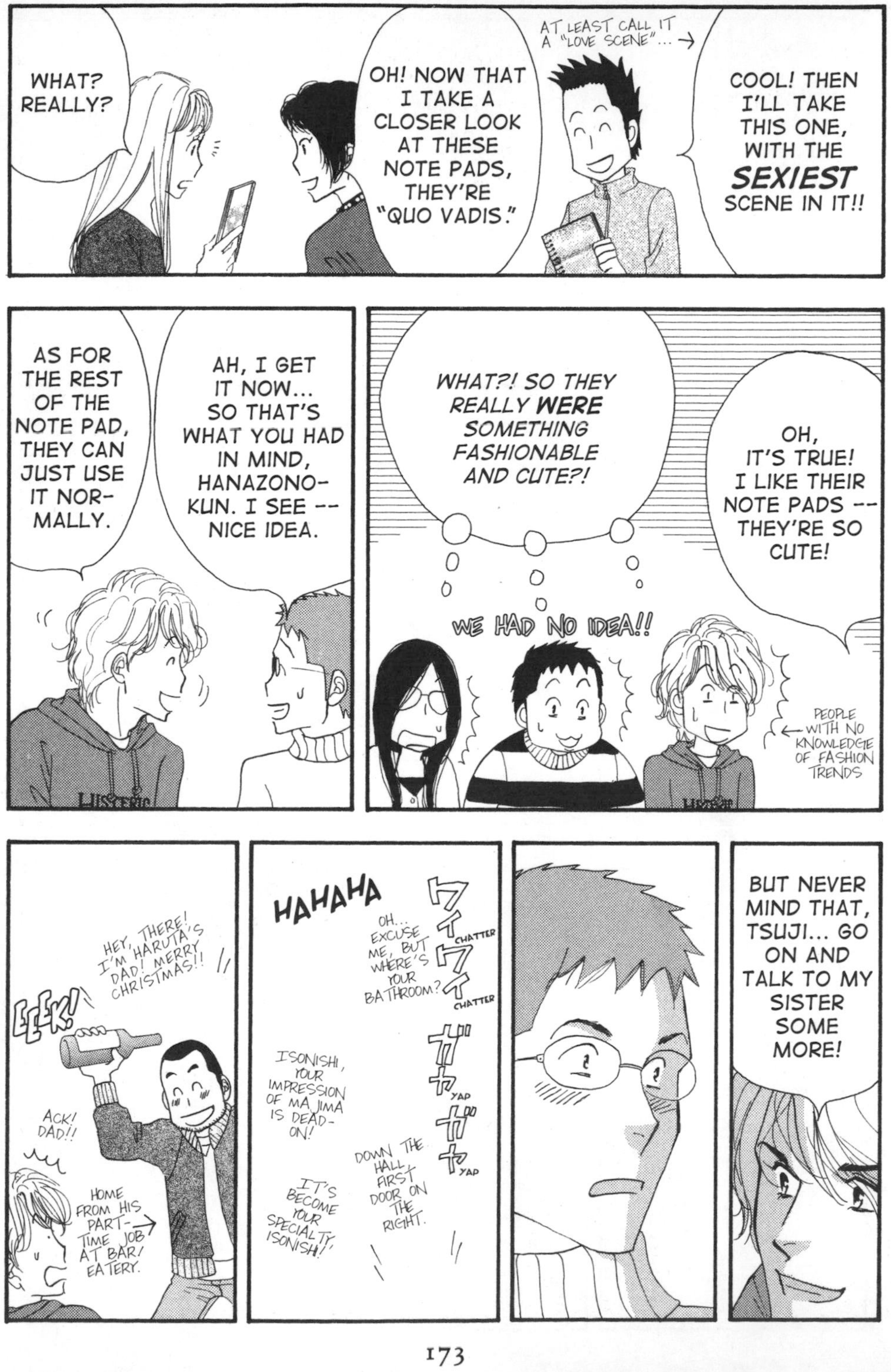
COOL! THEN I'LL TAKE THIS ONE, WITH THE **SEXIEST** SCENE IN IT!!
AT LEAST CALL IT A "LOVE SCENE"...
OH! NOW THAT I TAKE A CLOSER LOOK AT THESE NOTE PADS, THEY'RE "QUO VADIS."
WHAT? REALLY?
OH, IT'S TRUE! I LIKE THEIR NOTE PADS -- THEY'RE SO CUTE!
WHAT?! SO THEY REALLY **WERE** *SOMETHING FASHIONABLE AND CUTE?!*
WE HAD NO IDEA!!
PEOPLE WITH NO KNOWLEDGE OF FASHION TRENDS
AH, I GET IT NOW... SO THAT'S WHAT YOU HAD IN MIND, HANAZONO-KUN. I SEE -- NICE IDEA.
AS FOR THE REST OF THE NOTE PAD, THEY CAN JUST USE IT NORMALLY.
BUT NEVER MIND THAT, TSUJI... GO ON AND TALK TO MY SISTER SOME MORE!
HAHAHA
ワイワイ
CHATTER
CHATTER
OH... EXCUSE ME, BUT WHERE'S YOUR BATHROOM?
ガヤガヤ
YAP
YAP
ISONISHI, YOUR IMPRESSION OF MAJIMA IS DEAD-ON!
DOWN THE HALL FIRST DOOR ON THE RIGHT.
IT'S BECOME YOUR SPECIALTY, ISONISHI!
HEY, THERE! I'M HARUTA'S DAD! MERRY CHRISTMAS!!
EEEK!
ACK! DAD!!
HOME FROM HIS PART-TIME JOB AT BAR/EATERY.

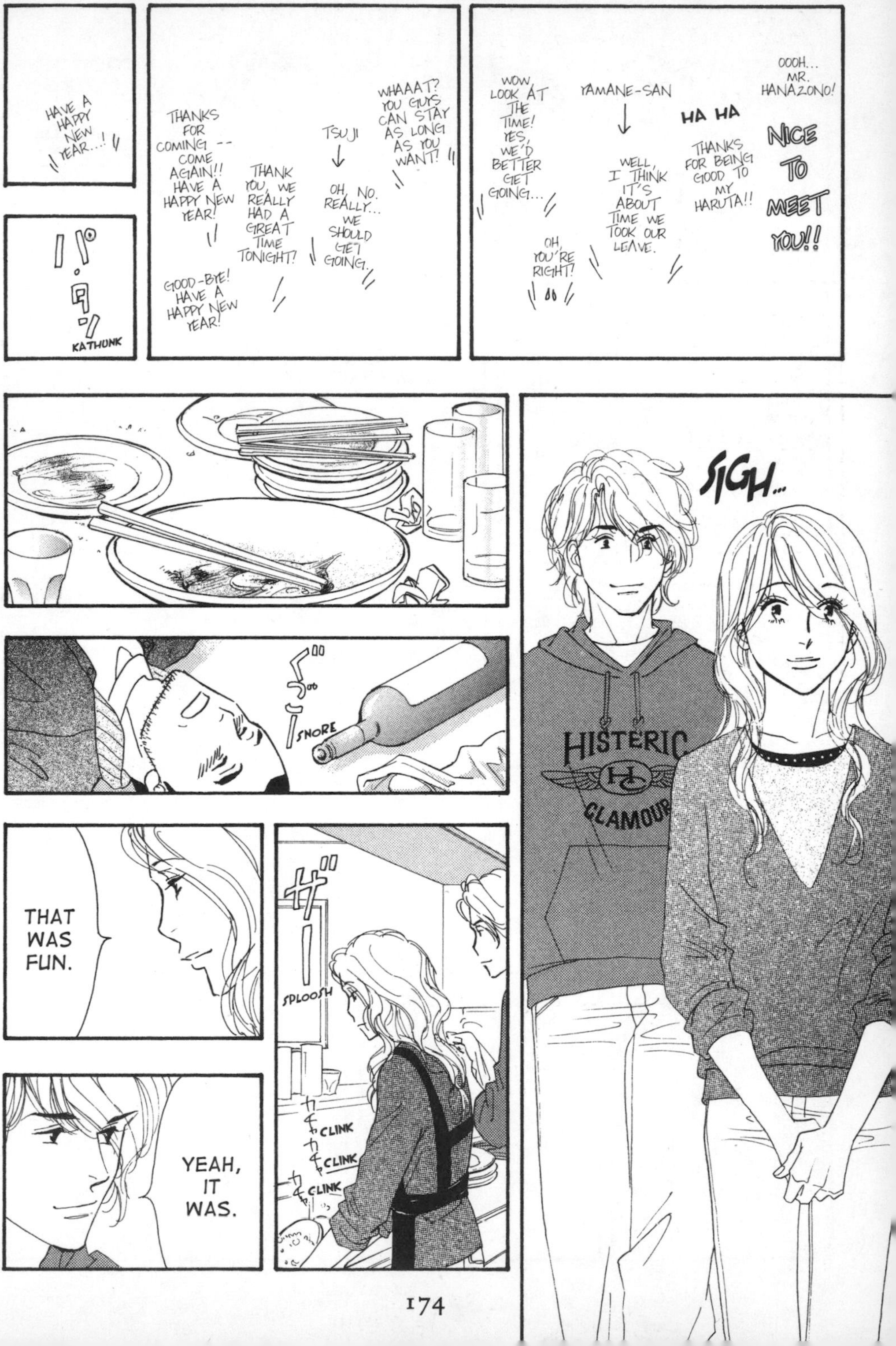
OOOH... MR. HANAZONO!
NICE TO MEET YOU!!
HA HA
THANKS FOR BEING GOOD TO MY HARUTA!!
YAMANE-SAN
WELL, I THINK IT'S ABOUT TIME WE TOOK OUR LEAVE.
WOW LOOK AT THE TIME! YES, WE'D BETTER GET GOING...
OH, YOU'RE RIGHT!
WHAAAT? YOU GUYS CAN STAY AS LONG AS YOU WANT!
TSUJI
OH, NO. REALLY... WE SHOULD GET GOING.
THANK YOU, WE REALLY HAD A GREAT TIME TONIGHT!
THANKS FOR COMING -- COME AGAIN!! HAVE A HAPPY NEW YEAR!
GOOD-BYE! HAVE A HAPPY NEW YEAR!
HAVE A HAPPY NEW YEAR...!
KATHUNK
SIGH...
SNORE
SPLOOSH
CLINK
CLINK
CLINK
THAT WAS FUN.
YEAH, IT WAS.

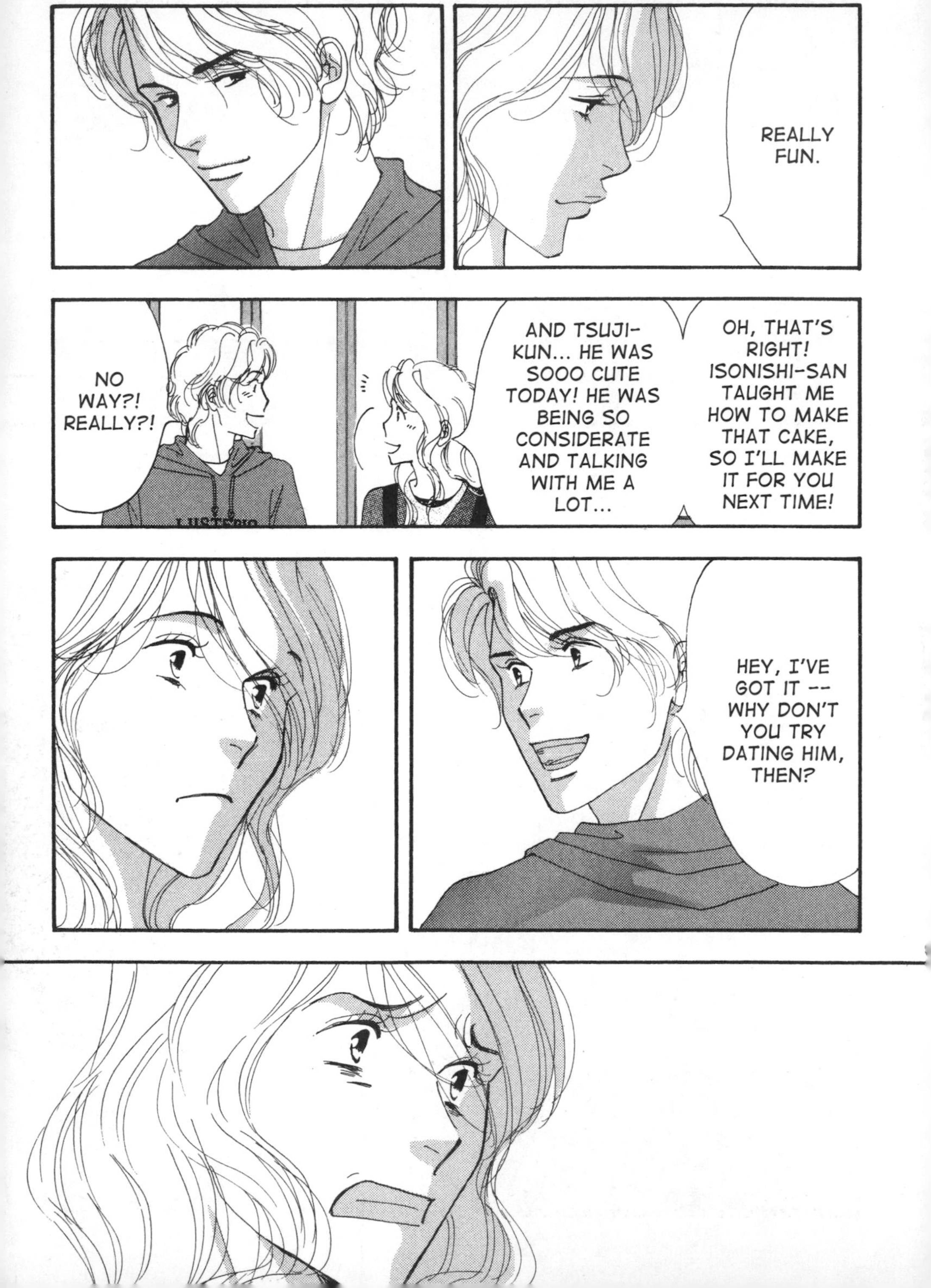
REALLY FUN.
OH, THAT'S RIGHT! ISONISHI-SAN TAUGHT ME HOW TO MAKE THAT CAKE, SO I'LL MAKE IT FOR YOU NEXT TIME!
AND TSUJI-KUN... HE WAS SOOO CUTE TODAY! HE WAS BEING SO CONSIDERATE AND TALKING WITH ME A LOT...
NO WAY?! REALLY?!
HEY, I'VE GOT IT -- WHY DON'T YOU TRY DATING HIM, THEN?

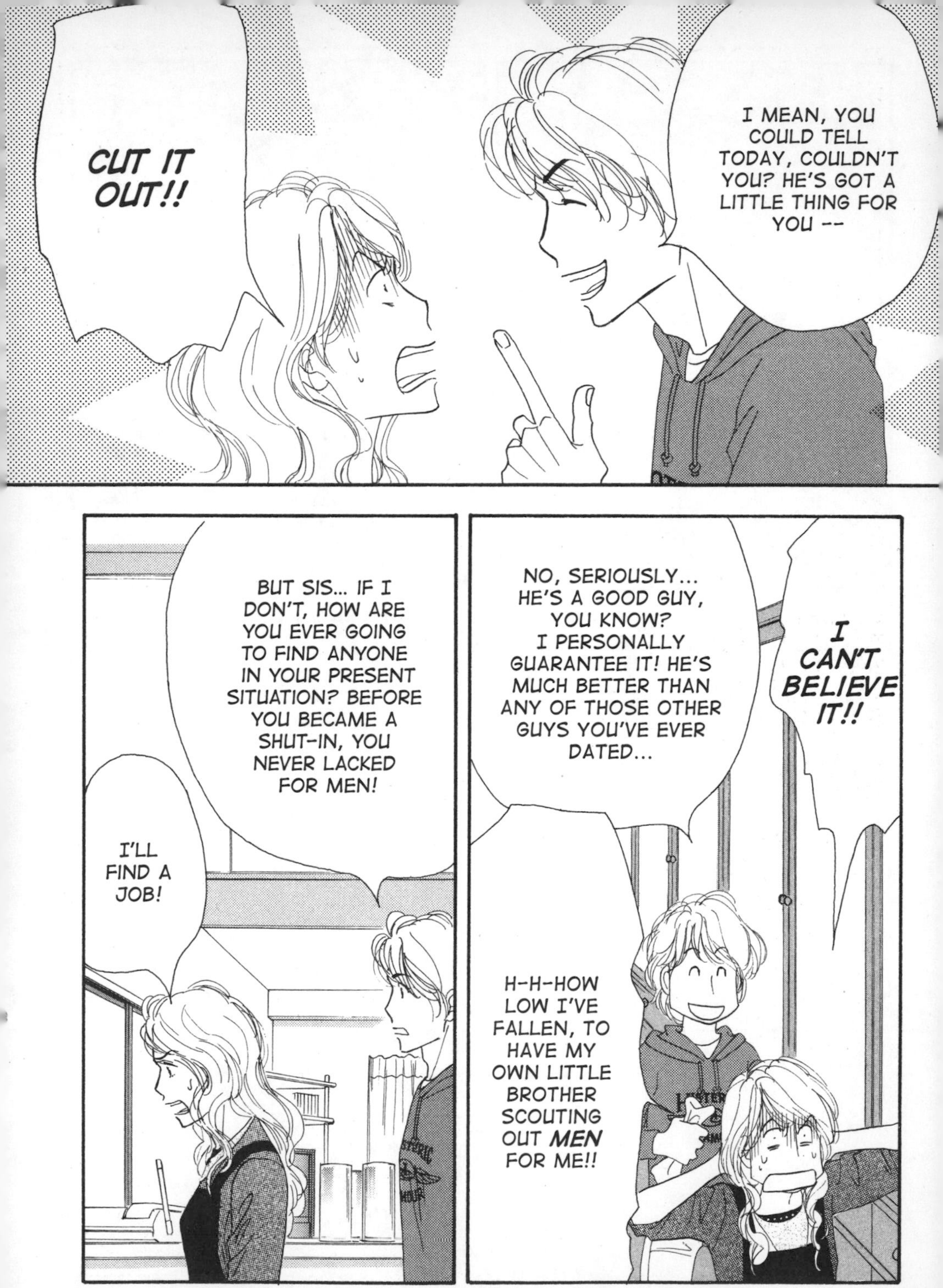
I MEAN, YOU COULD TELL TODAY, COULDN'T YOU? HE'S GOT A LITTLE THING FOR YOU --
CUT IT OUT!!
NO, SERIOUSLY... HE'S A GOOD GUY, YOU KNOW? I PERSONALLY GUARANTEE IT! HE'S MUCH BETTER THAN ANY OF THOSE OTHER GUYS YOU'VE EVER DATED...
I CAN'T BELIEVE IT!!
H-H-HOW LOW I'VE FALLEN, TO HAVE MY OWN LITTLE BROTHER SCOUTING OUT MEN FOR ME!!
BUT SIS... IF I DON'T, HOW ARE YOU EVER GOING TO FIND ANYONE IN YOUR PRESENT SITUATION? BEFORE YOU BECAME A SHUT-IN, YOU NEVER LACKED FOR MEN!
I'LL FIND A JOB!

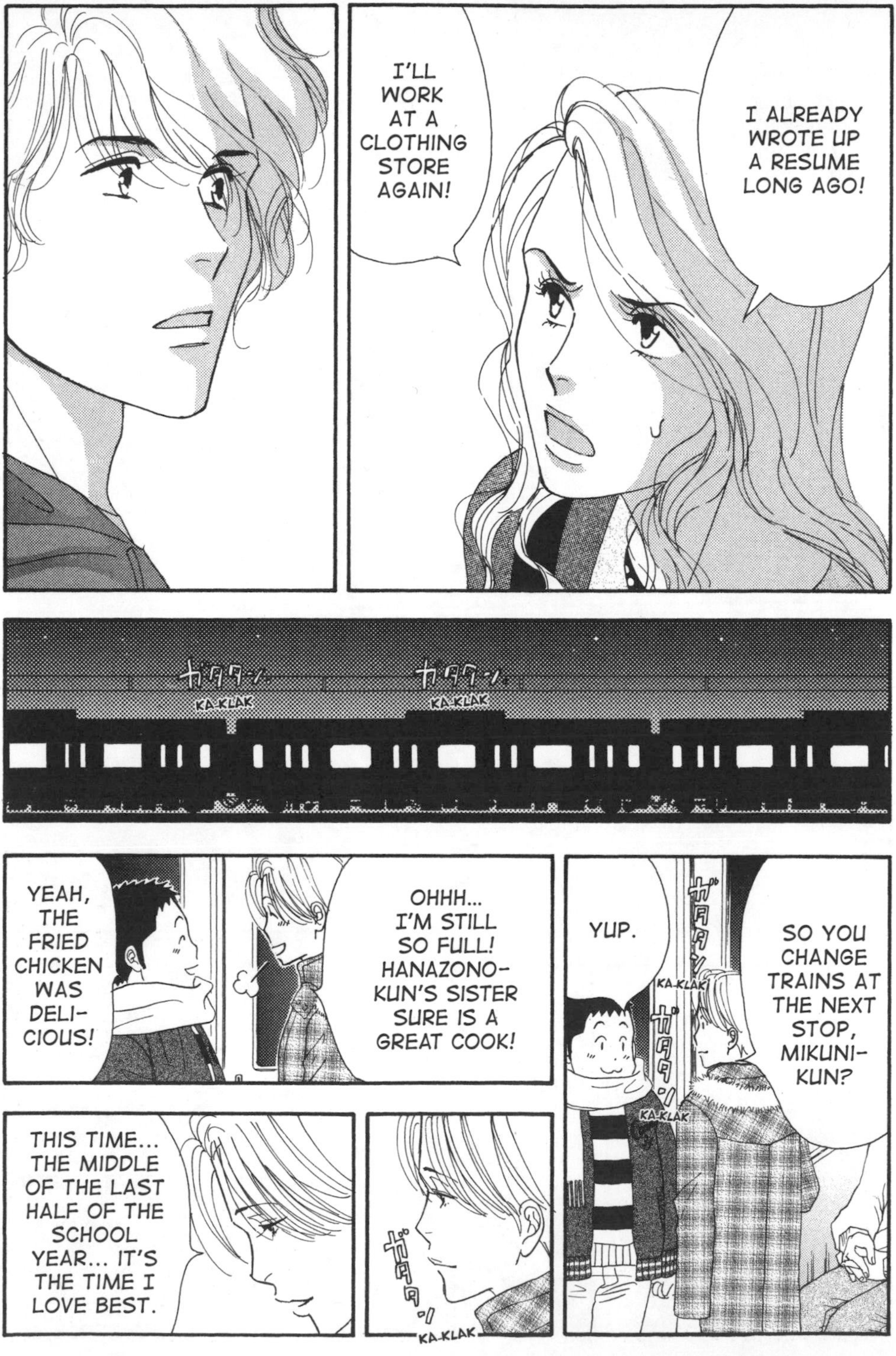
I ALREADY WROTE UP A RESUME LONG AGO!
I'LL WORK AT A CLOTHING STORE AGAIN!
KA-KLAK
KA-KLAK
SO YOU CHANGE TRAINS AT THE NEXT STOP, MIKUNI-KUN?
YUP.
KA-KLAK
KA-KLAK
OHHH... I'M STILL SO FULL! HANAZONO-KUN'S SISTER SURE IS A GREAT COOK!
YEAH, THE FRIED CHICKEN WAS DELICIOUS!
KA-KLAK
THIS TIME... THE MIDDLE OF THE LAST HALF OF THE SCHOOL YEAR... IT'S THE TIME I LOVE BEST.

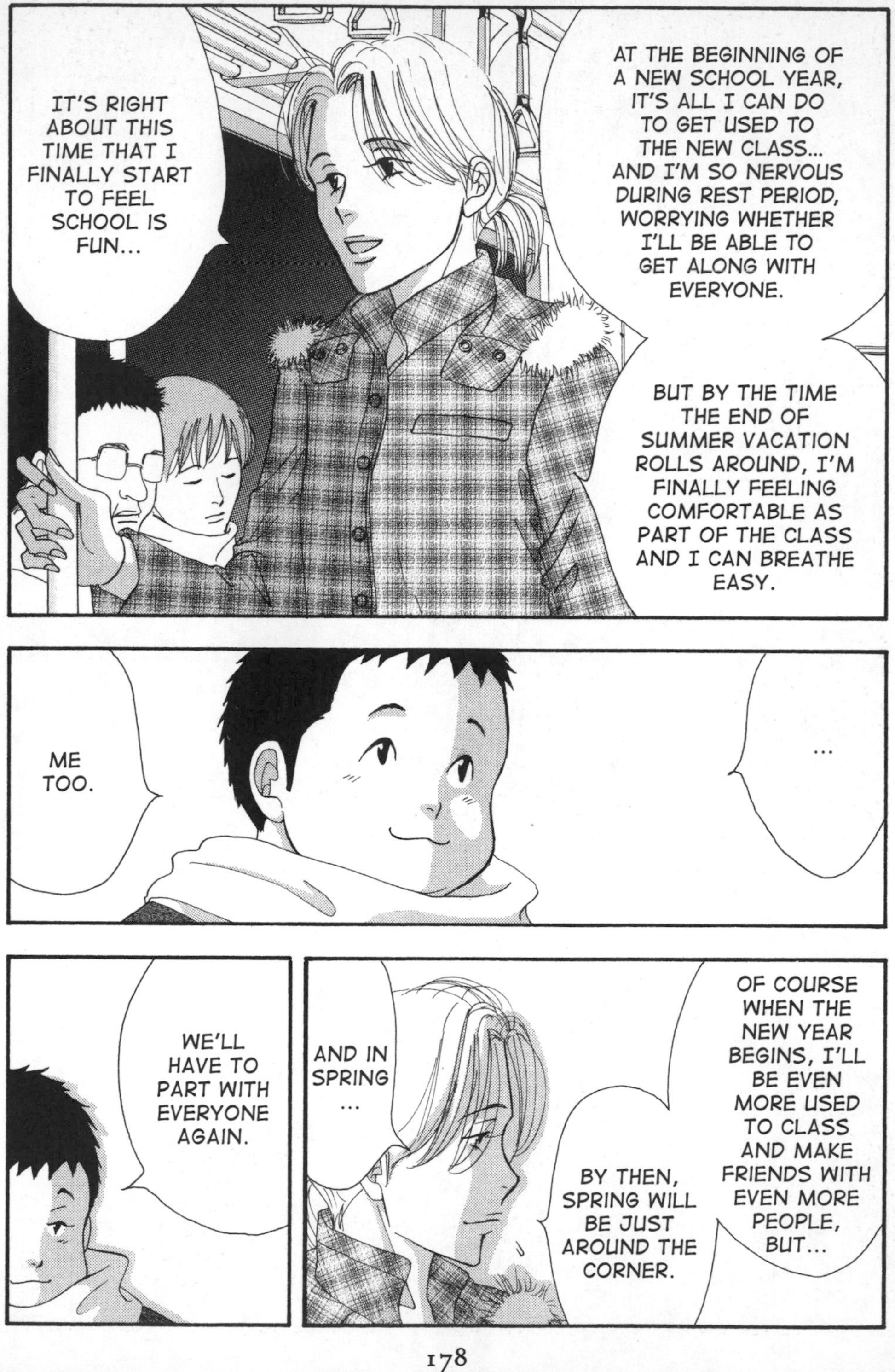
AT THE BEGINNING OF A NEW SCHOOL YEAR, IT'S ALL I CAN DO TO GET USED TO THE NEW CLASS... AND I'M SO NERVOUS DURING REST PERIOD, WORRYING WHETHER I'LL BE ABLE TO GET ALONG WITH EVERYONE.
BUT BY THE TIME THE END OF SUMMER VACATION ROLLS AROUND, I'M FINALLY FEELING COMFORTABLE AS PART OF THE CLASS AND I CAN BREATHE EASY.
IT'S RIGHT ABOUT THIS TIME THAT I FINALLY START TO FEEL SCHOOL IS FUN...
...
ME TOO.
OF COURSE WHEN THE NEW YEAR BEGINS, I'LL BE EVEN MORE USED TO CLASS AND MAKE FRIENDS WITH EVEN MORE PEOPLE, BUT...
BY THEN, SPRING WILL BE JUST AROUND THE CORNER.
AND IN SPRING ...
WE'LL HAVE TO PART WITH EVERYONE AGAIN.

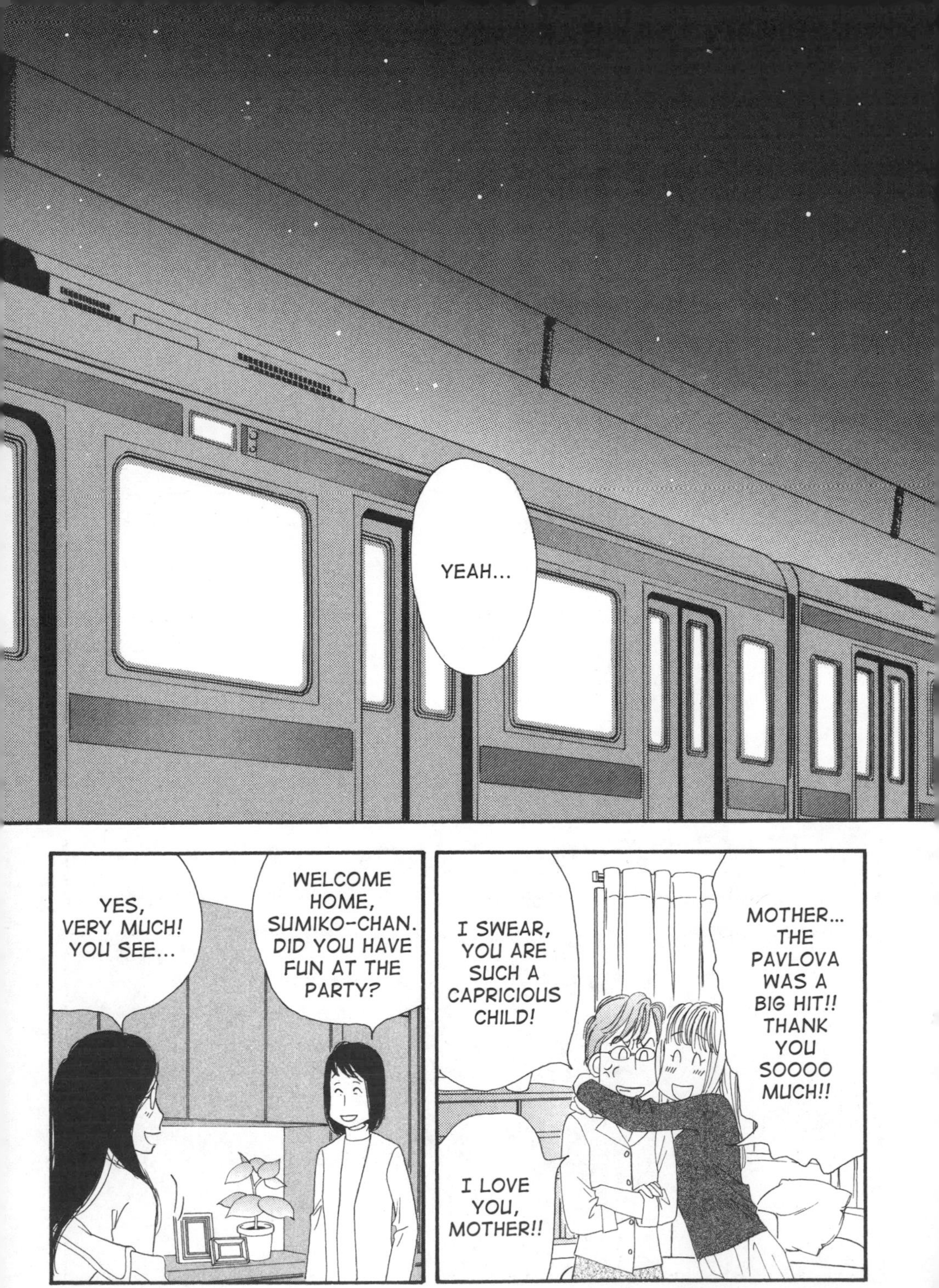
YEAH...
MOTHER... THE PAVLOVA WAS A BIG HIT!! THANK YOU SOOOO MUCH!!
I SWEAR, YOU ARE SUCH A CAPRICIOUS CHILD!
I LOVE YOU, MOTHER!!
WELCOME HOME, SUMIKO-CHAN. DID YOU HAVE FUN AT THE PARTY?
YES, VERY MUCH! YOU SEE...

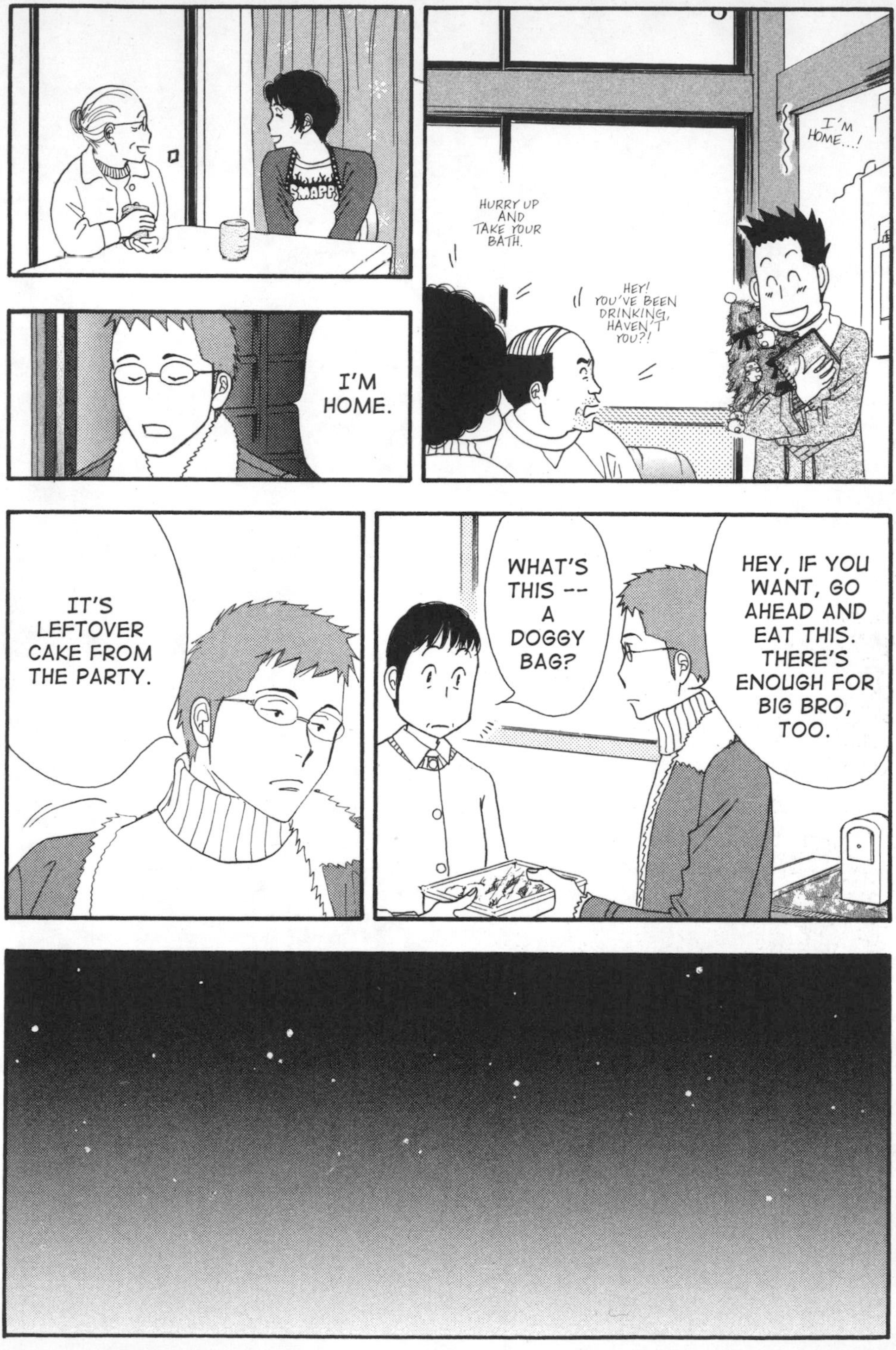
I'M HOME...!
HEY! YOU'VE BEEN DRINKING, HAVEN'T YOU?!
HURRY UP AND TAKE YOUR BATH.
I'M HOME.
HEY, IF YOU WANT, GO AHEAD AND EAT THIS. THERE'S ENOUGH FOR BIG BRO, TOO.
WHAT'S THIS -- A DOGGY BAG?
IT'S LEFTOVER CAKE FROM THE PARTY.

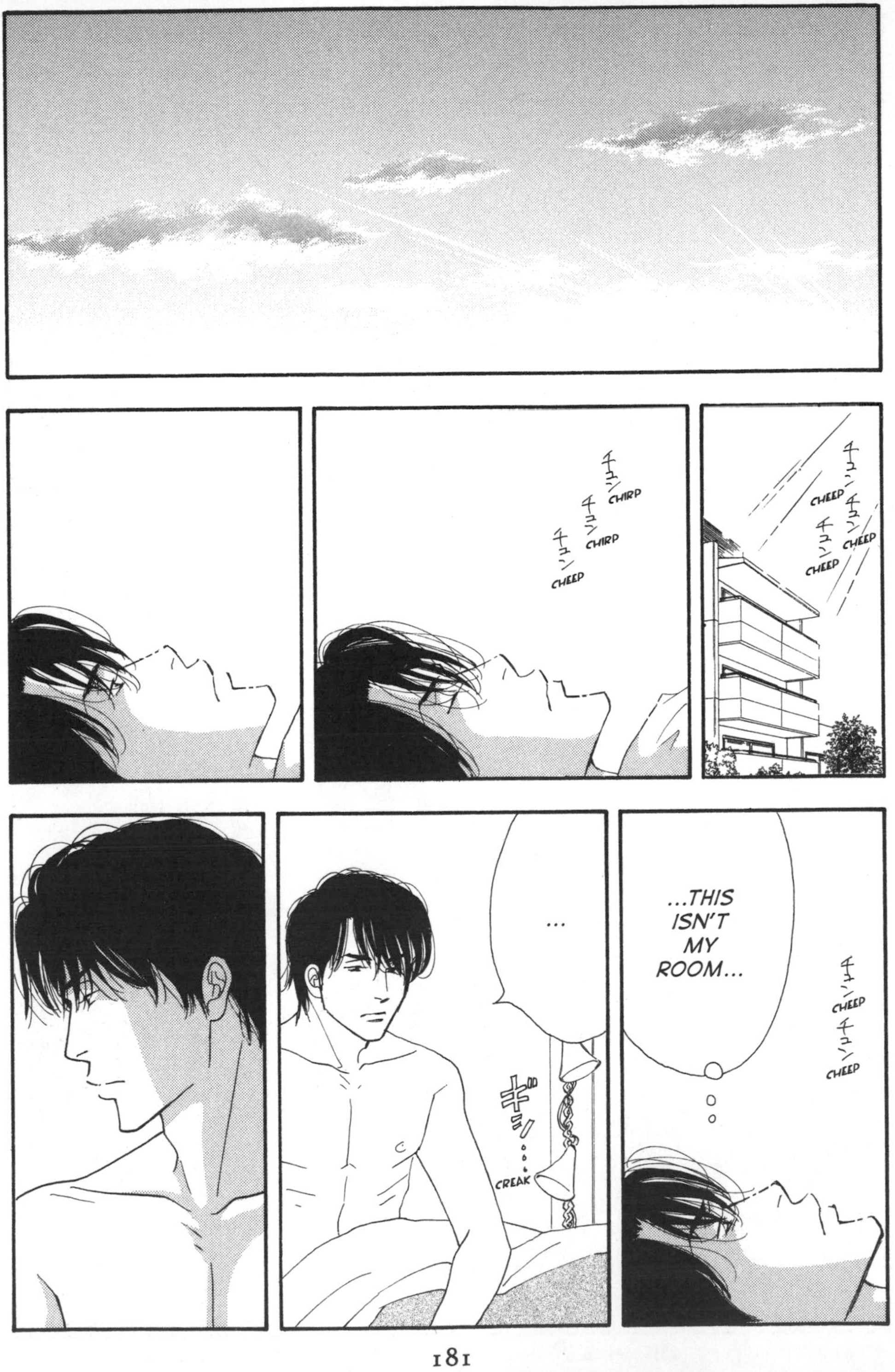

チュン CHEEP
チュン CHEEP
チュン CHEEP
チュン CHIRP
チュン CHIRP
チュン CHEEP
...THIS ISN'T MY ROOM...
チュン CHEEP
チュン CHEEP
...
ギシ... CREAK

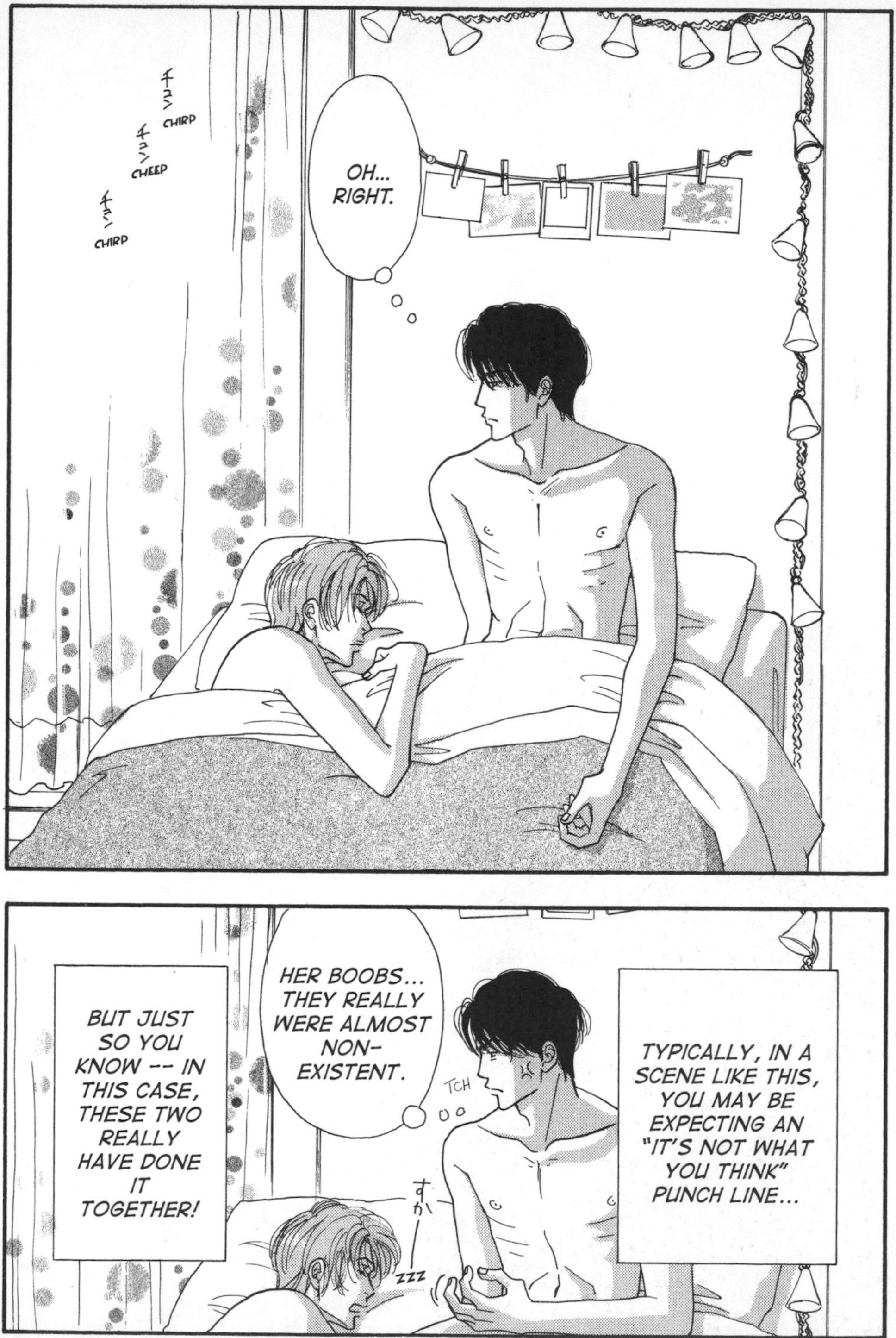
OH... RIGHT.
チュン
CHIRP
チュン
CHEEP
チュン
CHIRP
TYPICALLY, IN A SCENE LIKE THIS, YOU MAY BE EXPECTING AN "IT'S NOT WHAT YOU THINK" PUNCH LINE...
TCH
HER BOOBS... THEY REALLY WERE ALMOST NON-EXISTENT.
すか
ZZZ
BUT JUST SO YOU KNOW -- IN THIS CASE, THESE TWO REALLY HAVE DONE IT TOGETHER!

✻ CONTINUED IN VOLUME 4 ✻

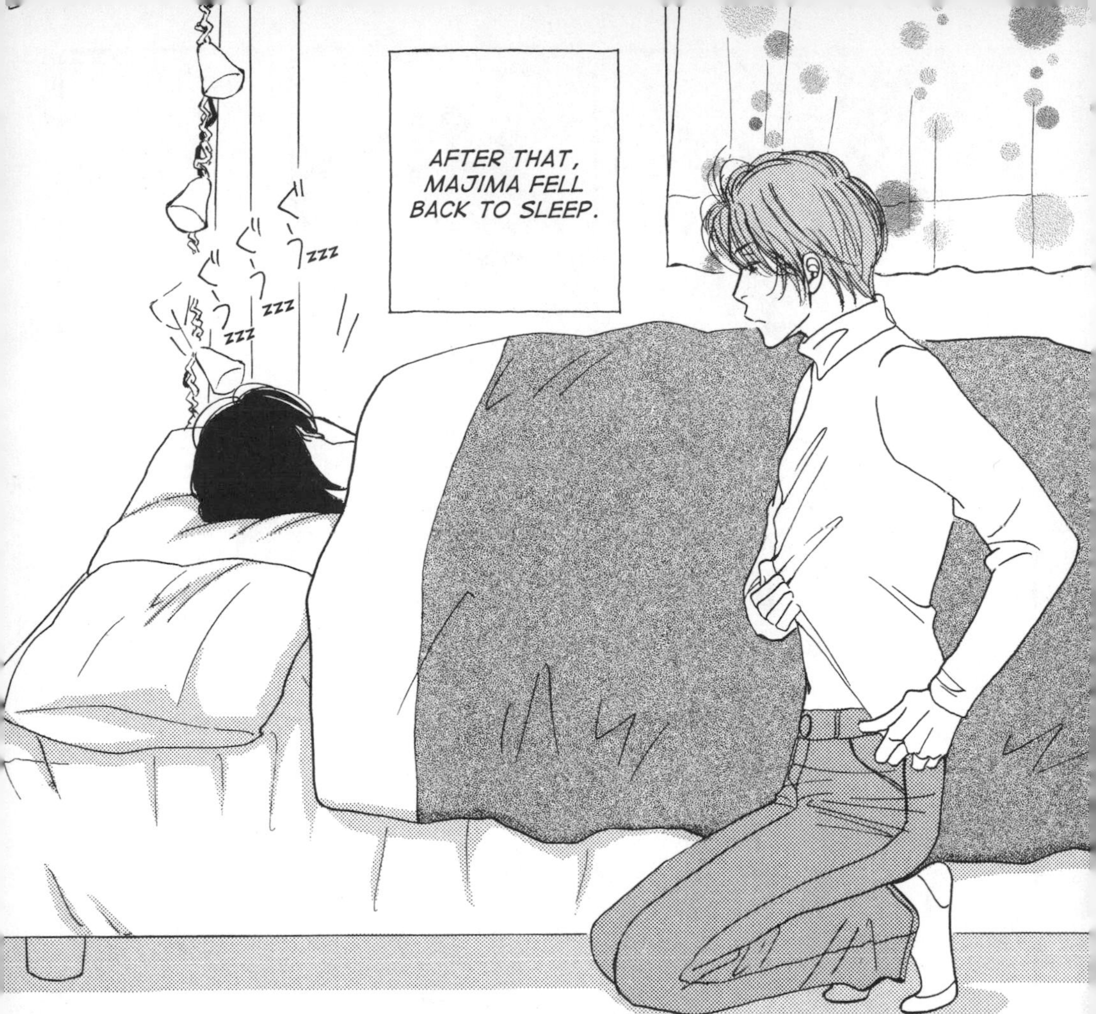
AFTER THAT, MAJIMA FELL BACK TO SLEEP.
ぐう zzz
ぐう zzz
ぐう zzz

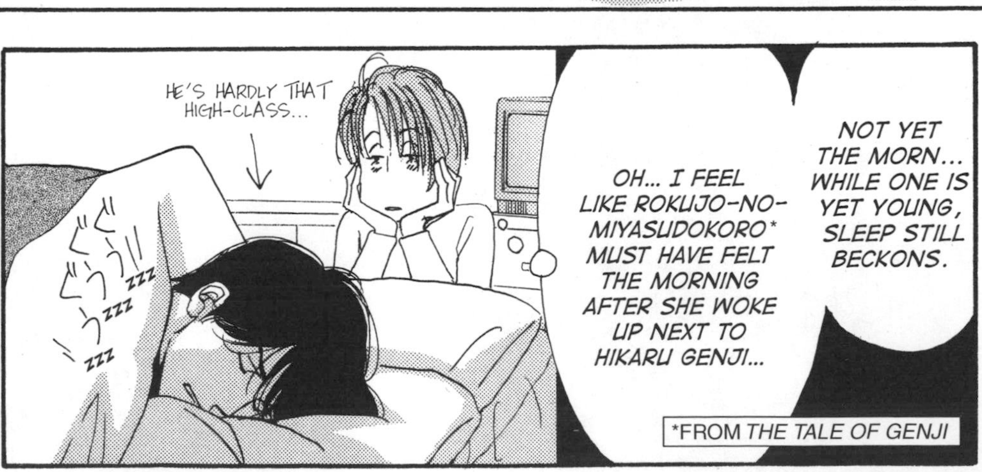
NOT YET THE MORN... WHILE ONE IS YET YOUNG, SLEEP STILL BECKONS.
OH... I FEEL LIKE ROKUJO-NO-MIYASUDOKORO* MUST HAVE FELT THE MORNING AFTER SHE WOKE UP NEXT TO HIKARU GENJI...
HE'S HARDLY THAT HIGH-CLASS...
ぐぐう!! zzz
う zzz
zzz
*FROM THE TALE OF GENJI

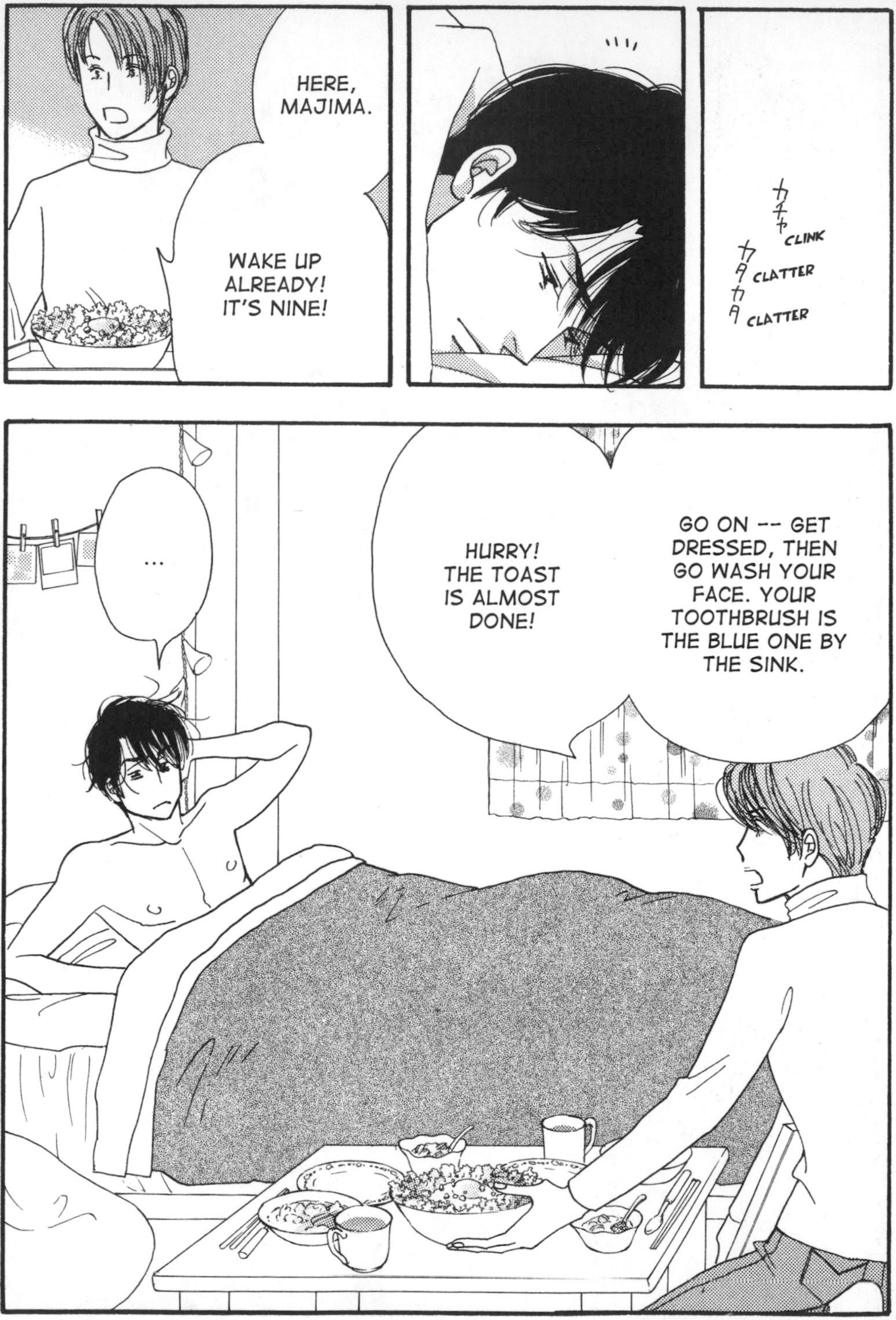
カチャ
CLINK
カタカタ
CLATTER
CLATTER
HERE, MAJIMA.
WAKE UP ALREADY! IT'S NINE!
GO ON -- GET DRESSED, THEN GO WASH YOUR FACE. YOUR TOOTHBRUSH IS THE BLUE ONE BY THE SINK.
HURRY! THE TOAST IS ALMOST DONE!
...

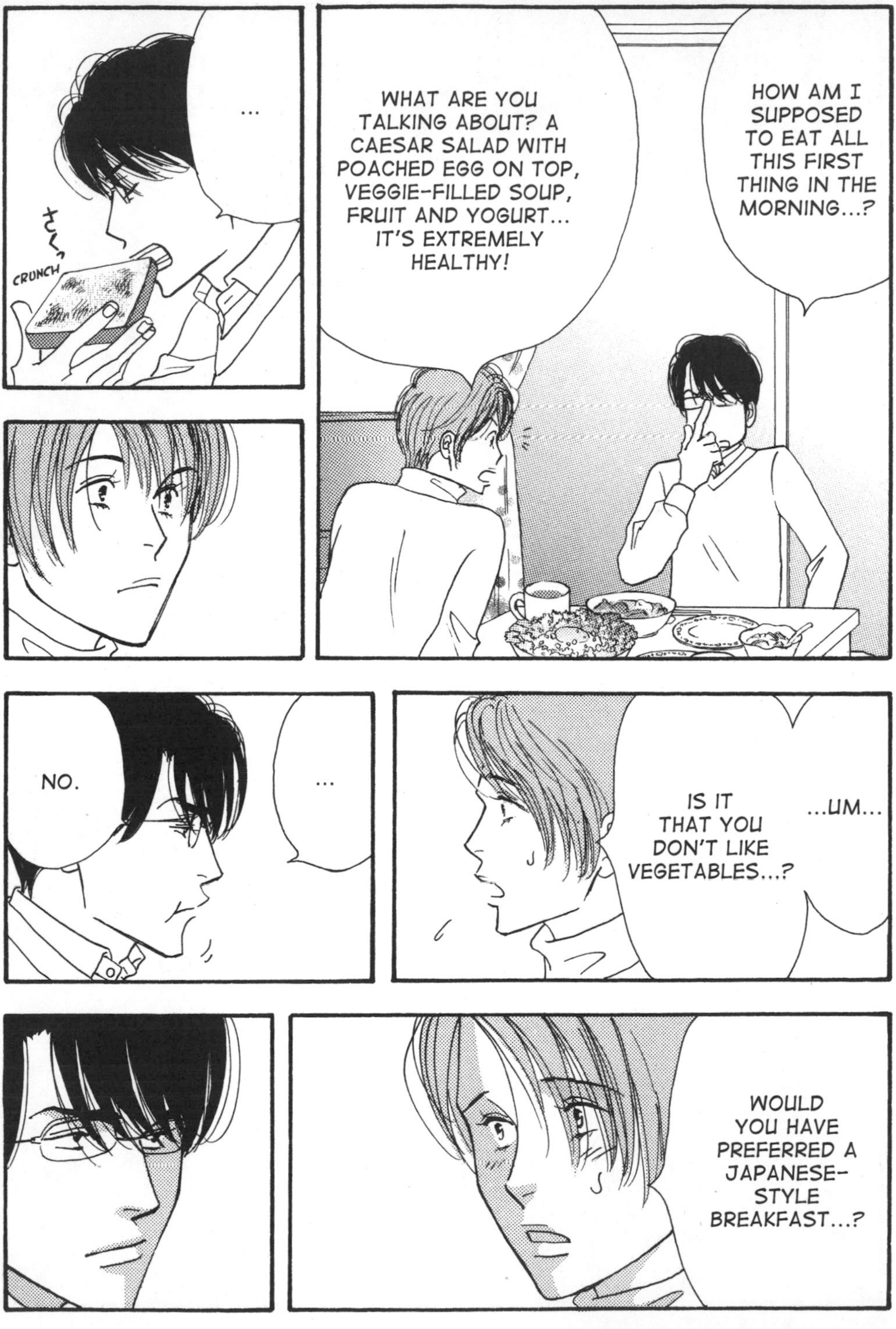
HOW AM I SUPPOSED TO EAT ALL THIS FIRST THING IN THE MORNING...?
WHAT ARE YOU TALKING ABOUT? A CAESAR SALAD WITH POACHED EGG ON TOP, VEGGIE-FILLED SOUP, FRUIT AND YOGURT... IT'S EXTREMELY HEALTHY!
...
さくっ
CRUNCH
...UM...
IS IT THAT YOU DON'T LIKE VEGETABLES...?
...
NO.
WOULD YOU HAVE PREFERRED A JAPANESE-STYLE BREAKFAST...?

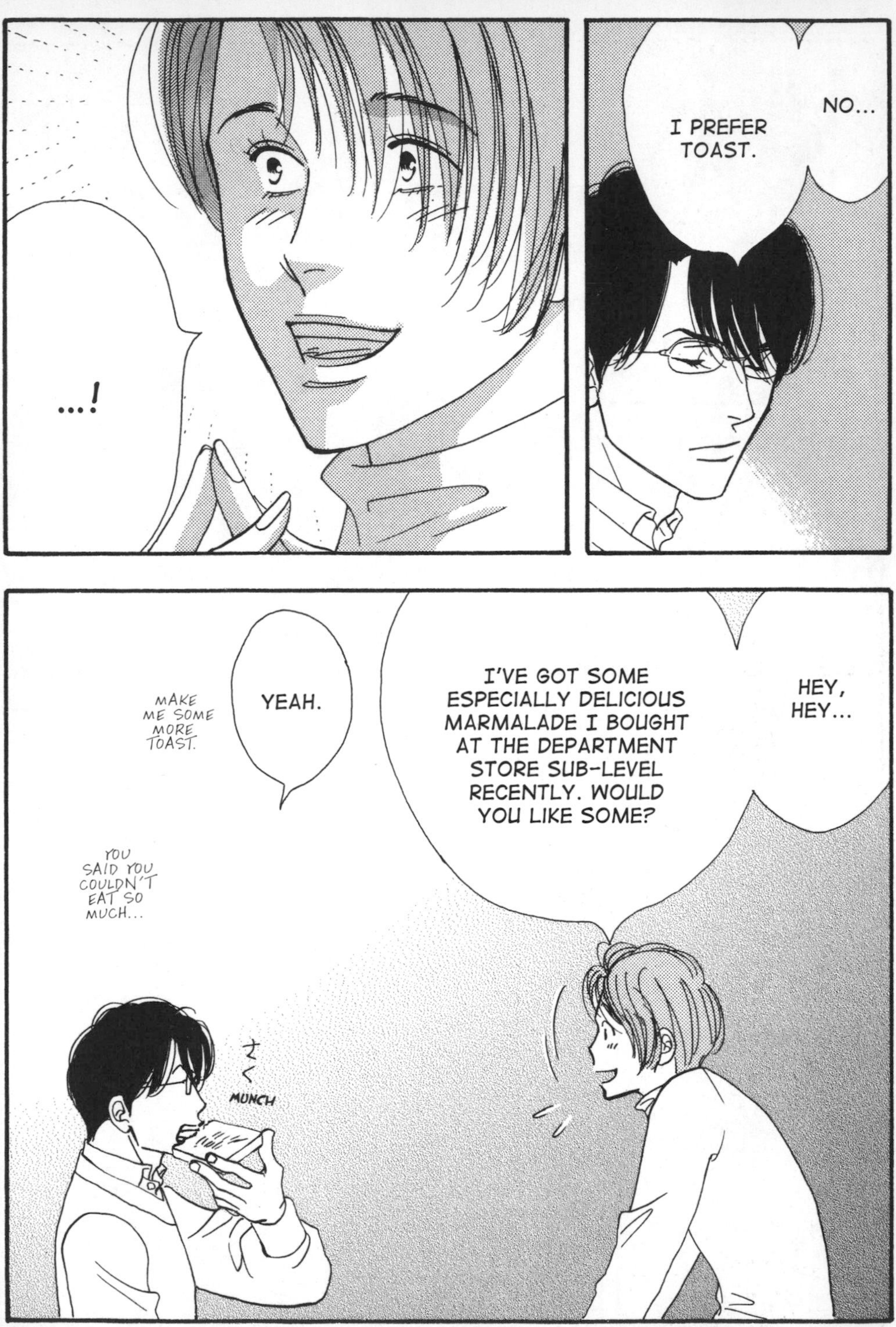
NO...
I PREFER TOAST.
...!
HEY, HEY...
I'VE GOT SOME ESPECIALLY DELICIOUS MARMALADE I BOUGHT AT THE DEPARTMENT STORE SUB-LEVEL RECENTLY. WOULD YOU LIKE SOME?
YEAH.
MAKE ME SOME MORE TOAST.
YOU SAID YOU COULDN'T EAT SO MUCH...
さく
MUNCH

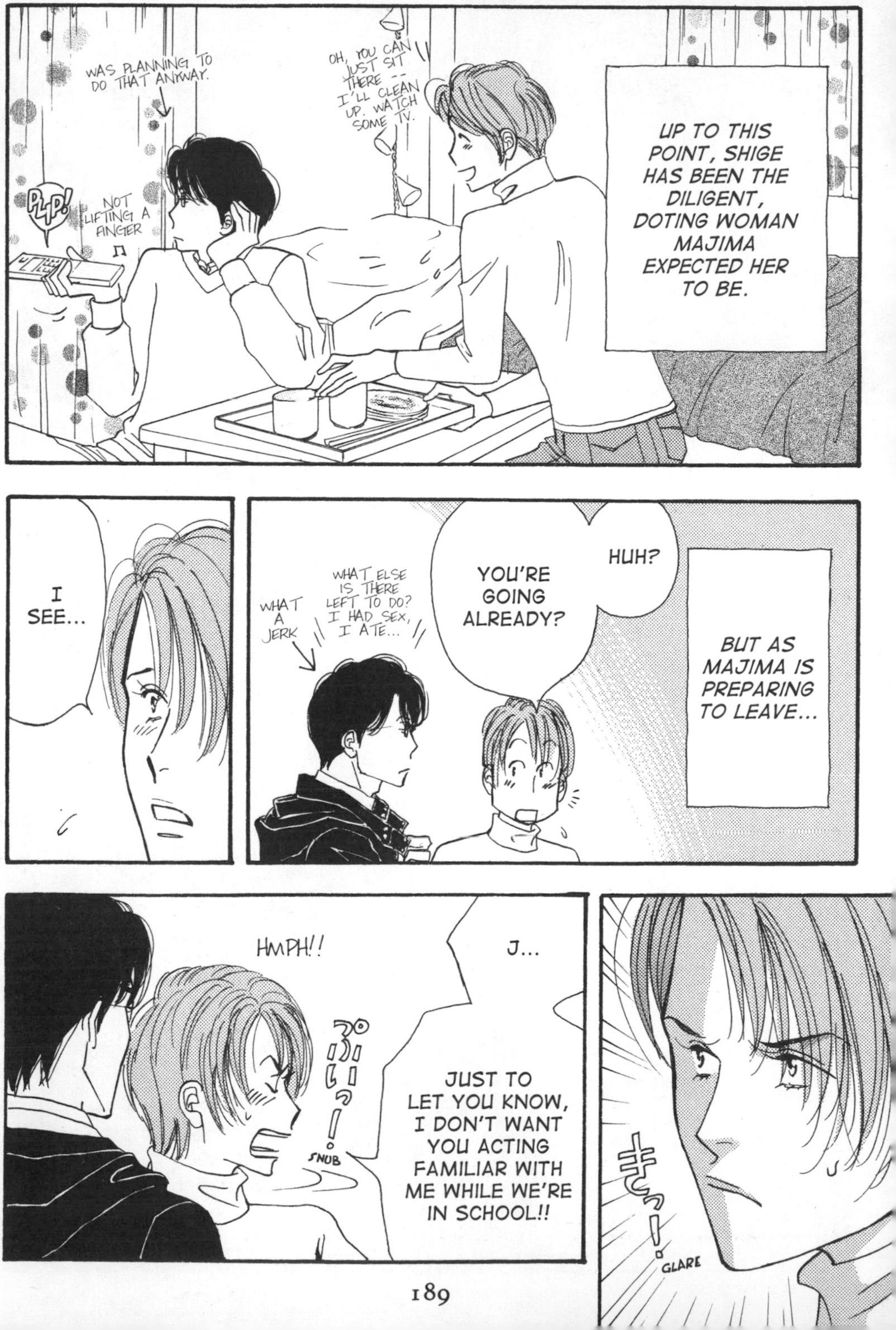
UP TO THIS POINT, SHIGE HAS BEEN THE DILIGENT, DOTING WOMAN MAJIMA EXPECTED HER TO BE.
OH, YOU CAN JUST SIT THERE -- I'LL CLEAN UP. WATCH SOME TV.
WAS PLANNING TO DO THAT ANYWAY.
NOT LIFTING A FINGER
PLIP!
BUT AS MAJIMA IS PREPARING TO LEAVE...
HUH?
YOU'RE GOING ALREADY?
WHAT ELSE IS THERE LEFT TO DO? I HAD SEX, I ATE...
WHAT A JERK
I SEE...
きっ!
GLARE
J...
JUST TO LET YOU KNOW, I DON'T WANT YOU ACTING FAMILIAR WITH ME WHILE WE'RE IN SCHOOL!!
HMPH!!
ぷいっ!
SNUB

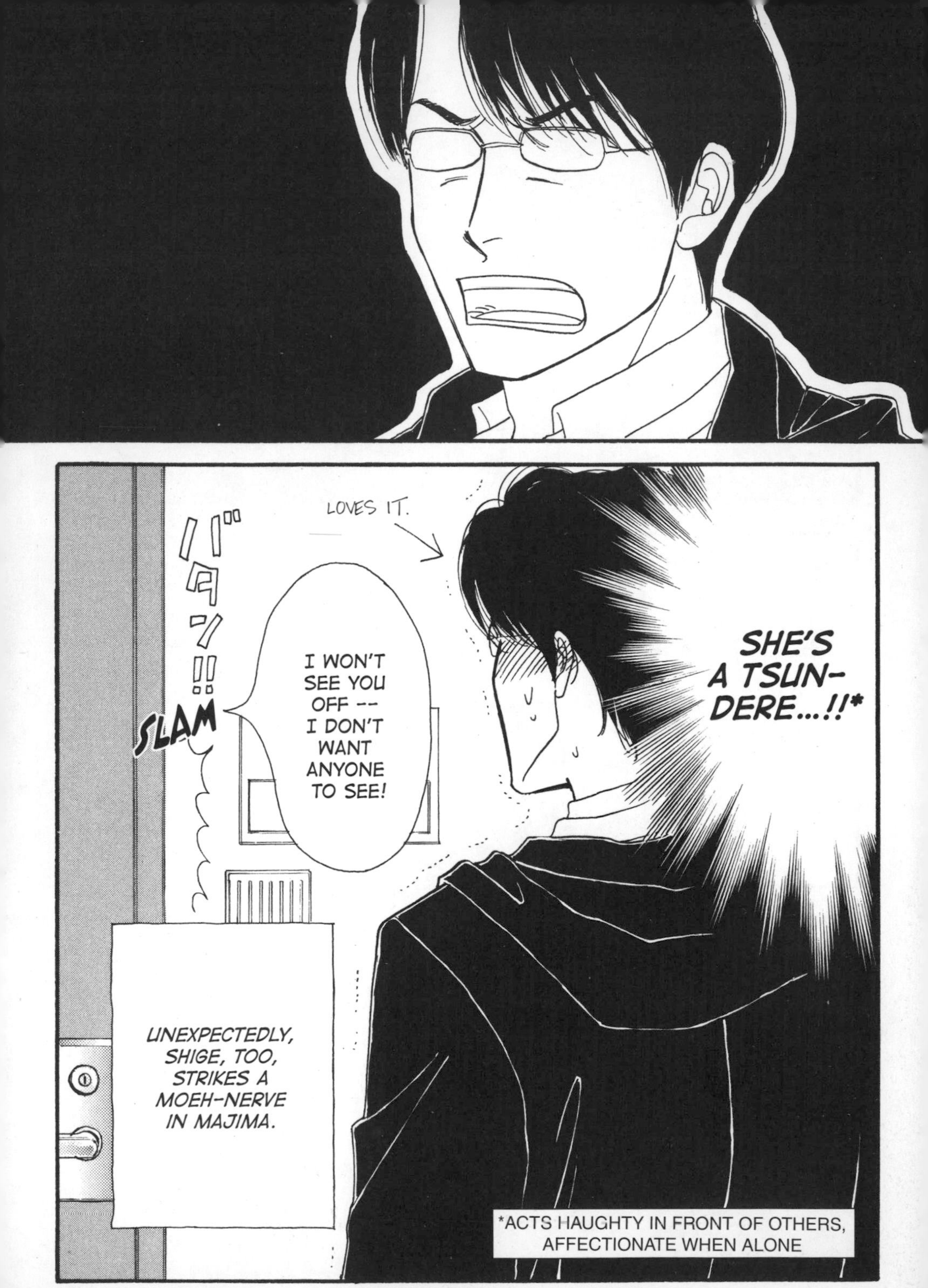
SHE'S A TSUN-DERE...!!*
LOVES IT.
I WON'T SEE YOU OFF -- I DON'T WANT ANYONE TO SEE!
バタン!!
SLAM
UNEXPECTEDLY, SHIGE, TOO, STRIKES A MOEH-NERVE IN MAJIMA.
*ACTS HAUGHTY IN FRONT OF OTHERS, AFFECTIONATE WHEN ALONE

From the creator of ANTIQUE BAKERY

A Duet Like No Other...

Solfège

Written & Illustrated by:
Fumi Yoshinaga

June™
junemanga.com

SRP: $12.95
ISBN: 978-1-56970-841-5

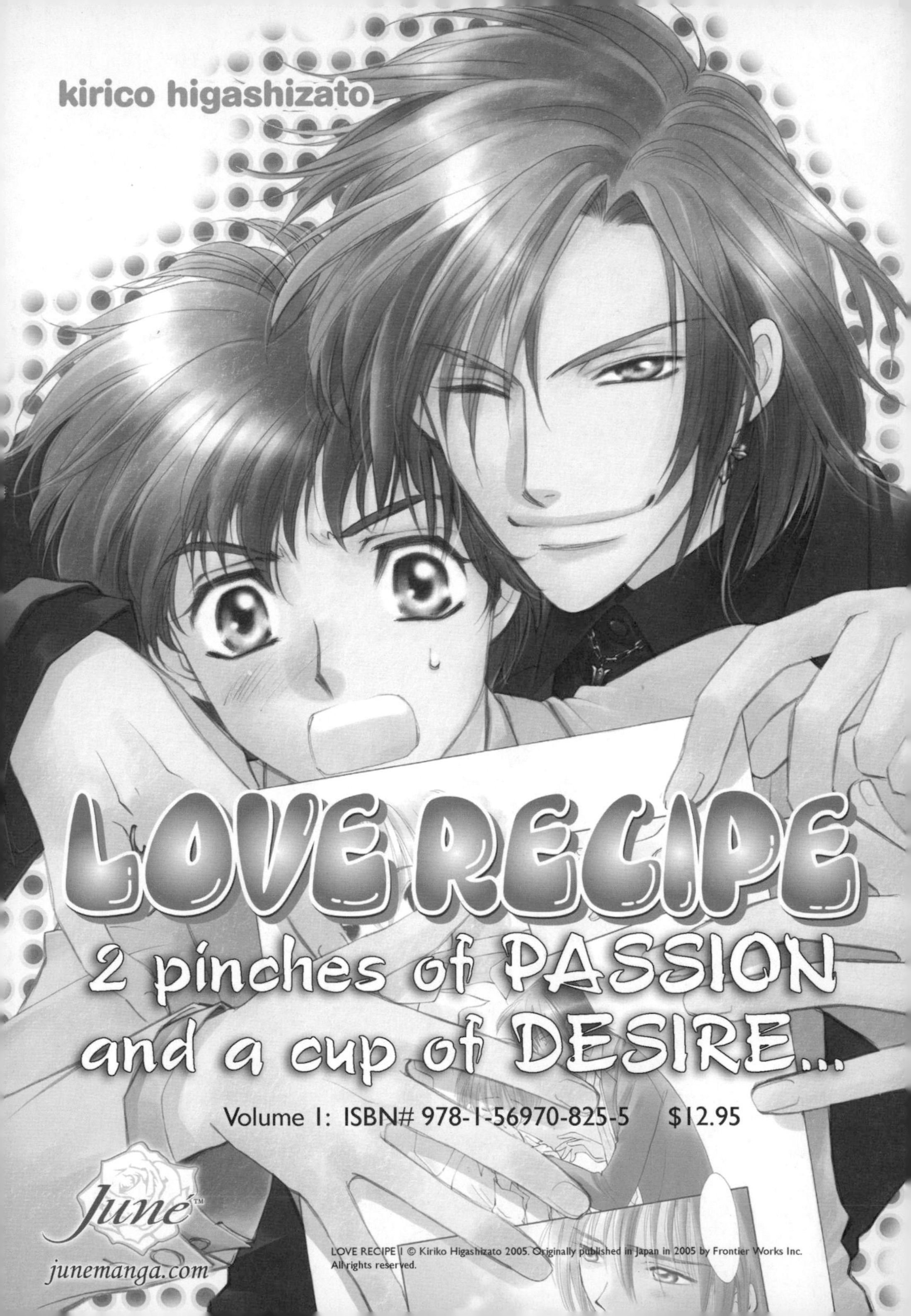
kirico higashizato
LOVE RECIPE
2 pinches of PASSION
and a cup of DESIRE...
Volume 1: ISBN# 978-1-56970-825-5 $12.95
June™
junemanga.com
LOVE RECIPE 1 © Kiriko Higashizato 2005. Originally published in Japan in 2005 by Frontier Works Inc.
All rights reserved.

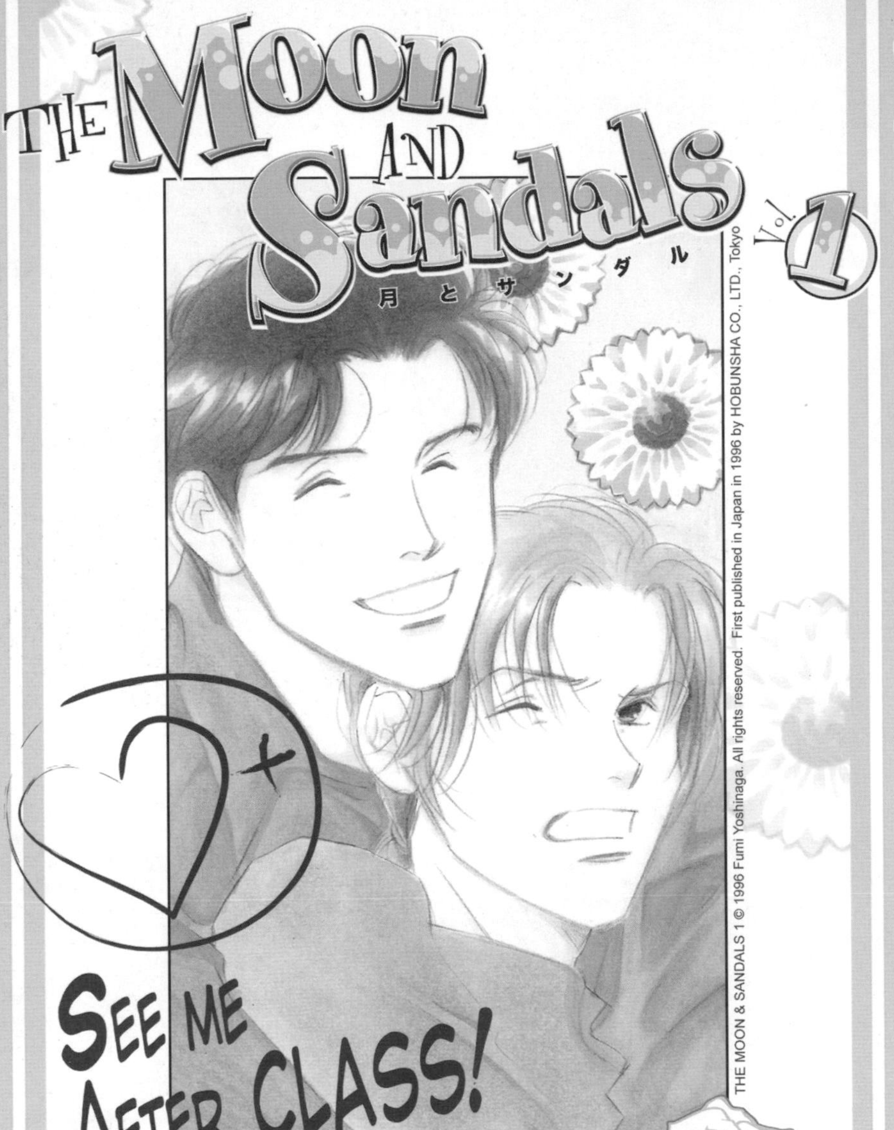
THE Moon AND Sandals
月とサンダル
Vol. 1
SEE ME AFTER CLASS!
June by DMP

ISBN# 978-1-56970-802-9 SRP $12.95

As a newly appointed high school teacher, Ida has yet to gain confidence in his abilities. His insecurity grows worse when he feels someone staring intensely at him during class. The piercing eyes belong to a tall, intimidating student – Koichi Kobayashi. What exactly should Ida do about it? Is it discontent that fuels Kobayashi's sultry gaze… or could it be something else?

Written and Illustrated by:
Fumi Yoshinaga

junemanga.com

Princess·Princess

By **MIKIYO-TSUDA**

Peer pressure...
has never been this intense!

When students need a boost, the Princesses arrive in gothic lolita outfits to show their school spirit! Join Kouno and friends in this crazy, cross-dressing comedy.

VOLUME 1 - ISBN# 978-1-56970-856-9 $12.95
VOLUME 2 - ISBN# 978-1-56970-855-2 $12.95
VOLUME 3 - ISBN# 978-1-56970-852-1 $12.95
VOLUME 4 - ISBN# 978-1-56970-851-4 $12.95
VOLUME 5 - ISBN# 978-1-56970-850-7 $12.95

DMP
DIGITAL MANGA
PUBLISHING
www.dmpbooks.com

A high school crush...

A world-class
pastery chef...

A former middle weight
boxing champion...

Winner of the
Kodansha Manga
Award!

And a
whole lot of
CAKE!

Written & Illustrated by
Fumi Yoshinaga

ANTIQUE BAKERY
1

Antique Bakery © 2000 Fumi Yoshinaga

DIGITAL MANGA PUBLISHING

THE DAY OF REVOLUTION

MIKIYO TSUDA

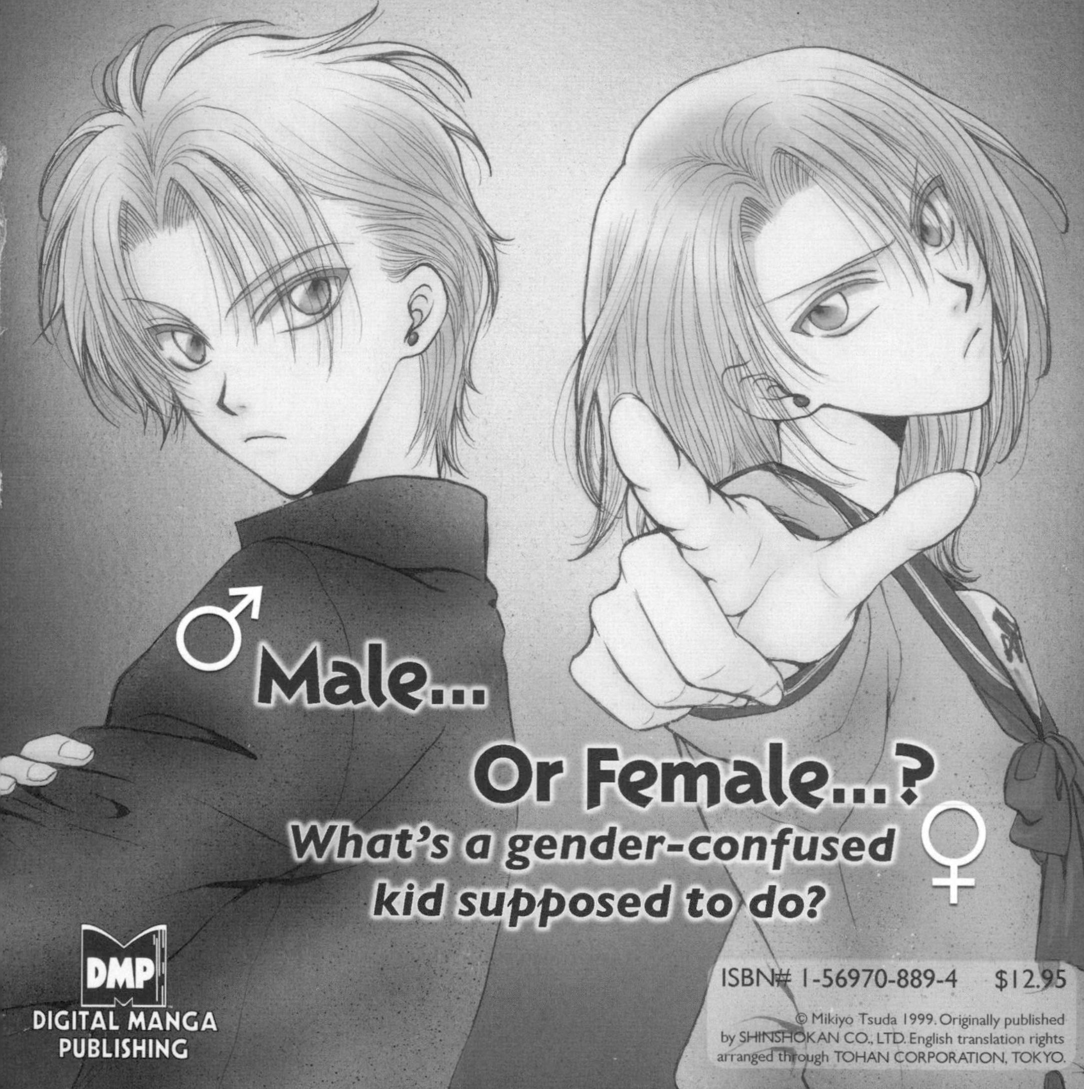

♂ Male...

Or Female...? ♀

What's a gender-confused kid supposed to do?

DMP
DIGITAL MANGA PUBLISHING

ISBN# 1-56970-889-4 $12.95

Cupid's arrows gone awry

RIN!

Only Sou can steady
Katsura's aim – what will
a budding archer do
when the one he relies
on steps aside?

Written by
Satoru Kannagi
(Only the Ring Finger Knows)
Illustrated by
Yukine Honami *(Desire)*

VOLUME 1 - ISBN # 978-1-56970-920-7 $12.95
VOLUME 2 - ISBN # 978-1-56970-919-1 $12.95
VOLUME 3 - ISBN # 978-1-56970-918-4 $12.95

june™

junemanga.com

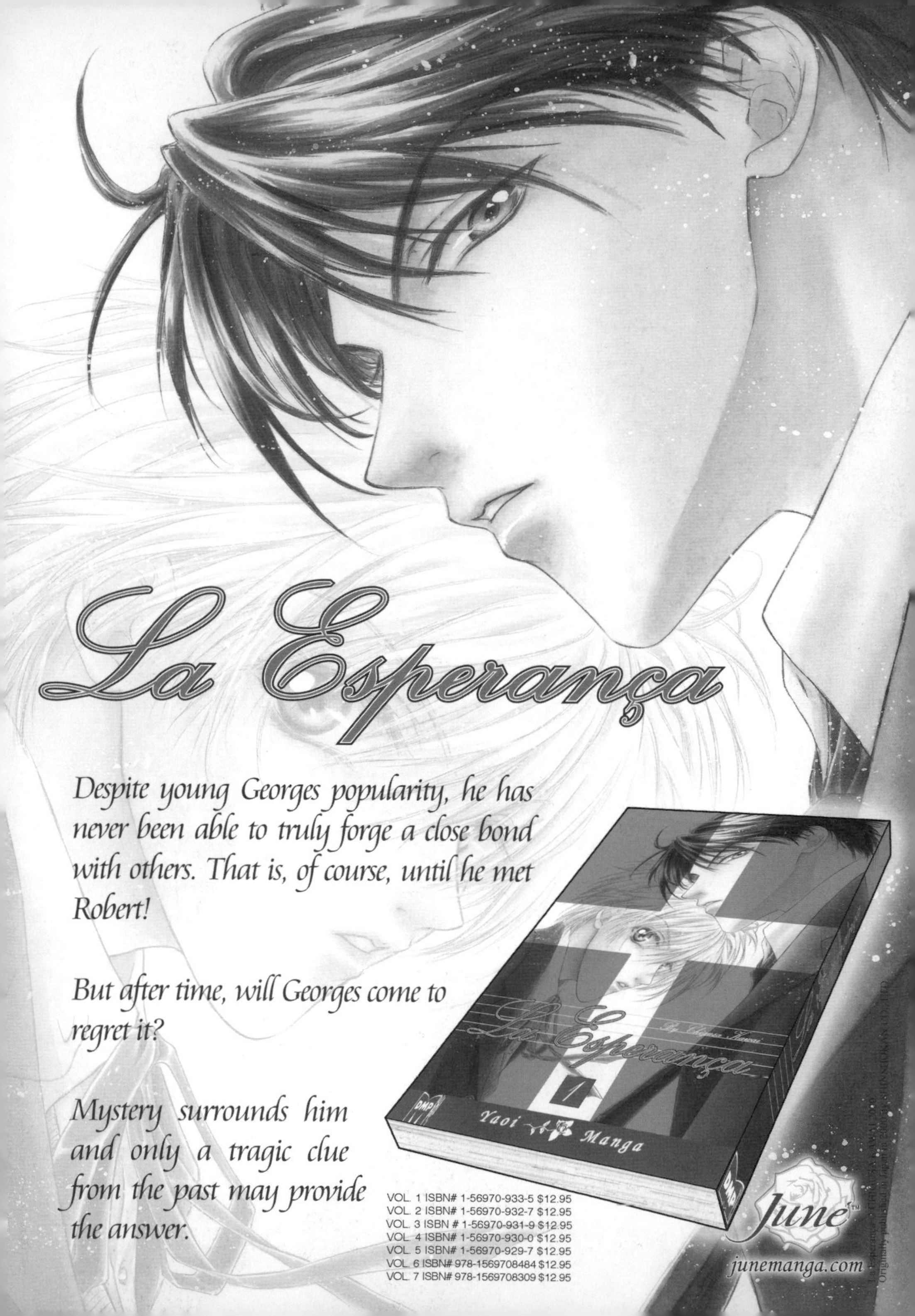
La Esperança
Despite young Georges popularity, he has never been able to truly forge a close bond with others. That is, of course, until he met Robert!
But after time, will Georges come to regret it?
Mystery surrounds him and only a tragic clue from the past may provide the answer.
La Esperança
By Chiharu Kawai
1
Yaoi Manga
VOL. 1 ISBN# 1-56970-933-5 $12.95
VOL. 2 ISBN# 1-56970-932-7 $12.95
VOL. 3 ISBN # 1-56970-931-9 $12.95
VOL. 4 ISBN# 1-56970-930-0 $12.95
VOL. 5 ISBN# 1-56970-929-7 $12.95
VOL. 6 ISBN# 978-1569708484 $12.95
VOL. 7 ISBN# 978-1569708309 $12.95
June™
junemanga.com
La Esperança © CHIHARU KAWAI 2000. Originally published in Japan in 2000 by SHINSHOKAN CO., LTD.

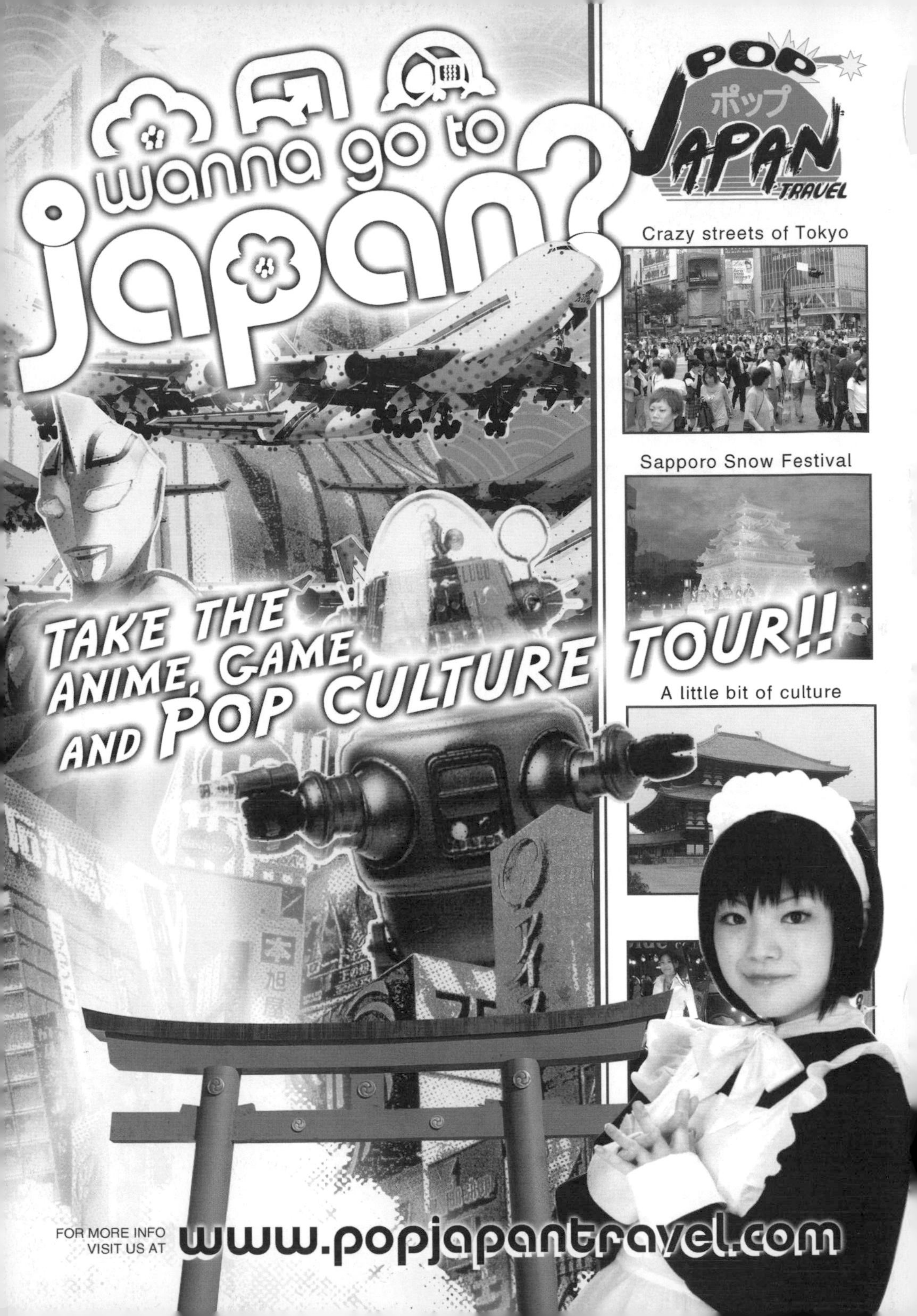
wanna go to
japan?
POP
ポップ
JAPAN
TRAVEL
Crazy streets of Tokyo
Sapporo Snow Festival
A little bit of culture
TAKE THE
ANIME, GAME,
AND POP CULTURE TOUR!!
FOR MORE INFO
VISIT US AT
www.popjapantravel.com

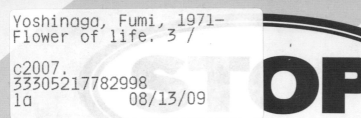

This is the back of the book!
Start from the other side.

NATIVE MANGA
readers read manga
from *right to left*.

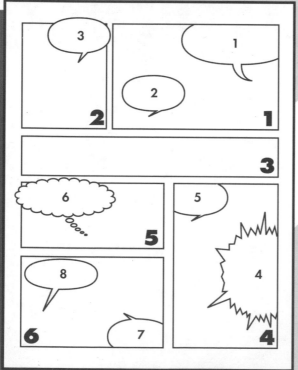

If you run into our *Native Manga* logo on any of our books... you'll know that this manga is published in it's true original native Japanese right to left reading format, as it was intended. Turn to the other side of the book and start reading from right to left, top to bottom.

Follow the diagram to see how its done. *Surf's Up!*

NATIVE MANGA
READ RIGHT TO LEFT